A Profile of Kenyan Entrepreneurs

Wanjiru Waithaka

&

Evans Majeni

Kenway Publications

Nairobi • Kampala • Dar es Salaam • Kigali

Published in Kenya by
Kenway Publications
an imprint of
East African Educational Publishers Ltd.
Brick Court, Mpaka Road/Woodvale Grove
Westlands, P.O. Box 45314
Nairobi – 00100
KENYA.
Email: eaep@eastafricanpublishers.com
Website: www.eastafricanpublishers.com

East African Educational Publishers Ltd.
C/O Gustro Ltd.
P.O. Box 9997, Kampala
UGANDA.

Ujuzi Books Ltd.
P.O. Box 38260
Dar es Salaam
TANZANIA.

East African Publishers Rwanda Ltd.
Tabs Plaza, Kimironko Road,
Opposite Kigali Institute of Education
P.O. Box 5151, Kigali
RWANDA.

First published in 2012

ISBN 978-9966-25-827-4

Printed in Kenya by
Printwell Industries Ltd.
P.O. Box 5216-0506
Nairobi, Kenya

Contents

Dedication

To the best sisters a girl can ever have. Ronnie, MaryG, Aggie and Jane (Kjni) – my biggest advocates and the ones who ensure I never give up on my dream of becoming a successful writer.

Wanjiru Waithaka

To my daughter Ruby Akinyi and my son Kwame Mayaka-Jabungu, the two people who have given my life a new meaning. I also wish to thank my mother-in-law Monica Ondeje who took care of my babies as I took time to concentrate on writing.

Evans Majeni

Preface

While Kenya is generally regarded as a haven of entrepreneurs, this is not reflected in the available literature. One only needs to walk into any bookshop where they are more likely to find large volumes on foreign business owners and almost nothing on local entrepreneurs. In fact, local politicians have had a head start when it comes to putting their stories to paper for future generations to learn from. It is against this background that we set out to write a book that will serialise successful Kenyan entrepreneurs.

The idea of documenting the profiles of local entrepreneurs was prompted by the need to unearth home-grown role models. These role models would inspire the Kenyan people to reach for higher goals especially as Kenya aims to join the newly industrialised economies by the year 2030. In the process, the exercise has proved quite enlightening indeed.

What proved to be even more controversial than anticipated was the process of selecting, interviewing and writing the respective stories. The mere act of trying to rank entrepreneurs in the elusive top 20, simple as it may appear, was daunting. At the beginning, just counting billionaires within the Kenyan borders was, to say the least, a walk in the park. However, picking out the ones who fitted in our criteria was not easy.

A spirited search for possible entries began in newsrooms where we picked the brains of some of Kenya's finest journalists, people who have over the years interacted, researched and written about business personalities in Kenya. We widened the search to entrepreneurs themselves and ordinary Kenyans by asking them to identify the top three most successful business owners they admire and whose businesses generate a turnover of at least KSh 100 million per annum. We ended up with a list of 80 entrepreneurs with solid companies and who had demonstrated financial success. This shows that Kenya has no shortage of role models in business.

The next step was to shortlist the top 20 based on our other criteria. The first and most important factor we looked for was inspiration. Such entrepreneurs needed to be people who had built successful businesses from scratch, proven rags-to-riches stories or individuals who had inherited a small business and taken it to the next level. The virtue of sacrifice and overcoming hardships needed to come out clearly. Innovation was another criterion; we wanted a business idea that has revolutionalised an industry, changed the rules of engagement or spawned new types of industries. Integrity was another key factor especially in a country where corruption is so deeply rooted. While we will not pretend to be moral purists, we made every effort to avoid people who have been obviously tainted in financial scandals in cases where the information was in the public domain.

Even though integrity was a key criteria, the exclusion of top entrepreneurs especially among the first 80 does not necessarily imply that they do not have integrity. For example, some prominent entrepreneurs declined to be featured in the book for personal reasons.

Lastly, we wanted to embrace diversity in gender, age, type of industry, geographical regions and ethnic affiliation. This last one was particularly important to dispel the widely held notion in Kenya that members of the Kikuyu and Asian communities dominate business in Kenya.

Once we had the shortlist of 20 entrepreneurs, the next task proved to be even more daunting – getting the chosen people to accept to be featured in the book. We expected difficulties given the common phobia that Kenyan business owners have of being in the spotlight. Indeed some declined to be featured for reasons as varied as 'personal reasons' while in some cases we did not get a response at all despite numerous letters, emails and telephone calls. The case of the coast region was particularly discouraging when four entrepreneurs did not respond or turned us down at the last minute. Mombasa is an important economic region, perhaps only second to Nairobi, and the lack of representation from there was a big blow for us.

But without doubt, the most disheartening aspect of this project was refusal by one major and well-respected entrepreneur to be featured. This was our lowest point when working on this book. We had sought this entrepreneur for several months and it was all the more saddening.

We ended up with a list of 14 entrepreneurs Our high point in the project was the men and women who freely gave their time to share their experiences both good and bad, expecting nothing in return but the opportunity to help a young Kenyan somewhere travel the often difficult road of entrepreneurship. We can never thank them enough for giving us the opportunity to sit at their feet and learn from them. We salute them; they are true Kenyan heroes and future generations will thank them for being motivators, teachers and torch-bearers.

There are those who dived into the world of entrepreneurship after being pushed off the cliff either through frustration at work, loss of a job, failure to secure gainful employment, lack of education or simply lack of better ways to earn a living. We also met those who had all the comfort and the best of job opportunities yet consciously opted for entrepreneurship either for the thrill of it or, as they put it, for financial independence, being their own bosses or making a contribution to the society.

Formal education has been widely touted as perhaps the fastest ladder to success. Admittedly, a number of those featured in this book have post-graduate degrees, but not all could attribute their immense wealth directly to formal education. The traits and habits that shaped their journey to the top were learnt more at home and in the business field with just little references to the classroom.

In our research, culture also emerged as a contributor to the spirit of entrepreneurship. Thrift and hard work in particular are overriding success traits in most entrepreneurs that were interviewed. These traits are either passed on through practice or genes. Partially, this could explain why some communities are more perceived as enterprising than others.

Our attempt to play the 'affirmative action' card by balancing the men and women in the top-flight entrepreneurs was futile. Women, though the obvious majority in the small and medium business sector, are poorly represented at the top management level. The reasons are beyond the scope of this work and could perhaps be the subject of another book. Helpfully, the few at the top had encouraging words for the sisters – we did it; you too can join us.

Family as a support system came out strongly as a factor in entrepreneurial success. Unless in instances of open defiance to expected family norms, most entrepreneurs adhered to family expectations. Inevitably, inheritance and privileged family position fuelled some great success stories. Those born into enterprising families often followed the footsteps of their mentors, the parents.

Spousal support in entrepreneurial success could not be directly traced although most entrepreneurs admitted, fleetingly though, that their spouses were their motivators. Some are unmarried, single, divorced or in some cases polygamous, hence rendering this theory highly contestable. However, family partnerships, moral support and goodwill of all partners seem to have an impact on overall family success.

Another emerging trend of much-talked-about and admired personalities are what one may describe as employee-entrepreneurs. These are corporate leaders whose career success is so conspicuous that they are almost always confused with entrepreneurs. Equity Bank's James Mwangi, Kenya Airways' Titus Naikuni and former CEO of Safaricom Michael Joseph are good examples, to mention but a few. Maybe these could be the subject of another book.

If there is one thing this writing journey has shown, it is that profiling successful Kenyan entrepreneurs will take several volumes; this book barely scratches the surface. Many worthy people were left out because of space and time constraints. It has been a learning experience and we hope that for subsequent volumes, Kenyan entrepreneurs who perhaps declined to be featured because they did not really understand what we were trying to do will be more open to tell their stories so that future generations of young Kenyans can be inspired to embrace their dreams and reach their highest potential as entrepreneurs.

Wanjiru Waithaka

Evans Majeni

April 2012

Acknowledgements

We hereby acknowledge the following people for their contributions to this book: the publishing staff at East African Educational Publishers, for conversations that clarified our thinking on this project, material support at critical and opportune times and for the care with which they reviewed the original manuscript.

A special thank you goes to Jeremy Ng'ang'a, the editor who fixed all of our grammatical errors and advised on sections that needed rewriting for clarity. His thoroughness and attention to detail enabled us to greatly improve the original manuscript.

We thank Linus Gitahi, Dennis Aluanga, Nick Wachira, Wanjiru's former colleagues at the *Business Daily* and all those who contributed ideas on the entrepreneurs to be included in the original list and their helpful suggestions on how to rank them in order to generate a shortlist.

Lastly, we wish to thank our families for their unwavering support. Over the many months it has taken to publish this book, they have been our greatest supporters, encouraging and inspiring us when the going got tough.

May you always be blessed.

Wanjiru Waithaka & Evans Majeni

April 2012

Abbreviations

AABA	All Africa Businesswomen Association
ABR	Africa Business Roundtable
ADB	African Development Bank
ADC	Agricultural Development Corporation
AG	Attorney General
AGOA	African Growth and Opportunity Act
ALAF	Aluminium Africa Limited
ALTECH	African Lakes Technologies
APDF	African Project Development Facility
ASBN	Africa Small Business Network
BA	Bachelor of Arts
BAT	British American Tobacco
BOAC	British Overseas Airways Corporation
BOP	Bottom of the Pyramid
BTL	Below The Line
CBK	Coffee Board of Kenya
CCK	Communications Commission of Kenya
CDs	Compact Discs
CCEE	Common Competitive Entrance Examination
CEO	Chief Executive Officer
CID	Criminal Investigation Department
CISPs	Corporate Internet Service Providers
CNN	Cable News Network
COMSOL	Communication Solutions Limited
CPA	Certified Public Accountant
CPE	Certificate of Primary Education
CSR	Corporate Social Responsibility
DC	District Commissioner
DEB	District Education Board
DFCK	Development Finance Company of Kenya
DJ	Deejay
DO	District Officer
DRC	Democratic Republic of Congo
EABL	East African Breweries Limited
EABS	East African Building Society
EACSO	East African Common Services Organisation
EADB	East African Development Bank
EBS	Elder of the Burning Spear
ECGD	Export Credits Guarantee Department

EIB	European Investment Bank
EPZ	Export Processing Zone
FM	Frequency Modulation
GM	General Motors
GSK	GlaxoSmithKline
HIV/Aids	Human Immunodeficiency Virus/Acquired Immune Deficiency Syndrome
IBEACo	Imperial British East Africa Company
ICDC	Industrial and Commercial Development Corporation
ICT	Information and Communications Technology
IFAW	International Fund for Animal Welfare
IFC	International Finance Corporation
IPO	Initial Public Offering
ISP	Internet Service Provider
IT	Information Technology
ITU	International Telecommunication Union
KACE	Kenya Advanced Certificate of Education
KAM	Kenya Association of Manufacturers
KAPE	Kenya African Preliminary Examination
KAU	Kenya African Union
KBS	Kenya Bureau of Standards
KCB	Kenya Commercial Bank
KCC	Kenya Cooperative Creameries
KCE	Kenya Certificate of Education
KCFC	Kenya Commercial Finance Company
KCPE	Kenya Certificate of Primary Education
KFC	Kenya Film Corporation
KIA	Kenya Institute of Administration
KIE	Kenya Industrial Estates
K-MAP	Kenya Management Assistance Programme
KNCC	Kenya National Capital Corporation
KPDA	Kenya Pharmaceutical Distributors Association
KPLC	Kenya Power and Lighting Company
KPTC	Kenya Posts and Telecommunications
KPU	Kenya People's Union
KRA	Kenya Revenue Authority
KSh	Kenya Shillings
KTN	Kenya Television Network
KU	Kenyatta University
KWFT	Kenya Women Finance Trust
LPOs	Local Purchase Orders
LPs	Long-playing (Phonograph records)

MBA	Master of Business Administration
MBS	Moran of the Burning Spear
MD	Managing Director
MIT	Massachusetts Institute of Technology
M-Pesa	Mobile sms-based money transfer service offered by Safaricom
MRM	Mabati Rolling Mills
MSK	Marketing Society of Kenya
NARC	National Rainbow Coalition
NCPB	National Cereals and Produce Board
NGO	Non-Governmental Organisation
NITD	Native Industrial Training Depot
NSE	Nairobi Securities Exchange
NTV	Nation Television
NYCPJ	New York Committee for Protection of Journalists
ODA	Overseas Development Agency
OERB	Oshwal Education and Relief Board
OTC	Overseas Trading Company
P1	Primary 1
PS	Permanent Secretary
PSI	Population Services International
PwC	PricewaterhouseCoopers
SMEs	Small and Medium Enterprises
SMS	Short Message Service
TI	Transparency International
TSC	Teachers Service Commission
TV	Television
UK	United Kingdom
UN	United Nations
UNIDO	United Nations Industrial Development Organisation
UoN	University of Nairobi
USA	United States of America
USIU–A	United States International University – Africa
UT	Untrained Teacher
VADA	Voluntary Agency Development Assistance
VOVC	Visa Oshwal Vanik Community
WWB	Women World Banking
WWW	World Wide Web

Chapter 1

Manu Chandaria

Most if not all households in Kenya possess at least one product from the Comcraft Group. From building and construction materials to kitchenware and other household items, Comcraft products are to be found everywhere in Eastern Africa with notable presence in Kenya, Tanzania, Uganda and Ethiopia. Comcraft's flagship companies specifically in Eastern Africa include Mabati Rolling Mills (MRM), Insteel Limited and Kaluworks Limited in Kenya, Uganda Baati Limited and Shumuk Aluminium in Uganda, and Aluminium Africa Limited and Metal Products Limited in Tanzania.

The Group operates in forty-five countries on five continents. Its over 200 companies generate billions of dollars in annual turnover. With its headquarters in India, it has additional offices in Singapore, Sydney (Australia), London (UK), Toronto (Canada) and Geneva (Switzerland). The Group's business empire employs more than forty thousand people and attracts the best and the brightest talent from around the world. For many young people, especially in the Asian community, working in the Group is a much sought-after career opportunity with the added attraction of gaining global exposure from among the over 200 companies in the Group. Sitting at the apex of the Group as Chairman is Dr Manilal Premchand Chandaria.

Known simply as Manu to many friends and business associates, he chairs the Comcraft Group which has become synonymous with excellence in manufacturing and is the first indigenous Kenyan business to go global. Dr Chandaria became a household name in Kenya and in the entire East African region not just from his business acumen but also his social and philanthropic activities. His pioneering effort in spearheading the private sector participation in the East African economies has been recognised and so has been his contribution to the welfare of both the citizenry and the business community. As a business manager, he was named the most respected Chief Executive Officer in East Africa, a position he went on to enjoy for three years in a row. Now an octogenarian, Manu has inspired many entrepreneurs all over the world.

Manu and the Chandaria family

Shortly after completing his studies in India and the United States of America, Manu returned to Kenya in 1951 to join the family business, a common practice with many children of Indian families. Indeed Manu grew up knowing that he would one day become part of the family business. As a trained engineer – he held a Master's degree in mechanical engineering – opportunities for getting a well-paying job were numerous; he could easily get a cushy job earning good money. He wondered if he might not be happier pursuing this option.

Although the business had flourished for most of his childhood, by the time Manu left university his father's holdings had shrunk to just two assets: Kenya Aluminium Industrial Works Limited, a small company in Mombasa that later came to be known as Kaluworks (it produced aluminium pots and pans), and Premchand Brothers Limited, a wholesale business of importing and distributing provisions throughout East Africa. Manu had to agonise over whether to stay in a business that could barely support the large family or to look for a lucrative job outside the family, which would perhaps make him happier. Eventually, he decided to stay on and be part of his retired father's business.

Joining the family business was to prove a great reward in coming years. He helped turn over the struggling businesses into multinational enterprises with a presence across the entire globe. To understand how a successful business operation shrank to plunge the family into financial hardship and then rose again, one has to go back to where it all began, with Manu's father Premchandbhai Chandaria.

Premchandbhai had come to Kenya in 1915 from Jamnagar Province in Gujarat, western India, to escape the grinding poverty in the family. In Kenya he hoped to earn enough money, go back to India and help his family. At the time, the family was making a living from farming in an unpredictable and harsh climate. Stories abound of people from the Shah community who had left India, gone to Africa and flourished. Indeed, it had become the dream of every young man to journey to Africa because this was the place where they could flourish and lift their families out of poverty. Manu's father therefore saw migration as an opportunity to escape the poverty that had become his life. However, his father (Manu's grandfather) was reluctant to send his son to Africa.

Before migrating to Jamnagar, Manu's father and his family had migrated from Kutch, also in Gujarat. According to the culture of the time, the firstborn did very little. Manu's great-grandfather had seven sons. Among these sons his grandfather was the eldest. Therefore, he was really spoilt. He wore soft, fine clothes and enjoyed life. He spent his days sitting in a shop while his siblings did the hard work on the farm. He accompanied Manu's great-grandfather to various places and as the great-grandfather was fond of a horse, the grandfather would ride with him.

Everything changed when the family split and all went their separate ways. Manu's grandfather had never learned to farm. Inevitably, this responsibility now fell on his son (Manu's father), who was still very young, and recently married to his wife Poonjiben. And thus began a life of toil for Premchandbhai who tried his best against the unpredictable monsoon climate. Every two or three years there was drought. Moreover, the land had very little water though surrounded by the sea. The Maharajas, who ruled the people under the British Government, added to the problems of poor farmers. In a good year they would pick up almost everything the people grew. Large families survived on collective labour, but families with few able-bodied people found the going rough.

Unfortunately, Premchandbhai suffered an accident at his young age. He fell from a tree and hurt his back. Given that tilling the land using ox-ploughs was so back-breaking, he found himself experiencing extreme difficulties. Some of his uncles tried to help him. But he had to look after the seven members of his family – his wife, two brothers, one sister and their parents. Soon he found it impossible to look after the large family. He could also not rely on the help of his uncles forever. That is when the idea of travelling to Africa came to mind.

It took a lot of pleading from other family members and friends to make Premchandbhai's father relent and allow him to travel to Kenya. He was still worried about who would look after the family. To get to Africa one needed to take a ship from Mumbai (then called Bombay) which was 500km from Jamnagar. As it was during the First World War (1914–1918), ships were very irregular and Premchandbhai had to stay in Mumbai for three months before he got a ship to sail to Mombasa.

By the time Premchandbhai arrived in Mombasa in 1915, a small Shah community in Kenya had grown in number. Initially, in its migration to Africa, the community had gone right up to Madagascar. However, many people in the pioneering group did not feel comfortable there and slowly they changed course and settled in Kenya. The first of the community people arrived in Kenya in 1898. They were three of them – a salesman, a man who could not find a job and ended up dressing stones, and another who carried cargo using handcarts.

Upon arrival, Premchandbhai got a job in a shop. He worked from 6.00 am to midnight, had three meals at his employer's home and at night slept on a bench on rolls of Americani (a grey cloth manufactured in the USA) with a few blankets to keep him warm. It was after six months that he plucked up the courage to ask for his salary. He was told it was 20 Indian rupees a month, equivalent to half a dollar.[1] His dream of earning 4,000 rupees and go back to India to help his family (possibly by setting up a shop) was shattered. He immediately decided to set up his own shop in Kenya. Consequently, he asked his parents to borrow money for him in India and send it to him.

At the time, it was common practice for people coming from India to start working as assistants in someone's shop before setting up their own and becoming independent. There was no fear of competition as there was enough business for everyone. Very often former employers helped new traders to set up their businesses. This explains how the whole country was dotted by Indian traders. They would go to an area before the British administrators got there and open it up by starting to trade. Indian traders flourished enormously because they offered reasonable prices and service with a smile. If one knocked on their door at midnight wanting something, they would open the shop and sell even small items to the customer. And since in those days Indians were not allowed in lodges or hotels, travellers from other towns would eat and be accommodated at home. The next morning they would buy something before leaving. The whole trading system was based on brotherhood.

Contrary to popular assertion, more than ninety-nine percent of the Indian workers who were shipped by the British to Kenya to work on the Uganda Railway (coolies) went back. Once in India those who returned told farmers to stop wasting their time farming the rocky terrain with no rain and move to Kenya. They spoke of a country that was so fertile that seeds thrown on the ground would grow.

Nevertheless, the British further imported labourers from India because they needed qualified people to run and maintain the new railway line. From northern India they recruited people from Punjab who were physically hefty and were mechanically trained. In addition, they could do hard manual labour and technical jobs. From Gujarat came the likes of Patels and Shahs to run the railway stations as assistant station masters, ticket collectors, ticket dispensers and clerks. This category of work required intelligence, literacy and the ability to handle money. As soon as the railway started running, there came the traders (Ismailias, Shahs, Bohras, Lohanas and so on) to support the labourers. After them came the masons, carpenters, other artisans and professionals like doctors, lawyers, architects and engineers. If people arrived and found that they were short of manpower, they would send for their relatives to join them. This explains how entire families ended up in Kenya. Soon there was a growing population of Indians many of whom had escaped the difficult economic situation back home.

---

1   Until 1922, the official currency in Kenya was the Indian rupees.

Upon setting up his shop business, Premchandbhai created a partnership with his brother-in-law's family who had emigrated after him. Their first shop in Nairobi dealt with sundry items specialising in stocking Indian food and rations. With time, they also started stocking products that would appeal to European and African customers. The shop grew bigger and both partners opened a second branch in Mombasa. By the time Manu was born in 1929, the family was reasonably well-to-do and the business was well established. However, the partnership between Premchandbhai and his brother-in-law had ended. It had lasted eleven years from 1917 and the partners had parted ways the year before Manu was born. The reason behind the split was that the older children of both families had got into the business. Premchandbhai's own children, while not old enough to join the business, would eventually do so. Thus, it was felt that it was better to separate the two families early enough. Each family got a half share of the business.

Early childhood and education

Manu was born in Nairobi on 1 March 1929, the fifth born in the family of Premchandbhai and Poonjiben Chandaria. In all, Manu had seven siblings, three brothers and four sisters. The eldest brother and sister were born in 1916 and 1920 respectively in India. All the others were born in Kenya.

During this time, Manu's two uncles and their children were staying with the family. One had six sons and a daughter and the other had only one daughter. Sixteen children living together with their parents made quite a large family. Manu enjoyed the experience because it was one big happy family. One was never alone. If one had a problem there was always someone's shoulder to cry on. Luckily, even if there was tension in the business or disagreements, the family members never brought them home. They were all very respectful of one another. Another thing that Manu observed was that being a toddler was fun because everyone wanted to play with it. But as one got older they became the child everyone wanted to send to fetch things.

Although Manu's father had only done three standards of vernacular while his mother was illiterate, both were committed to ensuring that their children got a good education. Even Poonjiben started teaching herself to read vernacular at the age of fifty-five. Manu's father felt that if he did not give his children a good education, their future would be the same as his and he didn't want that. In those days it was not possible to become anything unless you got educated first. This is how a farming community from India ended up building business empires in Kenya.

Manu attended a kindergarten school in a Jain temple opposite their house (the family was of the Jain faith). He also first went to primary school in Nairobi. When his father went to stay in Mombasa for a few years to look after the business there, Manu went with him and attended Alidina Visram Primary School. When his father returned to Nairobi, he again accompanied him and enrolled at Duke of Gloucester School (later renamed Jamhuri High School) which had both primary and secondary school sections.

Premchandbhai and three brothers had decided that their parents should never be left alone in India. So at any one time one brother would be in India while the other two stayed in Kenya. Manu's father went to look after his parents in India in 1938. While he was gone, his children went to live with their eldest brother Devchand (Manu's uncle) and his wife Pushpa whom he had married two years earlier. The couple had a young son named Praful. Unfortunately, Manu's elder brother Keshav had some problem with Devchand. Normally, the Indian family does not separate, but the brother decided to move out of the family home which was being shared by all. In effect, he now took responsibility for all members of the family.

The family went to live in a house with a tin roof (*mabati*) opposite the Kenya Power and Lighting[2] offices, Ngara. The house was just as crowded as the first home. Two families lived there. They shared the rent and also one sitting room. At night they would roll out mattresses on the floor to sleep and stash them away during the day. When Premchandbhai returned from India in 1940 the family moved to a new home that Manu's uncle had bought at the corner of Forest Road. It had four rooms and bathrooms inside the house. Manu's was the first Indian family to have moved that far in Nairobi; a majority of the families lived in the centre of the city.

Manu was excited by the new home. A house with a bathroom inside was such a novelty. But then his father decided to convert one of the bathrooms into living quarters and built bathrooms outside the house. In the evenings children would come out of the adjoining houses and happily play outside together for hours. The Second World War had started and it suddenly ruined the tranquillity that prevailed at the time. A small plane dropped a bomb in northern Kenya and the whole Asian community was shaken. It seemed they would be involved in the war. Families started sending old people, women and children to India where they would be safe. Only able-bodied men were left behind. Manu was then eleven years old and therefore a child.

In September 1940, young Manu was at the port of Mombasa waiting to board a ship to India. While the passengers had just started to embark, the siren went off signalling an impending air raid. The ship immediately pulled anchor

---

2   Now Kenya Power.

and headed for the open sea to wait until the danger had passed. After some hours, the siren went off indicating that the harbour was now safe. The ship hurriedly came back to the port and the remaining passengers boarded. Luggage was thrown in haphazardly. Finally, the ship left the shores as hurriedly as it had returned. In the open sea, it went so fast that in three days it had already covered half of the journey. This was not without discomfort and many of the passengers were seasick. Eventually everything settled down. Six more days and the ship reached Mumbai.

This was Manu's first visit to India. Seeing the big city (Mumbai) for the first time was a fabulous experience and an eye-opener for him. There were double-decker buses, which he had never seen before, trams and so many buildings some of which were five and six storeys high. He had to keep his eyes open all the time; he thought that if one blinked they would miss something. He was taken on a tram ride. Wow, what a wonderful life this was for Manu! Later, they travelled to Jamnagar where his uncle had rented a part of an eight-roomed house where the family stayed together. Manu and the other children were soon enrolled in school. Manu enrolled at Navanagar High School where the medium of instruction was English and Gujarati. However, English was hardly spoken.

Manu found the education system very different and intense. So was life in general. The fight for independence was ongoing and the teachers were all pro-independence. Unlike in Kenya, children read a lot of literature, which Manu enjoyed. His uncle bought the children one bicycle. Almost all the children in the neighbourhood had a ride on it. It brought a lot of pleasure. They also played cricket on the streets. Jamnagar was famous for the game as a result of its introduction into schools by Prince Ranjit when he became the Maharaja. He was a famous cricket player who played in English cricket teams as a student. Education was free although students paid a quarter rupee, equivalent to thirty-five cents in Kenyan currency. Of this amount, an equivalent of twenty-five cents was sports fee, which was used to fund the cricket teams. The students were also charged an equivalent of ten cents to get clean water to drink in school.

After high school, Manu joined the University of Bombay in 1944. At the university, he got immersed into the Gandhian philosophy and the independence movement. The next four years shaped his future life. He started reading, understanding and appreciating the philosophy of Mahatma Gandhi and became his ardent follower. The philosophy was based on *ahimsa*, meaning non-violence. Another philosophy was 'use local' because if people stopped using British goods then their coloniser (Britain) would not be able to sell anything to the people. It was also a way of ensuring that employment was sustained; for instance, in cloth-making, if machine looms replaced hand

7

looms people would lose jobs. The students would also hold demonstrations and, according to the philosophy of non-violence, if they got hurt, they were not to respond with violence. Manu and other students even wore *khadi* – a hand-spun and woven cloth. They spun the cloth themselves, then they got someone to weave it and stitch the clothes.

All this gave Manu a firm foundation for his later life. He learnt that leadership has to be attained and even if one has bright ideas they must work for leadership status so that people would respect and listen to them. Leadership requires a tremendous amount of sacrifice, low ego, humility and the capacity to work with people.

Manu graduated in 1947 with a Bachelor of Science degree in chemistry and physics. Going to university was a great achievement in those days and he was among the first members of his family to do so.

Another business split and study in America

After completing the first degree in 1947, Manu's family wanted to send him and Keshav to the USA for further education. But it was a difficult time because the family business had split for the second time. The initial split had been in 1928 just before Manu's birth. With this split, financing the education of the two young men in the USA presented a real problem.

A member of the Shah community, the Hirji Kara Family, had set up a factory in Mombasa for making pots and pans. However, the company had collapsed in the 1929 recession and had been repossessed by the bank. Aruna's father (Aruna was Manu's future wife) also known as Premchandbhai[3] – Premchand Raichand – joined forces with ten others each contributing ten thousand shillings as capital which they used to buy the company. The company was called Kenya Aluminium Industrial Works Limited (later to be known as Kaluworks Limited). Premchandbhai, who had immigrated to Kenya in 1911, became the first chairman of the company.[4] In 1933 Premchandbhai's family also set up Thika Tanning Factory but it ran into financial difficulties. They decided to turn to Manu's family for help, which gave them a loan. In 1935 the families became even closer and Manu's family acquired twenty-five percent shareholding in Kenya Aluminium and Kenya Tanning.

---

3   Bhai is a respectful way to address your elders like father or uncle in the Asian culture. It is like saying "Sir" in English and is added to a person's name. Manu could not address his father by just his name Premchand. He called him Premchandbhai. The same applies to his father-in-law. He also refers to his eldest brother Devchand (who has since died) as Devchandbhai. In the same way his employees (mainly of Asian origin) cannot just call him Manu. They address him as Manubhai as a sign of respect.

4   Later, Manu was to become chairman of the same company.

The same year Premchandbhai proposed his eldest daughter, Aruna's sister, as a bride to Devchand. Subsequently, the couple got engaged. They married a year later in 1936 and got their first child, a son named Praful, in 1938. At the time, Premchand Raichand's business was the second largest in the Shah community.[5] The family had originally started off in Maragwa then moved to Thika, which became their main base before they invested in Kenya Aluminium. Premchand Brothers, the wholesale business that Manu's family had built, was the third largest. All these businesses competed fiercely against each other. Eventually, Premchand and his brothers suggested that the two family businesses merge to form one strong group. In the process, it became the number one business in the Shah community.

In 1938 the businesses merged and then bought Muhoroni Sugar. Three years later in 1941 Premchand Raichand decided to go to India. The families set up a couple of industries in Jamnagar including a textile plant, oil milling and refining plant, and invested in a salt-cultivating business on 1,800 acres of land producing 150,000 tonnes of salt. While this was going on, they went into speculation and commodity trading. In those days commodity trading was done on around 10–12 items including gold, silver, oil, peanuts, peanut oil and linseed oil. This was a very different kind of venture but very risky because of its volatility. One could either make or lose millions. When they lost money in speculation, they borrowed heavily from the Kenyan businesses to finance the commodity trading in India.

In the Kenyan operation the shareholding structure was such that the Shah and Chandaria families each had around forty-two percent while other partners had fifteen percent. Their managing director in Kenya was MP Shah (after whom the hospital in Nairobi is named). He was a minority shareholder with only seven and a half percent. He continuously refused to take part in the business that required speculation because of his principles. He told both families that if they wanted money from the business, they would have to sell their shares to him. Gradually, the families' share of the business reduced until they were minority shareholders and MP Shah had a controlling stake in the business. The families totally lost out in commodity trading. In 1947, Manu's brother went to India and told his father and uncle that the family was in a precarious situation. He urged them to return to Kenya. By then, the business was almost collapsing.

Consequently, the businesses were split. The Chandarias only managed to keep their original business, Premchand Brothers. They started to negotiate the buying of Kenya Aluminium. Trufoods, a business Devchand had started, and Muhoroni Sugar went to Bharmal Riashi Shah, an uncle in the Chandaria

---

5   The largest business in the Shah community was Karman Mepa which even today maintains a small shop on Biashara Street.

family who had seven and a half percent shareholding in the business. The Chandarias were so keen to have Kenya Aluminium that they ended up buying it at double the price. The reason the family was willing to bid so high to get the company was that, with four children leaving university in another year, it needed a better base to absorb them. With degrees in engineering and commerce, Manu's parents realised the children could not sit in the provision store. With most of the family wealth now gone, the parents knew that if they did not give the children a platform to work, they would end up working for multinationals yet they were determined to keep them in the family business. This is a classical example of the determination of the Indian families to plan ahead of time so that the family can remain together.

How the generation of Manu's father lost control of the family's thriving businesses to a dormant shareholder is the irony of many African businesses. Often business owners think that turnover is profit. If one bought goods worth Ksh 5,000 and sold them, they may have only made Ksh 5,000 as profit. If one was to draw more than the business was generating they would lose their business. The family kept selling shares to the partner, MP Shah until he grew to a maximum size and got control of all the assets. Now Manu's family was fighting to get complete control of Kenya Aluminium, which they so badly wanted. Eventually, the consolation was in the fact that they still had their original business Premchand Brothers and Kenya Aluminium with which to make a fresh start.

Later, the Shah family decided to set up the first galvanising plant in East Africa to manufacture galvanised roofing sheets under the name Steel Africa Limited. The Chandaria family set up their own galvanising plant in Tanzania and later asked the Shah family to join hands. This is how the two families got into partnership again. Presently, although the Comcraft Group is worldwide, only one part of it is in partnership with the Shah family. They are partners in the steel industry in Kenya and the Eastern and Southern Africa region – Uganda, Tanzania, Ethiopia, Zambia, Malawi and South Africa. Subsequent investments by the Comcraft Group in Nigeria, Ghana, Ivory Coast, Cameroon and elsewhere in the world were done exclusively by the Chandaria family.

Although the business split had left the family with big financial problems, Devchand was determined to see that his siblings got further education. It was difficult for Manu's parents to decide if they should send the children to America. Devchand and Ratilal urged them to let Manu and Keshav go. Once in the US, they would find a way to support them. The parents finally agreed and the two brothers left for further studies from India.

At the time aeroplanes were rare and the biggest in India was the Dakota DC–3. Manu and his brother planned to travel to America via Nairobi in order to see the family. It would be their first time on a plane. The plane journey was to take two days with night stops in Karachi and Iran. Even before leaving India, they encountered peculiar incidents. On the day that their journey was beginning, it was raining hard when they took off. Two and a half hours into the flight, the air stewardess announced that there was a problem and the plane would be returning to Mumbai. Everyone started panicking and praying. Passengers had to be rearranged to balance the weight of the plane. Luckily, the plane landed safely in Mumbai. The next morning half the passengers did not come back for the flight out of fear.

On this day, Manu's relatives who had already bid farewell to them the day before came back to the airport, most of them in tears. When they were set to leave, the plane's engine wouldn't start. The flight was postponed again. They succeeded in taking off on the third day, finally getting to Nairobi where they stayed for three weeks. They were overwhelmingly pleased to be with the family. By then only the younger children were studying in India. Building bonds with each other in the family is one strong element of the Indian families.

After the three weeks, Manu and Keshav left for New York. This time, the plane was a little bigger than the Dakota one. It was owned and operated by the British Overseas Airways Corporation (BOAC), the British state airline at the time. The first night stop was Libya. From there they flew to the east coast of France. On the third day, they arrived at Croydon in the United Kingdom where they were met by a family friend who took them to the hotel where they were to spend the night. In London, Manu was fascinated to see a beautiful city, big buildings, wide roads, and beautifully well-laid-out parks.

After a couple of days in London, the two brothers took a flight to New York. During the night, they stopped at a Scottish airport located on the tip of England. Here, they had their first encounter with British five-star dining. Dinner was laid out on a huge table with a lot of cutlery, three forks on one side and three knives on the other, a butter knife for the bread and so on. Manu and his brother had never used a fork before because in India food is eaten by hand. Every time, they found themselves picking the wrong knife or fork. A huge Scotsman standing behind them would come up, with his eyes popping out, and sternly say "Sir!" pointing out the right cutlery. This happened several times. The brothers felt so intimidated that they left the food and walked away.

Other than constant airsickness, the rest of the journey was uneventful. There was another overnight stop in Greenland before landing at LaGuardia Airport in New York. A family member of one of their agents in India was on hand to welcome Manu and Keshav. He hosted the pair at his home where they had their first home-cooked meal since leaving Kenya. They spent the night in a hotel in Manhattan but could not sleep because of the time difference.

They were fascinated by the tall skyscrapers until late into the night. The fast elevators in their hotel made them wonder at the speed with which America had developed.

At the railway station the next day, Manu bid farewell to Keshav who was going to California. Manu boarded a train for the two-day journey to the University of Oklahoma. That was in September 1948. For the first time in his life he was now completely alone and he immediately felt homesick. Every so often he would go to a corner and cry out of loneliness and misery.

At the university, there were only four students of Indian origin. Luckily, one of them was Manu's friend and a distant relative. He played a critical role as he helped him to survive the first few days, especially because his arrival coincided with the start of the fall, hence it was beginning to get cold. Within a week, he had lost confidence in his ability to survive at the university and called his friend in New York expressing his wish not to stay. His friend however, encouraged him to stay a little longer. This helped, for when the studies began he got busy and regained his confidence.

Even when he had regained confidence, other adjustments at the university presented considerable difficulty. Diet, language, education system and sports were some of the things he had to deal with. Indian food was not readily available; there were all sorts of restaurants but none served Indian food. Manu decided to survive by drinking a lot of milk in a day, almost two pints, and eating rice, spinach, maize (corn), boiled carrots, salads and yoghurt. These became his daily menu. Milk was particularly important as it served as an alternative to the coffee and cola that were so popular in America. Being Gandhian, he would not take them. With time, he tried to get used to eating the Italian and Mexican vegetarian food in order to get variety into his diet. After six months of taking milk, he got so fed up with it that every time he saw a glass of milk he would get sick. This particularly affected his health, with his weight falling to a hundred and two pounds (around 46kg).

Language also presented a major hurdle. Having come from a Gujarati-speaking community, Manu initially found it difficult to understand the American accent of his professors. In addition, he experienced a remarkable change in the education system since the American system was based on continuous assessments. Spot tests were often given, which contributed to the final grade. This meant studying continuously in order to be prepared. This was unlike in India where one used to wait until the end of the year and cram everything in the last few days. However, the system suited Manu well and he worked on the accent. Soon, he began to get good grades.

With regard to sports, the college in Mumbai did not have any playgrounds, so he played indoor games like table tennis and badminton. In America, the most popular sports were American football and basketball. Manu's ignorance of other games and his small size put him at a disadvantage. He could not participate in any of them; hence, he opted to join the cheering squad for the football team. As a result, he attended most of its matches which helped him to make many friends. He was also able to make friends with a lot of young war veterans, as they seemed to accommodate his dietary difficulties. With the war now ended, some of those in their mid-twenties joined the university.

During the summer vacation Manu would do extra courses to earn credits. As a result, he completed his course in two years instead of the normal three. After the first semester, he had changed his course from petroleum engineering to mechanical engineering, reasoning that mechanical engineering was a more relevant course for a student living in a country with no oil. Manu would spend the December vacations every year with Keshav in California. Luckily, there would always be an Indian friend with a car in which they would take a drive and tour the country. His favourite spots were the Grand Canyon and Glacier National Park in Canada. The latter had beautiful huge glaciers.

As an international student Manu received invitations to speak about India in clubs. During such public holidays like Thanksgiving and long weekends, he would be invited by the other students to spend the days at their homes. These talking and interactive experiences broke his shyness and eliminated the fear of public speaking. His speaking ability developed tremendously and he completely opened up. Soon he became the President of the international club and also joined two national fraternities for students in engineering.

At the end of his first engineering degree he decided to take another year to do a Masters, which upset his parents who thought that he would not go back home. He had to reassure them earnestly that he had neither lost his culture nor had he gotten into a love affair to be induced to stay on in America. Nevertheless, he found life in America fantastic with high possibilities of growth. As long as one worked hard there was always ample reward. After completing his studies, he returned to Kenya in 1951 and subsequently joined the family business.

Joining the family business

Upon his return home, Manu went straight to the only remaining industrial asset of the Chandaria family, Kaluworks Limited. He was given a job as a second engineer at the plant, which now had forty employees. The chief engineer, to whom he was reporting, was a long-time employee but not a family member.

At the plant, Manu found six other family members. They were three of his brothers, two uncles and a cousin. The three brothers were Devchand, Ratilal and Keshav. Devchand, who had joined the family business in 1936, was now the head having taken over the reins after their father retired. Ratilal had joined the family business in India in 1942 and relocated to Kenya in 1945. Keshav, who had been in America with Manu, had returned home and joined the business a year earlier. Maganlal and Chaganlal, the two uncles, were working in two separate sections, one at the plant and the other in sales. Kapoor, the cousin, had joined the business from Mumbai and was looking after sales, having just completed his university education in India.

Manu not only found the business crowded with his family, but the home was also crowded. More than thirty members of the family lived together in four apartments of three bedrooms each. One apartment had been converted into a kitchen, dining room and two formal sitting rooms – one for men and the other for the women. The three other apartments were all living quarters. Rent for the apartments was about Ksh 1,200 a month. Only one servant was employed and he used to work until 3.00 pm every day. The family also shared one car. It was indeed a time of financial difficulties given the small nature of the business and expenses were kept to the minimum. Everyone had to make adjustments to suit the circumstances. At the end of the month, every working member of the family would hand over their salaries to Devchand who would pool the money and use it for family expenses. With such a large family, there was no money left over for a young man of twenty-two years to entertain himself, so Manu had a limited social life. During such moments, Manu would reflect on whether he really needed to remain in the family business.

However, thoughts about his family overwhelmed him coupled with reflections on his college days in India and the subscription to the Gandhian philosophy. Their parents and the family had gone through problems in life educating them and building a base for their future. Although the base had significantly reduced, they still had ambitions and dreams. Would leaving at this time be the right thing to do? The values that Manu had cultivated in his life came to the rescue. He immediately and with finality made up his mind that, irrespective of the size of the business, he would serve the family and use all his intelligence, business acumen and knowledge to make sure that the business succeeded. Once his mind was made up he never again thought of leaving; there was no turning back.

With a new resolve, he got into a daily routine. He would wake up at 6.00 am, have breakfast and join the rest so that by 6.40 am they would be at the plant to open the gates. A siren would go off at 6.50 am and again at 7.00 am signalling the work to begin. He would eat lunch at home with the family members and go back to work, ending his day just before 6.00 pm. A whole new revival started. They embraced a whole new way of thinking including looking at new opportunities, products and markets, systems and financing. Everything was looked at afresh with a view to growing the business.

The main challenge now was how to expand the business because at its present size it could not sustain seven family members, three of whom had joined after their university education. The family had paid such a high value for the business. The business had to pay for itself and grow or vanish.

As a strategy for growth, they first decided to import an aluminium rolling mill. Until then they had been importing aluminium circles to make the pots and pans. To finance the venture, they sought a loan (amounting to £25,000) from Standard Bank, a decision that demonstrated the first of several major generational differences in opinion between the family members. Manu's father and uncles always felt that one should never borrow money and make any commitment unless they have money in the account. Their ideology was that you can only grow with savings. But the youngsters were saying that one can use other people's money to expand and grow much faster. Fortunately, this opinion prevailed and financing was possible.

With money from the loan, they imported equipment from Italy and set up what would become the first aluminium rolling plant on the coast of East Africa at Mombasa. The plant was for manufacturing the raw material required to make pots and pans. Keshav went to Italy for six months for training. He returned with two people to train the workers in Kenya. The plant was officially opened in 1954 by Sir Evelyn Baring, the Governor of the Kenya Colony.

Inviting the Governor to open the rolling plant was of strategic importance. Government help was required because there were always roadblocks during the colonial days. The government was not responsive to petitions such as reduction of duty on machinery or on finished products. The economic policy encouraged trade but not industrial investment; in fact, there were no incentives for manufacturing because Kenya was considered more as a market for goods from overseas than a manufacturer. In other words, the government did not encourage local manufacture of products.

Racial discrimination was also a conspicuous feature during the colonial times, not just in the economic field but also in social circles. Around 1954, amid the racial segregation, Manu briefly took up golf after he had been allowed to join the exclusive white golf club. One day the manager of Standard Bank Mombasa branch where Manu's family banked had asked Manu why he did not play golf. Manu told him that he didn't think the private clubs would allow him to join because brown and white people did not mix. The manager went to the club and said he wanted to sponsor Manu, an Asian, to join. He was told that it wasn't possible to take an Asian for membership. At that time, the bank used to sponsor golf tournaments. Furious, he told them that if they didn't accept his Asian applicant as a member, the bank would stop sponsoring the tournaments. Fearing to lose the sponsorship, the club hurriedly accepted Manu as a member and he began to play. Fortunately, there was another Asian member. He was glad he had company.

However, the golfing did not last long. Usually, the family members in the business would hold daily meetings in the morning at ten o'clock for half an hour. When Manu missed two such meetings, Devchand got alarmed and summoned him to explain his absence. Manu replied that he was taking golf lessons. The other members looked at him strangely. Devchand, making use of his seniority, reprimanded him and told him to stop chasing the little ball to put into a hole; the company had a bigger hole that needed more attention. There was seemingly no time to play golf. That was the day Manu left golf and has never played since.

The Chandarias had been making pots and pans for twenty-three years. They had a competitor, Narshidas & Co., who had started production in 1930. The resulting price war was such that at times both companies did not make any money (they did not register losses either). It was time to diversify; hence, the decision to produce a raw material. Making the raw material (aluminium circles) would not only open a new line, but it would also give them a logistical advantage over their competitor in terms of flexibility (in respect of making different sizes). Now it was possible to make any new sizes immediately the market demanded, whereas the competition would need to order the raw material three months in advance to do the same.

Next, the company diversified into steel and wire manufacturing. It started producing steel fencing, barbed wire, nails and steel, weld mesh and BRC of thicker material for construction purposes. BRC West Indies Limited started manufacturing welded wire mesh for concrete reinforcement in 1980. There was also competition in the steel business, so the Chandarias decided to diversify further and started making hurricane lanterns and then pressure stoves, known as Primus, that used kerosene. By then the workforce had grown to five hundred employees.

In 1952 the Chandarias had spotted an opportunity for setting up an aluminium pots and pans plant in Usumbura (later renamed Bujumbura and capital of Burundi). This was during a trip that Devchand and Ratilal had undertaken in a car, in which they visited northern Uganda, Kigali and Bujumbura. At the time, Burundi was part of Belgian Congo. Consequently, the Belgian Government gave them permission to set up a small plant for manufacturing *sufurias*.[6] However, the government later realised it had made a

---

6   *Sufuria* is a Kiswahili term referring to a commonly used cooking utensil in East Africa made of metal. Before its introduction, earthen pots were universally used.

mistake, as allowing a plant to be set up would open up the country to Indians. With Belgian policies as discriminatory as apartheid in South Africa, the consent had to be reversed. Since the government had already given a letter allowing the investment, all manner of tactics were used to build frustration. One such tactic was to block the money transfer, amounting to five thousand pounds sterling and equivalent to one hundred thousand shillings, which had been used to purchase the equipment. Consequently, the equipment was now lying idle in the country.

When they sent the money via London it was blocked. Then they tried sending via New York, but it was blocked too. Fortunately, a friend in Bujumbura asked them why they had not started running the plant and they explained their predicament. He immediately offered to help by providing the money to the required amount. Within no time, the plant was up and running; the manufacturing began. Thanks to the brotherhood among the Indians, the problem was solved. In fact, such brotherhood was not just in Kenya but in other neighbouring countries. People joined hands and helped each other.

When the government realised that manufacturing had already started, it allowed the money into the country. Manu's cousin, Kanti, who was also an engineer by profession and had joined the business in 1952, was sent to Bujumbura to run the plant. This was the family's first expansion outside Kenya. By 1958 the company had eight hundred employees.

Marriage and further business expansion

Despite the social family problem within the Chandarias and Shahs as well as their business split, Manu and Aruna fell in love with each other. Manu courted Aruna for three years before the family agreed to the marriage. He married Aruna in 1955. As an American-educated young man, he wanted to go for a honeymoon, but pressures of work could not permit.

Initially, Manu was concerned about the imminent misery that would engulf his new bride. Aruna was joining a large family with more than thirty people. How was she going to fit in, especially coming from a home where she had never cooked? There were servants always to look after the family. Adjusting into the new large and joint family would not be easy. It required a philosophical understanding, strong commitment and humility. She had to accept him and the family as they were. It made Manu realise that truly women make a home. For one to give up so much freedom to accommodate a joint family like his was no doubt a major sacrifice.

Manu and Aruna had their first daughter Priti in 1956. Aruna went to India to be with her parents. They had not returned to Kenya since they left. According to the Indian culture, the first child is usually born at the home of the wife's parents. As a result, Manu did not see his daughter until she was six months old.

In early 1958, Manu was asked to relieve his cousin in Bujumbura, Congo, for a few months because his cousin's wife was about to give birth. This was going to be a major challenge because he did not know a word of French, which was the official language. In Congo, Manu became the manager, accountant, engineer and delivery boy as it was a one-man show. Besides, it was a small plant with only twenty employees though it was profitable. His wife, Aruna, helped him with the administrative duties.

Kenya Aluminium was well known for its *sufurias*. It was supplying the products as far as Kinshasa and all over the western coastline of central Africa. People used to buy the aluminium *sufurias* and stack them outside their homes as a sign of prosperity. It was amazing that as early as the 1950s aluminium *sufurias* made in Kenya had found their way through to eastern Congo and beyond. Manu stayed in Bujumbura for about eight months and then returned to Mombasa.

Soon after returning to Mombasa, the family met Sir Ernest Vasey whose advice changed the company's direction significantly. His contribution in developing the family's businesses and the family code of conduct was something that the Chandarias would always remain indebted to him for. Sir Vasey was then Kenya's Minister for Finance and a man of tremendous vision. He advised the Chandarias that, to survive and grow, they had to expand into the neighbouring territories. His argument was that once the countries became independent they would each want a share of their investments. When Tanganyika gained its independence in 1961, Sir Vasey left Kenya and became the country's first Finance Minister. Much later he was to become chairman of the Comcraft Group.

At around the time the Chandarias were meeting Sir Vasey, the East African Community decided to allocate different industries to different countries. Aluminium was allocated to Tanzania although the Chandarias were operating from Kenya. Sir Vasey felt that Kenya Aluminium should have a presence in Tanzania. Subsequently, he offered to help the company get started. In addition, he asked the family to think about getting into other countries like Uganda and Ethiopia. At that time, Uganda was the richest of the three countries in the East African Community. The country had established businesses owned by the Asian community like the Madhvani Group, the Mehta Group and Vaderas. The Chandaria business was very small in comparison; for instance, the Madhvani had sixty-five manufacturing units. To the Chandarias, the thought of getting into Uganda was good, but not to compete in that league.

In 1958, the family in partnership with the Khimasia family bought a match-manufacturing plant at Kinangop in an auction. Earlier, the families had a partnership when Manu's father had just arrived from India. This partnership had ended just before Manu was born. This was a revival of the old partnership. Since it was not possible to operate the plant in the White Highlands, the partners hired a European engineer to dismantle it, put it on trucks and send it to Mombasa. The plant was later set up in Mombasa. The partnership was extended to an investment in a chemical plant managed by a joint partner in India. This implies that the growth of the Chandaria businesses was achieved through various partnerships and understandings. One always has to look forward to finding opportunities for growth. Partnerships only work if relationships remain cordial irrespective of businesses.

Late in 1958, Manu and his wife decided to take a month-long holiday in Europe. They left young Priti with Aruna's sister Pushpa who was married to Devchand, Manu's eldest brother. They went to Britain, France and Germany and, on their way back via Italy, their vacation was interrupted. An urgent telegram from Devchand reached them asking Manu to return immediately and take care of a crisis. He obliged and returned home to find that the problem was not manufacturing but marketing. The company was producing too many goods that were not being sold. Although Manu was in charge of production, Devchand asked him to go to Uganda to do marketing. This was not Manu's area of expertise, but he obliged given that in those days there was no room for arguing in the family. According to Indian customs, once the head of the family decided something, one just packed their bags – and obliged. This is what discipline means. When a job had to be done, even if it did not fit in with one's thoughts, they just got on with the job at hand. That's how Manu found himself struggling to crack the Uganda market.

Before leaving for Uganda, Manu bought a new two-door Opel in which he drove his family to Nairobi. In Nairobi, Manu and his family spent a few days with his brother before driving to Kampala. Based in Nairobi, the family had closed the Premchand Brothers wholesale provision stores two years earlier to focus its energies on manufacturing. The Nairobi company office, which was headed by Ratilal and an uncle, Khetshi, became the base for procurement of equipment and raw materials. It was also the marketing office for Kaluworks. The company had also entered into an agency kind of agreement with Steamship Company of India Limited, a shipping company belonging to the Indian government, as its sole agents in Kenya. The company plied the route between Mumbai and Mombasa. Ratilal had proved an astute entrepreneur and negotiator with a vision of taking the family businesses to greater heights. He travelled all over the world looking for opportunities, ideas and equipment.

Once in Kampala, Manu and his family stayed with the Steamship Company's agent in Uganda while they looked for a place of their own. After some search, they got a rental house in an exclusive area at an equivalent of Ksh 800 per month. However, when Manu told Devchand about the house, his brother was furious. How could he rent such an expensive house? The house for the entire family in Mombasa cost less than that. He couldn't understand how two people and a child could spend that much on a house. Manu explained to him that he needed a decent place. It was only after some protracted debate that Devchand finally relented. Again, the significance of the head of the family was immediately visible; Manu had to seek permission to rent the house. The family's financial conditions were still not so good, which explains why Devchand objected to spending a lot of money on a house.

Manu had been sent to Uganda because the country was the biggest market in East Africa. However, there was strong competition in the name of East African Aluminium Works Limited. The company was so strong that it hardly gave any room for the Chandarias to sell. Its plant was in Kampala, which made it easier for it to sell at a cheaper price than the others. Manu had a big disadvantage because he had to bring in products from Mombasa in railway wagons. He had to device a formidable strategy if he was to make any inroads into the market. And that is what he did.

In a bid to outshine the competition, Manu adopted a more personalised approach. He started doing the rounds to recruit customers. First, he engaged them in personal conversations, listening to them when they asked about local, regional and international politics, about currency and taxes, as well as advised them on what to do about a son who was going to matriculate. After a hearty discussion they would reward him by placing an order. Then he would pool several orders to make it cost-effective to send the goods from Mombasa. However, as soon as the *sufurias* landed in Uganda and the competitor got wind of it, the latter would drop the prices to undercut Kenya Aluminium. What was he to do when he was up against an established competitor, didn't know the people, was cut off from the market, and most people did not have the capacity to buy from him, and those who could buy significant quantities like 5,000 sets of *sufurias* got such a low price from the competitor that he couldn't match it?

At the beginning, Manu sold very little, but the friendships he had cultivated from those who often asked his advice about their personal problems started to bear fruit slowly. He knew that the social aspect is what would help him to break into the Uganda market. But building the social relationship was not easy. He had succeeded in building good relations with other people in his university and working days in America and Mombasa respectively, but Uganda had posed a challenge as he was faced with business people. Wooing the customer needed lots of charm, ample time to listen and being able to take an interest in their lives. This presented one big test. He had to survive, and he knew there was no room for failure.

Eventually, his competitor's customers who were fed up with the impersonal services switched allegiances. Manu had now won their hearts and had built not just a business relationship, but a personal one too by taking an interest in their personal affairs. This gave him a totally new perspective to growth.

To build up on his modest success, Manu had to lead a very strenuous life. Every week he would travel around the country, once to the western parts of Masaka and Mbarara with a night's stay, and another time he would go to Jinja, Tororo, Mbale and Soroti to the east often staying two nights out of Kampala. His wife Aruna gave him tremendous support during this time as he would leave her without a car. Moreover, she had to stay alone for days in a new city. Luckily, the Manus had cultivated a few close friends who looked after Aruna and his daughter during this absence. Although security at that time was not a problem, one could get lonesome.

After a year, business was picking and Manu decided to buy three warehouses in Kampala. With the warehouses, he could stock up and service orders faster. He also procured a truck, a driver and a salesman. His customers appreciated the improved services. Meanwhile, the competitor had become abusive, didn't care about the customers and would shout at them when they were late in paying him. Slowly, the customers got so fed up with the services that they started turning to Manu. This served Manu well.

Normally, in line with Indian traditions, wives do not get involved in businesses. However, the wife of Manu's cousin in Bujumbura was assisting her husband. Aruna also started helping Manu to do the invoices and to look after the warehouses while he visited customers and did the salesman job. Often the driver would not show up for work and Manu would drive the seven-tonne truck with the salesman who did the deliveries. Thus, he did not lose a single chance to get the goods into the market and serve the customers. Many customers did not even know that he was the son of the owner of Kenya Aluminium. They thought that he was a salesman. Manu did not mind because it allowed the customers to speak freely with him. Such adaptability helped him to break into the Uganda market, even though it was still controlled by the competitors.

After gaining some ground, Manu gathered enough confidence to approach his competitor – East African Aluminium Limited – directly and try to bring the price war to an end. He politely reminded them that they had been fighting with his family since 1932 and told them that neither of them was making any profits, instead they were slowly killing each other. He warned them that if they would not allow Kenya Aluminium to make profits, then the Chandarias would not allow them to sell anything in the market. After all they were only a manufacturer and supplier while the Chandarias, besides being manufacturers and suppliers of pots and pans, were also producers of raw materials. In addition, he reminded them that customers now regarded the Chandarias as friends.

During the meeting, Manu proposed that the two families get together and set up a joint company in which both would provide the goods and sell at the same price. Their patriarch found it difficult to understand the proposal, but the family agreed with Manu and they took it upon themselves to convince him. Eventually, the families agreed and together they created a joint company called Sufuria Sales Limited. Immediately profits started rolling in and the aluminium business in Uganda started making money.

Manu was in Uganda for three years. Summing up his experience, he says: "The first year I was just building relations, in the second year was to bring our competitor to his knees, and the third year was for setting up the joint business." It is the Uganda experience that gave him new insight into the power and importance of marketing. First, he learnt that relationships with clients are most important. Customers should believe in the producer or seller. Secondly, he learnt that one should establish the market first and then produce goods that the customers want instead of producing goods and trying to sell. Manu realised that they had been doing the latter. And it is only after the market is established that one can introduce new items. A producer cannot take it for granted that the market will take the goods he or she has produced. This is why Manu's company was not doing well initially.

Before the Uganda experience, Manu's concerns as an engineer had revolved around finding ways to manufacture more quantities, at cheaper rates, and of better quality. Now he knew that without a market it was not possible to succeed in business.

Overall, Manu's family was happy with his achievements in Uganda. Now that the business was well established he returned to Mombasa in 1961. By this time the family was living in two homes. Manu's father and his children were living in one, while the uncles and his cousins were living in the other. In 1962 Manu opted to get his own home. Subsequently, he rented a four-bedroom house in Tudor estate where he stayed with his wife and children.

Regional expansion drive

As soon as Manu came back to Kenya, he was off to see Narshidas & Co., another of their competitors. Like East African Aluminium Limited, they had been in a price war for years. Manu tried to replicate his Uganda solution with the new target. He told them that the families had been fighting for so long and so viciously that they were only making enough money to survive, which was not right. He told them that the goal ought to be to expand the industries, get bigger and create more employment and wealth. By undercutting each other such growth would be impossible to achieve.

At first, Narshidas were hesitant. Manu knew that they did not have a market in Uganda anymore as a result of their partnership with East African Aluminium which had made both companies very strong. So he offered a sweetener. He told them that if they produced an agreed quantity and gave it to the Chandarias they would sell and pay them. This way both companies would make money. If demand was lower than what Narshidas produced, the Chandarias would have to work hard to sell the excess goods and if it was higher they would gain. Narshidas family agreed.

Although banding competitors together could lead to consumer exploitation through monopoly, Manu looked at it from a long term perspective. If competition is so cut-throat that no one gains, companies cannot expand and create more employment. It makes no sense to lose thirty years in cut throat competition against each other and not be able to produce significant volumes and value or create employment. Being tied up in such a way eventually leads to companies killing themselves. They undercut each other and fail to pay duty and other taxes because they have to make ends meet.

Consumer exploitation is not necessarily obvious. For instance, it doesn't translate that because two competitors have come together this will double the price of the products. In Uganda where Kenya Aluminium merged with East African Aluminium, there was a third manufacturer who kept the new alliance in check. Importation of finished products (especially in Kenya) was always an option and a possibility. In the case of Narshidas, Manu's proposal was borne out of the fact that the Chandarias had grown vertically and horizontally producing many more different products while the Narshidas had remained a *sufuria* manufacturer.

In 1960 while Manu was in Uganda, the family decided to close down the aluminium rolling mill in Mombasa and move it to Tanzania. Subsequently, Ratilal, Praful (Manu's nephew) and later two of Manu's cousins, Kapoor and Anil, went to Dar es Salaam. Within a year they had a fully fledged office and were prepared to set up a new rolling mill. The Chandarias had to buy new equipment of a bigger capacity to increase production because they would be serving a larger market covering the East African countries. While the Mombasa plant had been producing two thousand tonnes a year, the new plant tripled the capacity to six thousand tonnes. The new mill in Tanzania was not only bigger but also enjoyed more space which made it possible to produce better quality.

With this investment, the Chandarias also expected the respective governments to provide them with the necessary incentives given the governments' pledge to support local industries. They especially needed protection from import and external competition. For a start, President Julius Nyerere of Tanzania made available thirty-nine acres of land to put up the mill and other industries. The Chandarias went ahead and put up five manufacturing units. The first was an aluminium-rolling plant which started running in 1963. They also put up their first galvanising roofing plant which started manufacturing in 1962. This particular plant gave the family entry into the steel business and opened up their relationships with the Japanese machinery and raw material manufacturers and trading companies.

Relationships with Japanese companies started with Marubeni who introduced the Chandarias to the then Yawata Steel (now Nippon Steel) and Yodogawa Steel.

Marubeni is a renowned international corporation with interests in various industries. It started out as a supplier to the Comcraft Group and today also invests in the Group's cold rolling mills in Africa by taking out an equity stake in projects. Its main business is handling products and providing services in a broad range of sectors. These areas include import and export; transactions in the Japanese market related to food, textile materials, pulp and paper, chemicals, energy, metals and mineral resources, transportation machinery, and offshore trading. The Company's activities also extend to power projects and infrastructure, plants and industrial machinery, real estate development and construction, and finance, logistics and information industry. Marubeni also conducts business investment, development and management on a global level.

These companies were pioneers in and best quality manufacturers of thin roofing products. For a long time, the available galvanised roofing sheets that were being sold were between 0.6mm and 0.3mm. The know-how from the new relationships allowed the Chandarias to manufacture roofing up to 0.18mm. With this capability new lower prices were possible as the number of running metres per ton would almost double. The implication was affordability, which helped many people in Africa to roof their homes.

Manu's family also set up Paper Products in partnership with East African Stationery, which was owned by the Manilal Shah family (Manilal was brother-in-law to Devchand and Manu). The company manufactured exercise books in a highly automated manufacturing line; one put a roll of paper on one side and exercise books would come out on the other end. It was a German plant and technology.

Other plants that started during this period were Metal Products, Casement Africa Ltd and Tanzania Cables. Metal Products produced *sufurias*. Though it was a smaller unit, it was similar to the one previously installed in Mombasa. Casements Africa was a unit that made steel casements and doors. Finally, Tanzania Cables produced copper and aluminium cables.

By this time, Manu had been promoted to a management position within the family. He was sent to Tanzania in 1966 to take control of the Group's operations there as they were experiencing severe cash flow difficulties. He had remained in Kenya helping to run other manufacturing businesses into which the family had diversified. He was concerned with marketing their products as well. In 1968 the Chandarias bought Ideal Casements Limited, a subsidiary of the UK-based Ideal Casements. The company was a manufacturer of casements and the leading supplier of casements and steel doors throughout East Africa. To meet the purchase price the family decided to sell a number of properties they were holding in Nairobi. Giving up prime properties demonstrates the family's commitment towards industrialisation.

The Group expanded rapidly into the region between 1961 and 1965. The family put up a PVC pipe and tube plant. In partnership with the Khimasia family they set up a plant to manufacture matches in Moshi, Tanzania. As a result, they got into board manufacturing to cater for the matchboxes, which propelled the business further.

Encouraged by the business growth, the family started expanding aggressively into the East African region starting with Uganda. Rashmi, Manu's nephew, was sent in 1964 to set up an aluminium pots and pans plant to be known as Uganda Aluminium Limited. In addition, he was to set up a galvanised roofing sheet plant, Uganda Baati Limited. Keshav, who was in Bujumbura at the time, was sent to Ethiopia starting with Asmara and then in Addis Ababa to set up an aluminium pots and pans plant, which they called Ethiopian Aluminium Limited. He was also to set up a galvanised roofing sheet plant and black and galvanised steel pipe and tube plant, Ethiopian Steel Limited.

In 1965, one of the Managing Directors Hirji Shah was sent to set up a series of plants in Zambia. He was later joined by Anil, Manu's cousin. These included a galvanised roofing sheet plant under Steelco, black and galvanised pipes and tubes under Pipeco, PVC pipes and tube plant under Plastico, and zinc oxide used in the rubber industry under Metoxide Limited.

The Chandarias had a formula for expansion. They focused on three lines where they had experience – aluminium pots and pans, galvanised roofing sheets, and steel galvanised pipes and tubes. Along the way, they would pick up other items like printing and cable manufacturing, which were not their core business. The principle was to pick on the items for which they knew the suppliers of the requisite raw material, had the know-how and technology to manufacture, and had people who could move from one place to another to run the plants. Multiplying the manufacturing units was the major success of the family business during this period. Members of the family were sent to these countries to oversee the plants. Their operations in Tanzania remained their largest during this time.

To finance the expansion the Group used internal resources, borrowed from banks and development institutions, and bought machinery on long term contracts. Their Japanese suppliers in particular played a key role in helping to finance them. Once the suppliers knew that they kept their commitments, financing was not difficult. In effect, they made sure that the equipment came in time, was installed in time, production started in time, and the products were sold in time. With this operational principle, they could meet the targets. To achieve this, everyone was kept on their toes.

With the expansion programme, the difficult part was the physical establishment in new territories. Normally, the Group used a greenfield strategy which involved building a new plant from scratch as opposed to taking over existing industries. Many African countries, having just gained independence, did not have built structures. Moreover, adapting to new regulations in the respective countries was a big challenge. To operate in different countries and dealing with different governments was itself a major challenge. In every country the Group had to deal with a different set of banks unless the principal banks with whom they were operating in Kenya were also present in the other countries. In Tanzania, when after a few years of operations President Nyerere nationalised everything (including the industries), the Group had to establish its credibility with the new management of banks. In Ethiopia the language and legal system were different from East Africa. However, the zeal to expand and become a pan-African manufacturer was so strong that the Group found answers to all the impediments.

Sir Ernest Vasey, who had introduced the family to the Tanzanian government, had left the country after a year to take up a new position as the World Bank resident representative in Pakistan. The four years he was stationed in Pakistan coincided with the period when the family was aggressively expanding into the region. During that time the family continuously sought his advice on how to set up businesses in foreign countries.

The rapid expansion gave birth to the idea of professionalising the management of the Group's various operations. With plants in each of the surrounding countries (sometimes several of them), the family members were stretched and thin on the ground when it came to managing them. This intimated that if the Group wanted to expand further, the family could not do it by themselves; they needed other people. And it meant not just hiring people in management positions, but also delegating authority to them. "This is very difficult for Asian businesses worldwide because it means surrendering your power to someone else. It took considerable time to find suitable people on a constant basis and to subsequently spruce them into our family's philosophy," says Manu.

An example of such people was Hemendra Modi. He used to be the CEO of Insteel Limited before he was moved into a three-year programme that was meant to create a company called Bahari, a forwarding, insurance and transport business, which he was to turn into a big group. Previously, the family used to carry out the clearing function in-house. With the setting up of the company, it took up the clearing and forwarding for the Group's companies, subsequently building up external business. The insurance segment brought in business from outside, while the transport business grew from six to eighteen trucks, subsequently doubling the number. Overall, the new company grew the business by forty percent.

Professionalising the Group became the second major battle within the family. Devolution or delegation of power is one of the most difficult areas in a family business. To convince oneself and others that delegation of power can be done is a difficult undertaking. The Chandarias' success vis-à-vis other Asian families is due to the fact that they realised early enough that one cannot run many organisations. One has to delegate authority and make the managers responsible for the business. In effect, the Chandarias delegated authority systematically country by country in the same order in which they had expanded starting with Tanzania. This was done in either of two ways, through the Group or through partnerships. Even where it was done through partnerships, they insisted that the businesses must be run by professionals.

Expansion across Africa and overseas

Considering the growth of the family with regard to size, especially the rate at which the children were coming out of school, Sir Ernest Vasey advised that the family should establish a base outside Africa. This explains why the family went to India in 1960 and subsequently to the United Kingdom in 1965. Sir Vasey was to become instrumental in guiding the family on where and how to expand in new territories. At the time, he was the Chairman of Comcraft Group and was also serving as chairman of several other companies in Kenya including Bata Shoe and Carbacid. He brought this experience to the Group.

Another factor that pushed the Group's expansion worldwide was personal space. To avoid treading on each other's toes, the family had a policy that not more than four to five members should live in the same centre. They also had a policy that a family member could settle anywhere he wanted after retirement.

Whenever the family made the decision to open a plant, it worked as a team. This had been encouraged by the principle of delegation of power, which the family had adopted. However, Devchand was still the head of the family and therefore the final authority. The family team would meet regularly to decide what to do and where to expand. Sir Vasey's involvement with the management of the Group was deserved. He knew that the business had to run in a proper manner. Board meetings would take place in a regular fashion, a board paper would be presented, and regular reviews would be done before the board meeting. With time this became more elaborate; from a one-page set of minutes and a small report to voluminous board papers.

During the sixties and early seventies, the younger generation qualified in various capacities and joined the family business. They had studied in the best universities in the UK and the US. Sunil, Manu's cousin, completed his education in engineering, while another cousin, Anil, attended London School of Economics and did his MBA at Harvard. Two of his nephews, Praful and Rashmi, and another cousin, Chand, all completed their education in the UK and joined the business in Kenya. Subsequently two of them moved to Tanzania and one back to the UK. A nephew, Indu, completed his MBA at Harvard, joined the business in Kenya and subsequently went to set up an office in Geneva. Each of them came with new vigour, outlook and excellent education and started making strides in building the Group. Later, Rohit, Manu's youngest nephew, joined the Group bringing in the speciality in his area of knowledge. The most important was their drive, dedication and teamwork.

New countries, newer challenges and an environment of encouragement pushed the Group into a new league. Teamwork, formulating strategies and blending the strengths and weaknesses of individuals gave the family new dynamics. A multinational Group started emerging. It was a win-win situation and before long the Group, as a family, started to make its presence felt in many countries. This is what a joint family is all about.

At the end of 1965 Manu's brother Ratilal and nephew Praful were sent to the UK to scout for new business opportunities as the next generation of children started getting into the business. They did several small acquisitions including a trading company and a manufacturer of kitchen furniture. Later they acquired a steel trading and distribution company in Switzerland, a steel roofing and cladding company and a company manufacturing plactic hangers in Italy.

These acquisitions in Europe opened up new challenges because the management of these companies had to remain local. Although the Group had bought Ideal Casements in Nairobi in 1968 and inherited the English manager, the acquisitions in Europe marked the official shift in policy with regard to hiring Indian professionals only to manage the Group's investments. The family no longer directly managed these companies; instead they supervised the local managers already in place. It also marked a new level of professionalising the Group. Professionals from other countries and nationalities could now be hired as opposed to only professionals of Indian descent. In all cases the family only dealt with the top management, not staff on the shop floor. The non-Indian professional managers were groomed to sell the family ideology and implement its vision.

At around 1973, an opportunity presented itself for buying a plant in Nigeria. Manu's cousin, Sunil, was sent there. The plant was manufacturing aluminium pots and pans under the Tower brand. The brand products were very popular. Despite the popularity, the UK owners wanted to sell it off. This was a welcome breakthrough into the West African market and it became the Group's first acquisition in the region.

Expansion to South East Asia took place in 1972. Ratilal and Praful (Manu's eldest nephew), went to Singapore and set up the office. They started looking for investment opportunities there. Many years later, Praful was joined by Manu's younger nephew Vimal, a graduate of the London School of Economics, Manu's son Neal, a Stanford graduate, and a son of Manu's nephew Paras, also a graduate of the London School of Economics.

In 1978, Keshav, who was in Ethiopia, was relocated to Canada. The investments in Ethiopia had been nationalised following the entry of a new socialist regime. In Canada, he set up a fully fledged office in Toronto to look at possibilities of investment not only in Canada but also in the rest of North America, South America and the Caribbean Islands. Keshav was later joined by Chand, his cousin. A nephew, Pulin, joined them after completing his education in Canada. Over the years, the family decided to send his two other nephews Kuntesh and Raj.

Unfortunately, in 1978 Devchand passed away. Ratilal took over the leadership of the family. He subsequently moved from Singapore to London.

The Group's operations in Africa were considered as being in the 'sunset industry' because developed countries had had such economic activity years before. Only in Papua New Guinea, India, Bangladesh, Nepal and Caribbean did the African experience work. In countries like the United States, Canada, Australia and New Zealand the Group was investing in 'sunrise industries' like media, ICT, manufacturing of electronic parts and software.

Challenges in the expansion programme

Expansion of the family business was not without challenges. When a company is expanding as fast as Manu's business was, the first casualty is usually cash flows. Comcraft Group was no exception. In 1966, Manu was sent to Tanzania to take control of the Group's operations which were experiencing severe cash flow difficulties. Until 1965 there were five Chandaria family members and a horde of managers sitting at the Tanzania office. Naturally, the load on expenses was noticeably high and the business was making losses. Before Manu arrived there, the family members were redistributed. Ratilal and Praful were sent to the UK to open up Europe for the Group, Kapoor was sent to India to look after the Group's partnership there and Anil was sent to Zambia. Therefore, Manu replaced the four of them. Later his cousins, Sunil and Chand, joined him.

When Manu took over the Dar es Salaam operations, he found that it was top-heavy. Every operation had a general manager, financial controller, accountant and production engineer. There were at least sixteen top-level managers. He retained four of the managers and gradually let go of the rest as there was nowhere to absorb them. Being an engineer and not an accountant, his next challenge was how to get the accounts organised. He got junior accounts staff and distributed the work among them such that if there were ten items in accounts to be attended to, he trained five people to do two items each. Someone else consolidated the whole thing. He got them to be efficient in those few items and moved them around to do various jobs. In no time he was quickly getting all the accounts information. Consequently, he could continuously update the family because he knew what was happening in the business every day.

Cheques were written twice a week. Previously, they were being written daily. This new arrangement reduced the amount of time spent doing the ledger. He insisted on getting daily information on certain fundamental items such as stock levels, daily sales and debt collection. He would ask stock levels for 20 items to be taken daily. With around 500 total items in stock, everything would automatically have been checked by the end of the month. He would also walk daily in the warehouses and make sure that the raw materials were stacked in a particular way so that he could visually take stock as he walked around. That way, it was possible to see what was short and what needed to be done. These were the various little systems that he introduced. The systems made it possible to know what was happening on a daily basis. It also served to let everyone know that he had his eyes open. This is what is referred to in management as hands-on supervision.

Today, the Comcraft Group has developed elaborate financial control systems with annual budgets broken down into monthly projections for sales, variable and fixed costs, and cash flow projections and realisation (the difference between revenue and costs) for each product line. When the Group was smaller Manu used to sit on the boards of many companies and go through all the board papers making his comments. Now he only sits on the boards of a handful of flagship companies, namely MRM, Kaluworks, Aluminium Africa Limited (ALAF), Uganda Baati, and Metal Products.

The hands-on approach ensures that people are responsible for their tasks. It is not micromanaging people, but leaving them free to perform their duties while allowing the manager to see what they have done on a daily basis. For example, Manu did not keep the books, but every manager knew that he must have all his previous day's production, sales figures and debt-collection figures on Manu's desk by morning.

Manu holds that many small steps of good management do not cost much. An entrepreneur should create a form of discipline in the people working for them to do things on a daily basis that are a fundamental means to success. For Manu, it entailed working long hours. He woke up at 5.30 am daily and his day didn't end until 11.30 pm. This is a routine that he still maintains to date. The hard work paid off and he managed to turn the company around in two years.

Manu's experience in Tanzania highlights a critical but very sensitive issue in family-owned businesses – what to do when companies overseen by family members do not perform well. Also, things can go wrong because in business there are always ups and downs. In a family situation, it is difficult to fire people when things do not go right. To begin with, it is best to put family members in areas where they have the capability. When things go wrong, it is advisable to move people around to provide them with an opportunity to give another shot. Manu's family policy has been that wherever there is a crisis in a business, the family moves in. Wherever they want to expand the businesses, acquire other businesses, sell major assets or make decisions involving doubling or tripling capacity, the family moves in.

When a plan was mooted to grow the steel production capacity on the eastern coast of Africa from 250,000 to 500,000 tonnes in three years, the family's presence was necessary. This was because, to achieve this goal, it required so many minor inputs. Another example was the USD 30 million worth of investment in a new aluminium zinc-rolling mill for MRM. Of the total required, USD 10 million came from the Group's own resources, while International Finance Corporation (IFC), the private sector arm of the World Bank, put in USD 12 million and the European Investment Bank (EIB) put in USD 8 million. This was a team effort. Members of the family and members of the partnership's family together with professionals made it happen.

Another major challenge in the expansion programme was change in the political environment. In 1968, President Nyerere decided to nationalise every industry in Tanzania. Fortunately, the group's investments were not touched at the time principally because they had been set up in 1961 at the President's invitation. Therefore, they were not considered part of the country's colonial past. However, in 1973 the government came calling again. By then the government had already nationalised 350 companies. They told Manu's family that they did not want to nationalise their investments, but they could not have such a large foreign-owned corporation in the country. They offered to discuss how the government could acquire 60 percent of the shares. By then Tanzania was their largest business operation in Eastern Africa.

Manu's family offered a takeover instead, but the government declined, saying that they wanted the Chandarias to manage the company. The government would invest in the company on condition that the money did not leave the country. They asked the Chandarias to determine the monetary value at existing market rates of 60 percent shareholding. The Chandarias went ahead and did what the government asked; in any case the money would be used to expand the business. With this injection of capital the group put up a steel-rolling mill, asbestos roofing sheet plant, and a plant to manufacture pipes. They continued to manage the company although they were the minority shareholders. Such issues come up in a political environment and an investor has to take them in their stride.

New frontiers into the 21st century

As the Comcraft Group has expanded worldwide, its African business has declined relatively in terms of size (capacity, employment, revenues and so on). Africa now accounts for 26 percent of the Group's size. Europe, including North America, accounts for 40 percent, while South East Asia and Australia account for 35 percent. As evolution of markets takes place, changes continue to take place. A good example is Eastern European countries like Hungary and Russia which have opened up. The largest companies in the Group are Metecno (producing sandwich panels), Mainetti (producing plastic hangers), and the Group's set-ups in Australia and New Zealand. The first two are substantive Group's in their own right with operations in many countries.

In Africa steel is the third largest product category, although the Group has a large investment in steel in other areas. West Africa has grown to become the Group's largest aluminium operation on the African continent largely driven by the large population in Nigeria (over 150 million people), a much bigger market than the three East African countries combined. The other countries on the West African coast where the Group has businesses are Côte d'Ivoire, Cameroon and Ghana. The eastern coast of Africa is a rapidly growing market incorporating their companies in Kenya, Uganda, Tanzania, Ethiopia and South Africa. The Group has smaller set-ups in IT, media and BOP (outsourced services) mostly in Australia, South East Asia, India, Europe and the USA.

In terms of growth, the size of the businesses kept on increasing year after year by almost 25 percent. The markets became bigger and the Group increased its plants' capacities to meet the increased demand. In the 1990s MRM was doing 50,000 tonnes which doubled to 110,000 tonnes. By the time of writing this book the Group was to add another 70,000 tonnes by installing a new rolling mill to get a total capacity of 180,000 tonnes per annum. The size of the Kenyan steel market is around 80,000–100,000 tonnes and MRM exports 50 percent of its annual production to over 40 countries, a majority of them in Africa and a few countries outside Africa.

The Group opened a new vista of marketing; it's a different ball game from marketing only in Kenya. In the last few years it is the skills, quality of people and management structures that are responsible for meeting this demand which has made the Group grow to this size. The Group is poised to get even bigger on the eastern coast of Africa. It closed its biggest financing deal for USD 150 million worth of new investments out of which USD 35 million went to MRM in Kenya, USD 25 million to ALAF in Tanzania and the bulk (USD 90 million) to South Africa. The deal was partly financed by internal generation, IFC, EIB and other financiers. In Tanzania the Group put up a new Alu-Zinc coating plant and in Durban a steel-rolling mill, Alu-Zinc coating plant and a colour coating line. These expansions doubled the Group's capacity from 250,000 tonnes to 500,000 tonnes. The plants came in phases with the last plants completed in 2010.

The Group principle is that when the base is created and it becomes sound one must grow by greater multiples each year. When the growth is well rooted and the plant is being looked after, the size of the tree is noticeable.

To break into new fields and territories, the Group used the next generation of family members to spearhead their efforts. They all had strong educational backgrounds and were familiar with new fields. When the third generation completed their studies – Vimal, Kuntesh, Pulin, Raj and Neal – all the five of them were sent to Nigeria, a station they found challenging. This demonstrates how the family members were moved from place to place, continent to continent, using their strengths and complimenting their weaknesses. This is the discipline that resulted in a fast growth of the family businesses.

The younger generation had, say, computer training, which the older generation did not have. In effect, this generation plays the role of continuously educating the older generation on new business areas. They often pitch new ideas and seek the family consensus to implement them. They have been made the major engine of growth and this is where many businesses fail because the older generation is not willing to let go. If Manu Chandaria is the heart and soul of many things and gets off the scene, would the family get stuck? For Manu's family business, things will still continue. Everything is well laid out and the responsibilities are spread among many others. The fire will not die.

The Comcraft Group shifts its manufacturing operations from place to place as the environment changes and new opportunities come up. For example, the Group's main garment-manufacturing plants used to be in Italy. Subsequently manufacturing units were set up in France, UK, Germany and Holland. However, garment manufacturing has now shifted to South East Asia – Sri Lanka, India, China, Bangladesh and Vietnam.

Another frontier is to expand the Group ownership from private to public. Although the Group has invested in public-quoted companies, the family would like to shy away from being publicly quoted, for now. As time goes by, and the companies get bigger, those running them will probably go public. The Group recently went to the securities exchange and floated a bond of KSh 2 billion. It was at the most difficult time in the financial market, but the bond was fully subscribed. This demonstrated that as and when the Group decides to go public it will have overwhelming support.

Entrepreneurial and management skills

One may ask how Manu managed to reach the apex of such a multinational company. To achieve this requires hard work and above all teamwork where the smallest person is part of the chain. If the chain works alright it will hold. Creating ownership in employees of whatever they are doing is also important as well as continuous training. One has to keep challenging themselves every day then use their capacity to meet that challenge. One should not feel that since they are on top and they are the boss that they should not bother. That leads to mediocrity.

Manu has a proactive and can-do attitude. He believes that anything is possible, something that even his staff can attest and admire him for. He is always up to date and on top of things. His pulse is on the business and he knows what is going on even when he is overseas. Many a manager has been woken up at 6.00 am with a call from Manu asking about an issue in the company. To the top managers under him, he will always give advice but he does not insist that they must take it. He lets them take their own decisions. If they make a mistake, he will not say "I told you so" by way of admonition. That way he tries to encourage and motivate staff. He is also good at managing company politics at board level – a fact of life in any business – to ensure the companies run smoothly.

Manu also believes in giving responsibility to someone who then becomes accountable for his own work. According to him, this is how the Group grows. Even for MRM, the flagship company in the Group, Manu does not interfere with the day-to-day running of the company. Up to a few years ago he would attend quarterly review meetings but today he only attends the annual board meeting.

Another of Manu's attributes is his ability to be modest. He mixes with and can relate to anybody irrespective of economic status. His social work is very important to him. As such each manager is required to do something by way of contributing to social work. In cases where the manager works in the steel plant, he may be required to supply crutches to a physically disabled association. Managers are also required to work with charitable organisations like the Lions Clubs.

It is the principle of constantly challenging oneself that has made Manu accept so many invitations to committees and task forces set up to solve certain issues. A most recent invitation was to chair a thirteen-member consultative group formed to spearhead the implementation of a regional plan to upgrade East Africa's railway network. When he was first asked to join this committee he could have said that he didn't have the time. But he accepted the challenge because he feels he has a responsibility to this country. He doesn't want to see children going to bed with empty stomachs. Moreover, at his age, he feels that time is short and he wants to catch more miles and leave a legacy that people will remember. This is the challenge he has set for himself.

Manu is no longer involved in the day-to-day running of the companies. One of his key roles is brand ambassador for the Group. His knowledge and involvement in upper circles of government and his ability to rally people around the Group are very helpful in getting the business done.

Best and worst moments as an entrepreneur

Manu's best moment was the clinching of the USD 150 million deal under the Safal Group for new investments in steel. What an achievement! However, he prefers to view this more as teamwork than individual effort. This team included a member of the Shah Family (who are the partners), Mr Neelesh Shah, and Mr Narayanan, Mr Goshal, Mr Ashutosh, together with many other members of the operating companies. Having the team which got this new investment was a great thing for Manu. They negotiated, fought, argued and finally got it.

On the other side of success, Manu's worst failure is when he allowed the Tanzanian government to take over the management of ALAF in 1988. Having acquired a 60 percent stake in 1973, they now decided to take over the management, something that was triggered by a botched succession at the company. What happened was that the Managing Director, who was from the Group, decided to retire and his deputy (from the government) was appointed to the position in an acting position. He told the Group that he was ready to take over, but the Group said no. He had to be tried out first. Immediately, he went to the authorities where he gave totally wrong information. Subsequently, the government decided to take over. The Group probably took its position in Tanzania for granted because it had been there since 1960 and its relations with the government had remained good. When the Group finally got back the management of the company after ten years, it was a former shell of itself. It had been mismanaged. It was such a shock to see a large profitable company with an accumulated loss of USD 20 million and its reputation destroyed as well. It took the Group another eight years to wipe out the losses and bring it back to profitability.

Manu considers staying in Kenya as his most difficult decision. Of all the family members, it is only Manu and his cousin Sunil that live in Kenya. The other members are in other centres where the Group operates. While he can afford to live anywhere in the world and whereas there are better returns elsewhere – such that Kenya is not the easiest place to live – he decided to live in the country anyway. The country has had periods of insecurity, periods when standards of service went down , and periods of increasing poverty. The question is, what keeps him in Kenya?

According to Manu, initially his desire to remain in Kenya was motivated by the fact that he was born here and subsequently liked the country and its people. He now feels that Kenya has been good to him. Hence, he now feels a sense of duty and responsibility not just to Kenya, but to the whole of Africa. There is so much to do to bring the countries in Africa out of poverty. He feels very strongly that there is a wide difference between the haves and the have-nots. Consequently, he spends quite a bit of his time advocating policies that will bring hope to the people. His vision is multiple growth for the business, which is connected to equity. To do good, he must earn and provide services to the community at large by involving himself and his people.

But growth is a very difficult task and it creates lots of problems; it inflates egos, reduces humility and makes one to feel very important. Growth creates its own momentum which, if not properly checked and if it has no roots in a value system, will make one lose their way. Manu's family remained together because they had a philosophy which basically stated that they wanted to live and survive together. The family has an eighteen-point code of conduct based on their value systems which is engraved on a little plastic card that Manu carries in his wallet. Point Number Fourteen has to do with inheritance, a thorny issue in many businesses. It states: "To dispense with the traditional practices of inheritance and the resultant inequalities."

Based on the code of conduct, Manu's family cannot hire or fire its members. They hold the philosophy that a brother is not bigger than the other and that each has a place to survive. The principle behind this is to do good ultimately. This is not the usual practice in Asian families. Under normal circumstances, wealth is distributed equally irrespective of how many children one has. If one brother has five children, another has only one, and a third has nine, each brother will get 33 percent. Sharing the wealth further among their children creates a sense of inequality and bitterness where there are more children. This increases the risk of breaking families. In the Comcraft system all the wealth is held in the family not by individuals.

Passing the baton

Over the years, Comcraft Group has expanded tremendously with a presence all over the world. It operates through centres in Nairobi, London, Geneva, Singapore and Toronto. As mentioned earlier, five of the young family members – Vimal, Kuntesh, Pulin, Raj and Neal – came into the business. Before being deployed to work, they were given on-the-job training under the managing director of the Group's company in Nigeria. The training gave them a strong base for their future growth. It is absolutely necessary that younger people work under a person who is not a family member so as to instil in them the requisite discipline to face the future. This prepares them adequately to take over the running of the businesses.

The family management team meets once a year to plan strategy and expansion. The entire family, which has sixty-eight members, meets every two years. The management team is comprised entirely of men. In Indian culture, when girls get married they are taken care of by the husband's family. Thus, women have not been involved in the family business. However, this thinking may soon change because there are now more women than men in the family. In addition, the family has had its first incident of divorce where a daughter went back to her father and she needs to be catered for.

Looking back, Manu feels that it was an enormous challenge for the eight brothers and their cousins to create a base from nothing. With a lot of teamwork the younger Chandarias took over the challenge to create what Comcraft Group is today. To have younger people join business and older members to let them succeed is the most difficult issue. This is what succession is all about.

Going back to the issue of women, it is possible that there is going to be more women in the family than men. Such change is anticipated and the family hopes to be more flexible as time goes by; after all nothing can remain static. One of the family codes that are missing is to maintain the joint family system in such a way that it is modified to meet the changing environment. When the overall code was made, this particular one was probably not felt to be important. In view of the fact that the Indian families are becoming more westernised, there will be pressures to meet the aspirations of younger members. To continue to keep a joint family with its strong values, positive strengths and negative environmental pressures is a game that needs fine balancing. These values can only be maintained with deep understanding and generosity of giving rather than taking. Manu believes that continuous preaching of the family philosophy and living by example is the only way a joint family can succeed.

Social projects and philanthropy

Manu is as renowned globally for his charitable activities as he is revered for his business acumen. According to him, the biggest happiness that he gets is from doing good and remaining happy. Every day there is always something that is not right but if one frets about it they hurt themselves unnecessarily. As Manu says, "Forgive and forget and live the day because once it is gone it is not coming back."

Most of Manu's charitable work is carried out through family trusts set up in regions where the Group operates. In Kenya, he works through the Chandaria Foundation. Through such organisations, it is possible to involve the people in management in charity work, which is the policy of the Group. In Kenya, focus is mostly on two main areas: education and health. Education support is done with a bias to girls. Every year the charity gives one hundred partial scholarships to students in secondary schools, and fifteen in universities and polytechnics. In the area of health, the organisations have supported the building of Chandaria Accident and Emergency Centre at Nairobi Hospital, Pandya Hospital in Mombasa, and 15 Chandaria health centres all over the country.

Personally, Manu provides guidance, time and mentorship through leadership positions in associations such as the Rotary Club, Heart Foundation, Kenya Association of Manufacturers (KAM), Kenya Private Sector Alliance (KEPSA), and East African Business Council. Some of the Group's management staff also donate their time in these associations.

Other charitable organisations that Manu is involved in are the Asian Foundation, Limuru Girls' Centre, Starehe Girls' Centre, Kenya Ear Foundation, Undugu Society of Kenya, Council of Watoto Kwanza Trust and International Fund for Animal Welfare (IFAW). He is the Founding Chairman of the Asian Foundation, which built a hawkers' market on Limuru Road, and in Kibera and Kisumu. The Asian Foundation is looking after two polytechnics built by the United Nations Industrial Development Organisation (UNIDO).

Apparently, Manu has a clear bias on girls' education. He was the Founding Chairman of Limuru Girls' Centre and Starehe Girls' Centre. The latter is a classic example of an attempt to bring out bright young girls who cannot afford higher education and give them life skills and confidence to face today's challenging world. Manu has expressed a wish that there could be Starehe Girls' Centres in every region of Kenya, which would give a chance to the bright girls and provide them with challenging opportunities.

Manu is considerably involved in higher education in the country. He sits on the Council of the University of Nairobi on behalf of Mahatma Gandhi Memorial Academic Society. He also chairs Gandhi Smarak Nidhi Fund at the same university. The Fund provides thirty scholarships for Master's degrees. He also sits as Director and Trustee of United States International University– Africa (USIU-A), the premier institution of management studies. All this clearly signifies his deep interest in education.

Indeed the history of higher education in Kenya started with the Gandhi College which was started in remembrance of Mahatma Gandhi after his death. The Asian community decided to build an institution of higher learning and subsequently collected funds from the Asian communities of East Africa and the then Nyasaland (Malawi) and Northern Rhodesia (Zambia). The Foundation stone of Gandhi College was laid by His Excellency Dr Radhakrishnan, the Vice President of Indian Union and one of the greatest living philosopher-statesmen of the world at that time. The Asian community's contribution in building excellent primary and secondary schools is very well known.

For his contribution in all areas of social and economic endeavours, Manu has been conferred with many awards and honours (see list for selected awards). In a recent survey he was mentioned as one of the most influential hundred people in Kenya. In a second survey he was mentioned amongst the most lovable in the list of lovable and hated hundred people in Kenya.

Role models

Manu's role model is Mahatma Gandhi. He admires him for fighting an entire colonial government without resorting to violence. He also has great admiration for Mother Theresa who visited his home four times while on visits to Kenya. In the area of business, Manu has always admired the philosophy of the Tata Group in India which is one of the biggest philanthropists in India. Other businessmen that he admires are Henry Ford whom he describes as a great engineer, George Welch, the former CEO of General Electric, and Bill Gates, another philanthropist. Of the latter, he admires him for being intelligent, for revolutionalising the ICT industry worldwide, and for creating the largest living charity.

Tips for aspiring entrepreneurs

To aspiring entrepreneurs he says: "Success is not achieved in one jump. To go high up, you've got to climb steps, and all steps must be climbed, which will make you achieve success. It is a difficult but a possible journey. One has to put in hard work and have a sense of purpose in what one does. Successful people have almost similar experiences. It's always hard work, consistency, low profile, humility and approachability."

He hastens to add: "It's also important to create challenges for yourself every day. Without putting hard work and your soul into what you do, you can never do your best. We need to do unusual business. Our country is poor because we are multiplying zero by zero which is always zero. Once we reach to one and multiple one by one, it will be only one. It takes extra effort, passion, strength, capacity and fire in the belly to reach to two and when you multiply two by two it becomes four and four multiplied by four is sixteen. This is what we need. It's not easy but one needs to tell oneself on a continuous basis that it can be done."

Awards

The following is a summary of Manu's awards.

Date	Description of the award
2008	The Lifetime Achievement Award, Delhi, India
2000, 2001 and 2002	Voted East Africa's most respected CEO
2003	He was in Her Majesty Queen Elizabeth II's New Year Honours List, was made an Officer of the Order of the British Empire (OBE) in recognition of his work for the community in Kenya and promotion of Kenyan economic and British interests in Kenya.
2003	In the first year of inauguration, he was one of the 10 recipients of the Pravasi Bhartiya Sanmam Puraskar award from the Government of India. This is an award given to the 10 most distinguished persons of Indian origin overseas in recognition of exceptional services rendered to their countries of domicile.
2003	Conferred the Elder of the Burning Spear (EBS) by Kenyan Head of State.
1997	Awarded the degree of doctor of science by the University of Nairobi in recognition of outstanding achievements in the industrial, manufacturing and business sector and his contribution to the economy of Kenya.

Chapter 2

Samuel Kamau Macharia

There's hardly anyone in Kenya who has not felt the influence of Samuel Kamau Macharia, popularly known as SK Macharia. From his Madhupaper, Royal Credit and then Royal Media Services, SK Macharia has not only touched everyone in Kenya, but has extended his reach in the Eastern Africa region and beyond. Many in business circles, and even in the political field, have described him as a radical and a maverick who resorts to unorthodox means to get what he wants when conventional means fail, something that he has continuously dismissed as a misconception. "I just fight for my rights," he says.

SK Macharia's business enterprises have been characterised by perennial fights, physical and legal, that lasted over decades. And indeed fighting he had to always do in order to keep what he has built with his own hands and sweat, often at great personal cost. Not only has he suffered a systematic pattern of harassment at the hands of the state, which saw him lose three companies (Madhupaper, Royal Credit and the original Royal Media), but he has also been arrested, threatened with detention and shot at. At the height of the Madhupaper saga, his car was sprayed with bullets outside his home in Karen as he waited for the gate to be opened. Miraculously, out of the seventeen cartridges that were recovered from his car, only one bullet got him. It blew off the little finger on his left hand, which had to be reattached with a piece of metal.

Despite these hardships, SK Macharia has never given up. After every defeat, he gets up, dusts himself off and starts again from scratch. After losing Royal Media when its operations were closed down and the equipment confiscated, he restarted it in 2003. After only five years, the business grew again like the proverbial phoenix, rising from the ashes in a spectacular fashion. The media empire is today home to nine hundred employees, a television station and eleven radio stations. A 2011 first quarter survey covering all the districts in Kenya by Ipsos-Synovate, a media-monitoring firm, showed that Citizen Television (Citizen TV) had 50 percent share of the total viewers in the country. When it came to radio, Royal Media stations were the top listened to stations in nine out of twelve geographical regions in Kenya where Ipsos-Synovate measured listenership trends. By any standard, this was a remarkable achievement considering the station had overtaken stations like Kenya Television Network (KTN) and Nation Television (NTV) which had been in operation for much longer.

To understand this phenomenal achievement, one must trace the life and times of SK Macharia. His story illustrates that if something is one's destiny, no power on earth can stop it.

Early life and education

SK Macharia was born and grew up in grinding poverty. Before he was ten years old, he had gone through some experiences that many adults never go through in their lifetime. First, he was separated from his family for over two years and lived like a nomad, herding cattle with Maasai boys in Arusha. Then he had to trek back to his home amid grave personal danger. These childhood experiences instilled in him the toughness and discipline necessary to survive the challenges in the years ahead and were to ultimately shape his future life.

"I am told that my family moved to Sabatia, now Nakuru county in the Rift valley when I was a few days old. The exact date of my birth is not known but elders in my family told me I was born between 1942 and 1944 in Ndakaini Village in Murang'a county. In Kikuyu Ndakaini means 'the place of mud'."

His father, Macharia Karigi worked as a labourer on European settler farms. His mother Nyanjiru Muracia was the daughter of a man who rose to the status of a senior chief in the 1930s. SK Macharia was the only son in the family. His two older sisters died, one in infancy, leaving three – Njeri, Wanjiru and Wambui. His mother died around 1947, soon after giving birth to his youngest sister, Wambui. The young children were looked after by their grandmother Wanene when their father was out working in the fields.

The family was extremely poor and would spend their days picking pyrethrum. Only their father was paid a salary of two shillings and fifty cents a month, which was too low to sustain a family even in those days. The children got *mathace* (remnants of skimmed milk) daily. This daily ration was doled out by the white employer.

In some parts, the white settlers would still allow their workers to use a tiny piece of their land to grow food. However, the plots were usually not big enough to grow food that would sustain the family. In order to get extra food or income, SK Macharia and the other children would go back to the fields after the maize was harvested to pick the grains that had fallen on the ground. This practice was called **kūhūra kīrĩiyū**. The European farms were so large that often they would get half a bag and sometimes even a full bag particularly if they were many children. This is how they used to survive.

43

The family moved around a lot following their father as he sought work on settler farms. After staying in Sabatia for a while, they moved to Molo then Njabini in Kinangop.

Life in Njabini was harder because unlike Sabatia and Molo, workers were not given any land on which to grow their food. Thus, they would depend entirely on *mathace* and maize flour doled out by their employer. In addition, they were not allowed to go home during the day so they would have to take lunch with them. Lunch would comprise a piece of cold, hard *ugali*[7] (cooked maize meal) with nothing to wash it down as the *mathace* was doled at the end of each day's work. The *ugali* would be often bitter from handling pyrethrum; there would be no water to wash hands before eating.

The family stayed in Njabini for two years then moved to Ngaramtonia settlement on the south-western flank of Mount Meru, 12km from Arusha Town in Tanzania (then called Tanganyika). Life in Ngaramtoni was again one of bare survival. Their father was not employed; therefore, the family found itself relying purely on collecting peas for survival. After the harvest the family used to scavenge for peas and exchange them for bananas at the market in Arusha town. They would barter a small quantity of peas in exchange for a bushel of ripe or raw bananas and these would keep them going for a few days.

Up to this time, none of his sisters had gone to school. SK Macharia had attended for a few months while at Sabatia and Molo but he always dropped out due to lack of school fees. When the family moved to Ngaramtoni, an opportunity presented itself for the children to attend school. However, the Kikuyu community living in Ngaramtoni forbade children of those who had not taken the *Mau Mau* oath from going to school. The entire community had taken the oath, while SK Macharia's father had not. As the European farms where he had previously worked were not accessible to the oath administrators, he didn't get to be oathed. Thus, Macharia and his two younger sisters did not go to school until much later. The firstborn sister never went to school. Nevertheless, their father genuinely wanted to send his children to school.

After the colonial government in Kenya declared a State of Emergency in 1952, the crackdown on the *Mau Mau* was extended to Tanzania. In the two years that the family lived in Ngaramtoni, SK Macharia would spend most of his time grazing cattle with Maasai boys, often staying in the bush for weeks; hence, he would be away from home for long periods. It was during one such stint and absence that colonial soldiers invaded the Kikuyu community in Ngaramtoni at night, burnt down their houses and rounded up every Kikuyu person living there. They were all shipped back to Kenya and his father was

---

7 Even presently, *ugali* is a popular meal among societies in East Africa and beyond.

subjected to several days of interrogations by the colonial soldiers before the family was sent to Ndakaini. They had nowhere to stay and his grandfather Karigi took them in. But SK Macharia found this out much later.

When he went home, he found everything had been burnt down and there was no one to recount to him what had happened. So he thought the safest thing to do was to go back to the bush and join the Maasai boys. He went back to the boys and they continued with their search for pasture, wandering all over. It was while in the bush that SK Macharia finally learnt what had happened to his family. He was told that the Kikuyu in Arusha had been taken back home to Central Province. To a ten-year-old boy, figuring out where exactly they had been taken seemed an impossible task. He did not even attempt to trace the way home and instead continued his nomadic grazing life. Almost two years had elapsed since he had last seen his family. Then one fateful event changed his life.

Even in those days, Maasai herdsmen would roam far and wide covering large distances in search of pasture. From Arusha they would travel all the way to Nairobi and sometimes as far as Thika. It was during one of those grazing treks that SK Macharia one day ended up in Thika. As it was not something that he had planned, he even did not know that they had reached Thika until it was mentioned. As he was growing up, he had heard the mention of Thika whenever a visitor would visit their home. They would narrate how they had boarded a train at Thika. What a moment of fate, he thought. He must have come close to 'home' and now could trace where his family was.

It so happened that whenever Maasai boys got to a town they would go to the market and steal bananas. Thika town was no exception. The market was fenced off and there was a restaurant at the entrance through which one had to go to enter the market. Once inside the market SK Macharia learnt that they were indeed in Thika. He decided not to go back with the other boys. Thanks to the curfew imposed due to the Emergency regulations, he found a place to spend the night. People did not move around at night; therefore, in the evening, those working around the market would sleep on the restaurant's floor. Rather than go back to the bush, he opted to join the rest of the people and spend the night in the restaurant. This was to be his home for more than a month.

Meanwhile, his father back in Ndakaini was still frantically looking for his only son. However, he had made little progress as getting out of the communal villages during the Emergency was a cumbersome process. It involved obtaining a pass from the District Commissioner (DC) who was then based in Murang'a town over fifty miles away. To get to the District Commissioner, a person had to go through the Chief and then to the District Officer (DO). At every stage, one had to explain why they wanted to leave the district. SK Macharia's father would explain to the DC – in those days DCs were all Europeans – that he had left a son in Arusha and that he wanted to go and find him. Every time he went to see him, the DC wouldn't give him a pass. He was now desperate. The desperation was further aggravated by sustained pressure from SK Macharia's grandfather. Whenever he got drunk, he would sing a song with innuendos insinuating that SK Macharia's father had gone to Rift Valley looking for greener pastures than in Kikuyuland, but he became so poor that he had sold a son. This used to make SK Macharia's father really angry.

As SK Macharia hopelessly roamed around Thika, once again fate intervened. An old friend of the family called Ephraim Mutaki came calling one day while on a visit to Thika in the restaurant that SK Macharia was spending the night. This man was well off and he owned a lorry, which was a big deal in the 1950s. On this particular day, Mutaki came to eat and SK Macharia noticed him. He decided to sit opposite him and stared at him as he ate. After some time, Mutaki asked him why he was staring at him. SK Macharia told him that it was because he had recognised him and went ahead to tell him who he was. Fortunately, the story of how SK Macharia's father had lost a son had spread far and wide. So when Mutaki heard the name he was so shocked that he stopped eating. He promptly took SK Macharia's hand, led him out of the restaurant, put him in the lorry and took him all the way to Ndakaini. That was in 1954.

SK Macharia was naturally overjoyed to be back with his family. However, their economic conditions had deteriorated when the family was returned to Ndakaini. They had become even poorer; in fact, they were so poor that how they managed to survive was unimaginable. To illustrate the depth of their desperation, they would plant sweet potato vines one day and dig them up the next day to see if any tuber had sprouted overnight. Even at this point, none of the children had yet started school. Certainly, it was now clear that something drastic had to be done. That is why their elder sister, Njeri, was married off to an old man named Machora. From the dowry, their father could get money to send Macharia to school.

Machora was an employee of the government. He worked as a fish warden supervising Thika River and ensuring that Africans did not fish in the river. Only whites were allowed to do so. In those days being employed by the government meant that one was doing very well. After marrying Njeri, Machora undertook to pay SK Macharia's school fees as one of the terms of the marriage contract agreed between him and SK Macharia's father. Looking back, they laugh at this forced marriage with Njeri often reminding him that he was the reason why she never went to school. It is a sacrifice that SK Macharia has never taken for granted and he acknowledges that he owes his education to her. Subsequently, he has always ensured that she is taken care of.

Immediately, SK Macharia was enrolled at Ndakaini Primary School where he started Standard One. Soon he turned out to be a bright pupil. The intermittent schooling he had had at Sabatia and Molo had clearly not been a waste. After only one term he skipped two classes and joined Standard Three in second term because his teachers found him to be substantially ahead of the other pupils. After the second year, he sat the Common Competitive Entrance Examination (CCEE), a national exam for Standard Four pupils which determined those who would proceed to intermediate school level. He passed well and subsequently enrolled for Standard Five at Gituru Intermediate School, then a boarding school. (It was later converted to a secondary school.)

At the time, the Emergency and the war against the *Mau Mau* war were still on. Gituru was surrounded by a military camp. As SK Macharia used to be very good in playing draughts, he immersed himself into the game and for two years he did nothing else but play with Johnnies (a nickname given to British soldiers). He did not prepare for the exams. When he sat for exams at the end of Standard Six he failed but he didn't even know it. After the school holidays he reported to join Standard Seven only to be told that he was not supposed to be in the class because he had failed the exam. Consequently, he went back home and told his father what had happened. His father enrolled him in another school called Gichagi-ini, which had only Standard Six. In those days such schools were called 'primary top'.

At Gichagi-ini SK Macharia repeated Standard Six and this time round passed the exam the following year. Now with good results, he rejoined Gituru Intermediate School in Standard Seven in 1957. For the next two years he was the school timekeeper. Macharia credits the two years he spent as school timekeeper at Gituru Intermediate School with giving him the discipline that became the foundation for his success.

As in many boarding schools, Gituru had a very regimented programme and the timekeeper rang the bell at intervals throughout the day signalling when it was time for students and teachers to move on to a different activity. In effect, he would be the first person in the school to wake up at 5.00 am. The first thing would be to go and wake the headmaster up. Together, they would then synchronise their clocks after which he would ring the bell for everyone else to wake up. Throughout the day he would ring the bell for cleaning dorms, attending parade for inspection, and for lessons, breaks, meals, sports, preps and for time to sleep. He used to ring the bell around 60 times in one day.

No doubt, the timekeeper was instrumental in the smooth running of the school and was highly respected. It was quite a heavy responsibility because it required a lot of discipline. SK Macharia enjoyed it greatly. However, it was not without a little mischief especially if it helped out some fellow classmates.

Caning was allowed in those days and sometimes two or three teachers would join forces to really whip the pupils. If a teacher came to the class in a bad mood and started to whip the pupils, SK Macharia would ring the bell and everyone would get up before the end of the lesson and go to a different class. The practice was that if the bell rang everyone must move on to the next thing. Naturally, this would land him into trouble with the headmaster. To escape being punished he would come up with creative explanations. For instance, there was a time when he claimed that his watch had fallen and changed the time. Whatever the mischievous incidents, SK Macharia credits the two years that he spent as school timekeeper as being responsible for instilling discipline in him.

SK Macharia sat the Kenya African Preliminary Examination (KAPE) in 1958, marking the end of his primary education. In those days there were only a handful of high schools in the country, among them Alliance, Kagumo, Mang'u, Yala and Kigali (in Embu). Usually, the principals of these high schools would visit intermediate schools like Gituru and admit the top students in the KAPE exam from each school. In the year that SK Macharia sat KAPE, a new school called Njiri's High School was opened in Murang'a. Its first intake included five students from Gituru. Unfortunately, he was not among the students that were picked to join high school in spite of always believing that he would be among the best performing students. He couldn't believe that he was not going to high school.

Students who did not make it to high school were usually offered jobs as untrained primary school teachers. That is how SK Macharia found himself going to teach at Makomboki Primary School. He was paid a salary of eighty shillings a month. After a year teaching at Makomboki, he was offered a chance at Kahuhia Teacher Training College where he enrolled in 1960. For the next two years, he trained as a teacher attaining a P3 level of teacher education. Most of the teachers at the college were Europeans and every weekend a few students would accompany a teacher to his home where they would be taught table manners – how to use a knife and fork, place a napkin, and how to eat the different courses like soup, dessert and coffee. The college took these etiquette lessons very seriously and even if one was brilliant academically they could still fail the entire course if a teacher wrote a bad report on the etiquette part of it.

While teaching at Makomboki, SK Macharia had bought a second-hand radio and a bicycle. In those days car batteries, which were bigger than the radios, were used to provide power. Interestingly, the battery was even more expensive than the radio. In Ndakaini there was no other radio except SK

Macharia's. Thus, in the evening everyone would come to their house to listen to the news, which was very crucial as Kenya was going through a period of intense political activism. Leaders such as Jeremiah Nyaga would often give lectures about what was happening in the country. They would talk about other leaders like Tom Mboya and others like Kenyatta who were in detention. In Ndakaini, Dr Julius Gikonyo Kiano[8] was greatly admired and idolised. People would often listen to him on radio speaking in English.

After completing teacher training, SK Macharia was posted to Gituru, his former primary school. He had wanted to go to Uganda for further education to avoid being looked down upon by his former classmates who had gone to high school and P1 teacher training. In village life, P1 teachers would not mix with P3 teachers. Anyone who had been to Makerere University was really admired from a distance. When teachers wearing the Makerere uniform were seen around, no one dared approach them. But even as SK Macharia was thinking about how to get to Makerere, he encountered rumours about the Mboya airlifts which took people to America to study. He decided to travel to Nairobi to find out more.

When he got to Nairobi, he found out that Dr Kiano and others had formed an organisation called Cosak. The organisation vetted potential candidates for the Kennedy–Mboya airlifts. Successful candidates were then sent to the immigration department to obtain a passport to enable them to travel outside the country. They were also required to pay four Ksh 4,000. SK Macharia was successful in his application but he was unable to raise the required amount of money. Consequently he missed that year's airlift, which turned out to be the last one. That was in early 1962.

SK Macharia was devastated especially since his family had worked so hard to raise the money. They had held a *harambee* (fundraising) in their rural village which had only managed to raise a portion of the money. His father finally sold their piece of land, the only asset he had, but it only fetched fifty shillings. The whole village had struggled for months but all their efforts yielded only one thousand two hundred shillings.

Not one to give up, SK Macharia's heart was set on going to America for further studies. He started looking for alternative ways to get there and discovered an Indian travel agent who also took people abroad. The agency was called Nilestar and was located at Hotel Ambassadeur on Tom Mboya Street (then Victoria Street). After explaining his predicament, the Indian at Nilestar asked him how much money he had and SK Macharia told him that

---

8   Both Jeremiah Nyaga and Dr Kiano later became two of President Kenyatta's longest-serving cabinet ministers.

he had one thousand two hundred shillings. With that amount of money, the Indian agreed to take him to America.

Promptly, SK Macharia went home and withdrew the money from the post office without telling his father. He handed over the money to the Indian who gave him one hundred dollars and an airplane ticket to the United States. Then he went to the US Embassy (then situated at Mitchell Cotts House) where he was given a visa upon showing the embassy officials that he had a plane ticket and pocket money to spend in America. He went back to the Indian and gave him back the one hundred dollars and plane ticket which he tore up. The Indian had used a fake ticket just to help them get a visa. They agreed to meet three weeks later and start the journey to America.

A hundred-day journey to America

After obtaining a visa to the United States, SK Macharia went back to his teaching job at Gituru and waited for the planned day of departure. He did not tell his father about his plans to go to America but confided in two friends from Ndakaini, Samuel Mwangi Kariuki and Muiruri wa Koogi. He asked the two to accompany him to Nairobi on the eve of departure and they spent the night in a hotel along Tom Mboya Street which the Indian travel agent had rented for him. They had agreed with the Indian to meet at the agent's office at 5.00 am. the next morning. Before going to the office, SK Macharia swore his two friends to secrecy because the route he was to follow was so hazardous that he was not sure if he would make it to America, yet he did not want his father to worry over him.

SK Macharia knew that they would not be using the usual route to America. Neither would he be using the traditional procedure for departure. In those days people would hire buses. The whole village would go to the airport to see someone off. In addition, he knew he would be taking a risk and was not sure how he would be travelling. Thus, he decided not to tell his father until he arrived in America. Fortunately, he usually stayed in the school where he was teaching. Therefore, he knew that his father would assume he was still in school. Gituru was quite a distance from their home village and his father was unlikely to come looking for him there.

At Nilestar offices SK Macharia found five Overseas Trading Company (OTC) buses. This was the only bus company in those days doing long-haul routes. He boarded one of the buses with his little box containing two suits and a shirt. There were only two Africans on the trip; all the rest were Indians.

The buses travelled in a convoy and after three days they reached Kampala. All along he did not know where they were going. He only learnt that they were in Kampala when they saw the whole city decorated in preparation to celebrate Uganda's attainment of independence.

The convoy stayed in Kampala for a day, spending the night in the buses. The Indian spent the day preparing food and other provisions for the long journey ahead. Meanwhile, SK Macharia discovered why there were so many Indians on the trip; they were running away from Kenya because independence would be announced the following year (1963) and they were not sure of their future in the country. This was just one of many such trips organised for those who did not have the money to take a plane or ship to London.

The following day the convoy travelled towards Juba in Sudan. After three days on the road they reached the River Nile. There was no bridge and so the buses could not cross the river. The passengers crossed the river on rafts – three logs tied together which floated and followed the current. In effect, they were instructed that wherever one landed on the other side of the river, they must walk back to the point opposite where they started. Depending on how the log moved some people ended up far downstream. After crossing the river they walked for two days to reach Juba where they stayed for three days. At night they slept on the floor in a big hall. The Indian carried their food – dry bread, crisps, maize and beans washed down with water. The fourth day they boarded six buses and started the long journey across the desert heading to Benghazi located at the tip of Libya.

The journey to Benghazi lasted around forty-five days. It was so gruelling that had SK Macharia had an opportunity to turn back he would have done so. Sometimes they would be forced to stop for days because of sandstorms that would have covered the buses and blocked visibility. Other than going for short calls they spent all the time in the buses, day and night. The heat, not knowing where they were going and what dangers were ahead, and being covered by sand all the time were the hardest part of the journey. According to SK Macharia, at no other time in his whole life was he ever scared of dying as he was during this journey. He was sure that he would die in the desert.

When the party finally reached Benghazi, they stayed there for five days before being put on a ship to cross the Mediterranean Sea to Europe. The journey took almost two weeks and they eventually landed in a small city. From there they were put in buses for the rest of the journey. SK Macharia remembers this leg as being more pleasant compared to their desert crossing. They were now staying in good buildings and had hot food, not the dry stuff that they had been eating since leaving Kampala. Life was coming back to normal. Soon they got to the English Channel and were put on a boat to Dover, a one-day's journey. After spending a night in Dover they were put on a train to London the following morning which took a few hours.

Now in London, the Indian passengers had reached their destination. The Indian travel agent, who also acted as their guide, booked SK Macharia into a hotel where he spent the night. The next day the Indian picked him from the hotel and took him to the airport where he was put on a plane to New York. This part of the journey normally took two days. From this point on he would travel alone. He still had the brown sealed envelope which contained his visa. In those days visas were not stamped onto passports but were papers contained in a sealed envelope that a person carried to his destination where it was opened by the immigration officials. Once the officials opened the envelope at the airport and saw that one's papers were alright, they stamped the passport and one was allowed through.

SK Macharia had arrived in America during summer which was hotter than what he was accustomed to. While he was overjoyed to have finally arrived at his destination – America – he had not realised that the distance from New York to Seattle in Washington State where he had been admitted to a college was almost equivalent to that from Nairobi to London. He only had his clothes and not a cent on him. He wandered around the airport trying to figure out what to do next. Now he was all alone without the Indian who had guided them all through the journey to the UK. It felt strange and alien. For the first time he saw people kissing in public which amazed him. It looked queer and he thought that people in America eat each other.

After wandering around the airport for some time he saw a policeman and asked him how to get to Seattle. The policeman asked where he had come from and SK Macharia replied that he had come from Africa and was going to high school. The policeman told him to take a plane. He told him that he did not have a ticket. Then he said "Can you take a bus?" SK Macharia asked him what kind of bus could get him there. The policeman told him the Greyhound buses which were involved in long hauls in the US. SK Macharia asked him how to get to the bus station and he wrote the address on a piece of paper. He told him to give it to a taxi driver who would then take him there. SK Macharia told him he didn't have money for a taxi. That's when the policeman decided to take him to the police station inside the airport.

At the police station, SK Macharia was booked and asked for the admission papers to the school where he had been admitted. The police telephoned the Seattle Technical College which confirmed that Macharia had been admitted there but they did not pay travel expenses for students. The police were left with two choices. One, to incur the expense of shipping him back to Kenya or two, to arrange for his transport to Seattle. He spent the night in police custody.

The following day the police took him to Greyhound and gave instructions to the bus company that he should be taken to Seattle and given food along the way. They travelled day and night for ten days, only stopping for short periods to change drivers.

SK Macharia finally arrived in Seattle, but his troubles were far from over. The Mboya airlifts used to arrange for students going to America to stay with a host family. Since he had already been processed and had only lacked the money to travel to the US, he hoped he could find the family that had been assigned to host him. He had their telephone number. So he tried to locate them from the bus station. He kept calling but the telephone was never answered. Unknown to him, the couple had divorced and gone their separate ways. Once again he was reduced to being a street boy to survive. A week went by. He was still staying at the bus station and was now begging for food. By the third week he was in dire straits. He hadn't even mentioned the school to anyone focusing all his efforts on finding the host family.

Fortunately, the wife discovered that SK Macharia was looking for them. She went to Greyhound bus station where he was staying and asked for his papers to establish his identity. With a nod of satisfaction, she left promising to come back the next day. True to her word, she kept her promise. She took SK Macharia to an abandoned house and told him to stay there. She explained to him that she was no longer with her husband and therefore would be unable to support him. The house had a lot of sheets. She told him to make a bed out of them. She showed him where the school was; it was not very far from the abandoned house so he could walk to and from the school. He went and registered. She also made arrangements at a nearby shop where he could collect food. She must have paid because any time he needed food he would get it from there. That was the last time he saw her.

Winter soon set in and the house had no heating. For three months SK Macharia suffered through the terrible cold with nothing to keep him warm except bed sheets. It was colder in the house than outside and one could die easily in such conditions. While in school, a rumour went around that he was living in an abandoned house with no heating. A priest in a Presbyterian church nearby heard about him and one Sunday he came to see him together with other church officials. The priest took him to his house and he stayed with him for a few days until the following Sunday when he took him to the church. He told the congregation SK Macharia's story, then asked for volunteers to take him in.

The same week, a couple called Andertons, who didn't have children of their own, offered to look after him. It was a black American couple. He stayed with them for eight years. Although they were comparatively poor, SK

Macharia really enjoyed his stay with them. The husband was employed in a supermarket as a cleaner mopping the floors. There was plenty of food. For them it may have been a poor life but considering where he had come from, it was a good life for him. When SK Macharia returned to Kenya, he kept in touch with the Andertons. He even brought them to visit the country several times on holiday. Mr Anderton has since died but SK Macharia still talks to the wife regularly over the phone. He never went back to Seattle.

As SK Macharia was struggling in Seattle, his family back home thought he was still teaching in Gituru. It took nine months from the time he left Kenya for them to learn of his whereabouts. In those days, letters used to take months to get to their destination. He wrote his first letter when he got his new host family informing his father that he was in the US and had started school.

Life in America

While SK Macharia's host family would provide a roof over his head and ensure he was fed, he had to provide for all his other expenses – tuition, books, clothes and entertainment. Students from the Middle East used to be paid salaries by their government to go to school in addition to being paid for school fees. Some of the students even had cars bought by their governments. Nigerian students always had money. But the rest of the students from Africa had to survive by working. So SK Macharia had to work to earn money. During the three months of summer the students worked two jobs for sixteen hours a day in order to save for the tuition money which amounted USD 3,600 per year.

To further supplement his income, SK Macharia also worked throughout each semester juggling classes and a full-time job; he had one full-time job for eight hours a day. The good thing about the US was that one could select to work during the day or at night because work was round the clock – 24/7.

SK Macharia took the minimum number of lessons required to retain his visa. He attended classes and went to the library during the day and then worked at night. Some of the jobs that he took up were manual ones like cleaning supermarkets at night, collecting garbage and mopping floors. Other manual jobs were at Northwestern Glass Company (which made bottles), at the Boeing Company, at a shop making cutlery, and in road construction.

Meanwhile, his family had been left even poorer after selling their piece of land to raise money for his US journey. His younger sister was by then in high school and SK Macharia would send money for her school fees in addition to financing his own education.

After completing high school at Seattle Technical College, SK Macharia enrolled at Seattle Pacific University where he got his first degree – a Bachelor of Arts in political science. He then decided that accounting would be a more relevant degree for his future and enrolled at University of Washington for a BSc degree in accounting. He followed that with a Masters degree in accounting at the same university and later did Certified Public Accountant (CPA) examinations for professional certification.

"All work and no play makes Jack a dull boy," so the saying goes. It was not all classes and work for SK Macharia. As still a young man, he also made time for fun. Students used to hold parties and every Friday he would join other students and go out to dances. The practice was that the host only provided the venue and music; guests brought their own drinks. If one ran out of a drink they went to the nearest supermarket and bought more then came back to the party. He would also join up with others and visit Kenyan students in other states. By this time, most of the students had cars because with fifty dollars one could get a good car. However, whenever they wished to take a long journey they would not use their personal cars. SK Macharia learnt from other students a trick or two on how they managed to do it. Usually, they would go to a second-hand car dealer and ask to test-drive a car. The dealer would allow them to test the car for a day or two. Naturally, these dealers wouldn't imagine that African students would take these cars on road trips.

One time SK Macharia and his four friends decided to attend the graduation of their other friends in Eugene, Oregon, about three hundred miles (or roughly 482km) from Seattle. They went to a car dealer and got a car as was the norm. Unfortunately, the car broke down on the way. They didn't have the money to call a mechanic. So they abandoned it opting to hitchhike back to Seattle at night. They did not go back to the dealer and report the incident figuring out that he wouldn't be able to trace any of the five African students among so many in the country. They were wrong! Within no time, they found themselves reckoning with the efficiency of the US police. After three months each of them was picked up and arrested. They were taken to court and charged with stealing a motor vehicle, a very serious charge at the time. If they were found guilty they would be deported.

In a classic illustration of the craftiness of foreign students or perhaps their will to survive overwhelming odds, when the judge asked them which language they wanted to defend themselves in they said Kikuyu. By choosing their indigenous language, they reckoned that an interpreter fluent in the language would be difficult to find. As it turned out they were right. At that time, Kenya did not have an embassy in Washington; it had just a United Nations representative in New York. A hearing date for the case was fixed and on the material day the prosecutor told the court he had been unable to find an interpreter. The judge insisted that the students must defend themselves in the language they understood as anything else would not amount to a fair trial. The prosecutor wrote to the education attaché asking for a Kikuyu interpreter for the case. Meantime, the students had alerted the attaché about their plight requesting him to say no to any such request and he agreed to help. He replied the prosecutor's letter saying if a Kikuyu interpreter was needed one would have to be brought from Kenya. With no interpreter available the judge dismissed the case.

While SK Macharia was doing his CPA studies, a recruiting team from Kenya visited his university in 1969. The team comprised Jeremiah Kiereini, Habel Nyamu and John Malinda[9] and was looking for students to take over civil service jobs from the Europeans in the ongoing Africanisation programme in the country. Malinda was then the Secretary of the Teachers Service Commission (TSC), Kiereini was in administration, and Nyamu was at the Kenya Institute of Administration. SK Macharia was among the students who were interviewed by the team and subsequently offered a job in the civil service. Everyone who was recruited received their letters of appointment while still at the university.

SK Macharia was posted as a provincial local government financial officer (supernumerary) in the Ministry of Local Government. As a supernumerary, this meant that he was going to work under a *mzungu* (white man) for one year and, upon recommendation, he would replace him. He came back to Kenya in 1969 but started the job in January 1970. At this time the government paid all the transport expenses of Kenyan students recruited from America to work in the civil service. This is how SK Macharia came back to Kenya.

One of the best things about America that SK Macharia admired was the freedoms that its citizens enjoy besides the abundance in role models. He observed that this level of freedom was not something that Kenyans – and Africans in general – could understand because they were not born with it, a factor that has resulted in continued underdevelopment. People in Africa are unable to create role models because they tolerate stealing from each other; for example, people engage in cattle rustling which they justify by saying that it's an old tradition. When a community does not have a theory of stealing and believes that everything belongs to them, even if one was to place them at Central Bank they'll do the same thing because to them it's not stealing.

Moreover, once leaders are elected they become kings instead of servants of the people. An American President who hurts citizens would not be in office

---

9   Jeremiah Kiereini was later to become the Chief Secretary and later Chairman of East African Breweries Limited (EABL), and Habel Nyamu became head of Kenya Institute of Administration (KIA) and member of the Electoral Commission of Kenya (ECK).

the next day because individual liberties are very important. In Kenya, there is the wrong view of leadership whereby when people are elected to parliament, instead of asking their constituents what they need and in so doing actually represent them, they become arrogant and unreachable. There is no respect for the electorate or individual freedoms. For instance, while in America one could freely hold a protest demonstration even outside the White House, if one was to try the same in Kenya they would be shot or beaten up by the police. SK Macharia found this to be the fundamental difference between Kenyans and Americans. Consequently, many people started to brand him as controversial, but in actual fact all he has been doing is to insist on his rights, something he learnt from the Americans. He strongly held that nobody, not even the President, should tell him he cannot do what he wants to do to improve his life, improve his parents' life, and to improve his country.

According to SK Macharia, what is needed for Kenya to develop is re-education. A sweeper from the United Kingdom could visit Kenya, call the Treasury, ask to see the Minister for Finance and be given an audience in an hour because he's speaking the Queen's English and is white. A local businessman would spend a year trying to see the same minister and yet he's a Kenyan. Presently, there's no American who can say he wants to see a government official and be prevented because these officials are there to serve the citizens and solve problems without being bribed. This is the difference between Africa and developed countries; in Africa, citizens have agreed to be terrorised by the people they elect. Until governments know that they are there to serve the people, nothing will change.

A stint in the civil service

In 1970 there were seven local government financial officers. They were all Europeans. Eight Kenyans were recruited to understudy them and eventually take over these positions. Remuneration for these positions was 800 pounds per annum (equivalent to KSh 1,330 gross per month). SK Macharia was recruited together with Eric Kotut with whom they sat in the same office.[10] After three months they were to be transferred to different provinces where they would be stationed within the Provincial Commissioner's (PC's) office.

He also bought a new car, a Datsun 1000. When he reported on duty he and his colleagues were given a government loan to buy a car and all they had to pay was 10 percent. SK Macharia had come with some money from the US and walked to DT Dobie and put a down payment of one thousand shillings and drove out with a new car.

---

10   Eric Kotut was later to become Governor of the Central Bank of Kenya.

One morning SK Macharia received a letter informing him that he had been transferred to Kakamega and that he should report to the PC, then Paul K Boit, within fourteen days. Having just arrived from America, he could not see how he was going to a place like that. He refused to go. At the time, refusing to move to a posting was a very serious offence because he had signed a code of conduct which stated that one could be transferred anywhere in the country. Dietrich, the Principal Local Government Financial Officer in Nairobi, who had written the letter to SK Macharia, reported his refusal to take up the appointment to the Permanent Secretary (PS), then Timothy CJ Ramtu. The PS summoned him and ordered him to report to Kakamega. He advised that failure to do so would lead to disciplinary action and he would be dismissed from the civil service which would make it difficult to get another job elsewhere in the country. Despite the advice, SK Macharia remained adamant.

Two days later, SK Macharia came across a letter that Ramtu had written to the Director of Personnel, the late Joseph Gethenji, recommending that disciplinary action be taken against him. The letter was copied to him. When he read it, he knew that he was in hot soup. Consequently, he rushed home, packed a few utensils and clothes and drove to Kakamega. The first thing he did on arrival at Kakamega was to go straight to the PC and inform him that he had reported for duty. He asked him to call Ramtu and inform him that he was on duty. After that he was taken to the government house where he would be staying. It was huge with fourteen rooms in all. With his few belongings, he had to close all the rooms except the kitchen and the bedroom. These were the only rooms that he used during his short stay in Kakamega. Some of the things that bothered him were the thunderstorms; they really scared him. Never had he heard such loud thunder.

A few months later a copy of a letter written to Ramtu by Gethenji came to SK Macharia's notice. The letter made reference to Ramtu's earlier letter and noted that since the officer had reported to Kakamega and Ramtu was satisfied, his earlier letter recommending disciplinary action had been withdrawn. Having seen the letter, SK Macharia packed his bags the following morning and left Kakamega without even telling the PC. He drove to Nairobi. Knowing that his file was clean, he went to Ramtu's office and handed him his letter of resignation. The letter was accompanied by a cheque for one month's salary as per the requirements of his job tenure. He had been in the civil service for only nine months.

A taste of business in the quasi-private sector

Upon quitting the civil service, SK Macharia started looking for another job.

Fortunately at the time, there were plenty of jobs available for graduates. Within a short time, he got two job offers for an accountant position; one was from the University of Nairobi and the other from Industrial and Commercial Development Corporation (ICDC) to be attached to Kenya Industrial Estates (KIE) which was owned by ICDC. He chose the ICDC offer principally because of the things KIE was involved in: developing small industries and lending money to cottage industries. Five months into the job he was assigned to KIE situated in the industrial area of Nairobi (he was effectively still an employee of ICDC).

KIE had put up sheds, which were meant to be operated by individuals as well as groups. Its main objective was to get Africans into small industries. In effect, it would fund those who wanted to start a business by buying machinery for them. Once it was convinced that a business was viable, the entrepreneur was only required to pay 10 percent as working capital. KIE put in the rest of the required money. It was funded by the Government of India, an expert on small cottage industries. Being the one carrying out the feasibility studies, KIE would import the equipment and get it installed as they knew where to procure it. They would also give one a shed to operate from and one's work now would just be to run the business with the working capital of 10 percent, which was used to pay salaries and meet other expenses. KIE also provided technical support so that if the equipment got damaged they would repair it.

SK Macharia's first assignment was to do a feasibility study for an industry to manufacture *pangas* and *jembes*.[11] He negotiated with the experts who were to partner with ICDC to build the factory. The result was the company that is now called Kenya Engineering Industries. Thus, at KIE SK Macharia had his first taste of enterprise and was now in the world of real business. This is where he had always wanted to be.

Apart from doing his job he started organising groups and encouraging people to get into small industries. He got a group of twenty people together, mostly former students in America, and they started a project to manufacture clothes pegs. The group was called Ngwataniro Enterprises. He became the chairman as his presence gave them confidence. In any case they insisted that he should be there to ensure that they didn't make mistakes. The project was funded by KIE.

At the same time, Kenya Railways advertised for people to build restaurants along Enterprise Road on its land to cater for workers in the surrounding

---

11   *Panga* and *jembe* are common implements in peasant farming in the East African region and beyond. The former is widely referred to as a machete, while the later is a hoe.

industries. The group applied and got approval to build a restaurant. However, the project, that is the restaurant business, did not succeed.

Later, the group, in the name of Crescent Investment Limited, started an industry to manufacture carbon paper using technology from Germany. From inception, the company did very well and it always made money. It paid dividend to its twenty shareholders every year; hence, the industry was very valuable. However, with the development of computers, which gradually replaced the need for carbon paper, the industry died out and it became necessary to sell.

Overall, KIE was exceedingly successful in getting Africans involved in small businesses. In fact, it was to be the platform for Kenya's industrialisation supported by ICDC and the Industrial Development Bank (IDB). There was a policy that if one grew big and started making profits, they got out of the KIE shed and KIE would help them to build their own factory. This paved the way for other people to come in and be assisted in the same way. ICDC was also directly funding people, including foreigners, who wanted to set up industries in Kenya.

At this time, entrepreneurs of Asian origin were not in manufacturing on the scale they came to operate in later years, virtually dominating the industry. They were predominantly in the retail trade and were commonly referred to as *dukawallas*. President Jomo Kenyatta's government had come up with a policy of Africanising businesses. The policy was being implemented under the Ministry of Commerce with Dr Julius Gikonyo Kiano as Minister. As an employee of ICDC, SK Macharia was incorporated in the scheme that was Africanising the commercial retail trade. Government officials would go to retail areas like Biashara Street and take down the details of all the *dukawallas*. Then they would advertise them in the newspapers for Africans to apply and buy them. Those who were picked would get a letter from ICDC and take it to the respective shop that was allocated to them. Together with the previous owner, they would take the stock and sign a document ascertaining the value of the shop plus the stock. ICDC would then pay the owner an equivalent amount of money and the African would take over the shop. The money paid to the previous owner was a loan that the new African owners were expected to repay to ICDC.

In this way many shops in Nairobi were taken over by Africans. So long as the Africanisation policy was ongoing, the Africans could not sell back the shops. Consequently, Indians were left without business having been replaced in the retail trade. They had to find an alternative and this is how they started moving into manufacturing. Given that they could not go through KIE, they used the savings from their retail businesses to consolidate capital to start the industries. In a way, finding capital to set up the industries was not a problem for most of them. Nevertheless, most of the new African owners later sold the shops back to the Indians. Presently a majority of these shops are still run by Indians. And even when they took back their retail businesses, they continued with their industries. To this extent, Africanisation flopped.

Despite KIE's success in getting Africans into industries, it received less support with the change of government in 1978. When the Moi government came in, it started removing local people from trade and industry. A country that wants to develop must put its own people in both trade and industry; it cannot develop in any other way.

While SK Macharia was still at KIE, another government body, the Agricultural Development Corporation (ADC), was collapsing. ADC was in charge of national farms that mainly grew maize seeds and bred cattle and sheep. At the time, it was the largest supplier of milk to Kenya Cooperative Creameries (KCC), it owned huge sugarcane plantations, and it was also redistributing the land that had been acquired from European settlers. Now the government had decided that ADC was no longer viable. Consequently, a team of three people was appointed and given the assignment of liquidating it. SK Macharia was one of those in the team. The other two were Joe Muchekehu and James Mburu; the former was then working for Pannell Bellhouse Mwangi, an audit firm, and the latter was the Director of Agriculture.

The team was given an office within the Ministry of Agriculture headquarters. After studying the ADC for a year, the team concluded that the parastatal could be saved. It handed over its report, which gave details of what should be done to save ADC, to Geoffrey Kareithi who was the Head of the Civil Service and Secretary to the Cabinet. Kareithi gave a copy of the report back to SK Macharia and told him to go to ADC and implement the recommendations. Subsequently, he left KIE and was moved to ADC in January 1974 to become the Financial Controller. With time the management team, which SK Macharia was part of, converted ADC into one of the most profitable and viable government organisations.

Getting into private business

SK Macharia first toyed with the idea of starting a business immediately upon returning from America in 1969. The first thing he did with the little money that he had was to invest in a *matatu*.[12] Having come from America where the transport system was very good, he noticed that in Kenya people were still

---

12   A *matatu* is a low-capacity commercial vehicle usually used to ferry passengers over short distances and is the common mode of transport in Kenya.

walking very long distances. According to him, transport looked like a business that needed to be done. The idea was to buy a number of *matatus* to operate between Thika and Ndakaini. So he purchased a brand new Volkswagen from Cooper Motors Corporation (CMC) for twenty-one thousand shillings. All he was required to pay was 10 percent. Then he got a good friend, the late Muhika Kageni, to drive it to Ndakaini.[13] He had met Kageni when they were both in America.

However, the *matatu* business did not last. Two months into the business, the *matatu* rolled and was seriously damaged. Fortunately, no one was hurt. SK Macharia repaired it and put it back on the road. But it rolled again two weeks later. This time a passenger was injured on the leg. Although the insurance company handled the claim, SK Macharia was so traumatised that he decided to get out of the *matatu* business altogether. He reckoned that if people died in an accident, he would be in real trouble. He continued paying the loan from his little salary as there was no more income from the *matatu*. Eventually he decided not to repair it and instead took it to Pembroke, a company that used to sell trucks with the intention of trading in the *matatu* for a lorry. He thought that a lorry would not be very risky because it would carry goods like charcoal and wood from Ndakaini to Thika.

Pembroke valued the *matatu* at seven thousand shillings. SK Macharia decided to order a seven-tonne lorry costing forty-five thousand shillings and used the amount valued for the *matatu* as the down payment for the lorry. When the lorry was ready Pembroke wrote to him to collect it. However, he had by then changed his mind. Since he was still paying a loan on the *matatu*, he figured out that if the lorry rolled like the *matatu* he would be left with another loan. That would send him to bankruptcy. So he wrote to Pembroke and told them that he did not want the lorry. Therefore, they should refund the down payment. But they refused, saying the lorry had been built and he had to take it. They argued about it. Eventually, he decided to forfeit his deposit. That marked the end of SK Macharia's involvement in the transport business.

The formation of a group to start a cottage industry and thereafter the founding of Crescent Investment Limited saw SK Macharia get involved in the next business. When he joined ADC, he got together with three friends and bought Tina's Bar and Restaurant, which was located opposite the ADC offices on Moi Avenue in the city centre. It was a very popular place with patrons. It is at Tina's that he first met Daniel arap Moi (the second President of the Republic of Kenya) as this is where he used to have coffee all the time.

His other partners in the bar business were Muhika Kageni, Munai Njoroge,

---

13   Muhika Kageni was the father to Maina Kageni, a renowned radio presenter.

Njama Karanja and James Kieme. They have all since died.

In running Tina's, SK Macharia would leave work in the evening and go to the bar where he would sell beer until midnight. The business was doing so well that they rented another bar in Lang'ata, a suburb in Nairobi. While at Tina's they were selling beer from East African Breweries Limited, at the bar in Lang'ata they started selling *muratina,* a traditional Kikuyu beer. Among the patrons at the bar were army personnel from the Lang'ata Barracks who would drink and beat up everybody. After the resulting mess, they would retreat to the barracks. Once in the barracks, the police could not follow them. The losses incurred from the constant fights drove the business to its knees and they had to close it. They found that they had been putting all the money they made at Tina's into the bar at Lang'ata. As the Lang'ata business affected the original investment, the other partners sold their shares in Tina's bar to Kageni who continued to run it until his death when his wife took over.

The founding of Madhupaper International Limited

Once when he was still working at ADC, SK Macharia went on an official trip to Italy to see the cross-breeding of cows and buffaloes. The idea of implementing the method in Kenya appeared attractive because the resulting animals called Beefalo were huge and good for meat production. Over one weekend he came across a cottage industry where a family was making paper using a hand-operated machine. The family would go around offices and homes collecting waste paper which they would put in water and beat with a stick to turn the paper into fibre. Then they would process the fibre using a steam-roll to make tissue paper. All this was being done by hand and would produce about twenty rolls of tissue paper which they would sell.

SK Macharia was fascinated by the process. For the first time, he wondered how many people used toilet paper in Kenya. When he came back he went round and found that toilet paper was only found in the big hotels. He went to Hilton Hotel to inspect the toilet paper and carried a roll which he took to KIE. Having worked with KIE he was familiar with its procedures and he knew that he just needed a sample of the product he wanted to produce and KIE would find out if there were local producers. Accordingly, KIE established that toilet paper was imported from Andrex in the UK. After conducting a feasibility study they also concluded that there was enough waste paper in Kenya to produce toilet paper. They pegged the cost of establishing the factory at Ksh 5 million. However, KIE was restricted to financing projects of up to Ksh 3 million. So they could not finance it.

Officially, SK Macharia incorporated Madhupaper in 1976. Armed with the feasibility study, he approached National Bank of Kenya (NBK) for a loan. He spoke to RS Atwood, the General Manager, who promised to look at the application. However, there was no response from the bank for six months. Meanwhile, Stanley Githunguri whom SK Macharia had met while in America had been transferred from the NBK Mombasa branch where he had been working to Nairobi. He replaced Mr Atwood as General Manager. He went to see Githunguri and told him that Atwood had been sitting on his loan application. He asked him to look into it. Two days later, Githunguri called him and asked him to go to his office. He asked him if he knew where he was going to get the machinery for the factory. SK Macharia replied in the affirmative. He told Githunguri that he needed to pay a deposit of two million shillings. NBK agreed to finance the company. According to SK Macharia, Githunguri really believed in entrepreneurship; he helped a lot of people get into business when he was at National Bank.

The next step was to look for land on which to build the factory. At that time, the government was very efficient. SK Macharia walked to the lands office and told the lady at the reception that he was looking for land for a factory. She went inside the office and got a young gentleman who introduced himself as Daniel Wainaina and asked how much land he wanted. SK Macharia said ten acres. Wainaina brought a map of Nairobi and told SK Macharia that the only area they were allowing factories was Lunga Lunga Road in Industrial Area. SK Macharia did not know where Lunga Lunga Road was. Wainaina offered to take him there. Once they reached the designated area, he asked SK Macharia to select the spot he wanted. Once he selected his spot, he got a letter of allotment in two days. Immediately, he took it to NBK, which paid the standing premium. In three weeks he had a title deed.

SK Macharia bought the machinery from an Italian supplier who installed it. Production of tissue paper started in 1977. Over the next three years he added a second paper machine to produce facial tissues and wrappers. By 1981 he had completed building the factory and supplied toilet paper called Rosy in Kenya, which he also exported to Uganda and Tanzania. Total production was twenty tonnes of tissue and ten tonnes of wrapping paper per day. The factory had three hundred employees and was operating twenty-four hours a day, seven days a week.

With the success of the venture, SK Macharia was already thinking about expansion: to building a factory the size of Pan African Paper Mills (Pan Paper). The first thing he wanted to produce was folding-box board which was mainly used for packaging food, medicine and cigarettes among others. Folding boxboards, also called paperboards, are produced by taking several sheets of paper and pressing them together after stuffing the middle with cheaper raw materials like sawdust. The result is a thick high-quality paper used for packaging.

Meanwhile, SK Macharia decided to have a ceremony to officially open the factory. He liaised with Dr Munyua Waiyaki, Minister of Industry, to invite other government officials including the President. The President agreed to open the factory. However, just three weeks before the material day, Dr Waiyaki changed his mind about the invitation. He went back to SK Macharia and suggested that he should go back and tell the President that it was just a small factory and not worth being opened by him. However, SK Macharia turned down the suggestion. Having known the President from Tina's Bar and from his dealing with land issues at ADC where he was still working, he told Dr Waiyaki that the party had already been made for the Head of State. His mind was set that it is he who would open the factory and plans for the party continued.

On 21 January 1981, the President arrived at three o'clock in the afternoon accompanied by several high-ranking government officials including GG Kariuki, Minister of State in the Office of the President, Charles Njonjo, the Minister for Constitutional and Home Affairs, Mwai Kibaki, the then Vice-President, and the Lang'ata Member of Parliament, Dr Philip Leakey. At that time the Lunga Lunga area was part of Lang'ata Constituency. In his speech, SK Macharia spoke of the high demand for paper and his plans to put up a fully fledged paper industry in Thika. While the current factory was using waste paper, with such high demand, it would be necessary for the new operation to produce the raw material (trees). The President received the speech very positively. In his statements he said: "If I had ten Macharias this country will have developed." SK Macharia took this as a sign to continue and went the full hog with the Thika project.

The original estimate of setting up an integrated pulp and paperboard mill with an annual capacity of twenty thousand tonnes was USD 100 million (roughly Ksh 1 billion) which was a lot of money in the early 1980s. SK Macharia approached International Finance Corporation (IFC), the private sector arm of the World Bank, for funding. At that time IFC would only fund projects through the government, either through ICDC or KIE or directly through the Treasury. Even after conducting a feasibility study and concluding that a project was economically viable, they would still seek a government guarantee from the Treasury as a condition of lending money. They sent a team to Kenya for six months to study the proposed project. It identified a fifty-thousand-acre sisal farm in Maragua where a nursery could be set up and entered into an agreement for Madhupaper to buy it. The plan was that when the trees were cut from the forests authorised by the government, Madhupaper would move in farmers to plant normal food crops like maize and vegetables as well as tree seedlings from the Maragua nursery. The farmers would take care of the trees for two to three years and when the trees were able to stand on their own, the farmers would be moved to a new piece of land and repeat the process. This is how reforestation is normally done.

The government had set aside land for building the plant near Thika and Chania Rivers because paper mills require a lot of water. After the feasibility study was concluded, IFC approved the project and advanced one hundred million dollars without asking for a government guarantee. The IFC board paper said that for the first time they had located someone in Kenya who could actually be given money from the World Bank without requiring a government guarantee. This was because 'what he has done already is enough security for ourselves'. The loan was syndicated, meaning that several financial institutions came together to fund the project. The other players were: Export Credits Guarantee Department (ECGD), a body of the British Government; Finfund, a subsidiary of the Finnish Government, which lends to the private sector; and, KfW, a German Government-owned development bank. The nature of syndicated loans is such that financiers often get equity in a company until their loans are repaid and this was the proposed plan with Madhupaper as well.

Government-owned financial institutions in Kenya were also involved. These were: East African Development Bank (EADB), Industrial Development Bank (IDB) and Development Finance Company of Kenya (DFCK). Standard Chartered Bank of London was appointed by IFC to be the lead bank to oversee the whole process and ensure all other stakeholders were paid. The paper mill was to come from the UK, machinery to produce pulp was to come from Finland, and equipment to cut and transport the trees was to come from Germany.

The Madhupaper project had been approved at all levels of government. The tree licences and land for building the factory at Thika had been given by the government and Central Bank had given full consent for the loan. In those days one could not borrow money overseas unless they had been given approval in writing by the finance committee of the Treasury and the Central Bank. This approval was called a Certificate of Approved Enterprise usually given to foreign investors. It assured exchange control permission to facilitate payment of loans, interest and dividends using foreign currency.

The IFC board comprises the Ministers of Finance of member countries of the World Bank. For a project to get approval and get IFC financing, the Minister of Finance in the home country where the project is to be carried out must appear before the board in person and table a letter indicating that his own government has approved the said project. In other words, sending a letter of approval to the board is not good enough; the Minister for Finance must appear in person. Professor George Saitoti was the Minister for Finance at the time and he tabled a letter before the IFC board. This clearly indicates that the government had approved the Madhupaper project and that they were part and parcel of the project. This was in addition to the fact that some government institutions also participated in the syndicated loan.

The law firm of Kaplan and Stratton prepared all the documents and the signing ceremony was conducted in July 1985. Given the size of the deal, the signing ceremony made news in all the major news media in the country. Unfortunately, as SK Macharia came to find out later, the President was soon after told that the Ksh 1 billion borrowed overseas was not for a project but to overthrow his government. He was told that there's nobody who gets that kind of money from the World Bank and that even for the Treasury to organise this kind of funding would take years. The President reacted by calling a special cabinet meeting whose outcome was to halt the project. Members of Parliament from Central Province wrote a petition to the President asking him to rescind his decision. IFC also got involved and tried to get the project back on track, but it was all in vain.

As the agreement between IFC, the other financiers and Madhupaper had already been signed, the government had to quickly look for a way to nullify it. The easiest way was to call in the debts associated with Madhupaper. Kenya Commercial Bank (KCB) – a government-owned financial institution – was instructed to demand payment from Madhupaper. Failure to pay the same day was to see the company put into receivership. (Once a company is under receivership all the agreements it has signed become null and void.) This is how KCB got involved.

Around the time the Madhupaper factory in Industrial Area was being officially opened, Philip Ndegwa, then the Executive Chairman of Kenya Commercial Bank, came to visit the plant. After a tour, he had a chat with SK Macharia in which he observed that NBK would not be able to handle a project of the magnitude of the one proposed in Thika. At the time, Madhupaper was banking with NBK. Consequently, he advised that Madhupaper should move its account to KCB. He even offered to fund the company's own feasibility study and initial preparations like buying land to build staff houses for one thousand eight hundred members of staff. SK Macharia agreed and they ended up spending Ksh 53 million of KCB's money. The loan agreement with IFC stipulated that KCB would be paid off once the project was running. Thereafter, Standard Chartered Bank in Kenya would take over the Madhupaper account.

On 25 October 1985, an official of KCB accompanied by Robin D Cahill and RLE Kerr of Peat Marwick Mitchell and Company went to the offices of Madhupaper and demanded immediate payment of the KCB loan. SK Macharia and his friends scrambled around trying to get the money, but it was not available. When the money was not immediately forthcoming the receiver managers from Peat Marwick took over the company. Apparently, the bank had only one agenda – to keep the company in receivership. As it became clear later, KCB had been ordered not to accept a single cent from Madhupaper. It was not just enough to kill the Thika project, even the current Madhupaper had to be taken over. They were determined to finish SK Macharia completely. He was kicked out of the office and left with nothing, not even school fees to pay for his children's education. Even the car that he was driving, which was in the company's name, was repossessed. He was now forced to start commuting by bus.

As SK Macharia continued struggling to get his company out of receivership, he came to find out who had told the President that he was going to use the IFC money to overthrow the government. Stephen Muriu, who was among those trying to help raise money to pay the KCB loan and had started a small bank, Mid-Africa Finance (one of the local banks started by Kenyans during this time), was the banker for the late Kariuki Chotara, a powerful and close confidant of President Moi. In a conversation with Muriu one day, Chotara let slip that two assistant ministers from Central Province are the ones who told the president that the money borrowed from IFC was to be used to overthrow his government. The two assistant ministers had told Moi this falsehood while at a function at Mary Leakey High School.

The day after Muriu passed on this information to him, SK Macharia woke up at 3.00 am and drove all the way to Kabarak, the President's Nakuru home. He arrived at 6.00 am. Leaving his car some distance away, he walked to the gate and demanded to see the President. The guards told him that the President was not there, but he insisted. The guards talked with someone inside the house on their walkie-talkies then they told him the President had said he would not see him as he did not have an appointment. SK Macharia responded by telling them he was going to stand on the road for as long as it took. He knew that was the only gate the president could use and reckoned that when the President came the guards could do two things, shoot him and remove him from the gate for the President to pass, or run over him with their vehicles. So he sat on a rock at the side of the road and waited. Five hours later at 11.00 am he saw a motorcade approaching and moved to stand in the middle of the road. When the vehicles neared the gate the convoy stopped; someone jumped out of one vehicle and ran towards him. He asked if he was SK Macharia. When he said yes, he was, he told him the President wanted to see him. They both went to the President's car which was the fourth in the convoy. The President had rolled down his window and he asked him: "*Wewe Macharia unataka kitu gani?* (Macharia, what do you want?)" SK Macharia told him that he only wanted to say something to him briefly and asked for one minute of his time. Moi told him to enter the car. He went round the vehicle and entered through the other side. For the first time he was in the Presidential limousine. The other vehicles were all turned around and they went back to the house. However, they did not go inside the main house but sat outside on the patio where people often drank tea. SK Macharia told him, "Your Excellency, I just came to tell you one thing. I know why you stopped Madhupaper from being built. You were cheated by two of your assistant ministers that the money was borrowed with the assistance of Mwai Kibaki and Njenga Karume so that they can overthrow your government. I came to tell you that it is not true. I got this information from one of the Ministers."

At the mention of this name, President Moi jumped up from his seat and got very agitated. SK Macharia cooled him down and said, "I did not come to tell you so that you can reverse your decision. I just want you to know that I know why you stopped it and tell you this: All things being equal you are older than me and if we're going to die due to age, you will die before I die and the things you have prevented me from doing, I'll do when you are dead."

Then he walked out and left him shouting after him. The house was quite a distance from the gate. As he walked, the Presidential convoy passed him but no one stopped him. It had been a huge risk confronting the president like that but he didn't care. At that moment, he was ready to die.

Fighting for Madhupaper – battle goes to the courts

Having failed to reverse the President's decision, SK Macharia decided to take the government to court. The first thing he did was to file a case against the Attorney General. The company had already entered into quite a number of agreements for supply of the equipment, and with the architects and consultants who were to build the factory. The company had even made the deposit for the machinery for making pulp and the paper mills, it had acquired two hundred acres of land in Thika from the Commissioner of Lands for the factory, and it had paid a deposit on the fifty thousand acres of land in Maragua for the tree nursery. It had also incurred over Ksh 50 million on preparation costs for the project which was borrowed from KCB. Therefore, the state was sued for compensation.

In all, SK Macharia was asking for more than Ksh 1 billion on the grounds that it was the state that approved the project. For example, the Forest

Department had issued all the necessary approvals to harvest forests and to replant, which explained why the company had bought the farm in Maragua. A letter dated 8 May 1984 from the Ministry of Environment and Natural Resources, and signed by OM Mburu, Chief Conservator of forests, stated: "With regards to several applications we received from you to assure you of a continuous adequate supply of pulpwood, we indicate that the Forest Department's stand on the issue is as follows. (1) The department will be able to offer you an annual supply of pulpwood of 130,000 cubic metres o.b. as has been communicated in earlier correspondence. (2) Consideration will be given to procuring the pulpwood requirements from the closest forests as much as possible. (3) A felling plan will be worked out specifying all the details of felling in accordance with existing silvicultural requirements."

Another letter from PH Okondo, Minister for Commerce and Industry, addressed to his counterpart in the Ministry of Environment and Natural Resources, PJ Ngei, and dated 23 May 1985, said: "It would appear to me that there is no substantial objection to allowing this company (Madhupaper) to start making paper pulp. I therefore accord my approval subject to (a) Ministry of Finance having no objection regarding foreign exchange implications and (b) the full availability of timber for the project in the forests managed by your ministry. From an industry point of view I fully support this project and hope there can be a way for it to start at once."

The Commissioner of Lands, JR Njenga, approved Madhupaper's application for land for the Thika project in a letter dated 19 April 1985, which read: "Reference is made to your application dated 13 March 1985 applying for plot LR No 4670 within Thika Municipality to be incorporated with the land that Madhupaper International Limited are buying for their above mentioned project. I wish to confirm that the Government approved your application and a letter of allotment will be issued as soon as possible."

Clearly, the government had made ministerial commitment to go through all the necessary approvals in order for the World Bank to approve the project. So SK Macharia took the government to court because he did not find any reason for stopping the project. At that time he really believed one could get justice from the courts, that one could sue the government and the courts would protect the litigant from the excesses of the highest political level. In this case the President was involved heavily and he had to be mentioned, although he was not the one SK Macharia was suing. What he was saying was that he had been given all these approvals and after he had incurred massive costs, the project was arbitrarily stopped. He felt that if there was something that he had done that required approval by law and he hadn't got it, then the government could stop him by getting a normal court order. But the government did not do that.

As required by law, Madhupaper International Limited, through its lawyer Gibson Kamau Kuria, gave the Attorney General a 30-days' notice of its intention to sue the state. There was no reaction after the notice period had lapsed and the company proceeded to file a case in the High Court. KCB was also sued with the intention of removing the receivership; this was necessary for the project to go on. In the meantime, SK Macharia had organised to raise the loan repayment money; Africa Finance, Continental Bank and a few other people had chipped in to raise enough money. However, when he attempted to pay, the bank refused to accept the money.

As the cases were going on Madhupaper was still trying to negotiate with KCB and the government to get the receivership lifted. One day three years later SK Macharia received a phone call from the President. It was becoming embarrassing for the government because the World Bank was involved and every time they would approach the World Bank for money they would be told to settle the Madhupaper case. The President told SK Macharia, "We want to settle this matter once and for all." The President suggested a meeting to resolve the issue. Others present at the meeting were Joseph Leting, then head of the civil service and secretary to the cabinet, Dr Benjamin Kipkorir who had replaced Philip Ndegwa as Executive Chairman of KCB, and the late Hezekiah Oyugi, Permanent Secretary for Internal Security.

They thrashed out a deal acceptable to all the parties and this was reduced into writing in various letters exchanged between SK Macharia, Dr Kipkorir and Mr Leting. Three basic points were agreed upon. SK Macharia was to pay the banks Ksh 54 million in full and final settlement of Madhupaper's loans. This was the amount that the company owed the banks on 25 October 1985, the day the receiver managers took over. He was also to withdraw the three cases Madhupaper had filed in court against the government and KCB. In return the banks would lift the receivership on Madhupaper and hand the company back to him.

Subsequently, SK Macharia paid the Ksh 54 million, which according to the written agreement was to be the full and final settlement of the debt owed to KCB. Then he withdrew the three court cases, and resumed control of his company on 7 March 1989.

A week later, on 13 March 1989 Mr Leting called him at the factory and informed him that the President had directed that the receiver managers be returned to Madhupaper and that KCB had been ordered to return the money he had paid. Immediately, SK Macharia drove to the offices of Waruhiu and Muite Advocates and told Paul Muite what had happened. As they were consulting, a clerk arrived from KCB with a banker's cheque for Ksh 54 million. Even more bizarre, the bank was now demanding one hundred and ten million shillings as payment for the same debt arguing that this was the amount they had been offered by potential buyers of Madhupaper.

What transpired was that the bank had already received a 10 percent deposit of the Ksh 110 million from Ravi Investments which wanted to purchase Madhupaper for its agent Malde Transporters Limited. SK Macharia was now in a very difficult position. He had withdrawn the court cases in good faith believing the matter was settled, but in so doing he had reduced his options for getting compensation because once a case against the government is withdrawn it cannot be resumed. In addition, he was about to lose the company he had worked so hard to build. Clearly drastic measures were needed.

Muite advised that SK Macharia looks for Ksh 110 million and pays KCB to prevent the company from being sold. Then once the bank had returned the company, SK Macharia would go back to court and sue to recover the difference between what he owed and the Ksh 110 million; the difference was Ksh 54 million. Once again, SK Macharia got together with friends including Muite and Muriu and they applied for a loan. However, getting the money proved to be another headache. They went to Standard Chartered, but the bank was called and told not to deal with SK Macharia. They rushed to Barclays Bank which quickly processed the loan application, but they were also stopped from giving SK Macharia the money. Barclays suggested that he should try to get the money from its head office, Barclays Bank PLC in the UK. So SK Macharia flew to the UK and negotiated for the loan. They told him that they wanted a bank guarantee. He knew well that no bank in Kenya would give him the guarantee and he called IFC who were familiar with the whole story of Madhupaper. After briefing them on the situation, they agreed to give a guarantee to Barclays Bank Plc. The loan of Ksh 110 million roughly equivalent to £ 3 pounds would be issued by Auger Investments, a subsidiary of the bank.

With the one hundred and ten million shillings now in place KCB threw another spanner into the works. The bank agreed to accept the money on condition that SK Macharia instructed Barclays Bank to pay the money to Trust Bank. Ravi Investments agreed to rescind its sale agreement with the receiver managers on condition that it was reimbursed all the costs it had incurred in the transaction. The amount came to Ksh 14 million. KCB insisted that SK Macharia pay this amount even though he was not involved in the deal between Ravi Investments, the receiver managers and the bank to buy his company. But securing Madhupaper's assets was paramount; so SK Macharia, having no money, borrowed fourteen million from his lawyers Waruhiu and Muite

Advocates and did as instructed then made plans to go to industrial area at 4.00 pm the same day 17 July to take back control of Madhupaper.

At 3.00 pm Ketan Somaia, Ajay Shah and Isaac Githuthu came to SK Macharia's small office at National Bank Building on Harambee Avenue. They told him that the President had directed them to go with him to Madhupaper and take over from the receivers. They said if he refused to hand over the company to them he would be detained. What made the demand even more outrageous was that Ketan Somaia was the chairman of Trust Bank, the same bank that KCB had instructed Macharia to pay the Ksh 110 million. Ajay Shah and Isaac Githuthu were directors at the bank.

SK Macharia called Paul Muite who crossed the street from his office at Electricity House and joined them. Muite asked the trio if they would pay for the company. They replied in the affirmative, but they would determine the price at which they would buy it after SK Macharia had handed Madhupaper over to them. Muite called SK Macharia aside and told him that he may as well give up as it had now become clear that the government would not let him set foot in Madhupaper again; it was determined to dispossess him. That's how SK Macharia lost Madhupaper.

With Madhupaper gone, SK Macharia was left with the huge loan of Ksh 110 million from Barclays Bank Plc. The money to pay Ravi Investments/Malde Transporters was a loan from Waruhiu and Muite Advocates. With Madhupaper gone he had no means of repaying all this money. And since he had withdrawn the court case against the government, now the only people he could sue were Ketan Somaia, Ajay Shah and Isaac Githuthu. Consequently, he went to court and filed a case. The case has never been heard.

After taking over Madhupaper, the trio through Mutune Investments Ltd offered SK Macharia Ksh 250 million as the purchase price for the company. This was a gross undervaluation considering that the World Bank had valued it at Ksh 750 million. In a short one-page agreement they proposed to pay an initial deposit of Ksh 125 million which would be used to pay off the Ksh 110 million loan from Barclays Bank Plc plus interest and other bank charges that had accumulated. This money would be paid directly by them to Auger Investments Limited, the subsidiary of Barclays Bank Plc. The balance on the sale price was to be paid to SK Macharia over a year in two installments – Ksh 70 million after four months and Ksh 55 million after nine months. For these two payments SK Macharia insisted on a bank guarantee, confirmed and irrevocable, payable to his bankers, Standard Chartered Bank.

Standard Chartered bank rejected the initial guarantees issued by Trust Bank and Mutune Investments went to Alnoor Kassam, owner of Trade Bank, and asked him to provide alternative guarantees. SK Macharia got the first seventy million shillings, but when he asked about the second payment Standard Chartered could not trace the money although it had confirmed in writing on 9 March 1990 having received Ksh 55 million. Consequently, he sued the bank and the case is still ongoing (as at the time of writing this book). So the only money SK Macharia got from Madhupaper was Ksh 70 million.

Out of this money, he refunded Waruhiu and Muite Advocates Ksh 14 million which they had loaned him to pay Ravi Investments/Malde Transporters. Over the next two years SK Macharia tried on numerous occasions to get a refund of the Ksh 14 million he had been forced to pay Ravi Investments/ Malde Transporters but to no avail. Finally, he got fed up and in July 1991 instructed his lawyers to sue the company on the grounds that no services had been provided by them to warrant the payment.

The case was still in court in 1997 when the company asked for an out of court settlement. Ravi Investments/Malde Transporters agreed to pay back the money with interest and paid Ksh 20 million after which they entered into an agreement terminating the court case. By this time SK Macharia had incurred a lot of debt as a result of the years spent in court over Madhupaper and the rest of the money was swallowed up by legal fees. Thus, in reality he got nothing out of Madhupaper, a company he had spent nine years building (1976–1985) and which was thriving by the time it was taken over.

SK Macharia continued following up the issue of overpayment to KCB of the Ksh 56 million. It was only with the advent of multiparty politics in 1992 that he felt confident enough to go to court. Madhupaper sued KCB, Kenya Commercial Finance Company (KCFC) Limited and Kenya National Capital Corporation (KNCC) in 1992.[14] These are the institutions that Madhupaper collectively owed Ksh 53, 780, 000 (which was rounded off to KSh 54 million). After almost a decade of litigation, a ruling in SK Macharia's favour was made by Justice (Rtd) Richard Kuloba of the High Court on 23 January 2003.

Justice (Rtd) Kuloba delivered a judgment in which he analysed and applied the principles of economic duress, restitution and unjust enrichment. He found that SK Macharia and Madhupaper had been subjected to illegitimate pressure and had been coerced through the unconscionable conduct of KCB and the other lenders to pay surplus monies over and above what they actually owed. Part of the judgment read:

"While a chargee, mortgagee or debenture holder is entitled to seek ways under the charge, mortgage or debenture, to recover monies owed to it, the ways it employs must be reasonable, and not in a manner which frustrates or impedes the borrower to reasonably carry on his business under such peace of

---

14   Civil Case No. 1263 of 1992

mind free from excessive anxiety caused by the creditors' terror tactics such as those employed by the defendants herein." It continued: "In the instant case one cannot sensibly accuse the defendants of having refrained from instilling inexcusable terror in the plaintiffs to thereby wring out the monies paid from the plaintiffs. If it was not for the only purpose of creating terror in the plaintiffs, why did the defendants enlist the assistance of the Permanent Secretary in the Office of the President and the Head of the Civil Service, who was not a director of any of the defendant companies?"

In finding for unjust enrichment Justice (Rtd) Kuloba said, "Involving the government or the Chief Secretary conveyed to the plaintiffs clear knowledge or belief that they had no means of escape from paying the extras and surpluses demanded of them. The plaintiffs were forced to abandon the pursuit of justice. They had to withdraw court cases or suffer losing their assets. The plaintiffs withdrew the cases but in the end still lost their assets. They paid off the monies demanded but in the end they lost their assets. This is a case of vitiated judgment. There was illegitimate pressure, unconscionable conduct on the part of the defendants, coercion, inequality between the parties, and lack of real choice for the plaintiffs."

Accordingly, judgment was entered in favour of SK Macharia and Madhupaper in the amount of Ksh 56 million, representing the surplus monies paid to the financial institutions. KCB and the other lenders filed an appeal against the decision and in July 2008 the Court of Appeal ruled in favour of KCB. While the Court of Appeal agreed with the High Court's exposition of the principle of unjust enrichment and its application to Kenya – generally, that a person who has received an unjust benefit at the expense of another should not be allowed to retain the benefit – it differed with the manner in which the High Court had applied the principle to the facts of the case. Restitution or repayment cannot be ordered where the benefit in question was conferred through a valid legal obligation owed by the claimant to the defendant, the Court of Appeal observed. In other words, a person who has an honest claim in law to the money of another person, whether through a loan agreement, charge and so on cannot be said to have been unjustly enriched if he is paid that which was legally owed to him. The judgment of the High Court was set aside and substituted with an order dismissing SK Macharia's claim who, together with Madhupaper, were ordered to pay to the other parties the costs of the appeal.

Since the 1980s the courts in Kenya were not dispensing justice to Kenyans. They had been corrupted and operated like an auction; those who had money just went and bought justice. A country cannot develop until there is equal justice for all, irrespective of one's economic status or position in society.

A new business initiative – Royal Credit Limited

Madhupaper was gone. However, life had to go on and SK Macharia started thinking of a new business to start. He was thinking along the lines of a hire purchase system where the service is offered by a third party, not the retailer. He wanted to organise a system where an individual could go to a shop and buy things like furniture on credit; for instance, a teacher goes to a shop, fills a form, brings it to a third party, the third party pays the shop and the teacher pays the third party slowly in instalments after paying a small deposit. Therefore, SK Macharia's original idea was not to start a credit card business. His experience with Madhupaper also influenced his choice of business as he didn't want to have any physical assets that someone could lay their hands on.

In the process of investigating how he could start the hire purchase system he discovered the existence of credit cards and felt the need to go to the UK to research on how these products worked. He could not travel because his passport had been confiscated in 1985 when he first started having problems with the government over Madhupaper. His wife Purity Gathoni, a partner in the new business went instead. She visited the offices of American Express in the UK and read leaflets, asked questions and so on. In addition, there was a new Managing Director at Standard Chartered Bank who had followed the Madhupaper history and knew that the bank had been told not to give SK Macharia a loan. Anthony Groag was however sympathetic and he promised to help him once he found something else to do. This is how the couple got financing for Royal Credit.

At that time their only competitor was Diners Card, the oldest credit card in Kenya, which was a franchise of the Chicago-based Diners International. The franchise had first been run by Pannell Bellhouse Mwangi and was later bought by Alnoor Kassam of Trade Bank who operated it until the bank collapsed in 1993. Royal Card became very successful and six years after inception the company introduced an international credit card after getting a licence from Diners Club International. By then the company had thirteen thousand cardholders and became the first wholly owned local card company to go international. By 1997 the company was operating a one-hundred-million-shilling overdraft facility with Standard Chartered Bank. However, once again politics interfered and SK Macharia lost his second business.

In February 1999, the President gave instructions to the Managing Director of Kenya Power and Lighting Company (KPLC), and one of his ministers to go to Macharia's Bank and tell the Managing Director to close the Royal Credit account failure to which the bank would lose the KPLC account. Of course the latter's account was huge compared to the former's. The Bank's Managing Director called SK Macharia and told him that he didn't want to close his account and advised him to write a letter to the London head office. Without mentioning the Managing Director's name, he was to say that he had heard a rumour that the bank had been instructed to close the Royal Media account. Then he was to make a request that London writes to the local branch to ensure this action was not taken.

SK Macharia wrote to the head office on 3 March 1999 and the London office replied on 17 March seeking more information which he provided. The local branch was then told not to close the Royal Credit account. The Managing Director of the same Bank called the Managing Director of KPLC and told him they had consulted with their London office and decided to keep the Royal Credit account. That afternoon, the Managing Director of KPLC went to see the Managing Director of the Bank with a letter closing all the accounts of KPLC in the Bank. When the Managing Director faxed the letter to London, he was instructed not to let those accounts go. He called SK Macharia and said the Bank would not renew its overdraft facility. He offered to assist him look for another Bank. SK Macharia managed to persuade the MD to give them more time before withdrawing their line of credit. In August 1999, the Bank agreed to give them four months (which was inadequate and much less than they had requested) to reorganise their finances, pay the existing overdraft and move their account to another Bank.

Having a line of credit was crucial because this was the money the company used to pay retailers such as supermarkets, fuel stations and hotels where its cardholders purchased goods and services on credit. Royal Credit usually billed each cardholder at the end of each month for purchases made using the card during that month. The customer usually got a grace period of 15 days to pay the bill. This meant that the total credit period was 45 days. While Royal Credit needed to wait for this period to elapse in order to collect its money, retailers or 'merchants' would present invoices to it before then which had to be paid so that they could keep offering credit to its cardholders. A line of credit from its bankers was therefore crucial to finance day-to-day working capital requirements, hence the overdraft facility. The Bank withdrew the line of credit in January 2000.

Losing it meant that the company could not pay merchants in the short term. Given the sensitive nature of the credit card business, which relies heavily on trust between the players anchored on the reputation of the service provider with regard to its financial viability, just the rumour alone – that Royal Credit was in trouble – was enough to finish the business. Retailers began to drop their card. The only thing that SK Macharia could do was to thank the Bank's Managing Director and to express his gratitude for his help. All through he had suspected that the closure was imminent, but he knew the MD had done his best. He told him that he was still going to sue the Bank together with the Managing Director, KPLC.

When he went to court, SK Macharia was suing for compensation on the grounds that the bank had withdrawn Royal Credit's overdraft facility under political influence and he had correspondence to that effect. In addition he would not pay the Ksh 100 million overdraft. He also wanted the bank to pay all the monies owed by Royal Card customers. This case was filed in 2001 and has never been heard.

According to SK Macharia, he lost faith in the Kenyan courts after the Madhupaper experience. Therefore, although he sued after Royal Credit's account was closed, he does not hold out too much hope of getting justice. He goes to court to make noise, not necessarily to seek justice. After all, he was not the only one who suffered the consequences of an imperial presidency. There were many businessmen, who also had their businesses closed down for no good reason. When the powers that be decided that a particular businessman must be finished they would finish him completely. What saved SK Macharia was that he was always loud; he did not care if he was going to be killed or not. But he did not give the power barons any peace. He would go to court knowing he was not going to get justice, but would still go because newspapers would report and he would write letters and copy them to the media. He survived by making noise in court so much that one time he met a lawyer who said, "Why can't you build an office here?" SK Macharia was always in the court corridors and he spent a fortune on lawyers.

Nevertheless, despite the frustration, he has never allowed himself to become emotional or bitter about all the hardships and injustices he has suffered. This is yet another reason he has survived. No matter what he loses, he always laughs about it. He used to have a cassette in which an American psychologist explained how laughter comforts someone. He would say that if one had a problem, they should find a reason to laugh and they will forget it. So SK Macharia laughs at all his problems no matter how big. When he lost the case for Ksh 56 million, which was so straightforward, his wife cried. He comforted her by telling her that if they lost one million shillings they would find another million shillings somewhere else. Despite everything he feels that God has been good to him.

Royal Media Services Limited

During the 1992 elections SK Macharia was annoyed by the way the Kenya Broadcasting Corporation (KBC) handled publicity from opposition candidates. SK Macharia's presidential candidate was Jaramogi Oginga Odinga. In effect, he used to fund his campaigns, especially by paying for advertisements in KBC. The adverts were never aired. When Oginga Odinga lost the election, SK Macharia went into shock; he did not believe that he would lose. When he got over the shock, he thought that most likely Odinga lost because KBC refused to cover him in the same way they were covering Moi. There and then he decided that he would have his own TV and radio station.

At the time SK Macharia decided to launch his own broadcast station, he didn't even know who was supposed to give broadcast licences. Subsequently, he wrote a letter to KBC asking for a licence to broadcast on radio and television. KBC's Managing Director called him back, laughing over the phone and telling him that KBC was only a broadcaster and did not give broadcast licences. He advised him to write a letter to the Office of the President, which he did. That letter was subsequently passed to the Ministry of Information and Broadcasting. SK Macharia was not even aware that it existed. The Ministry's Permanent Secretary, David Andere, wrote back to him saying that he could not be given a licence to broadcast as a private person. SK Macharia wrote back giving him seven days to give him the licence failure to which he would take him to court. The PS did not respond. At the expiry of the seven days SK Macharia instructed Gibson Kamau Kuria to go to court. For four years the case was in court.

The government argued in court that it could not give SK Macharia a licence to broadcast because there were no frequencies. With this development, he needed to challenge the Attorney General's stand. However, there was a problem because he knew nothing about frequencies. Therefore, he decided to go to the International Telecommunication Union (ITU) in Geneva, Switzerland, where he spent two months learning about frequencies and how they are allocated. They explained that frequencies are international. Countries apply and are assigned blocks. Each country then distributes the frequencies within its block to its citizens. Each frequency covers a radius of about one hundred kilometres and they have to be allocated in such a way that one person's signal does not interfere with another person's communication. Within each block are frequencies defined as military communication, police communication and for general public use. At the end of the visit, ITU gave SK Macharia a diskette containing all the Kenya frequencies.

SK Macharia printed out the contents of the diskette and tabled them in court. The document showed the total number of frequencies Kenya had and those already in use, showing that there were frequencies available for distribution. The High Court issued an order stating that the government should consider giving Royal Media a licence to broadcast. This order was however vague. The company decided to go to a higher court – the constitutional court – seeking to have the court order affirmed on the basis that SK Macharia had been denied his rights and no one, not even a government, should deny a citizen the right to private broadcast. The court affirmed the order.

Once the constitutional court affirmed the order the next thing was to compel the ministers concerned to act on it or go to jail. The company went to the Court of Appeal seeking for an order to have the Minister for Information and Broadcasting and the Attorney General, the late Johnstone Makau and Amos Wako respectively, to be committed to jail for failing to obey a court order which was contempt of court. The ensuing order, which was flashed by *Daily Nation,* immediately stirred the government. President Moi, during a public meeting in Naivasha, declared that no Minister in his government would go to jail. Effectively what the President was saying was that his 'government cannot obey court orders'. It probably appeared minor because it involved an individual, SK Macharia, only. But the implication in the country was huge because it meant that the government did not recognise and follow the law. Then why was it a government? It meant the laws were only what the government interpreted them to be. Then why have the courts? It left *wananchi* (citizens) feeling that if an officer in government decided to take their piece of land, then they have nowhere to go for justice.

Meanwhile, Royal Media was determined to enforce the court order. It succeeded in getting warrants of arrest from the police for the Minister and the AG. When they were on the verge of being arrested, President Moi summoned SK Macharia to State House where he found Johnstone Makau and Amos Wako already there. With them was Joseph Kamotho. President Moi asked SK Macharia why he wanted to take his ministers to jail. SK Macharia told him that all he wanted was a broadcasting licence as ordered by the court. The President asked SK Macharia if he would support him and KANU in the elections later that year (1997). SK Macharia replied in the affirmative. The President asked him if he would agree to stand on a KANU ticket in Gatanga. Again SK Macharia replied in the affirmative. Then Makau was ordered to go and give Royal Media a licence. Surprisingly, minister Makau did not even know how to write it. SK Macharia accompanied him to his office and helped him to draft the licence, then waited for it to be typed. When it was ready, Makau called his PS Andere to sign. Thus, after a four-year struggle, SK Macharia finally succeeded in getting a licence to broadcast on 22 April 1997.

According to SK Macharia, he had no interest in running during the coming elections. However, he knew that the licence could be withdrawn at any time. That is why he complied. President Moi had also requested him to form a group to campaign for him in Central Province. This is how the Central Province Development Support Group got started. It used to go around talking to *wananchi*. And because it was widely believed that President Moi would go back for another term anyway, the members of the Group would tell the *wananchi* that it was better to be there when the meat was being shared; at least one could negotiate and get a little piece. Expectedly, SK Macharia lost the Gatanga parliamentary seat in the election.

Once the elections were over, SK Macharia focused his energies on getting his broadcasting stations up and running. Subsequently, he went overseas to procure the transmitters and other requisite equipment. This was before Royal Credit ran into problems and so he used revenues from the company to finance the project. Once he procured the equipment, he began assembling the stations. The whole process took about one year. On 1 March 1999, Citizen Radio and TV came on air for the first time. Both stations were operating from AmBank House within the city centre.

At the time, both SK Macharia and President Moi were still on good terms. The President visited his home in Ndakaini twice. SK Macharia had also visited President Moi's home many times. The President's ability to interact with anyone and his genuine warmth masked a ruthless streak. It often led people to underestimate him. According to SK Macharia, President Moi had this ability to really bring himself down to anyone's level, which could really mislead someone. For instance, if tea was brought by the cooks or waiters in his house, he would tell them to go and would serve the guests himself. Meat would be brought and he would take a knife, cut it himself and hand out the pieces. What a display of humility!

SK Macharia had such an experience one day when the President visited his home in Ndakaini. Usually when the President was outside State House or his home, he was not supposed to eat food that was cooked in the absence of his security people. The security team carried everything including drinking water and cooking utensils. During the visit to Ndakaini, it was different. The Central Provincial Commissioner, Wilson Kiprono arap Chepkwony and his security people came four days before and camped at SK Macharia's home. One of the places to be secured was the kitchen. SK Macharia's wife, Purity Gathoni, called the PC and told him, "If the President wants to come to my house I will provide and cook the food. I do not want any security person in my kitchen, otherwise he can stay and not come." When President Moi was informed about Mrs Macharia's stand, he ordered the security people not to get involved. Subsequently, she did all the cooking and served the President assisted by Mrs Monica Kibe, a friend.

The friendship between SK Macharia and President Moi lasted until the Millennium celebrations in January 2000. During the celebrations, the owner of Kunste Hotel (in Nakuru) asked Citizen Radio to air their New Year's Eve party live. It was common practice during Moi's presidency that a party was held on New Year's Eve at State House, Nakuru. Therefore, while the president's function was being covered live by KBC at State House, the party at Kunste Hotel was being covered live by Radio Citizen. Some people at the State House party were listening to the radio. When they heard the party at the hotel being aired live they went to Kunste Hotel. The following morning jealous people were briefing President Moi and putting a completely different spin on the event. The President was told that SK Macharia had set up another State House at Kunste Hotel and that his party was aired live by his own radio station. It was designed to anger the President and had the desired effect. The President ordered Citizen Radio closed immediately.

When Royal Media set up broadcasting stations, it rented masts in Limuru, Nyambene and Nyeri from KBC instead of building their own masts for setting up transmitters. In Londiani where KBC did not have a mast, Royal Media had rented a mast from Telkom Kenya which had its own masts. According to SK Macharia, this was a blunder because for President Moi to close Citizen, all he needed to do was call KBC and Telkom and order them to shut down the Royal Media transmitters. Within hours the stations were off the air. The corporations were also ordered to make sure that nobody from Royal Media got near the masts. Therefore, Royal Media was also barred from removing its equipment.

Contrary to the insinuations of the President's men, there was no political angle to the transmission at Kunste Hotel. It was purely business. The station was not doing the transmission for fun; neither did it have anything to do with State House. So what was the issue? Unfortunately, this is how politics and business get mixed and the businessman is the one who suffers. This was the first time Royal Media was shut down.

SK Macharia kept on begging and sending politicians as intermediaries to convince President Moi to reopen the stations. The pleas fell on deaf ears. Now they had become enemies and SK Macharia could not get anywhere near him. He tried going to court to force the government to reopen the station, but with no luck.

The stations stayed closed for almost a full year. In November 2000 the President summoned SK Macharia, Dr Sally Kosgei, then the Head of the Civil Service and Secretary to the Cabinet, and Samuel Chepkonga, the then Director-General of CCK to his house. In their presence, he ordered that Royal Media should go back on air and that CCK should issue a letter to that effect. But when SK Macharia attempted to get the equipment from KBC and Telkom, he was told that they had not received official instructions allowing him to do so. It turned out that President Moi had been cheated that Royal Media was using KBC's equipment and that the original letter shutting the station down stated that KBC was to confiscate the equipment. Everyone was afraid of going back to Moi to ask for a letter to release it. In effect, SK Macharia was left with no choice but to start afresh – from scratch. Consequently, he went to the US and asked for assistance from Voice of America. The broadcaster gave him two transmitters, which he installed in Nairobi and Nyeri. Citizen Radio went back on air in February 2001.

By now SK Macharia was so bitter that he started attacking the government on its corruption record, injustices and lack of press freedom using two main programmes – *Yaliyotendeka* and *Wembe wa Citizen*. It was not surprising that the station was on air for only two months before armed police and GSU (General Service Unit) officers raided the station, destroyed equipment and carted off what was left. Citizen was shut down for the second time.

Royal Media went to the High Court demanding the return of its equipment. It was never returned. But SK Macharia swore that this time he would not go to beg the President to put Citizen back on air. He and a few leaders including Kiraitu Murungi, Matu Wamae and Matere Keriri got together and decided to mobilise the Kenyan public and also get the support of the American government to apply pressure on the Kenya government. Collin Powell, the US Secretary of State, visited Kenya to see President Moi on the issue of freedom of the press. However, the latter did not budge. Unable to pursue that line of lobbying, SK Macharia finally bowed to pressure from his supporters to appeal to President Moi.

When SK Macharia went to see President Moi, he asked him if he would support KANU and his preferred presidential candidate. He asked him who his candidate was and he told him that it was Uhuru Kenyatta; the Uhuru candidacy was a closely guarded secret at that time. SK Macharia agreed to support Uhuru, just because he wanted his stations back. According to SK Macharia, in reality he had already decided to campaign against KANU. Having agreed with President Moi, Citizen went back on air. It was shut down again two days later. However, this time round, owing to pressure from the public and the American government, the stations were back on air after four days.

Management style and company structure

Royal Media had started broadcasting again at the end of 2002 with the two transmitters that were procured from VOA. However, the real growth began in January 2003, when a new government came into place. The company was issued with new licences to broadcast nationally. In 2003, Royal media had a staff of twenty-four; at the time of writing this book, the staff had grown to over nine hundred with a monthly payroll of about Ksh 60 million.

The growth was evident from the expansion in facilities. By 2011, Royal Media had one television station (Citizen TV) and 10 radio stations, namely, Citizen Radio (which broadcasts in Kiswahili), Hot 96 (which broadcasts in English) and eight vernacular stations – Mulembe FM, Inooro FM, Egesa FM, Ramogi FM, Muuga FM, Musyi FM, Chamgei FM and Bahari FM.

Royal Media is a family-owned business with SK Macharia and his wife as directors; SK Macharia is the chairperson of the company and his wife Purity Gathoni is the vice-chairperson. SK Macharia focuses on the technical side of the business, building transmitters, while Purity markets the stations. According to SK Macharia, Purity has done a tremendous marketing job; if she had not been in charge of the marketing function, the company would not have achieved such growth. Being the one who knows how to sell airtime, he admits that she's very good at marketing. So SK Macharia focuses on building the stations with the aim of reaching as many Kenyans as possible with radio and television. Then he leaves it to Purity to make the money which in turn helps SK Macharia to build more stations.

Below the directors is the Managing Director.[15] Under the Managing Director are four heads of department, namely the marketing director, programming director (radio), programmes manager (television) and the chief engineer. Before the Managing Director was hired in 2006, SK Macharia used to handle all aspects of the day-to-day running of the company. However, the company had grown very fast, becoming a very complex operation, especially with some of the radio stations like Citizen, Ramogi and Inooro having presenters for 24 hours; the others were run by a computer after 4.00 am till morning when the breakfast show crew would take over. The directors soon realised that they needed a full-time energetic younger person to handle the day-to-day operations.

Another reason why SK Macharia gave up the day-to-day running of the company was that he was never the type of boss who sits in the office and just gives instructions. With more than one hundred sites, which were mostly in

15   At the time of compiling the profile, the Managing Director was Wachira Waruru, who has wide experience in the media.

the field, he felt he needed to be out there. He has been involved in climbing hills and erecting masts and transmitters on all of them. In some places, there are no roads to get to the sites and they would spend about five days hauling equipment to the top of a hill in order to erect a mast. Thus, SK Macharia worked very hard at the initial stages doing everything. Now that he was getting older he also saw the need to slow down.

Future of Royal Media Services

With the expansion of the company, the directors plan to make it public in the long run. SK Macharia's dream is to build a strong company that will outlive him, hence the plan to have Kenyans buy into it. He is concerned that everyone who talks about Royal Media only sees him; they do not see the institution or the nine hundred employees. The company is still involved in a lot of construction to expand its reach to remote areas like North Eastern Province and improve the reception of its signal in some areas. In all, it plans to install transmitters all over the country. His aspiration is to change the perception of a one-man show and also take a step back and let the company grow as an independent institution. Then it can be taken over by the public through an Initial Public Offering (IPO). Before that, however, he would want to see the management properly structured.

The company also plans to go regional. It plans to take Citizen Radio and TV to Tanzania where it will cover the whole country being a Kiswahili-speaking country. Expansion is also planned for one installation each in Kampala (Uganda), Bujumbura (Burundi), and Kigali (Rwanda). In tandem with this expansion, SK Macharia is spearheading efforts to put up new headquarters for Royal Media. The company would have to spend about three hundred million shillings to put up new offices and studios (planned in the medium term) for which the company acquired a one-acre piece of land in Upper Hill, Nairobi. The new offices would take up seventy thousand square feet of space, more than double the area where the premises moved to at Communications Centre in Kilimani, after AmBank House. Other than offices and studios, the new headquarters would also have a theatre with a seating capacity of five hundred people to produce local dramas and host live conferences.

The intense competition in the media industry is an ongoing challenge as companies try to hold on to their best presenters. An incident in May 2004 illustrates that when SK Macharia is backed into a corner he will fight back by any means necessary. During this incident, Patrick Quarcoo, the owner of Radio Africa Group (which includes Kiss 100 and Classic FM), poached five Citizen Radio employees at a go; they all resigned the same evening without giving any notice. A furious SK Macharia wrote two letters to the Minister for Information and the Minister for Transport. He told them what Radio Africa had done with the intention of closing down Citizen Radio. He told them that he needed action within a few hours – to ensure that all other media houses were protected against such action as Radio Africa had taken – failure to which he would take the law into his own hands. Upon inaction by the authorities, he did exactly that. He went ahead to interfere with their signal and blocked it intentionally. For three days all that the Kiss 100 listeners heard was vernacular music. As would be expected, this led to another confrontation with CCK which subsequently disabled Royal Media's transmitter at Limuru. SK Macharia remained unrepentant and told CCK that it could close everything; it did not matter anymore. At midnight CCK reversed its action.

SK Macharia's vision is that Royal Media will play a key role in helping Kenyans to live free lives with access to information that will improve their lives and enable the country to go forward. For example, he went ahead to install radio transmitters in the north-eastern region of the country knowing very well that he couldn't make money there. However, he reckoned that even if one person became more exposed, stopped being a *shifta*[16] and did something more constructive with his life, this was good enough. If he could talk to the Pokot and Turkana in their own language, not get a cent out of it, but it stopped cattle rustling, then this was good enough.

SK Macharia started a newspaper called *Leader* in 2007. It did not last long and he closed it early in 2008. He says it was meant to be a short-term venture for the elections as print lends itself to better record-keeping than electronic media. He is passionate about the latter and that is where his focus remains.

Family and legacy

SK Macharia has four grown-up children with his first wife Njeri Karanja and two sons with Purity Gathoni. He has been very straightforward with all his children that it is not automatic they will inherit his company. He makes it clear to them openly that what he has worked for is for himself and his wife. He tells them not to sit back and wait to inherit his property because he could as well write a will giving all his wealth to charity. Nevertheless he will give them the best education he can possibly afford and whoever shows courage to go out there and work hard he will support.

Out of encouragement for hard work, SK Macharia's oldest son now owns one of the large insurance underwriters in Kenya. He helped him obtain the

---

16   *Shifta* is a derogatory word used in the north-eastern part of Kenya to refer to a bandit.

licence, but he is not involved in running the company. His other son and a daughter operate Mobile Planet, a company that provides value-added SMS services to cellular provider Safaricom and Zain (now Airtel). For example, during the 2002 and 2007 general elections in Kenya, their platform provided up-to-the-minute election results. As the results were tallied, subscribers were sent updates via SMS. In August 2008 Google bought 12.5 percent shares in the company. Another daughter works with Royal Media as traffic controller. Finally, his last two sons with Purity Gathoni are in university in Kenya, one studying law and the other commerce.

SK Macharia says his highest achievement is showing Kenyans that they can succeed. Even where his failure is because of the government he laughs, goes forward and tries something else, going all the way. When the failure is one's fault, let them just forget it and move on.

SK Macharia's role model is the American citizen. Everyone is treated equally by law and there is nothing a citizen would not do for the good of his family or his country. He admires Bill Gates for recognising early enough that his abilities lay in computer science, leaving university midstream to focus his energies on it and becoming the richest man in the world.

On vernacular radio stations and media consolidation

In response to claims that media owners who own radio, television and print media are a threat to free competition Macharia says: "This is just propaganda by politicians because first you want to be internationally competitive and being big helps you to do that. It also enables citizens to get free information because governments all over the world will never give their citizens information until they are forced or until they know they are going to be discovered. Which government in this world is going to touch CNN, for instance? Not even the US President can afford to talk ill of CNN. If there is no strong fourth estate no government would be democratic. Having big media houses is not bad, what is bad is having monopolies because that impedes competition."

Is the explosive growth of vernacular radio stations a lasting trend? SK Macharia believes that vernacular stations are here to stay. One can only consume information in a language they understand fully. For instance, if one took a book like the *Government Inspector* (by Nikolai Gogol) which is taught in schools and interpreted it into vernacular, relating it to how their own government operated, people especially in rural areas would understand the theory of it better than learning it in English.

On the claim especially by politicians that vernacular radio stations cause tribal hatred and clashes he says: "Tribal clashes are caused by politicians because radio stations host politicians in talk shows or cover their rallies and merely report what they say. Speaking on behalf of the major media houses, I can tell you that they know they have a responsibility to the country not to be misused by politicians. As far as Royal Media is concerned I cannot order Ramogi to go and fight Raila, Mulembe to fight Mudavadi or any other leader for that matter. I sit with my employees and tell them the radio stations were set up for the good of their communities and because I don't understand the language I pass over the responsibility of doing this to the presenters."

He further argues: "And it works very well because these people become responsible to their own communities who question them. I will know when the Luos are fighting Ramogi or when Kalenjins are fighting Chamgei FM and at that stage then I would get involved because if you're not being listened to by your own community, then you must be doing something wrong. If you keep feeding people parochial, cheap and negative stuff and denying them information about national issues, they will switch you off and yet you get advertising revenues on the basis that you have listenership. It is as simple as that and I can tell you that these communities have benefited from Royal Media stations. They have been educated and know their rights better than politicians think. It is because of vernacular radio stations that politicians can no longer go to rural villages to cheat *wananchi*."

On local and foreign investment

SK Macharia believes that Royal Media could still go the same way as his other companies. As foreign companies are protected by their governments, closing them down (despite being a possibility) would mess the country's reputation overseas. If the Kenya government was to try and close the Nation Media Group, for example, it would be a fight against the Aga Khan. Messing up with East African Breweries Limited would see the British come calling. But local companies can be messed with and one can go to court and shout, but they will not get justice. Fortunately now, Kenyans can come to one's defence to a certain extent, but not the government. So in Africa it is still the case that if a government wants to destroy a local business it will do so with ease. As a result, Africans who can develop their economies have been kept at kiosk and *jua kali* level by their own governments with individuals in these governments ready to be corrupted by foreigners to make sure their fellow citizens never rise.

As SK Macharia says: "You cannot depend on foreigners to develop as a country. This is what I have been saying but nobody in government hears me. All politicians in this country and in government do not talk about anything else other than foreign investment, and of course foreign countries which fund them encourage this because it is their people who come here to invest. A foreign investor contributes less to the development of a country's economy than local investors. His investment mostly develops the economy of his home country."

Giving the example of an investor who brings in USD 1 million into Kenya, SK Macharia observes the irony of the accompanying incentives. The investor is given all the advantages including being given land, getting duty exemption on machinery, repatriates profits back to his home country and so on, the normal conditions investors give before investing in the country.

Says he: "The USD 1 million is usually in form of equipment and chances are that he will borrow working capital from here. He will manufacture his products and sell to the local market. At the end of each year he will make a profit which is transferred back to his country. That profit which is made in Kenya is invested in his home country and ends up developing that country. At the end of it all, having transferred his profit every single year and investing it in his own country, he can sell his factory for USD 2 million because he'll now be talking of goodwill and go back to his home country yet he only brought in USD 1 million. So in essence he'll have left nothing in this country other than the salaries he's paid workers."

Furthermore, he says: "If on the other hand this profit that was made here was also being reinvested here, that guy would be developing Kenya. This is what African governments have never been able to comprehend. This is why despite all this foreign investment they talk about, the African is still going without food, remains poor and the economy cannot move. This is why Singapore in 1970 was poorer than Kenya and today it is among the developed economies. How would the European countries or America have developed if all the profits that their companies make in billions were to be transferred to other countries? They would never develop."

African governments not only encourage foreign investors, but they also often frustrate local business people who want to start industries. Later, they turn around and bend over backwards to accommodate foreigners who express an interest in starting similar ventures. In 1985 SK Macharia made a detailed application to Kenya Posts and Telecommunications (KPTC) for a licence to operate a mobile phone company. The Managing Director replied stating that SK Macharia could not be allowed to start such a company in the country. When the first licence for mobile phone was advertised SK Macharia was the first to apply. But because of the big circle of foreigners with access to the President, local investors were not given the licence.

In reality, SK Macharia observes that Kenyans do not lack the skills to start industries. If one were given a licence all they would do is buy equipment and install it. SK himself had built a factory to make paper; he saw it being made in Italy and that's how he got the idea. He did not employ even a single foreigner to run the business. Neither had he ever thought about broadcasting; he knew nothing about it. In the broadcasting business, he has not employed any foreigner because he believes all one has to do is learn. He made a lot of mistakes but he learnt. And one thing he knows is that he employs a Kenyan who is supporting himself, while he develops, and if he makes money he ploughs it back into the country; the money does not go overseas.

SK Macharia believes a change in attitude within government is needed. It is better for the government to borrow money overseas and distribute it to local people to build industries. Once they set up the industries, the government should let them learn how to run them. In the process, the local people will make mistakes but ultimately the country will develop. In fact, all the government needs to do is to support citizens to go out there and get money themselves like SK Macharia did with Madhupaper, by creating an environment which guarantees justice and security, and where businesses are not interfered with.

Tips for aspiring entrepreneurs

Having built such a media empire within a short period of time, SK Macharia has a few tips for aspiring entrepreneurs. One of them is commitment. When one starts something they should be committed, doing it all the way and when they fail they shouldn't give up. They should start something else and go all the way. It is also important that an aspiring entrepreneur should learn how to take risks. One must be prepared to take risks for what they believe is good.

Young people must also participate fully in deciding who goes into government by the power of the ballot because they are the majority. Tomorrow's Kenya is for them, not for the previous generation. And their future is dependent on the political environment. A good environment will allow them to think for themselves, be able to work freely and improve the welfare of their families which ultimately benefits the whole country. The next step is: once an election is held, they should accept the verdict of the majority and end the tendency of Africans to be sore losers instead of joining together to build the country until the next election.

Another tip is to respect everyone. An aspiring entrepreneur should treat every employee well because they are human beings just like them. For example, the rule at SK Macharia's home is that everyone eats the same food whether it is the children, the drivers or the watchmen. This is in recognition of the fact that if the watchman who guards them when they are asleep is hungry, and the watchman knows that the employer did not sleep hungry, what would stop him from opening the gate and accepting ten shillings from a thief to go and buy *mandazi* while the employer is robbed?

SK Macharia also believes that it is important to give back to society. After registering considerable success, he returned and built many schools and churches all over the country. He has also assisted many families and individuals in cash or by paying medical bills.

Chapter 3

Nelson Muguku Njoroge

During his early life, Nelson Muguku Njoroge was always told that he could not do anything. Education officials told him that he would die an untrained teacher (UT). Years later, he would prove these prophets of doom wrong. From six hens, which he raised in the backyard of his house at Kabianga Government School and with no experience, he started a commercial poultry business that was to make him one of Kenya's largest poultry farmers.

As if this was not enough, people continued to frown at many of his business ideas. When he set out to get into hatchery, they thought he was mad. Nevertheless, he went ahead and started what was to be the only African-owned hatchery in the country in 1972. Years later, when he withdrew money from a reputable stable bank to put it into a building society at a time when African-owned financial institutions were collapsing, everyone, including his bankers, told him that he was crazy and that he had made the biggest blunder of his life. Muguku Poultry Farm in Kikuyu was to become one of the top three hatcheries in the country. Nelson Muguku Njoroge also became the single largest individual shareholder of Equity Bank with shares valued at over KSh 3 billion by 2008.

Many admirers came to refer to him as the 'poultry king', but Muguku continued to carry his wealth with grace, humility and that rarest of qualities – service to his community. On the streets, he would attract little attention because of the simple life that he led. Nevertheless, the story of how he rose from an untrained carpentry teacher to build a business empire is one of a legend. His journey amply demonstrates the value of trusting one's instincts and taking well-calculated risks. It also demonstrates how, given a chance, African entrepreneurs can conquer mountains.

Early childhood and education

Nelson Muguku Njoroge was born on 25 July 1932 in Kanyariri, Kikuyu, in the present-day Kiambu County. He was the firstborn child in a family of ten children, seven boys and three girls, born to Stephen Njoroge and Edith Wambui, both farmers. Muguku's father had at one time been employed by the Europeans, but he later decided that employment was not for him. Subsequently, he went into farming, growing vegetables for the Nairobi market. Later in the 1950s when Africans were allowed to keep grade cattle, he also went into livestock farming. " He even tried to grow coffee but the climate around Kikuyu is not suitable for the crop," says Muguku. The family was average in terms of income; their father, Njoroge, was able to earn enough to put food on the table and ensure his children were educated.

Muguku had a typical rural upbringing where children were expected to help out on the farm and fetch water from the river. He also helped his mother to look after his younger siblings. His father was a Christian who did not drink beer. "My father was very hard-working and also very strict. He was a Christian and did not drink beer. We were not allowed to play and we spent all our time working on the farm. Even after I started school, I was expected to help out on the farm after school. I grew up working hard and still do," says Muguku.

Muguku began his education near his home where he attended Kanyariri Primary School. After sitting the Common Competitive Entrance Examination (CCEE), a national examination that pupils sat in Standard Four to determine whether they would proceed to intermediate school, he was one of only three pupils in his class who qualified. Subsequently, he was admitted to Kagumo Intermediate School in Nyeri where he completed Standard Eight in 1948. However, he did not qualify to go to high school. His father wanted him to repeat the class, but he was not keen. His father insisted and he was enrolled at Kabete Intermediate School where he repeated Standard Eight in 1949. "I did not really make any effort because I had not wanted to repeat but surprisingly I passed and had the best marks in my class. However, my name was omitted from the list of those admitted to high school and I did not know why, since other students with lower marks were called to go to high school. I came to learn later that some students in our school had foreknowledge of the exam and my class was blacklisted," he says.

Despite his earlier reluctance to repeat the class, he was disappointed this time round about not going to high school. So he decided to look for employment and earn money. However, his father would hear none of it, insisting that his son was still too young and should pursue his education. By this time, Muguku had sent an application to the Kenya Bus Service Company and been called for an interview. Still his father did not allow him to go. Instead, he suggested that he should go for technical training to learn a craft. He approached a teacher at Thika Technical School who told him that the school offered courses in masonry and carpentry. "The masonry class had vacancies, but my father said I was too small to lift building stones. The teacher said he would try and find a slot for me in the carpentry class which was full. In the teacher's house, I was impressed by the beautiful furniture and, although I did not really like carpentry, I thought that if he could make furniture like that, then it wouldn't be a bad course to take. Thus, I joined the technical school once a carpentry vacancy was available in 1950," says Muguku. The course usually took four years.

An interesting challenge that Muguku faced immediately was one of uniform. "The school made uniforms in three sizes – small, medium and large. The smallest size was too big for me, so I was the only one sent to the tailor shop to have a special uniform fitted," Muguku reminisces. Despite his small size he thrived in the course and discovered that he had a talent for the craft. He did so well that in his second term at the school, he was promoted to second year. He continued to do well in the course surpassing some of his colleagues who had been doing the course. However, in a classic case of colonial bureaucracy, when it was time to do the final exam, he was told that he could not sit for it because he had not completed four years. "Thus, despite being promoted and being the best in my class, I could not sit for the exam. They insisted that the curriculum rules stated that a student must complete four years before doing the exam yet I knew that I was ready and would pass. I knew I was gifted in carpentry and could have sat the exam after two years," he states as a matter of fact.

Part of the reason why Muguku was denied the chance to sit for the exam had to do with the colonial mentality that Africans were not that bright. It was held that there was no way a student could complete a four-year course in three years. Muguku remembers, "The teacher who used to teach us the course used to say: 'You are not trained to be rich, you are expected to be good *fundis* (artisans). A good *fundi* should be trained for four years. After working for a year, you can apply to do a second grade. You cannot pass one grade today and next month apply for the second grade'." In that case, Muguku had no choice but to accept and do another year. The irony was that some of his classmates were employed as teachers at the school and he would ask them: "What do you expect to teach me because I was even better than you when we did the course together?"

Teaching career

Upon eventually completing his carpentry course after another year, Muguku sat the exam and started looking for a teaching job. At that time, carpentry (for boys) and domestic science (for girls) were compulsory subjects in intermediate schools. Pupils had to pass these subjects to get a certificate. Several schools including Chogoria in Meru, Githumu in Murang'a and Government School Kapenguria in West Pokot had written to Thika Technical School asking for carpentry teachers. Muguku was posted to Kapenguria, a considerable distance from Thika. The posting was supposed to be temporary, lasting only four months, where he was to stand in for a teacher who was going on leave. "Since I was prepared to do anything to get out of Thika Technical, I agreed to go to Kapenguria." That was in November 1953.

At the time the crackdown on the *Mau Mau* was in full gear following the colonial government's declaration of a State of Emergency in 1952. Many members of the Kikuyu community, as well as Embu and Meru, had been confined in communal villages. To enable him to go and teach in Kapenguria, Thika Technical School had to process a special pass for Muguku which he was to carry at all times. Kapenguria was famous then for the trial of Jomo Kenyatta and others charged with managing the *Mau Mau* (commonly referred to as the Kapenguria Six).[17] By the time Muguku went to Kapenguria, the trial had been transferred to Kitale. "Kitale was the nearest big town and quite far from Kapenguria. Since every morning the magistrate had to travel from Kitale to Kapenguria for the hearings, it was decided that the trial should shift to Kitale. The court where the trials had been carried out in Kapenguria was just next to the school," says Muguku.

Muguku took the train from Thika and travelled to western Kenya. When he got to Kitale, he was unsure of which direction Kapenguria was and decided to ask a man at the station unaware that the man was a home guard.[18] The man asked Muguku where he was from. When he mentioned Kiambu, he asked to see his pass. "He looked at it closely and asked me whether I had a relative in Kitale. When I said no, the man questioned me further and asked, 'If you had someone, would you like to see him?' At this point I began to get irritated and told the man that he was becoming ridiculous because I had already told him that I didn't know anyone in Kitale. Also, I had already told him that I was going to Kapenguria to teach. Perhaps he didn't believe me because of my small size," remembers Muguku.

Little did he know that the man kept insisting on knowing if he had a relative because his boss at their camp was called Peter Muguku from Kabete.

Later, he came to learn that this Muguku was actually his father's cousin. He did not know he had a relative who was working in Kitale. Above all, he was occupying the high position of a chief.[19]

---

17   Other than Jomo Kenyatta, the others in the 'Kapenguria Six' were Bildad Kaggia, Achieng Oneko, Kung'u Karumba, Fred Kubai and Paul Ngei. Jomo Kenyatta, who was then the President of the Kenya African Union (KAU), was later to become Kenya's first Prime Minister and President (1963–1978).

18   Home guards were members of a native contingent that was employed by the colonial government to help keep order during the *Mau Mau* insurgency. The contingent was particularly active in central Kenya.

19   The position of chief was very powerful during the colonial era among the Africans. During the Emergency period, chiefs had sweeping powers and could arbitrarily determine someone's fate.

Muguku's denial about having a relative in Kitale coupled with his insistence on being given directions to Kapenguria, convinced the home guard that he was a criminal who was impersonating someone else. He promptly arrested him and took him to the home guard camp where he would be interrogated further. Muguku remembers well, "Fortunately, as we passed by Peter Muguku's office he (Peter) looked up and saw me. He told the home guard to take me to his office. It is only when we came face-to-face that I realised that I in fact knew him. Both of us were shocked at the sight of each other and he asked, 'Am I dreaming? Aren't you Muguku?' When I answered in the affirmative and explained what had brought me to Kitale – that I was going to teach – he was shocked even more. Promptly, he instructed the home guard (askari) to take me to a hotel where I could eat anything I wanted, and he would pay. Thus, I escaped the cold treatment." After eating to his fill, the home guard escorted him to the bus station and instructed the bus driver to take him to Kapenguria. He even helped him with the small box containing a few clothes which he had carried. This final ride would take him to the school.

On arrival at Kapenguria School, Muguku was met with stares of disbelief from the staff when he said that he was a carpentry teacher. His small size and the fact that he was still dressed in the Thika Technical School uniform did not help matters. "At the school, I found out that that the principal had a diploma in carpentry. However, the carpentry teacher that I was replacing was very old and didn't even know how to draw. With my new knowledge I began to transform the teaching of carpentry and the principal was very impressed," says Muguku.

Muguku started by teaching two streams of 40 students each. "It did not escape notice that I was smaller than the boys I was teaching, some were even older and had beards.", Muguku narrates, "during the first week, I accompanied the old teacher to class and some of the boys asked, 'We hear there's a teacher taking over from our teacher when he goes on leave. Could you be the one? If you are, you're too young. When did you start learning?' They couldn't believe that I had finished intermediate school and had even gone for training. It wasn't until the second week when I started teaching by myself that they believed I was a qualified teacher."

Unlike the old teacher who could only demonstrate what he needed students to do, Muguku used technical drawings on the blackboard to illustrate the work to be done. In so doing he was able to impart the important skill of technical drawing as well as the practical aspect of carpentry to his students.

Nevertheless, having not attended a teacher training college, he was considered and ranked as an untrained teacher (UT). "Anyone who had not gone for teacher training was employed as a UT. Such a category was paid KSh 220 per month. The teacher that I was replacing was a trained teacher;

therefore, he was paid more than me. I protested over this on account that I had trained longer for carpentry. If I had joined a teacher training college, I would have trained for only two years and received a certificate for a trained teacher. But I had trained for four years at the technical school. I further reasoned that they must have thought I was qualified otherwise they would not have hired me. Moreover, the older teacher was part of an earlier group of people who left primary school at Standard Three or Four and joined the Native Industrial Training Depot (NITD) at Kabete to learn basic carpentry skills," says Muguku. His protests however made no difference and he had to settle for a lower salary.

Two weeks after joining the school, colonial soldiers went to Kapenguria and rounded up all the members of the Kikuyu community as part of the numerous 'operations' to hunt down *Mau Mau* fighters. Muguku was the only Kikuyu teacher in the school. "Together with twelve other Kikuyu students, we were bundled into Land Rovers and driven off without any warning, neither were we given time to pack our belongings. At the time of the operation, I was not carrying the special pass identifying me as a teacher and was given no time to retrieve it from my house which was within the school compound.

"When my compatriots and I were arrested, we were told that we were being taken to the District Commissioner's (DC's) office which was near the school. However, the vehicles carrying us sped past the office without stopping. Now we did not know where we were being taken. We stopped at Makutano where we found many vehicles, heavily armed soldiers and other people who had been rounded up from the district. They all had blankets unlike myself and company who had not been given a chance to take anything from the school," says Muguku.

Immediately a chance presented itself, Muguku made up his mind to protest. He identified the person commanding the operation and walked straight to him. He told him: "I am a teacher and I have been rounded up with twelve boys. I do not know what is going on. All the other people have blankets except me and my students. We were not allowed to carry anything." The commanding officer demanded to know who was in charge of the operation at the school. A European soldier stepped forward and said he had forgotten to tell his 'prisoners' to take their blankets with them. The commander told Muguku, 'Too bad but the operation can't stop.' And with that they were packed into the waiting lorries and driven off not knowing where they were being taken.

Their next stop was Kitale Town. They were ordered to alight and squat in pairs. "I looked up and saw my father's cousin (and my namesake) at the high table where the commanders of the operation were sitting. That's when I realised that we were in Kitale. I stood up and went straight to him. On seeing me he said, 'Are you here again?' Then I explained to him what had happened. After I had finished, he said, 'Surely does this *serikali* (government) think that even children are *Mau Mau*? Didn't you come here with a clean pass?' Then I told him that we had been given no time to take anything, so I could not show them my pass. He reassured me and told me not to worry. Then he called an *askari* and explained to him that I was a teacher at a government school and ordered him to arrange for my group to be taken back to Kapenguria. While the rest in my group (who were mostly children) were put into a vehicle and taken back the same day, I was asked by my father's cousin to spend the night with his family and go back to school the next morning, which I did."

Muguku was indeed fortunate to have found a relative in Kitale. What lay ahead of him would have been catastrophic. The next step on arrival at Kitale would have been screening (with thorough interrogation) followed by deportation back to his home village in Kikuyu. Such 'operations' were dreaded because some people simply disappeared never to be seen again, while others were killed. Any of such fate could have befallen him.

The next three months at Kapenguria passed without incident. When the teacher he was to replace returned to work, he was subsequently posted to Government School Kabianga in Kericho in February 1954. He taught at Kabianga until 1957.

When it became apparent that he would always he ranked as a UT, Muguku got so frustrated that he seriously considered quitting the teaching profession. "At Thika Technical I had done the Grade 3 carpentry exam. While at Kabianga, I decided to apply for Grade 2 for which I would have to go from Kericho all the way to Kakamega to sit for the examination at a school known as Sigalagala. Out of all the people who sat the examination with me, I was the only one who passed," says Muguku.

When the examination results were released, Muguku gave them to the principal but he dismissed them and said that even if he had done Grade 1, that would not have changed his UT status. To be considered a trained teacher, he would have to go for teacher training for two years. This seemed unfair because if he did that he would have trained for a total of six years, taking into account the four that he had spent at Thika Technical. After that he would still be ranked at the same level as people who had trained for only two years.

To add insult to injury, his younger brother went through a new system – instituted by the government to encourage more people to teach carpentry – which involved a student training for two years at Thika Technical and two years at Kagumo Teacher Training College. When his brother started teaching carpentry, he showed Muguku his payslip. He was earning double what Muguku was earning yet he had trained for the same number of years and had less experience than Muguku. This really discouraged him. Subsequently, he decided to do something about his situation.

"At this time, I was pursuing another course in line with carpentry examined by City and Guilds. I had six months to go before sitting the exam. Nevertheless, I quit and decided I wanted nothing else to do with carpentry. I felt mistreated," remembers Muguku. "After passing the Grade 2 examination, I had also received a letter asking me to go ahead and do the Grade 1. This I also declined. All I wanted to do was to start something else. In poultry keeping, which had been my hobby until then, I found refuge."

Turning poultry farming into a business

"At Kabianga, all the teachers were provided with housing in the school. My house had a small compound in the front and at the back. Since I enjoyed farming I decided to grow vegetables instead of always trimming the grass in the compound. I also fenced off a small enclosure with wire mesh where I kept three chickens, two females and a cock."

The vegetables did very well and he started selling the surplus to other teachers. One day, the principal, who was a European, called him to the office. Noting his interest in poultry, he told him about a European poultry farmer nearby and suggested that he buys a few eggs from his white leghorn breed, which his hen could brood. Once hatched, he offered, they could share the offspring.

"I thought that it was a good idea because I hadn't known where to get white leghorn, a very good breed. Now an answer had presented itself and it wouldn't cost me anything," says Muguku. When his hen was broody, he went to the principal and asked him to buy the eggs for him. The following day, the principal gave him 13 eggs. All but one hatched successfully. Six were hens and six were cocks.

After four months when the chickens were grown, he found the principal waiting for him at home to take his share. The arrangement was that each would take half the chickens. However, the principal selected six hens leaving Muguku with the cocks. Muguku protested but the principal defended his choice saying he had four children and a wife. With six hens he was guaranteed an egg for each member of the family every morning. "I told him that even though I was a bachelor, I would also like to have an egg every morning. Thus, I asked him to be fair and take three hens and three cocks," says Muguku.

"The argument got heated up, eventually prompting the principal to say that I was too stubborn just like the *Mau Mau*. He even threatened to report me to the DC. When I realised that it was becoming a political issue, I gave in and told him to take whatever he wanted. So the principal took the six hens.

99

"I was left regretting why I had agreed to let my hens hatch the eggs," says Muguku. Fortunately when the hens started laying, the principal was transferred to another school. Here he was housed in a storeyed building, thus he could not carry his hens because he had no compound where to keep them. He sold them to the principal who replaced him at Kabianga without telling Muguku.

The new principal did not want chickens running around the larger compound. "He summoned me after a week and proposed to sell the chickens to me at KSh 15 each. He told me that much as he liked eggs and chicken meat, he could not stand chickens in the larger compound. I told him the price was too high, after which he shocked me when he said he didn't want my money. When I asked him what he wanted, he told me to take the chickens and sell to him all the eggs at a price of 25 cents per egg. He would only pay cash once the chickens were fully paid for," recalls Muguku.

Muguku agreed to the arrangement expecting it would take a year to pay off the chickens. However, he was surprised when they were fully paid for after less than three months. He realised that white leghorns are very good layers, but they rarely brood. Their eggs are normally given to other breeds to hatch.

The arrangement with the new principal had worked out so well that he became ambitious and started thinking how much more he could earn if he had 100 chickens. His teaching job had become very frustrating as all his efforts to change his status from UT to a qualified teacher came to naught. To make matters worse, his annual salary increment was something like KSh 5.

"After doing some calculations, I realised that, if the price of a chicken was KSh 5, I could earn more from 100 chickens than what I was earning as a UT if my experience with the six hens was anything to go by. Similarly, if I wanted to double my earnings, all I needed to do was to double the number of layers to 200," says Muguku.

With this realisation, he approached the principal and requested him to write a letter to the education department stating that if they didn't improve his terms of service he would resign. "I had done everything I could to improve my status from being a UT to a trained teacher; I had done examinations and passed and I kept on being told that unless I went to a teacher training college, I would never be promoted. Now I was reaching the end of the rope," laments Muguku.

Before sending the letter, the principal asked Muguku if he was really ready to resign because if the government perceived it as a threat, it may backfire on him. The principal's concern was indeed valid. Says Muguku; "I thought about it for some time. I had never seen anybody do the kind of large-scale poultry farming that I was thinking about; it was just an idea in my head based on the experience that I had with the six chickens. It was a risk but I calculated that with

100 chickens I would earn more than the KSh 250 I was earning as a UT."

Although at that time he was not ready to resign, he was also not going to put up with employment conditions that he felt were unfair. He now made up his mind regardless of the risks involved. So he asked the principal to go ahead and send the letter.

Within two weeks the reply came. The principal called him into his office and told him the government had accepted his resignation with immediate effect. "I was given a week to pack, close the workshop and clear out of the school without handing over." In the cold month of July 1957, he sold his six chickens at KSh 20 each, making a profit of KSh 5 on each, and packed his belongings. He was given a lorry to take his few items, including furniture, to the railway station at Kipkelion from where he took the Kisumu train. That evening, he left Kipkelion to arrive at Kikuyu station the following morning.

Leaving his luggage with the station master he went home. When his father enquired from him whether school had closed, Muguku told him he had resigned. His father was shocked but didn't question him further only saying they would talk later. He gave Muguku a vehicle to collect his luggage from the railway station.

Later that evening, he asked Muguku what his plans for the future were. Muguku told him that he was thinking of keeping chickens, upon which he asked, "What! You leave employment with the government to keep chickens?" Muguku told him he was resolved on the matter. He told him that since it was his choice he would accept it.

Subsequently, Muguku asked for a place to build a house for the chickens. His father told him that as he didn't know what ideas he had and since he knew their land well, he could build wherever he wanted. Thus, Muguku designed and built a house for 200 chickens.

At the time, Muguku had no knowledge of rearing chicken commercially. More so he had absolutely no idea of how to hatch 100 eggs because they couldn't be hatched in the traditional way (that is, where hens sit on the eggs). He figured out that there must be a very big machine that is used. Armed only with enthusiasm, he approached a commercial poultry farmer who lived nearby for help. The farmer agreed to import day-old chicks for him but refused to give him any more help in getting his poultry business off the ground.

Recalls Muguku, "This farmer had trained in Israel and was very knowledgeable but he wouldn't tell me anything. I then decided to seek details through secretive means. Since my cousin was married to the brother of the farmer, I would go to her and ask for information on how chickens are reared. Because she could walk freely on her brother-in-law's farm she was a big help to me in my business as she conveyed to me all the advice she could gather such as the kind of feed to buy."

In this way Muguku got started. By experimentation he learned the best ways to rear chickens amid the many challenges. Buying 200 layers and building the hen house had exhausted his savings. He was left with little money to feed them and was forced to ask his father to chip in. Unlike broilers which grow quickly and are ready for slaughter within six to eight weeks, layers take six months before they start laying eggs and hence generating income. "I realised that I was in a hurry to achieve my goal and had not factored in all that would be required. While my *kienyeji* (free-range) chickens at Kabianga used to feed on the plentiful left-over *ugali*, hence it cost me nothing to feed them, these chickens needed commercial feed. I soon discovered how expensive it was.

"By the time I saw an egg five months later, I was completely broke. My father complained daily about how much the chickens had consumed of his own resources," says Muguku. What made his father even more worried was that his own experience of keeping chickens some years before had ended in disaster, when his 100 birds died within a week. "He had started out with a few and increased them by breeding until he was running out of space. One day he borrowed a hen house from his neighbour whose birds had all died. Unknown to him, the neighbour's chickens had died from Newcastle, a common and highly contagious disease among chickens. The hen house was still infested. So his birds caught the disease and died," recounts Muguku. What was more amazing was that he was still willing to help Muguku venture into the same business on a much larger scale with the risk of losing big. His willingness to put his own money into the business was a testament of his faith in his son's abilities.

"I spent every spare moment with the chickens, subsequently learning a lot about their behaviour. If they started pecking each other, I would find out the reason. If it was because there was no water, I would fix it. I used my technical knowledge as a carpenter to ensure they had the best water troughs, enough air circulation and warmth, and that the house had no contamination which is a big problem when rearing chickens, (the reason why my father lost his birds). Eventually, I had the best chickens; they were even better than those of many European farmers. Later, many people would wonder how I came to know so much about rearing chickens and where I had trained," he says.

Remarkably, Muguku did not lose any chicken which was common for first-time poultry farmers. After five anxious months, he was rewarded when the chickens started laying eggs and he was earning much more than his previous salary as a teacher. However, he was not satisfied. "I wanted to double my income and hence added another 100 layers to my stock, now bringing the total number to 300 chickens. When the new stock started laying eggs I built another house and added 100 more layers."

All the while, Muguku had decided not to get married until he was financially secure. Says he, "The occupation I had taken up was risky and I wanted a wife who could assist me financially if the worst came to the worst. By then the few women in employment were mostly teachers."

Finding a spouse also proved difficult because he was considered crazy in his neighbourhood; how could he rear chickens yet he was an educated man? Before the first batch of chickens started laying eggs, he had no money to hire a worker to help him in the business. Thus, he would often go to the river and fetch water. Fetching water was mostly done by women and he would be the only man at the river. After filling his two jerrycans, he would leave the women gossiping and wondering loudly why an educated man was doing manual work instead of seeking employment. The women in his neighbourhood therefore did not consider him to be potential husband material.

"Convincing people that I was doing something that could become a serious career was very difficult for me. Thus, I had to look further afield. Eventually I met my wife Leah Wanjiku, a teacher, and we got married in 1960," says Muguku.

Getting to farm business

"By 1960, I was doing so well that I told my father that I wanted to have a farm as big as his if not bigger. I had realised that my father's 12 acres were not enough for all of us because even if he distributed it among his seven sons, the maximum I would get was two acres. This was not good enough for what I wanted to do. My dream was to keep some cows and expand the chicken business. However, I had no idea where and how to get a farm. Whatever the case, I had resolved that staying on my father's land was out of the question," says Muguku.

At this time, independence was looming and many European settlers had started leaving the country. They were selling their land to the government for the resettlement of Africans. One such farm in Sigona was advertised for sale (in 1960). "One day I came across a large group of people whom I thought were having a *baraza* (public meeting). When I inquired from them, they told me that landless people were registering to be allocated the farm. I decided to register as well. The farm had been divided by the government into 37 plots each measuring 15 acres," he says. After registering, he had to attend interviews conducted by the District Officer and local agricultural officers to select applicants with basic agricultural knowledge.

During the interviews he was asked questions such as how to plant crops like maize and potatoes, spray animals and what medicines to use. Successful applicants got a loan and two cows to start them off; the government did not want people squandering this opportunity. The loans were to be used for fencing and other things. One plot was given to an agricultural officer who would serve as a role model for the other farmers and give technical advice.

"The allocation process took a long time and some people got discouraged. There were also rumours flying around that after independence, those who were not willing to buy the land (it was not free) would be evicted and even beheaded," he says. A good friend encouraged him to hang on telling him that to get land, one had to struggle.

Muguku passed all the interviews and got a farm in the scheme after paying a 10 percent deposit of KSh 700 on the purchase price (which was KSh 7,000). But he did not move to the farm, fearing that people would be killed after independence. He continued with his poultry business at his father's farm in Kanyariri and kept some cows at the Sigona farm.

"During the distribution of cows, I asked for chickens instead of the cows; I wanted to expand my business. However, I was told that there was no provision for chickens in the loan. Contrary to what was expected, I used the loan for fencing to buy two cows to add to the two given to every farmer under the scheme. I also bought two more cows from my income from chickens. This made the total number of cows six, which I kept in the 15-acre plot. To me, this was a lot of land and I had plenty of grass."

Muguku's cows produced a lot of milk which he sold and within no time, he was able to buy fencing without having to get a loan. Nobody thought along these lines, not even the agricultural officers who were there. Meanwhile, the government had insisted that the farmers who purchased the Sigona farm organise themselves into a cooperative. When it was actualised, Muguku was made the treasurer.

In 1963, Muguku moved his poultry business to Sigona. Just before independence, the last colonial governor in Kenya, Malcolm MacDonald, who served from 1963 to 1964, visited the Sigona settlement scheme accompanied by the Minister for Agriculture and other government officials. He was impressed with Muguku's farm. "As he inspected the farm, he turned to his entourage and told them that they had been cheating him that Africans could not do anything successfully; neither could they sustain a business. He said that he had recently come from Britain and the chickens that I had were the same or better than the ones in Britain. Now he could see with his own eyes that given a chance Africans could excel," recalls Muguku.

The Governor asked Muguku what his target was. He replied that he wanted to have at least 3,000 birds. By then he had 800. The scale of his ambition surprised and pleased the Governor who said to the other officials, "Africans have ambition and you keep telling me they don't?" Before he left, he proposed that Muguku sends two dozen eggs to State House every week. Muguku agreed to this arrangement.

The arrangement was to continue even after the Governor had left. When Jomo Kenyatta became Kenya's first president, Muguku was still supplying the two dozen eggs. Unfortunately, after some time he was informed that he could no longer supply eggs to State House because he did not have a government tender. But as he later found out, it was the machinations of the State House comptroller that were behind the cancellation of the order. He had started his own poultry business and wanted the arrangement for himself. Muguku raised no fuss about it; he showed no disappointment at all and was content to let the business go. In any case, he says: "Getting the eggs into State House was a very cumbersome exercise because of all the security issues and the quantity wasn't worth the trouble."

Matters however took a turn for the better when Mzee Kenyatta intervened. One morning at the breakfast table, he noted how small the eggs were compared to the previous day. Mrs Mwathi, the housekeeper, was summoned to explain and she informed the President that the previous supplier had been stopped because he had no government tender. Kenyatta got upset and retorted sarcastically wondering why something good could not be eaten in State House and yet it was being eaten somewhere else. The housekeeper was ordered to restore the old supplier immediately. She went looking for Muguku who resumed supply to State House. "I would always select the biggest eggs for Mzee," says Muguku.

Specialisation in hatchery

Muguku started his hatchery in 1972. "Before venturing into hatchery, I had been told that as an African, I could not hatch chicks. At the time, there was no other hatchery owned by an African; that is why everyone thought I was crazy despite my 15 years of experience in the chickens business," he says. He set out to prove wrong those who had said that.

By the time he was getting into the business, Muguku had moved to a farm in Kikuyu Town. Part of the land on which Muguku Poultry Farm came to be situated used to be owned by a European veterinary doctor during the colonial period. "He specialised in treating chickens and was in charge of poultry at Kabete Vet Lab. I used to go to him for technical advice. The doctor was surprised that I knew so much about chickens yet my background was carpentry. He used to say that in his work he had never seen anyone who kept chickens like me. Later when settlers started leaving the country, I asked him to sell the farm to me whenever he was ready to go. However, the doctor told me that he had no plans to leave." As it turned out the Vet did leave the country and he sold the 20-acre farm to Muguku who later bought land around it bringing the total acreage to 27 acres. That was in 1965.

When he moved to Kikuyu, Muguku's priority was to increase his stock of layers from 800 to almost 10,000. Once he was done with that, he would start exploring the possibility of hatching eggs on a large scale to produce his own day-old-chicks instead of importing.

Before buying the farm, the Vet doctor had shown him an old machine and told him it was an incubator used for hatching chicks but he had never used it. In 1967, out of curiosity, Muguku decided to test it and see if it worked. The main ingredients required for eggs to hatch are warmth, air circulation and humidity. "It was a very crude machine where water was heated using paraffin and operated like the radiator of a vehicle to warm the eggs inside the incubator. It also had a small motor for blowing air to facilitate air circulation. The fertilised eggs were put on a tray inside with warm water below it," he narrates.

Regulating the heat in the incubator was a difficult task and it took some time to master. Normally a hen hatches her eggs by sitting on them and turns the eggs every hour. If this is not done the eggs will not hatch. Modern hatcheries are mechanised so that this is done automatically. With his incubator, Muguku had to do it manually which was very cumbersome and time-consuming. "I had to turn the eggs several times during the day and night and make a mark on each egg to show the position in which the egg was placed so that I could change to a different position each time."

After 21 days he got some chicks. He was encouraged by his success and continued to experiment with the machine. "After three trials I now thought of trying to do it commercially. First I would hatch my own chicks instead of importing which would be more profitable," he says. The machine he was using could hold 3,000 eggs per week. Out of these, 250 eggs would hatch and only 125 would be females. Thus, in a week he could only sell this number of day-old-chicks. "Demand was however very high; so I bought another machine from Britain. It was a reconditioned machine and was recommended because it was good for areas with frequent power failures as it could retain heat," he recalls with ease. It was wooden and very heavy, as it was supplied fully assembled.[20] It cost around KSh 8,000 and had a capacity of 9,000 eggs.

---

20   Modern machines of such magnitude are usually supplied as knocked-down units which the client puts together at the designated premises.

As demand for day-old-chicks grew, Muguku realised that he needed more machines. This time, he didn't want to buy reconditioned ones. He inquired from his supplier which machines were replacing the ones they were selling as reconditioned. The supplier was very sceptical. Instead of telling Muguku about the new machines in the market, he merely said they were very expensive and he doubted whether Muguku could afford one. When Muguku insisted, the supplier told him that the new machines came from the US and were the Rolls Royce of incubators. It was a brand called Robin.

Subsequently, Muguku wrote to the manufacturer in the US to inquire further about its specifications. He was informed that the machine could hold 42,000 eggs, but it was supplied as a set – one part for incubating and the other for hatching. The eggs are incubated for 18 days in the first machine (known as a setter) where they are placed on trays which turn automatically at an angle of 45 degrees, they are then transferred to the other machine (called a hatcher) for three days where they are not turned at all. "I concluded that this new machine was cleaner and more hygienic than the old machine where eggs were placed at the bottom of the same machine. Moreover, eggs ended up being covered with feathers from chicks which is not recommended."

With regard to capacity and pricing, he noted that he would need five reconditioned machines to match the capacity of the Robin machine. When he compared the prices he realised the difference was affordable – an additional KSh 5,000. Therefore, the choice was whether to buy a brand new Robin machine or five reconditioned ones. He opted to purchase the new machine.

The next step was to build a hatchery. Again he asked the suppliers of Robin to give him the plans for building a suitable house for the machine. "It was quite complex and so I asked for drawings for a hatchery with room for expansion so that in future if I decided to buy another machine I would not have to build a bigger hatchery. When I got all the drawings I decided that I would not compromise on the specifications and built the structure exactly as indicated." Fortunately, he did not need to borrow money to finance the building of the hatchery and to buy the machine because he was generating enough cash from selling eggs. By this time, he had one of the biggest commercial poultry farms in the country.

"The loan that I got to buy the Sigona farm was supposed to be repaid over 20 years, but I repaid it within three years. I got another loan to buy the Kikuyu farm also with a 20-year repayment period, but I was able to pay it back in three years. My accelerated repayment was because I did not like being in debt," he offers. While many people prefer to work with borrowed money, he does not. Part of the reason for this is that it was a long time before facilities like loans and overdrafts became available to Africans as most were banking through the post office. Therefore, for most of his early years in the business he relied on ploughing back profits from the business to finance expansion.

After starting the hatchery, Muguku continued importing day-old-chicks for some time until his hatchery became fully operational. Now he could produce enough chicks to meet the demand from his customers. He then gradually got out of the business of keeping layers to concentrate on hatchery.

The hen houses where Muguku had previously kept layers were now used for breeding stock, the birds used for fertilising eggs for the hatchery. "I needed fewer birds as breeding stock, but they were very expensive to purchase as they are imported from only three companies in the world which include Aviagen (which supplied the popular Arbor Acres breed of broilers) and Hendrix Genetics." These companies license breeders in other countries which they supply with birds (grandparents) that are then bred locally to produce eggs used in hatcheries which supply farmers with day-old-chicks.[21] This is what is known as a grandparent operation. In Kenya only Kenchic is licensed to run a grandparent operation. Other suppliers like Muguku import their breeding stock directly from Europe.

According to Muguku, specialising in hatchery is more profitable, but it is harder than keeping layers for eggs. "Quality is very important and you have to know how to keep the breeding stock because this influences the quality of the day-old-chicks you produce. Breeding stock requires more work and attention than keeping layers," he explains.

When he started the hatchery, the government had restricted imports of the day-old-chicks in an effort to encourage people to breed them locally. In any case, importing chicks was a hassle that was getting more complicated because of regulations. This, coupled with high demand, assured him of a good market and his business expanded rapidly. A big challenge however that came to emerge in the market is fluctuating demand. This makes it difficult to plan revenues with certainty. "Out of the blue, you will find that people do not want to eat a lot of chicken and the demand for broilers goes down. Tourism is a big market for chicken. When it goes down, it destabilises the market. Depending on what farmers think will bring in more money, you will find periods when most move from keeping broilers to keeping layers. A year ago, most farmers wanted to keep layers and today they are running away from layers and going back to keeping broilers, so it's a tricky business."

---

21   In Kenya there are only four big breeders which include Kenchic, Muguku Poultry Farm, Sigma and Kenya Bixa.

Scares such as the threat from the Avian Influenza (bird flu) outbreak in 2005 also depressed the market.

Management strategy

Muguku Poultry Farm employs 30 people and produces 20,000 day-old-chicks a week. The average price in the market is KSh 55. So the farm rakes in revenues of over KSh 1 million per week.

Muguku's wife Leah Wanjiku handles the administrative aspects of the business and marketing, while he handles the production and technical side of the business. Among his seven children (five sons and two daughters) his two older sons – Daniel and Jonathan – are in the poultry business. He got Daniel to do poultry courses in Britain and after getting a diploma, he told his father that he wanted to continue with studies and do business administration, which Muguku agreed. "I had bought a 60-acre farm in Ngong where I wanted to expand the business. When Daniel returned, I asked him to run the poultry side of the farm.

"My second son, Jonathan, is also based on the farm. He keeps pigs, as the farm is big." Muguku also set up a poultry farm for one of his daughters on a 15-acre farm in Naivasha. "I bought the farms on realising that the farm in Kikuyu was not big enough. I do not interfere with what my children are doing, as I consider the enterprises as their own businesses." With the three involved in farm business, his other children are in various professions including pharmacy, medicine and business administration.

Planning the future of the business was a complicated issue for him because he believed in letting his children decide for themselves what to do with their lives. His vision was for Muguku Poultry Farm to remain exclusively in hatchery because he believed that specialisation is the future of the industry. "In Europe, those doing breeding focus on that and don't get into commercial farming. Commercial farmers don't go into distribution. But this operation may not stay the way it is because my children have expressed a desire for integration and if they can, I can let them do it. I don't want to work for more than ten years. I will leave it to the new generation and see how they do it."

Diversifying into other businesses

In 1964, Muguku bought out an Asian who had a shop in Kikuyu. The Asian owner had been letting out the shop at KSh 400 per month to another. Now the tenant Asian was leaving the country. Without any consultations, he approached the owner who told him the price was KSh 10,000. He bought it on the spot and didn't even bargain.

"It was only after buying it that I did some calculation and figured that I would recoup my money very quickly. However, I was unable to find a tenant. I then tried selling the building but the most I could get for it was less than KSh 5,000. After three months of trying I realised that I had burnt my fingers and wondered what to do. That is when I decided to run the shop myself. Consequently, I started my own shop called Kikuyu Merchant. This turned out to be an even bigger mistake."

Muguku knew nothing about retail trade. He didn't know where to buy stock, was clueless about prices and had no customers. He spent another KSh 5,000 on stock, but the money was not enough to fully stock up the shop. As he was very busy with poultry farming, he hired an employee called Gideon to sell in the shop. "At the end of every day when I went to the shop to find out how much he had sold, I would find only KSh 20 in the till. I would tell Gideon that if we were both relying on the shop to eat, then it would not sustain us. However, I would encourage him to continue.

"At some point I asked him what customers wanted. He told me they wanted dresses. So I went to Nairobi and bought dresses and later *mitumba* (second-hand clothes). Subsequently, I tried selling every kind of product. Eventually, the shop would earn KSh 50 per day and KSh 100 on a good day."

At that time, there were price controls which the government enforced rigorously. Muguku was taken to court and fined several times because his employees at the shop would often round up prices to make it easier to give customers change (even 5 cents was enough to get someone into trouble with inspectors who usually posed as customers). "I would tell my employees to sell at the recommended price, say KSh 8.75, but they would round it up to KSh 9.00. The next day I would be hauled to court. Although the fines were small, I found it time-wasting.

"After some time, I decided to get into hardware which had no price controls," he says. Moreover, demand for building materials had shot up after independence as people began building houses in the area. Another factor that boosted his hardware business was a government policy that came up shortly after independence.

As a way of realising the goals of independence, the Kenyatta government introduced a policy of Africanisation, which stipulated that all retail businesses owned by Indians were to be sold to Africans. Areas that featured Indian businesses started having Africans' presence; for instance, River Road was declared an African zone. Subsequently, this policy was the turning point for Muguku's retail business. Manufacturers were now forced to channel their products through wholesale outlets such as Muguku's. "For a good number of years, I would sell *mabati* (iron sheets) for the biggest companies in Nairobi. They would send their customers to me and I would give them the local purchase order (LPO) after paying. Then they would use the LPOs to collect the *mabati* from the manufacturer. I would just collect a commission and no *mabati* would go through my shop," he reveals.

The hardware business did so well that it was rivalling poultry farming in terms of revenues. It even became one of the biggest shops in Kikuyu. This created a problem for Muguku; he had a difficult decision to make as he had to choose between the two businesses. Both were expanding rapidly and needed his full-time attention. "At the time, while my wife was in charge of the farm, I was doing the marketing and purchasing for things like feed. This meant that I was always on the move and could not even spend enough time in the hardware shop. A point reached when I had to ask myself whether I was a shopkeeper or a poultry man." He chose to focus on poultry and closed the hardware shop after almost twenty years in the business.

Closing down the hardware concern brought to an end his involvement in shop business – first as a general shop and next as a hardware outlet. However, he kept the building, which he later leased to Equity Bank. He also made extensive investments in real estate in Nairobi and other towns.

Investing in Equity Bank

Muguku had been approached earlier to put money into Equity Building Society. "I was reluctant to make the move because at the time I was banking with Barclays Bank which had better services; for example, Equity could only issue in-house cheques which could not be deposited in other banks. However, Equity's interest rates on savings were better than Barclays, which was attractive for me because I was not interested in borrowing money."

Once he understood Equity's business model, he approached the management to sell him shares but he was told that they were not selling. Nevertheless, he was promised that if they ever decided to sell they would let him know. A few years later, they approached him and told him they had shares he could buy. However, the timing was bad as this was in the mid-1980s, the period when banks owned by Africans were closing down. Nobody had faith in them. Other people, including his own bankers at Barclays, told him he was crazy to withdraw money from a bank and put it in a society. He went ahead anyway.

Muguku used all the money in his Equity account to buy shares. Most people would not have bought shares and they called it a 'blunder'. However, the 'blunder' paid off handsomely. Equity Building Society converted into a bank in 1994 and was listed on the Nairobi Securities Exchange (NSE) two years later. Muguku was to become the single largest individual shareholder of the bank with over 22 million shares. With the bank's shares trading at KSh 139 in October 2008, his nest egg was worth over KSh 3 billion. Despite his shareholding position, Muguku had no direct role in the management of the bank.

Social activities

All throughout his life, Muguku passionately believed in the cause of empowering Africans. He always wanted to show that Africans could do it; he wished his legacy to be that of demonstrating that Africans can conquer mountains. Despite other people's misgivings, he wanted to help African-owned businesses and so became a customer of a building society. Even when he bought the shop from an Asian he wanted to see if he could help transform Kikuyu Town by showing that an African can own a shop. Even to his last day he supported the idea of Africanisation and believed that people should support their own banks and not bank with foreign banks. It was this belief that prompted him to join in the starting of two primary schools.

The first was Kikuyu Township Primary School. "The District Officer at Kikuyu asked all the business people in the town to form a committee of traders for the purpose of uplifting the community. After forming the committee, I was selected as the chairman. The committee decided that the best way to help the community was to build a school for the children. They organised and held a *harambee*[22] using the proceeds to build the first class. I enjoyed doing the actual building since I was a carpenter."

Upon completing the first class, pupils were enrolled into the school. They subsequently built a class every year as the students progressed. This way they built the entire school after several years. The school became instantly popular and it was clear that it needed to be expanded. However, the headmaster said he didn't want a double stream so the committee decided to build a branch of the school in a different location which they called Kikuyu Township Primary School Annex with the same headmaster in charge of both schools. The annex later expanded and became independent. Its name was changed to Kidfarmco Primary School.

Muguku's involvement in the two schools ended soon after they were established. "However, my love for education drove me to buy a school recognising the fact that educational standards in Kikuyu area were very low with as much as 90 percent failure rates among the Form Four students. After

---

22   *Harambee* was the term used to describe an activity that was done together in a community, especially fund-raising. It was later used to describe fund-raising activities.

failed attempts to meet with teachers in Kikuyu to solve this problem and realising that they were not very keen, I decided to start my own school."

He realised this dream when he found a school, known as Greenacres, on sale in Tigoni, Limuru, situated on 50 acres of land. It had been closed for five years after the European founder died and his heirs had no interest in running the school. "For three years, the school had no buyers until I came along. I purchased it for KSh 150 million using a bank loan."

Upon taking possession of the school in August 2007, he renamed it Tumaini High School. The school took its first intake in January 2008. Unlike the previous two schools that he helped found, Muguku now had every intention of getting involved in the management of the school. "I found it enjoyable and very interesting. While I would blame the teachers in Kikuyu for the poor results of the students, in my own school I could bring in good teachers and get good results," he recounts.

Best and worst moment in business

Muguku considers his 'blunder' in buying shares in Equity Building Society as his best moment in business. He considered it a happy accident. "Nobody could anticipate that shares could rise from around KSh 70 to KSh 200; it was unheard-of. So was coming from a building society to a successful bank." He also considered it a reward from God for helping him to start two schools in Kikuyu many years before.

According to Muguku, buying the shop from the Asian was his worst mistake in business, although fortunately he turned it around and it became successful: "I learnt two things. That you should not rush into any business and you should not expect quick profits before you are known in the market. Give yourself time and have enough money to sustain you in the meantime. This is always where many people fail; when the business does not bring quick profits, they give up because they run out of money."

Tips for aspiring entrepreneurs

Muguku emphasises on discipline as a major character in entrepreneurship: "Be disciplined and always think before doing things. Remember, revenue is not profit. Think of your business as a tank with two pipes; one is an inlet and the other is an outlet. For the tank to fill, what is going into the inlet must be more than what is going out through the outlet. Always set a budget and stick to it. Self control is very important in business."

He singles out young people who frequently overspend while socialising. He advises them to drink to socialise and to quench their thirst when thirsty, but not to get drunk: "I drink two bottles and when I finish, I leave the bar, which puzzles many people who ask, 'You have money; why don't you drink?' When I say no they ask me to buy for them since I'm not drinking, but I tell them it's better for them to despise me than for me to buy them beer and encourage them to drink more than they can afford. This is the failure of many people who are so poor yet they spend so much money on alcohol."

He also advises people in business to stick to what they have started. "They should not be in a rush to try many things without giving enough attention to each one." Citing the example of his decision to close the hardware shop despite the fact that it was doing well, he stresses that it was because he needed to make a choice between this business and poultry farming and decide which one he would focus on.

Taking the bitter with the sweet is also very important in business. "Don't be afraid to be a laughing stock like in my case when I was fetching water from the river, a task normally done by women. I struggled for three years with no helper in the chickens business but whenever I achieved something I could see light at the end of the tunnel. Have faith in yourself and follow your dream no matter what other people say. I had been told I would remain an UT until I died but I had a vision, worked hard and made it. Many people said the things I wanted to do were unrealistic but I proved them wrong."

Above all, he singles out the main factor that led to his success as commitment: "Many people take business as part-time or a hobby so they are not fully committed to it. Many people also fail because they confuse revenues with profits and spend it all forgetting to allocate money for restocking. Taking the example of chickens, if you get a lot of money and you spend all of it forgetting that these birds get old and need to be replaced, then the business will suffer. In their prime, layers can produce an egg daily but as they get older they lay fewer eggs with weak shells. It is therefore wise to dispose of them after a year or eighteen months maximum. Even a vehicle has to be serviced and replaced when it is old because a time comes when it costs more to maintain than what it is bringing in as income."

He further explains: "When I was keeping layers, if I had 200 chickens and they started laying I knew that in a year I would have to replace them. But I didn't wait until then to dispose of them because that would interrupt supply to my customers as the new stock would take five months to start laying. Also when chickens first start laying, they produce small eggs so waiting would mean I could not supply orders for large eggs. To ensure I maintained a constant supply of all sizes of eggs throughout the year, I bought new stock every 4–5 months. In any business you have to understand the cycle of production and your market in order to succeed. Most important, understand that revenue is not profit so don't spend everything you earn.

"I spent so much time with my chickens that I understood their behaviour and I could tell when they were stressed. I learnt all these things from experience and now I teach others. Today I tell anybody who wants to get into this business that if they don't have time to go to the hen house they should forget about chicken business. You have to be involved because workers can wreak havoc, steal or even kill the birds and hide them. Being involved applies to any business not just chickens," he concludes.

Author's note:
Nelson Muguku Njoroge died on 10 October 2010. May his soul rest in eternal peace.

Chapter 4

Ibrahim Ambwere

One of the people who have individually transformed the landscape and economy of western Kenya is Ibrahim Omwenyi Ambwere. The bulky businessman straddles the western business region like a colossus. He is a farmer, contractor, hotelier, oil magnate, real estate mogul and chain supermarket operative.

From a stone cutter, mason and carpenter, Ambwere rose to be one of the wealthiest individuals and the most visible real estate developers in the western region. Also a renowned philanthropist, his name strides across county boundaries and dots major urban centres, from Chavakali, Mbale, Kakamega and Kisumu to Kitale. Added to these are significant business interests in the City of Nairobi, having developed prized residential properties in Westlands, the lush part of the city.

As one criss-crosses market centres and towns in western Kenya, it is difficult not to spot Ambwere plazas, complexes, shopping malls, petrol stations and superstores. A first-time encounter with Ambwere leaves one humbled for his physical features do not display the influential person that he is – dark-faced, wide shoulders, modest height with a deep voice. However, his no-nonsense attitude betrays the character of an astute entrepreneur. What Donald Trump is to New York in the United States is what Ambwere is to western Kenya with regard to real estate development, inevitably making his name the signpost in every urban centre in the region. Added to this is a nine hundred and fourteen-acre farm in Kitale, which produces thousands of tonnes of cereals to feed the nation. It also employs more than three hundred people.

A graduate of the 'University of Life', Ambwere's story is one of rags-to-riches. Having been abandoned by his father and bereaved of his mother at the tender age of ten, he started off as a destitute boy with no food, shelter, clothes and parental love. Subsequently, he was unable to acquire any formal education. However, this did not deter him from pursuing his entrepreneurial zeal which he nurtured to admirable success. At their peak, his business ventures provide a source of livelihood to thousands of households not just in western Kenya but also across the country.

Owing to his status, he rubs shoulders with the *crème de la crème* in all spheres of the Kenyan society. He has played host to Presidents Mwai Kibaki and Daniel arap Moi in their tours of the western region, some of which were to open his landmark investments. Ambwere is a member of the coveted United Kenya Club, an exclusive facility for distinguished academics, professionals, corporate leaders, business persons and respected politicians. Although Ambwere has been of immense influence, he has had no political ambitions but continues to support political leaders. But who is this person who has dominated the business scene?

Early life and entry into business

Born *Omwenyi*, a Maragoli word for 'one who searches', indeed Ibrahim Ambwere went out to seek and to get. He was born in 1936 in Rotego, Chavakali, in Vihiga County, western region of Kenya, the first son to Lwoyero Sagna who was the third wife to Francis Aura. Lwoyero was the third and youngest wife and Ambwere was her first child. Unfortunately, Ambwere did not experience the joy of growing up with his parents. First, his father was conscripted into the army in 1942 and went off to fight in the Second World War. No sooner had his father left than his stepmothers ganged up to send his mother packing back to her parents (Ambwere's grandparents). She had only two children then, Ambwere, and his sister Rhoda. She later got another son, a stepbrother to Ambwere, before she passed on in 1946. Thus, at only ten years of age, Ambwere and his two siblings were without parents. They were left under the care of their maternal grandmother, the late Midarano Ambwere. It was from his maternal grandfather that he derived his name, Ambwere. It is a name that he was to build into an enviable brand.

When Ambwere's mother passed on, any chance of attending school vanished as he could not raise the required fees. Any element of education that he got was self-taught or learnt on the job, especially carpentry and masonry. Life experience also played a great role in his education. With no chance to attend school, he had to start earning a living immediately. And so did his sister Rhoda, both of whom had to earn and learn at the same time. In later years, they supported their younger brother, Reuben Ngoya, through school. He went on to become a teacher.

Just as he had supported his younger brother, Ambwere undertook to give the best in education to his children. Having missed out on formal education, he decided to offer an opportunity for them to study up to any level of education they desired. Milly, Maximilla, Francisco and Harry managed to pursue studies to university level, which notably was not due to lack of financial support. By choice, Ambwere has extended this same generosity to his grandchildren for whom he pays school fees. He has bequeathed them further education support through his company. Their education, he says, will be the responsibility of his company even in his absence.

Young Ambwere started by herding his grandparents' goats and cows. At this time, Western education had taken root in western Kenya through missionary effort. However, Ambwere was not enrolled because only few families who were well off gave education a thought, especially those closest to the missionaries. The poor were either not exposed to education or did not recognise its value. Herding cattle was to them more valuable. After only one year in the grazing fields, he left for Nairobi where he went to work as a house help for a relative who was staying in Thika, a town forty kilometres from Nairobi. It was while in Nairobi that he met two building contractors, Karam Singh and Pretta Singh. These contractors were to change Ambwere's life forever. They hired him, a little boy then, as a cleaner in their workshop in Molo. It was while working with the Singhs that Ambwere learnt carpentry and masonry.

After working in the workshop for a while, he was later transferred to the quarry. Here, he learnt the art of stone cutting, which was to come in handy in later years. It was not long before he got employment as a stone cutter. At the quarry, he not only learnt to work hard, but he also saved whatever he earned. He earned money the hard way, so he had to manage his finances well; he relentlessly saved every coin he could. For example, he would save by buying a week's meal of chicken legs and heads for only 25 cents from Highlands Hotel (the current paramilitary base in Molo) which was ten kilometres away. Whatever he saved, he kept under his mattress as there were few banks available then and those few only served the white settlers. Thus, he could not open a bank account.

After a while, he returned to Nairobi where he was to demonstrate his business acumen by going into self employment. Armed with his rudimentary carpentry skills, he decided to go out on his own by setting up a carpentry workshop. As he did not have enough money, he approached the leader of Friends Church Centre, Maringo, for assistance. The leader, a white man named Walter, was sympathetic but he could not provide a suitable space for a workshop. Eventually, on realising Ambwere's determination, he decided to create space for him in his garage. It was at the Friends Centre Maringo that Ambwere opened his first workshop.

Upon securing some space, he set out to work. He would work at the garage during the day and carry his tools home in the evening to create room for his landlord (Walter) to pack his car. Despite the inconvenience, this makeshift garage-cum-workshop was not for free. He had to pay a rental fee of five shillings per month. Ambwere learnt early in life that indeed nothing comes for free.

Nevertheless, business picked up well. Within no time, customers started streaming in. Orders were now starting to overwhelm him mainly for tables, chairs and stools, the fastest-moving items at the workshop. He had to hire two workers to enable him to meet the demand. His customers were mainly Africans residing in Maringo and Jerusalem. At the time, a chair was going for Ksh 5 , a stool for Ksh 3 and a table for between Ksh 25 - 30 a piece. Maringo and Jerusalem were African quarters at the time because of racial segregation in colonial times. There was segregation that isolated Asians, Africans and the Whites.

While working as hard as he could, Ambwere continued to save relentlessly. Other than rent his own house, he preferred to share a house with a friend and pay a modest Ksh 8 at Ofafa Kunguni. Having paid for the house and workshop as well as setting aside some money for the basics, he would tuck the rest away safely. Considering that he was still single, and hence his expenses were minimal, he was able to save a lot during this time. He adopted the mantra, 'Save more than you consume'.

Although business was booming, there was considerable tension orchestrated by the struggle for independence. The unease that permeated the mood in the country made those in Nairobi, particularly those from the western region, think of going back to their rural homes. Although they were not particularly targeted for harassment by the colonial authorities, the urge to go back home persisted because every African was somehow exposed to colonial harassment at the height of the independence struggle. Fear and speculation were rampant. People would gather in small groups to discuss the unfolding events. There were fears that violence could break out any time in whatever portion. With arbitrary arrests by the colonial forces being the order of the day, life became uncertain. Most of these arrests were however directed at the Kikuyu with other ethnic groups sometimes spared the harassment. With every passing day, the option of going back home gained momentum. But Ambwere had no home to go to.

Search for identity and family

From an early age, Ambwere had no parental care. He hardly knew his father who had left to be recruited into the army when he was only six years old. Now a young adult, he only had vague memories of his mother who had died when he was just about ten years old. The closest he knew of his background was his maternal grandparents. According to the Maragoli tradition, he could not regard this as his home. Moreover, he could not put up his house there even if he wanted. He belonged elsewhere – his biological father's home.

Ambwere was constantly tormented by the growing uncertainty about his background. It plagued his mind so much that occasionally, he would slide into deep thought, which surprised his staff. In their world, they thought that everything was going well for Ambwere; after all, if business was good, why was he worried? But he chose not to share his troubles with them. Little did they know that his lapses were about to significantly change their workplace, and life.

Soon, his internal struggles prevailed upon him to travel back home in 1958. He left behind the good money he was making in Nairobi in search of an answer to the nagging question about his home. He wanted to know where he came from and where he would settle down as his home. The only thing he knew was that he was a Maragoli because he spoke the language, *Lulogoli*. But, a Maragoli from where? This worried him.

When he travelled home, he went straight to his maternal grandparents, the only home that he knew. From there, he enquired about his mother's marital home, which, supposedly, was to be his home. Luckily, his mother had been married within the neighbourhood. Therefore, it did not take him long to find the home, that is, Francis Aura's home. He walked over to the home and introduced himself to his newfound relatives. However, he got an exceptionally cold reception, which confirmed his fears that no one was ready to accept him back, let alone share with him his father's property, if any.

Fortunately, he had all along prepared for this kind of reception. What was important to him at the time was that he had found his home and there was no turning back. Rather than fight over properties, he looked for land nearby and bought a five-acre plot for Ksh 3,000. All he wanted now was to be close to his people and have a place he could call home. He was not interested in inheriting land.

Having bought his own piece of land at home, Ambwere went back to Nairobi to wind up his business. Now that he had a home, he could escape the tension-filled Nairobi. Although the Emergency regulations were slowly being relaxed, the numerous arrests and deportations of the Kikuyu had made his customer base thinner. Faced with an option to go home, he made up his mind to close the business and relocate home. Before leaving, he met with his staff and shared his plan. He gave them the necessary time to adjust. He also facilitated the buying of their own tools and starting off on their own. It was in 1959 that Ambwere packed his tools and went back to his home in Chavakali.

In his second homecoming, Ambwere did not have much money. After spending all his savings on the piece of land, he had only worked for one year in Nairobi, which had yielded little money. In all, he arrived in Chavakali with a total of Ksh 1,600 in savings. From this amount, he built a grass-thatched house, bought three cows, and paid dowry for the marriage of his first wife,

Zipporah. Dowry, which consisted of three cows and Ksh 300 in cash, left him with a balance of Ksh 50. Now he had family responsibilities and he could not live like he had been used to. With a wife and only Ksh 50, he had to think and act fast if he was to sustain his family.

Unlike other people in the village whose granaries were full of maize, millet, sorghum and beans, Ambwere's new family had nothing in terms of farm produce. There were no harvests to fall back on and he had to buy everything, from maize meal to vegetables. If he did nothing, there would be trouble soon. Fortunately, he easily fell on his trades, carpentry and masonry. He went to Kaimosi and bought six pieces of timber for thirty-eight shillings, which he carried on his head for a distance of over ten kilometres. He could not afford to hire transport.

Back at home, he made a bench in his compound and set out to work with his tools. He started by making two stools and a chair. These were quickly sold. At this point, his best customers were school teachers. A teacher would buy furniture from him and word would spread around the school. More teachers would come to buy. Business started to pick. He ploughed back most of the cash he got from sales into the business.

Ambwere not only utilised the skills that he acquired from the Singhs, but also adopted their work ethic. He worked like no other villager would, starting off at dawn and retiring at dusk with occasional breaks for lunch and porridge. Gradually, he won the admiration of fellow villagers.

After only three months, he realised that he had to relocate to a central point if he was to serve his growing clientele effectively. As a strategy, he needed to be visible to his customers. Although the workshop remained at home, he rented a small space at the Bendera market centre from Mzee Laban Akhatsa for Ksh 5 a month. This was to be his showroom. Later, he got bigger space from his uncle Mzee Imbugua Aradi where he moved his workshop. However, he retained the previous space as a showroom.

Ambwere's determination was inspired by the absence of his parents. Like in a timed race, he felt as though the whistle for the final lap had been blown for him. Since he had lost his mother way back, the message that he was on his own was firmly etched on his mind. When he went back home, he hit the ground running. His thirst for money far surpassed the ordinary villager. Maybe it was their family comfort or farm wealth, or their desire for wealth was low, but they watched with disinterest as Ambwere worked hard and whizzed past them. He did anything and everything to make money. He sold eggs on foot, literally hawking from hotel to hotel before Rhoda, his sister, bought him a bicycle. He grabbed every opportunity there was to make money such that the villagers thought he was crazy.

Break into big business

Ambwere's fortunes changed drastically when he was awarded a tender to supply seats and beds for children at Kaimosi Mission Hospital. The tender was worth Ksh 3,700, a fortune at the time. However, he did not have enough money to finance it. He approached the hospital administrator, a Mr Mills, who gave him the tender with a down payment. This was after he had explained his predicament. He was advanced Ksh 500 The money was not enough. He sought help from his uncle, Imbugua Aradi, who loaned him another Ksh 500. Now with a Ksh 1,000, he added his savings to this amount and excitedly embarked on the job. He regarded this as a chance to make money and create a good name among the white community whom he thought would pay better than the teachers. He gave it all his heart, working late in the evening to beat the deadline.

After working tirelessly, he finished and delivered the items on time. The job was satisfactory and Mr Mills was pleased. However, shock awaited him when it came to payment. The hospital did not have the funds. In order to settle the bill, Mr Mills deducted the money that had been advanced to Ambwere. For the balance, he offered him the grounded hospital ambulance. After all that work and excitement, he was left with a stalled vehicle and a debt of five hundred shillings to pay back to Mzee Aradi.

Despite the disappointment in payment, Ambwere was not discouraged. He never gave up but he quickly thought of ways to turn this lemon into lemonade. After reassessing his position, he stopped grumbling and took the vehicle. He examined it closely. Other than a broken spring, he found out that the vehicle was generally in good condition. As he could not travel all the way to Nairobi just to buy the spring, he thought of a way out. The vintage carpenter designed a wood plank to be used in place of the broken spring and the vehicle was back on the road. Now another business frontier was beckoning – transport. He put the vehicle up for hire and being the only vehicle in town, the demand was overwhelming.

With this new business venture, Ambwere started working day and night. During the day, he would work in the workshop. At night, he would ferry passengers with their goods in the van to their various destinations. He would leave home early only to return late in the night. Business was roaring and he was beginning to feel pleased with himself. Unfortunately, this plunge into business was taking its toll on his marriage without him knowing. His wife Zipporah could not take it anymore. She ran away during this time. When Zipporah left, the couple had three children – Rose, Emily and Obote. She went with the children. That was in 1962. Perhaps he was dedicating all his time to the business and she felt neglected, which may have been the cause of their disagreement.

Now on his own, Ambwere immersed himself in more work. He sold firewood, he was in transport and he did carpentry full-time. He also took on tenders to build people's houses using building bricks and blocks. It was out of this business that he bought a block-making machine in 1973. Later he opened a shop and got into cigarette and battery distribution. From the proceeds, he invested in hotels. His first hotel business was Kakamega Hostel which he ran from premises rented from Kakamega County Council; from the proceeds he built Bendera Hotel.

Literary, Ambwere sold anything to make money. Ambwere was to have a long list of hotels in western Kenya. In his stable were the Kakamega Hostel that he started in 1968, followed by Bendera Hotel, then Mbale Hotels in Vihiga, the Alliance Hotel in Chavakali, and Embassy Lodging and Hostels. His other buildings are the multi-storey Ambwere Complex Kakamega, Ambwere Towers; Ambwere Plazas in Kitale and Kakamega, residential and commercial houses in Kisumu, Kakamega, Kitale and Nairobi. At the time of writing this book, he was putting up Ambwere Furaha Centre in Kakamega. He also owns warehouses, chain stores and petrol stations. His palatial homestead where his wife Frida stays was built in 1969. Complete with a swimming pool on top and internal flush toilets, the building is unique in many ways.

At this level, the business environment was now characterised by cut-throat competition. Ambwere realised that some education would give him a niche in the business. Consequently, he hired a teacher in 1974 to give him lessons at home. His interest was not in academic certificates, but the ability to communicate with his customers. For this, he needed reading, writing and simple arithmetic skills. In between his busy schedule, he would make time to study every evening and full-time on weekends. The home-learning scheme went on for four years. His teacher was Lawrence Kisame whom he paid well. After he was done with learning, he gave his teacher a generous send-off package in the form of cash and a permanent house from which he drew owner-occupier allowance from the TSC, something that Kisame was forever grateful for.

The four years of learning paid enormous dividends indeed. With greater access to information, Ambwere was able to expand his business horizons. Turning to agriculture, he became a successful large-scale farmer having acquired nine hundred and fourteen acres in Kitale, which he put under mechanised maize farming. He also went into dairy farming and registered equal success. In addition, he established himself as a big-time contractor and acquired the most modern and sophisticated construction machines. Within no time, he was handling large figures in business transactions on a daily basis.

Sometime in the 1980s, he had a memorable encounter at his business premises that left him more aware of the need to protect his interests. This was the day university students came calling at his Mbale Hotel. In those days, university students were revered, not because of their academic prowess, but their absurd display of rogue behaviour. Whenever they attended the burial of a departed colleague, they would terrorise the host village. First they would descend on hapless villagers, raining sticks, kicks and fists on anything on sight. Then they would raid bars, restaurants and other drinking outlets, joyfully trampling over anything in their wake, feasting and not paying a cent for their indulgence. Nobody would dare raise a finger.

One such escapade took place in Mbale Hotel. They landed at the hotel, danced, and made merry. Before they left, they attempted to do what they had accustomed themselves to do in such situations – cause disturbance and leave without paying their bills. But this time they did not get away with it. They encountered a rare display of resistance. In a flash, what was a merry dance and a glamorous show of campus superiority turned into an ugly confrontation. Everyone scampered and ran for dear life. The provocative students were beaten senseless. What they did not learn at the university, they were taught at Mbale Hotel. Although the students were stopped, the resulting damage was enormous. The loss was aggravated when the insurance company refused to pay.

Ambwere was so angry about this incident that he took up the matter with the President (Daniel arap Moi at the time) who had his ear. The President was the Chancellor of all public universities. So, Ambwere thought that he could take his grievances to the top through Mark Too, a close ally of the President. But the President was reluctant to take any action. Instead, he advised him to take up the matter with the university concerned. Nothing came out of this. He ended up forgiving the students. Nevertheless, he remained categorical on one thing: nobody should play with his hard-earned wealth; not neighbours, not enemies and, certainly, not friends. Not even his family.

Many people have tried to make a go at his wealth, some taking advantage of his deficiency in formal education. However, they have been shocked to find that Ambwere is up to scratch with figures. Even when he was almost sank into bankruptcy, he bounced back into business with a fighting spirit. In 1989, he was admitted at Nairobi Hospital and he did not recover until 1992. All the while, he left the management of his businesses in the hands of his children. By the time he recovered, they had made a mess of his business empire. At the time he was admitted, he had left the businesses with enough stock. On return he found empty shelves in the stores and run-down petrol stations in addition to a huge bank overdraft totalling over KSh 40 million. They had even shared all his vehicles amongst themselves. According to Ambwere, this was the worst moment of his life. It drove him into a feeling of helplessness and hopelessness. Other than finding his businesses in near ruins, there was the hefty hospital bill.

Instead of running the businesses prudently, some of the children, now with the power of attorney, descended on the various enterprises like desert locusts, mowing everything in sight. In some cases, they became targets of fraud. In one case, one of the sons gave out goods worth millions on credit against cheques that eventually bounced. When the buyer was eventually contacted, he took back the cheques and offered to withdraw cash at Barclays Bank in Kisumu and settle the debt. While the son was waiting at the bank's reception, the buyer left through the back door. By the time it dawned on him that he had been conned, it was too late. In another incident, another son was duped into a fertiliser import deal that never was. But he had already paid KSh 10 million in cash to an Asian who flew out of the country immediately thereafter. Yet another son went into an indiscriminate asset-buying spree. Unfortunately, in order to hide some deals from Ambwere, he used a nephew's name. This was to come out much later when the ownership of some of the properties became contentious and were subjects of legal battles.

In yet another incident, another son who was in charge of battery distribution diverted business money into buying millet from Uganda. Later, he realised that he had been conned into buying sawdust instead. However, Ambwere has forgiven all of them and allowed them to operate their own businesses separately from his. Since then that has remained the case till today.

All these dealings left Ambwere's business empire on the verge of bankruptcy. Weak and recuperating, Ambwere found not only comfort, but also prudent business advice from Ebby, his youngest wife. Ambwere disposed of some of his properties, one warehouse and a residential house in Kisumu, four buildings in Kakamega and two buildings in Bungoma, in a bid to keep the auctioneers at bay. Together with his youngest wife Ebby, they took charge of the businesses and worked tirelessly to restore the finances and resuscitate the once vibrant empire. Ebby embarked on reviving the stores with Ambwere facilitating the negotiations to procure goods on credit from suppliers, especially batteries, cement and cigarettes, which they sold and made reasonable profits. It is from this effort that Ambwere made enough money to put up Ambwere Complex in Kakamega.

Ambwere's Kitale investments came by chance. Upon recovery and leaving the hospital in 1992, his doctor advised him to seek and reside in a place with cool temperature and clean air. Kitale came to his mind. No sooner had he moved there than he bought a plot on the main street at a cost of Ksh 20 million. On his newly acquired plot, he built a supermarket complex at a cost of around Ksh 47 million only to sell the property at Ksh 140 million several years later, thereby making a cool profit of over Ksh 90 million. From the proceeds, he managed to build Ambwere Plaza, also in Kitale.

Marriage and family

Ambwere is a family man. When his first wife Zipporah left him in 1962, he continued to support their three children. As the Luhya tradition dictates, children belong to the father. So the children returned home and he took them to school and provided for their upkeep. Later, he went for their mother and brought her home under the customary practice. When the children left, he built a house for her, for he felt obliged to take care of her. Rose, Emily and Obote are now grown-ups with their own families.

In Zipporah's absence, Ambwere married his second wife, Frida Kangeleha, in 1963. Together they got five children, Kenneth, Pamela, Ben, Lydia and Arisa. All of them are also grown-ups with their own families. When Frida got too involved in the affairs of her church, Ambwere found himself lonely. The Bendera Jaggery Factory which Frida was incharge of collapsed. That is how he found himself seeking comfort in the younger Ebby Ingado. He formally married her in 1994. They had been friends for many years.

Ambwere did not become polygamous by choice. He found himself one out of need. He married Frida when Zipporah left and married Ebby out of loneliness when Frida neglected him. Although he spends much time with the younger Ebby, he takes care of all of his family, especially the children. No doubt Ebby has been a useful partner and has helped him sustain the businesses to the present level.

Unfortunately, one of the key challenges that Ambwere had to face in his entrepreneurship had to do with his family. While Zipporah was less supportive preferring to desert him at the height of his struggles and the most crucial stage of the business, Frida went as far as maligning him and condemning business and business people as evil. For lack of support, he had to sell a supermarket business that he had built for lack of somebody responsible enough to run it. What a lost opportunity!

According to Ambwere, the day he tied his union with Ebby to become his third wife was his best moment in life. He was even more exhilarated when she lived up to his expectation as an effective director of the company. As a source of hope for the future of the business empire, she has made true the tenet that 'Behind every successful man there is a woman', that men too need women to succeed.

Business and management strategy

Central to Ambwere's business strategy are the people. It is not so much creating employment that he cares about, but the livelihood of the workers that the business supports. For instance, with regard to the farm, he is concerned less about the produce in relation to the livelihood of the workers that it supports. He then employs integrity and focus as the main pillars in his strategy. In effect, he has invested a lot in building trust and loyalty among business partners, the government and the general public. As a result, he has won the hearts of even the political class with most of his buildings being commissioned by senior government officers. As early as 6 August 1973, Mwai Kibaki, then Minister for Finance, opened one of his buildings – Chavakali Hardware. He hosted retired President Moi on 26 December 1998 at his homestead in Bendera. He had realised early that he needed to cultivate public sector cooperation for business success. A believer in private-public sector partnership, he holds that business people should work closely with administrators to influence, understand and profit from government policies.

Ambwere has found that it is important to build trust among the local community. Out of trust, he got a loan from his uncle Mr Aradi to deliver on his first contract, which essentially propelled his business to a greater level.

Being focused has worked well for Ambwere as yet another strategy to grow his business. For a long time, he was known as a hotel person. Indeed the greatest part of his investments after the initial carpentry business was in the hospitality industry where he built hotels and lodgings. This enabled him to learn more about the industry and discover how to make more money. From this experience, he believes that when you do one thing for a long time, you become efficient in the allocation of resources in the respective field. This efficiency boosts returns and gives a competitive edge over the newcomers.

As he advances in age, Ambwere is busy consolidating his businesses with a view to getting out of small trading to give space to young people. Consequently, he has adopted a strategy of concentrating in big-time construction, hotel and farming investments. Besides, he has found that trading is too rigorous for his age; it requires younger blood. Most significant however is his decision to diversify his investments.

With regard to real estate, Ambwere has this paradigm of 'buy low, sell high'. While this sounds obvious, it is not that easy; hence, only a few people have mastered the art of dealing in real estate. It is the few who are enjoying the party while the others are watching. For example, Ambwere bought three prime properties in Kitale, two on the main street and another out of town, which he intends to remodel and sell at tidy profits. Having been in this business for long, he understands good bargains and tidy profits. To succeed in real estate, you need to sharpen your judgement through experience. Only then is it possible to discern opportunities. By the time you make a decision to buy, you should have already booked your profit in the mind. It should not be lower; there should be no loss. Real estate business is so sensitive that an error in judgement can be fatal, especially given the figures involved.

In order to effectively run the business enterprises scattered all over western Kenya, Ambwere established offices in Kitale and Kakamega where he alternates, working with Ebby. The two, who operate jointly as directors, are supported by a team of middle-level managers and accountants. Property managers are deployed everywhere where there are properties. Their responsibility is to maintain the respective properties and ensure that they are in good condition. Other duties include collecting rent and paying staff salaries, taxes and other financial obligations whenever they are due. These managers are incharge of the staff under them and report directly to the directors.

However, at the farm, Ambwere is personally incharge of the over three hundred workers who include drivers, mechanics and casuals. Although they have supervisors who allocate work to them and ensure that they are paid for the work done, there are no formal structures defining lines of authority. Ambwere employs an informal management style where everybody reports directly to him. For example, whenever he is around, he is the one who pays the workers.

Ambwere also goes to great lengths to build trust among his employees, going as far as housing the most loyal employees within his compound. If after work he finds himself leaving together with his employees, he gives them a lift in his personal car. This personal touch with his staff has won over the services of his best employees who see him more as a father than an employer. As a way of motivating them, senior employees are provided with free accommodation in custom-built modern houses where all the utilities are also free. He believes that by employing this strategy, he has minimised the likelihood of deception and maximised loyalty among his employees.

Being a down-to-earth person has also been effective as a strategy for Ambwere to win the hearts of not only his staff but also potential customers. He has successfully applied this strategy to mingle with the ordinary people as well as the high and mighty. Driving across town, he is rarely conspicuous both in dress and demeanour. For those who recognise him and offer greetings, he replies humbly. *Boda boda* operators chat him up easily, casually calling him by his name. Those who bow to him in courtesy receive a similar bow in acknowledgement. Other than his palatial house which displays his opulence, even his vehicles are modest. He often drives around in either a weather-beaten Mitsubishi Pajero or an old Mercedes. This is in total contrast to Ebby who has a taste for the latest models. He has endeavoured to keep the lives of his younger children equally modest. He spoils them minimally and takes them to ordinary schools but offers them the best in non-luxury terms.

Just as he is down-to-earth, Ambwere has maintained a hands-on management style throughout his business life. He is aware of whatever goes on in his businesses at all times. It is not surprising that he knows everything in his big business empire, from the big earth movers to the tiny razors in his office. Within a moment, he can fish out any file (which he locks in his personal cabinets). He also knows all the government taxes, their rates and the dates when they are due. For his buildings, he knows all the tenants by name. To facilitate his knowledge of business further, he signs all the petty cash vouchers, including those for minor repairs or for what would ordinarily be considered as negligible amounts in relation to the scale of operation. However, he delegates some duties to Ebby.

As one used to hard work, Ambwere does not find such paperwork tiresome. On the contrary, practice has helped him to develop his capacity to the extent that he is able to do so much with amazing speed. There is never backlog on his desk, not even for filing. His in-tray is always empty and his wide desk an impeccable display of order.

Another important strategy that Ambwere has employed to build his multi-million business empire is financial discipline. From a mere thirty-eight shillings, which was loose change from what remained after he paid dowry for his first wife, he was able to start off business in earnest. His could be a case study of frugality. When he sold his first goods and earned some money, he reinvested the whole amount. Later, he came to adopt other sophisticated strategies of financing his businesses including bank and supplier credit, both of which he has used sparingly and carefully. He has demonstrated such a high level of financial discipline that he has been bestowed with numerous awards for his impeccable credit record.

Against conventional practice, Ambwere has relied more on overdrafts to finance his construction projects than any other form of credit. Experts often advise financial matching where one is supposed to match long term projects with long term finance. However, while Ambwere recognises that overdrafts are short-term cash flow management tools that are not suitable for long term projects, he also realises that loans are debited to a customer's account immediately and start earning interest even before they are prepared to use it. With regard to an overdraft, one only takes and pays interest on the amount that they need. Using his personal experience, Ambwere determines the type of financing that suits his interests.

Among his first formal financing was a loan of Ksh 20,000, which was advanced by the Industrial and Commercial Development Corporation (ICDC) in 1965 which was secured by the personal guarantee of a friend, a Mr Adolwa. He put this amount into cigarette distributorship and paid it off in a record two years. Immediately after repayment, he got his second loan of Ksh 20,000 from Standard Chartered Bank, which he used to buy his first house in Kakamega Town. Since then Standard Chartered Bank has supported him in his growth.

The future of the Ambwere business 'empire'

Although Ambwere's business interests are expansive, he has consolidated them and put them under two directors, himself and Ebby. Both are directly in charge of the business. Ebby has demonstrated her acumen and prowess in securing profitable deals. For example, she was able to negotiate for higher rents in one of the Kakamega properties, more than Ambwere himself could have, thereby increasing business returns. She also managed to bring on board corporate clients like Equity Bank to occupy the premises. By attending to the needs of clients and customers, say renovating buildings to suit their requirements, she is able to keep the relationships going to the benefit of the businesses.

Ambwere recognises that managing growth has also been difficult. As the businesses grow, they have posed a major challenge in tracking them; after all, running a chain of supermarkets is not the same as running a small shop. While in the latter one can take stock almost on a daily basis, the former requires an elaborate period and structures to capture the respective transactions. Thus, he has done away with the old manual systems and has embraced information technology by installing computer facilities. Use of modern systems allows the staff to carry out accurate record-keeping.

Upon retirement, Ambwere intends to hand over the holding company to his co-director Ebby and other directors whom he will appoint at an opportune time. They will then manage in consultation with professionals. Having had first-hand experience of what non-professional management could do, he would prefer that trusted professionals under the watch of appointed directors take over the management. He is understandably reluctant to hand over the baton directly to his children. In effect, he has already initiated a scheme of grooming such managers and formulated a will that will guide the future of the empire. Nevertheless, he has hopes that his younger children and other members of his family will acquire requisite training to enable them to enter into the professional cadres or directorship. He is satisfied that his older children are fully engaged in their own businesses, but could participate as shareholders entitled to dividends and other benefits.

The grooming of professional managers notwithstanding, Ambwere acknowledges that getting competent and trustworthy people to run his businesses has been a challenge. From experience, he has learnt that most workers want to fleece the employer. One has to keep following them to get things done. They abuse delegated authority and can take off with an employer's money at the blink of an eye. And it is not just employees, but also potential customers and other public who are out to fleece an entrepreneur. Ambwere has had a stint with conmen. A politician friend once swindled him of a large sum of money; he had sold to him a plot which he had borrowed against from a bank. He knew too well that he was lying. Ambwere has observed that once one gets money, people will spend sleepless nights devising schemes to get that money from them without a sweat. His satisfaction is that Ebby has demonstrated that she would be able to fit in his shoes as director.

Dreams and accomplishments

No doubt, Ambwere is an accomplished entrepreneur. The question is, what drove him that far? Unlike most entrepreneurs who are pulled by lofty dreams of a better future, Ambwere had, in the place of a dream, the push of a nightmare. The excruciating poverty that he and his siblings plunged into after the demise of their mother has always been a stark reminder of what awaits him should he slip. It is not surprising, therefore, that initially he was motivated by the need to earn a living. So, he just started running. First, he ran from home to be a house help in Thika. From Thika he ran to Molo to work with the Singhs, after which he ran to Nairobi to start a carpentry business. When he finally returned home, he did not cease running. Like a possessed man, he ran and whizzed past his peers in a mad rush to acquire wealth.

Many people could not understand why he kept running even when they thought he had enough to be comfortable. He would not stop; neither does he intend to stop. His advice is: if one gets a chance, let them run, run and keep on running. Run uphill and even much faster downhill, for life is a race and it never stops until one dies.

Even as he approaches the octogenarian mark, Ambwere is not done yet. He has in the pipeline huge projects. In particular, his targets are in Kitale and

Mbale where he has planned to transform the two urban centres by putting up structures with budgets running into hundreds of millions of shillings. In Kitale, he has already built a three-storey shopping mall with access ramps, staircases and all the modern accessories, as well as acquired a petrol station as a going concern. While running the station, he decided to put up a five-star hotel on the adjacent plot.

Having risen from modest projects, Ambwere stopped building simple houses. According to him, getting involved in simple projects would be denying young entrepreneurs the opportunity to grow. It is for this reason that he moved away from lodgings and small hotels to complex structures, such as classified hotels. Emphasis gradually shifted to shopping malls, huge residential estates and five-star hotels.

Ambwere's education has been no barrier to success. After running petty businesses for a while, he founded a construction firm with which he has erected some of the most modern buildings in western Kenya. His personal houses, also built by his construction company, are architectural marvels. His compounds are a showcase of modern building as well as construction and farm machinery. His family does not rely on municipal water supply. He has engineered an elaborate water-harvesting system with huge underground and overhead storage tanks that also serve the neighbourhood throughout the seasons.

Today, Ambwere has a vision. Within the next decade when he intends to retire, he wants to have transformed the Kenyan landscape into a beauty to behold through multi-million modern buildings. He also wants to give others a chance to earn a living by creating employment and producing food crops. He is already living his dream.

Social projects and philanthropy

Ibrahim Ambwere commands great respect among the elite from western Kenya for his progressive enterprises. Consequently, he has been appointed to chair several social and development committees. He is the present chairman of the National Council of Luhya Elders, an initiative that brings Luhya leaders together with the aim of integrating the community culturally.

Ambwere has great respect for the educated. This is manifested in the amount of resources and effort that he has put to promote education amongst his community. For example, he built and handed over Evojo Primary School to the community, complete with classrooms ranging from nursery level to Standard Eight. When he could not stand the frustration teachers underwent as their salaries were delayed during the donor stand-off in the 1980s, he offered to pay the salaries of all teachers in the then Kakamega District.

Other than his generous contributions in public functions and for community projects, Ambwere is also a renowned philanthropist. The once destitute boy who grew up knowing what it means to lack food, shelter, clothes and parental love, has taken philanthropy to a new level in the western region. In Kitale, Kakamega and Chavakali, he has single-handedly bought land, built and handed over complete churches to congregations. He is known for generous contributions in *harambees* (which were particularly common during President Moi's regime), all of which he does without any political inclination.

Role models

To attain his success in entrepreneurship, Ambwere learnt a lot along the way. From the Singhs who had employed him as a cleaner and thereafter a stone cutter, he picked his trade – carpentry and masonry – both of which started him off in the business. In addition to the trade, he also picked up their work ethic. He found them to be hard-working people who appeared tireless, were thorough in whatever they undertook and paid attention to detail. He considers them his most outstanding role models.

Dr Manu Chandaria is Ambwere's other role model for having transformed a small family business into a multinational corporation. Ambwere admires Dr Chandaria's choice to work on the family business after university and ignoring other job opportunities that could have given him a bigger salary and probably a more prestigious status at the time. Eventually, he was vindicated as he was to acquire a bigger stature than he would have if he would have gone into employment.

Ambwere also had a strong admiration for the late Dr Njenga Karume, the businessman turned politician. He considers Karume's achievements, though mired in politics, phenomenal. His struggle strikes a chord within him. Just like Ambwere, he started from scratch, something familiar to Ambwere who cannot help to admire his tenacity and resilience. According to Ambwere, it is unfortunate that politics shadowed his exemplary effort to lift himself from poverty and build an empire that today is the livelihood of thousands; hence, Ambwere's maxim of not mixing business with politics.

Legacy and the final word

Undoubtedly, Ambwere has played an important role in the transformation of the Maragoli community, and the western region in general, in modern times.

Among the landmarks that can attest to this are churches, schools and houses that have been built with his assistance. Other than supporting educational and religious institutions, he has supported lives by creating employment which has been a source of livelihood for many people. To the entrepreneurs, he has demonstrated the fruits of honest work.

Consequently, Ambwere encourages the youth to seriously consider taking up entrepreneurship as an option to attaining a fulfilled life, other than solely looking up to white-collar jobs. After all, the current population growth far outstrips the job creation capacity. The resulting unemployment has provided an opportunity for Kenyans to engage in entrepreneurial ventures. This is a challenge that is open to all, especially the youth.

For the youth who are aspiring to go into business or those who are starting off, Ambwere offers some advice from his experience:

"Do not get into unnecessary debts. Take a debt only if you are going to put it into a business that will generate more money. Do not take personal debt. Taking a debt to buy non-productive assets or to pay off your bills will only add to your misery. Throughout my business career, I have been very careful when it comes to borrowing. Whenever I borrowed, it was to acquire a productive asset or to stock sellable merchandise. That's how I have managed to keep a clean record with my bankers."

In addition to caution when it comes to amassing debt, Ambwere advises young entrepreneurs to exercise patience. Business is usually slow. Unlike a job, one cannot earn so much in the first few years in business. The first years are like the planting season with the harvest coming later. They should allow for gradual growth. Owing to its organic nature, every business should build itself if well managed. Growth is a slow process that should not be engineered overnight.

Further, it is important for the upcoming entrepreneur to set realistic targets and not to strain themselves by overreaching. What one cannot reach means that one cannot do successfully. In other words, one can only do that which is within their reach. Whenever necessary, it is important to seek advice from seniors and those with experience. Above all, hard work, integrity and reliable relationships are crucial ingredients of growing a business. Finally, one should not mix politics and business, for one cannot serve two masters at the same time.

Chapter 5

Esther Wanjiru Muchemi

As the old saying goes, 'Hell hath no fury like a woman scorned'. It is this fury that propelled Esther Wanjiru Muchemi into a multi-million business enterprise that is the envy of many Kenyans. Once bitten – by a false promise of a partnership in an audit firm – she decided to take the driver's seat in business. That saw the start of Esther Muchemi and Associates audit firm. Not long after, Saamchi, a respected brand in the telecommunication industry, joined the group. Saamchi, which has grown in leaps and bounds, is a leading mobile telephone dealership with over thirty-eight branches all over Kenya.

Almost three decades earlier, Esther was every man's dream girl; brown, slender, intelligent and roundly beautiful. She had great education and almost a perfect career as an auditor in an international firm. The girl was hopelessly in love, a relationship she believed would lead to marriage. Then, the husband-to-be dropped the bombshell: "Dear, I don't know how to say this: I'm getting married although I care so much about you. You are a great person and I promise to support you in any way I can …" As he bubbled on, Esther stopped listening. Her world came to a standstill. Coming just two weeks to the wedding, she was devastated. Obviously, he had been cheating on her all along.

Fast forward a decade and a half later. Esther found herself yet again in the middle of disappointment. While working her heart out at Mucheke and Associates as a senior auditor, the firm merged with Kassim Lakha and Associates. During the merger discussions, Esther was promised partnership in the resultant firm. The promise was never to be. This failed promise coupled with the choking culture at the firm sent Esther once again over the roof. This time, she decided to start her own outfit and she never looked back. She became an astute entrepreneur and award-winning business magnate.

An 'A' student throughout her school life, Esther holds a Bachelor's degree in Commerce and a Certified Public Accountant of Kenya (CPA-K). Though now beyond her youthful days, Esther maintains a trim figure and a deceitful girlish smile that makes guessing her age an instant puzzle. Her beauty is still captivating. Her enthusiasm in life, business and family is infectious. Most remarkably, she is a lesson in comebacks; she picked herself up from a broken heart, forgave those who wronged her to stand tall both in family and in business life. As the founder and a director of Esther Muchemi and Associates audit firm, she has given great inspiration to aspiring entrepreneurs.

Early life and education

Esther Muchemi was born to Moses Macharia Nderitu and Zelpa Nyambura. She was not only their first daughter, but also the first child in a family of nine. Moses Macharia was a renowned school teacher and head. He was also a respected elder in his village. He jealously guarded his reputation and taught his children the value of keeping a respectable name. They were taught to respect others and not to do things that might besmirch their name or that of the family. Such was the zeal to protect their reputation that Esther remembers having cried when her sister teased her about a false rumour that purportedly had soiled her name. Today, Esther is still very cautious of her reputation and is happy that she left an unblemished name back in her village.

A strict Protestant, Esther's father loved education. Little wonder he would exempt his daughter from manual work both at home and at school to allow her to concentrate on her studies. Even today, Esther's hands do not show signs of hard manual labour. In any case, she's not that endowed physically and given her size, she knew from long before that her strength lay elsewhere other than physical abilities. True to her thinking, she was to discover her academic prowess in secondary school.

At a tender age, Esther was compelled to walk long distances to school. Her father could not allow her to go to the Catholic schools nearby, perhaps because he believed that Catholic schools were not good for his children. He insisted that they attend only Protestant schools. To Esther and her siblings, this was like a punishment. It was only later that he somehow relented and allowed them to attend Catholic schools. At his mellowing, Esther would go to St. Michael's boarding school in Kerugoya from Standard Four. St. Michael's was a Catholic school.

Perhaps due to the absence of her strict father (he had gone to Germany in 1967 on a five-year education scholarship), Esther did not perform that well in Standard Seven. She could not therefore gain admission directly to a national or a provincial school. Luckily, her father came back the same year and swiftly used his connections to procure her a place in a secondary school. She gained admission at Kamahulu Girls' Secondary School where she dramatically emerged as an academic force. Maybe it was the fear of her father that drove her to work hard on her studies. She loved him so much and did not want to disappoint him. Another reason could be that she had matured and therefore took her academic work seriously. Whether out of fear or self discovery, she had woken up to a new academic reality.

To demonstrate her awakening, she led her class throughout her first year. Her father, sensing that maybe she had it too easy, sought a transfer for her to

Kahuhia Girls' Secondary School where she would meet stiffer competition. Even in the new school, Esther maintained her excellent performance – always a contender in the top three in her class. She was certainly a good student.

Like most of the girls, Esther fell for the ploy that Mathematics was too difficult for girls. Therefore, she gave the subject a wide berth, missing classes and boycotting revision sessions. Despite all this, she obtained a decent grade in Mathematics at the end of her final year. With hindsight, she believes she could have done better. Thus, her advice to girls is not to fall into the same trap. There are no men and women subjects.

In line with her conviction, Esther led her class in the Kenya Certificate of Education (KCE) examinations with an admirable Division One of 9 points. This outstanding performance earned her direct entry to the coveted Mukumu Girls' High School where she studied for her 'A' levels. Her academic star shone even brighter at Mukumu. She emerged a top student in the final Kenya Advanced Certificate of Education (KACE) examinations. Notably, the same year Mukumu Girls' was ranked the third best performing school in the whole country. This unequalled performance would qualify Esther for admission for the Bachelor of Commerce degree at the University of Nairobi.

Gaining admission at the University of Nairobi (known as Campus) was a major feat. Students were quite few – actually less than three thousand in the whole country – hence a feel-good factor. The few students commanded this aura of academic achievement that was respected in the city and revered in the villages where they stood out if not for anything else, the limited number. Campus was the ultimate dream of every ambitious student and the joy of their families. Ironically, Esther does not remember her parents celebrating her admission to the university. At the time parents appeared more conservative, unlike in later years when they began pampering their children with gifts for every little achievement. Esther's parents did not acknowledge her achievement loudly, but they were proud and may have been bragging to their compatriots in her absence.

Campus life turned out to be one of the best experiences for Esther. Everything pointed to the pinnacle of success. The pristine compound, well-manicured lawns, clean rooms and a great camaraderie amongst fellow students. Students were lavished with five-course meals – with catering rivalling five-star hotels anywhere. The generous boom – the allowance given at the university as pocket money – made students equal, at least socially. Somehow the boom diminished the glaring difference between those from rich and those from poor families. All could afford decent clothes and upkeep.

Socially, 'campus' students were greatly admired. They would turn heads – literally – in town. Girls especially were undoubtedly the object of affection to every ambitious man. If they were few in Nairobi, then in the villages they were like gold, so valuable and difficult to find. They basked in the glory of undiluted admiration. Such was the social pressure at the university that even the deeply religious Esther admits to have once slipped. She enjoyed her days at the university – and probably a little bit more – to the point of neglecting her academic work. Although she ended up with an Upper Second Class degree classification, she believes she could easily have attained First Class Honours if she had applied herself more. Her contemporaries then included some of the latter-day corporate executives such as Gerald Mahinda, who was to become the Group Managing Director of East African Breweries Limited (EABL).

At the end of her studies, Esther graduated with a Bachelor of Commerce (BCom) degree, accounting option, in 1983. She was among the few who were chosen directly from college to join Ernst & Young, the international auditing firm. This was a good job with a very generous starting salary. Esther found audit work quite demanding. While she worked, she took up studies for professional qualification in accountancy. Recruits into the firm were required to sit for their professional exams – Certified Public Accountant (CPA) – while working on strict client deadlines at the same time. Esther had to resort to her high school discipline to manage her work and studies. During this time, she seldom went to bed before 1.00 am and had to be at the office by 8.00 am the next day. Her life oscillated between work and study. Nevertheless, she enjoyed it, as the work environment at Ernst & Young was professional.

Marriage and family

Esther's first love affair ended in a terrible act of betrayal. No lady could withstand such shameless betrayal from someone she loved so dearly, not in the least the innocent faithful girl who had given her all to the only man she knew then. It is ironical that the astute business lady that is today Esther wept and cried. No amount of consolation, not from the brutal man or her friends, could stop the torrents of tears that drenched her. Her whole world, a world she had enviously built for so long, came crumbling to her feet. She had all along believed that she had everything a man would want in a woman. Indeed life can be cruel!

Esther could not believe that she was the innocent fool all along. The truth, now in the open, was too severe to contemplate. She survived it though. She got her therapy by crying her heart out and opening up to family and friends. She learnt an unforgettable lesson on which she advises young ladies: "Remember that others' judgement of you does not define your worth. They may reject you for their own insecurities and reasons other than your beauty, intelligence or ability as a woman. So do not take their rejection as a vote on your womanhood."

As the saying goes, every cloud has a silver lining. Unbelievably, the same man who betrayed Esther was to introduce his friend to her. The resulting relationship culminated into a successful marriage and a multi-million business partnership that is the envy of many Kenyans.

It was in 1984 when Esther was love-bitten once more when she met Engineer Muchemi, an army officer. They grew fond of each other and soon a relationship developed. She had to learn how to love and trust again. Luckily, the new man in her life was patient with her. At the time, she found the emotional demands quite distractive given that she was working and doing her CPA examinations. She never got a referral. The first and only referral came when she got late for the exam; she had relied on someone to pick her from work and drop her at the exam centre.

The two lovebirds tied the knot in an inconspicuous occasion, which was followed by a one-week honeymoon. Unlike modern honeymoons that have been hijacked by uncalled-for grandeur, they tried as much as possible to observe the original purpose: to bond and get to know each other better. It is doubtful whether nowadays newly-weds get to achieve the intended objective given the short duration and exotic locales besides being mainly a statement of financial ability.

The first five years of their marriage were difficult. To start with, their two children came in a quick succession with only a year in between. A woman at the maternity ward warned her of dire consequences if she continued giving birth at that rate, especially because she was small. Another woman looked at her and asked if this was her first child. When she answered in the negative and confirmed that it was her second, and delivered through a caesarean section like the first, she cautioned her that if she dared get a child again at such a close interval, then she should be ready for any eventuality. The woman's message sunk. Perhaps due to this message, the couple resolved to have only the two children. Esther's happiness was that they got only two children and they got them early enough in life, which gave her leeway to pursue other goals.

On parenting, Esther recommends commitment and patience. Though enjoyable, it is a difficult task, especially when it comes to the problematic house helps, clinics and intermittent children's ailments. Every stage in parenting requires a different approach as well as lessons to the children. As she observes: "I believe it is difficult to remedy a situation that was the result of skipped lessons at one stage by applying it retrospectively. Parents should be there to direct kids at every stage in life. Fortunately, today's parents are keen to assist their children understand life and their body development. As maturing teenage girls, we were not given adult talk or even advised on how to handle natural body changes like the menstrual cycle. We had to contend with the embarrassment and manage the changes as they came. Today, I am happy that parents are not shy to discuss such topics as sex and sexuality with their teenage children."

Esther advises that children should also be taught responsibility. She never did homework with her children even for one day. They were to do it on their own and leave it for her to check. Any corrections would be done by the teacher. This taught them that school work was their responsibility. They would only come to ask for her assistance and not her pushing them to do their homework. As the children grew older, Esther was not afraid to give them her car. She observes that by refusing them to drive the car, a parent would be sending the message that they are not responsible enough. A parent should show them that they believe in their judgement and they will return that trust by being responsible. Esther feels she's lucky that through this practice, her children have turned out to be responsible adults. To date they have credit cards that they have never misused.

Generally, Esther expresses worry that recent developments appear to threaten the survival of marriage as an institution. It is under siege and is being bashed from left, right and centre for all the right and sometimes the wrong reasons. It is commonplace to find the young swearing never to get married, perhaps due to the visible shortcomings of marriages. While Esther would not advise anyone to stay in an abusive marriage, she invites the cynics to consider whether they would rather bring up children in single families or in a setting of both parents. If one was to answer such a question honestly, then they might remedy the situation. In her opinion, just because marriages can be difficult does not warrant wholesome condemnation. It would be tantamount to throwing the baby out with the bathwater. In other words, she has no regrets and if she were to live her life afresh, she would marry again.

Esther hails from Nyeri, a region stereotyped for its no-nonsense women who have no patience with men who cannot carry their weight. Such is their wrath against ineptitude. With regard to marriage, some men would find the women overbearing. For the Nyeri women, however, as far as men are concerned, you either shape up or ship out. Perhaps it is this mythical fear that makes men chicken out of their grip. While unapologetic for coming from Nyeri, Esther comments on the legend: "That's a misunderstanding. We are neither hostile nor do we beat up our men ... my husband was a military man for heaven's sake; how would I beat that man? All we do, and our men have accepted this, is manage our homes. A Nyeri woman will do everything in the home; milk the cows, go to the farm, prepare children for school and all other chores and let the husband be. I think only insecure men who want to dominate the show may find this overbearing."

On their own they are pacesetters. The indefatigable Esther, a mother of two, has not only seen her children to universities in the UK, but she also runs high-flying businesses – a leading mobile telephone dealership and an audit firm, Esther Muchemi and Associates.

Career and business

Family life took its toll on Esther's career. With the babies coming too close, she was forced to extend her maternity leave, something that was unacceptable to her employer, Ernst & Young. Thus, she was put in a situation where she had to choose between her family and the job. Naturally, the family triumphed and she resigned. This to her was a typical case of an employer who fails to understand their employees. She saw herself as a good worker who needed just a little understanding during the rough time.

After quitting at Ernst & Young, Esther stayed home for four months nurturing her babies. Gradually though, she got bored and started scouting for work. She got a job as an accountant with EABS Bank a position she left in a huff months later after disagreeing with her boss. She found him an imperious boss who did not respect employees. Esther tried as much as she could to work with him, but she could not take it. One day, she called it quits and went back to being a housewife.

Fortunately, she had a supportive husband. As a family, they never sat down to discuss whether she should resign or not. She would just tell him that she had quit her job and he would understand. Sometimes he would pleasantly joke about it: "At least I'm assured of being served tea by a smiling wife from now henceforth." This also lightly confirmed that he had noted how distraught his wife was from the job.

Life was not easy then. The Muchemis had to live on very limited resources. Her husband was not that well-paid. The family was living in a house provided by his employer. However, after leaving EABS, Esther did not stay long at home. She got a job at Mucheke and Associates as senior auditor. Though a small company, the audit firm was a great place to work. For once Esther got an employer who gave her an opportunity to realise her professional goals as well as family obligations. She could go to work and leave at any time to attend to family matters without the hustle of bureaucratic authority. Indeed, at Mucheke, they were a family. It was a lovely culture. For that, Esther paid back by working overtime even at night to complete her assignments. She found herself doing a kind of flexitime in Kenya even before it was widely accepted in Europe. To her, this was great.

It was while working at Mucheke that Esther and her husband pooled resources to buy a plot at Garden Estate where they began to put up a house. Four years later, they took a cooperative loan to complete the house. In 1996, they moved in. The family still lives in the same house.

Despite the impressive culture at Mucheke, Esther was to suffer a rude shock and a disappointing moment when an opportunity came for Mucheke to merge with Kassim Lakha and Associates. During the merger discussions, Esther was promised partnership in the resultant firm, a promise that was never to be. This failed promise infuriated her and this time she resolved to start her own outfit. She had had enough of working for others and being let down. Now she wanted the feeling of being in the driver's seat.

With her credentials, experience and a supportive husband, she launched Esther Muchemi and Associates in 1996. Her husband helped her to set it up. Then they employed two more accountants after which they went marketing the firm to new clients. The response was overwhelming, thanks to Esther's experience and good record in the industry. It was this small audit firm that would finance the start-up stage of her business flagship today.

Although she was a good and loyal worker, Esther disliked the working environment. As an employee, she was particularly bothered by two things. One was the 8.00 am to 5.00 pm work schedule. She could not understand why employers would insist that she should stay at the work station, work or no work. She hated pretending to be busy just flipping through old files to wind down the clock. "I wish I had the freedom to work and attend to my other engagements after finishing whatever I was assigned to do without the rigidity of the work clock." Though desirable, such freedom was a tall order in any employment scenario. Even Mucheke and Associates, a more liberal employer, was at times peeved at Esther's persistent absence and she could sense it.

The other thing that got to Esther was the assurance of a regular income. Though good, it made one lazy and extravagant in expenditure. As long as one knows there is a salary coming the following month, they have no qualms spending all their money and even borrowing for that matter. She observes that, even though she was earning decent salaries wherever she worked, she had no significant savings to lay claim on.

If these two factors weren't enough to make her move to entrepreneurship, then the failed promises would have done it. She doesn't like being lied to; even her children are aware of this because if there is one thing they can never escape punishment for, it is telling a lie.

Another factor that motivated Esther to go it on her own was her strong belief that she was cut out for bigger things in life. "I always believed I could do more with my life than what I was doing at work. I had a strong belief in my abilities and did not envisage failure. This propelled me to take the risk and get into entrepreneurship." Moreover, like many people, she was scared of poverty. She may not have experienced that biting poverty while growing up, but she saw it as it was all over the neighbourhood. As she observed, "I knew families that were struggling and obviously it was not pretty. I never wanted to be in their position. Let me say that even today, the thought of going back to count coins drives me to work harder."

Esther Muchemi and Associates was Esther's first baby in entrepreneurship. The business picked up well. It could provide her with the much-needed basics and a little savings. Towards the beginning of 2002, her husband, an electrical engineer, hinted of a looming opportunity in the telecommunication industry. Suffice it to say that his profession may have been a key factor in enhancing his foresight. At the time also, the couple was widely travelled, something that exposed them to the emerging trends in the telecommunication industry. Mobile telephony especially had taken root in other parts of the world. They knew that it was just a matter of time before the revolution came home.

As a family, the Muchemis agreed to start a shop dealing with telecommunication equipment. Their main line would be telephone sets, fax machines and a sprinkle of mobile phones. Subsequently, they obtained a licence from the telekom authority to stock these products. During those days one had to apply to Telekom Kenya to be allowed to buy a line.

Armed with about Ksh 1 million, the couple set up a shop at Nginyo Towers in Nairobi's Central Business District. Esther's colleagues jeered at them at the beginning. They could not understand why two professionals would choose to open a shop instead of an office offering professional services. Their idea of a shop was that of a common shopkeeper, the *dukawalla*. At times, Esther too felt a bit uncomfortable at this outlook, a feeling that was enough to prompt her to splash half of her capital into furniture and refurbishment. Maybe this was to assuage her ego. Nevertheless, she felt that if she was to run a shop, it must be a decent one. This explains why by the time they were starting up, they just had about half a Ksh 500,000 worth of stock. The opening of the shop's doors marked the beginning of Saamchi, a nationally respected brand created out of the names of Esther's two children Sam and Ciiru.

At the time they started, Safaricom was a monopoly in the mobile telecommunication sector. It did not however take long before Kencell (now Airtel), the second mobile operator to be licensed in Kenya, hit the market with a bang. The trailblazers Safaricom instantly became the underdogs. The new company was more aggressive, and went ahead to brand Esther's shop, placing their posters everywhere. Significantly, she could sell more Kencell lines and airtime than Safaricom's.

Buoyed by the good returns from Kencell, Esther applied to be a registered dealer. Her request was however declined despite her capacity to do their business. Besides, she had the energy, experience, knowledge, time and ability to marshal personnel. Kencell could not see all these. All they wanted to see was money, money and more money. Esther's bank statement could not demonstrate that capacity.

Like in Esther's case, most businesses lose out on great opportunities by failing to see other strengths in their partners besides capital. After failing to secure a Kencell dealership, Esther didn't even bother with Safaricom; in any case they were the underdog. She could still sell airtime and lines for both companies and get her returns. Then one day, out of the blue, Esther got a call from the Safaricom dealership manager, a Mr Hussein. He introduced himself and asked whether Saamchi could consider being an exclusive dealer of Safaricom. To Esther, the word 'exclusive' here was tricky given that she was doing better business with their rival Kencell although they had refused her dealership. Still holding the manager on the line, Esther turned to her staff for advice. "Hey guys, am holding Safaricom here on the line. They want us to be their exclusive dealer. What do I tell them?" The members of staff were unanimous in their answer. Take it. And she confirmed there and then. The rest would be history.

The following day, Esther removed all the posters of the rival company and replaced them with Safaricom promotion material. Word reached Kencell about the new development. Promptly, she was honoured with a visit by the Kencell marketing manager who nearly shed tears when she saw Esther removing their posters. Her pleas however could not change a thing. The decision had been made. Although Esther was betting on a weaker horse, she now had a dealership, something that Kencell had refused her.

Esther and her team immediately got to work and work they did. She embarked on setting up a structured system that would make the work flow as they were dealing with near-cash items. Thus, a systems audit was important. She also set up a sales team that could help in moving volumes.

At the end of the first month, Esther was disappointed to note that, unlike her counterparts in dealership business who had booked huge commissions, she was trailing with nearly a million shillings. She was to realise that dealers were being paid on a graduated scale; the more one sold the higher the scale of commission. Her counterparts had discovered a way to outsell them. She had to find out. On investigation, she discovered her handicap – capital. Saamchi was buying lines at KSh 2,500 from Safaricom and was supposed to sell at the same price. The well-heeled dealers however subsidised the price of the lines, which they would sell for as low as KSh 500. Obviously they lured more buyers thereby graduating to higher commission scales.

Although now Esther knew their trick, she could not match it. She needed the money to make her next order. While Esther accepted that she could not take the big boys head-on (for doing so would be a financial disaster given her small financial capacity), she was also not prepared to be the underdog. Being the one on the run had never been an option to her all through her school and work life and this wasn't going to be her first time.

So she got thinking. Her first strategy was to sharpen her sales team. She would come up with the first-ever door-to-door mobile airtime and lines sales team in Kenya. She put up a team of about 20 salespeople who would deliver Saamchi products to the clients at their premises. It was a big gamble, as it involved giving employees airtime – which is money – to walk around with and bring back the returns. In business one has to risk and trust those who work for them. However, there were a few rotten apples that took advantage and disappeared with the merchandise. Overall, however, the strategy was a great success. On the month that Esther mounted her sales strategy, she got a competitive commission to the consternation of her competitor-dealers.

In addition to the sales team, Esther engaged in building relationships with her clients. She singles out honesty and integrity as the two qualities that every business person needs. She dealt with her clients honestly and, over time, she won their trust. Unbelievably, her clients, especially those of Somali origin, would give her cash in advance to buy lines for them. They could trust her with so much money that at times she wondered if this was her business or theirs. This boost put her at par with her well-capitalised competitor-dealers.

In business, just as in life, nothing is static; change is the only constant. Esther was rudely awakened to this reality when one morning she walked into the office but did not find her prized mobile sales team. As they used to report by 6.30 am she expected to find them in the office collecting their merchandise by the time she came in at 8.00 am. Not even one of the team members was in the office. The team leader was not picking Esther's phone either. That is when she sensed that something was amiss.

It was not until at 9.00 am that she confirmed her worst fear: they had been poached by the competition. Esther felt blank. She needed somebody to talk to. She called her husband who was out of the country to share with him the devastating blow. He listened and promised to get back to her within one hour. Sure enough he did, and he advised her to shuffle the staff among branches to fill in the vacant positions temporarily. He would be on his way back.

That was a bitter but vital business lesson for Esther. From then on, she vowed never to build her business around people. Instead she chose to build a structured branch network and systems that would be run by anybody in the organisation. This marked the beginning of Saamchi branch network expansion that stood at over 38 branches across the country by 2008.

From this blatant unethical episode Esther got another blessing. The remaining staff seamlessly took over the jobs of those who had left. They zealously stepped in with almost a silent vow to do better. Perhaps it was the feeling of betrayal that hung in the air or just a sense of added responsibility that got into them. But they got to work so hard that Saamchi never lost an edge in as far as the monthly commission was concerned.

Before long, Esther started to stretch her lead. The next three years in a row, Saamchi was voted the leading Safaricom dealer in various categories. Ever since, the company has won many awards, but the one that was most touching to Esther was the one they got the same year she lost her husband. As she was not there to direct the operations, it was therefore more of a reward to the staff who in her absence kept the standards high. This taught Esther something about loyalty from staff: "I think this can only happen if those who work for you feel fairly treated."

Esther is a believer in fairness. She believes in fair process and she personally gets unsettled by real or perceived unfairness. Consequently, a majority of her staff are not on a salary, but a retainer and a commission added on top to reward extra effort. She does not want those who put extra effort to feel short-changed.

Growth and management strategies

The shop that Esther co-founded with her late husband quickly grew into a giant company both in turnover, staff and resources. This growth quickly put Esther on notice. Luckily her business degree, professional training and experience had prepared her for the challenges of a growing business. While it is easier to start and run a small business, greater challenges set in as the business becomes bigger – it starts to demand in-depth management, more human and financial resources, and compliance in such areas as regulations and government taxes. Actually, the initial growth is a steady projectile but it becomes complex as it approaches maturity.

With time, Esther accepted that Saamchi was no longer her business but a company with its own life. It had its own stakeholders – creditors, suppliers and employees among others. That usually marks the point of transition. Entrepreneurs who fail to make that acceptance and transition end up strangling their own businesses. As she observes, "You cannot be everywhere all the time, check everything, hire, fire, order and still allow the business room to grow. When we came to that point, I humbled myself and accepted that I needed to hire more professionals and delegate responsibility and authority to them. We also decided to compartmentalise our work in departments for flow in administration. Subsequently, Saamchi today has a General Manager, Human Resource Manager, Sales and Marketing Manager, M-Pesa Administrator, Finance Manager and Operations and Logistics Manager. All the departments are headed by professionals. We recruit mainly based on staff referrals. This is the easiest way to check on character given that we deal in cash and near-cash items."

Robert Ringer, in his book *Million Dollar Habits,* lamented on the level of competence of the modern-day's workforce. Esther too has a grudge when it comes to employees, especially the youth. Getting a well-rounded person to hire has been so difficult. She always says that there is room for one better employee at Saamchi anytime, but still she cannot get good people. She thinks that this is a no-sweat society where people expect to be paid without working. Unfortunately, due to the nature of business, which involves modern telecommunication systems, Esther's workforce mainly comprises the youth. She's had a fair share of frustration: "We are living in an age where young people believe they should be rewarded just for being alive. A large percentage of them have a remarkably inflated perception of their abilities."

Some of the youth that Esther has employed are also dishonest and fraudulent. She has experienced such bad work ethics and integrity that she urges parents to teach their children that success comes after work. Parents should also make their children responsible and help them to develop a respectable work culture. For example, if domestic workers were to do everything for them, when and where will they learn? If they are to be exempted from housework, then they should study hard at school and show results. Esther too was exempted from housework and she did well in school.

How does Esther manage such a growing business? "I am a decider. When confronted with situations, I believe in making fast decisions. I'm also humble enough to accept and make amends whenever I make a wrong decision. I think being undecided puts your fate on others. If not careful, you can become a victim of other people's decisions. I believe you are better off with the consequences of your own decisions than those of others. When I accept that I have made a wrong decision, I move on. That is the best way I know to improve on yesterday's mistakes."

Saamchi's strategy to grow the business has been the development of lasting and mutually beneficial relationships with the principal, suppliers, staff and customers. With regard to staff, Esther trains and personally mentors them to grow in leadership. Through these interactions, she's able to feel her employees. Actually, she tries to know all her employees by their names.

Challenges in the business

According to Esther, looking at it from another angle, anything that one undertakes in entrepreneurship is a challenge. It starts with the courage to quit the comfort of one's job. She's happy that she left when the stakes were not that high – a huge salary with perks such as a prestigious house and school fees for children in high cost schools. It would have been more difficult for her and the drop could have been steeper and perhaps scarier. Looking at the things that were at stake, she felt there was not much to threaten her. She already had a roof over her head and her children were going to modest schools. She also had a car. With that, nothing worse could have happened to her.

In the line of business that Esther is involved in, frauds are an inherent risk. Security is a big issue given that the main merchandise is cash. Esther's challenge as the leader is to try and design controls that reduce frauds but do not stifle business.

Another area of challenge is from the competition. Esther has had to contend with undercutting from the other dealers. As a company, Saamchi chose to be fair in their pricing, maintain a decent margin and let those undercutting fry in their own fat. Price wars in the long run only hurt the proponents. In addition, they also chose to invest in other areas of business such as relationship, product variety and staff training other than direct competition.

Like any other growing organisation, staff issues are a major challenge to the company. For example, there is the issue of promotion as the company grows. Experience has taught Esther to promote from within instead of hiring from outside with regard to senior positions. Besides the obvious resentment from existing staff, most of the recruits fail to mesh in the organisation culture; hence they end up frustrated and also frustrate the employer. Moreover, some of the employees price themselves so high without any idea of their capacity to contribute to the business. However, promotion from within has its shortcomings. If one is promoted and left at the same branch, usually they may not easily command the respect of their juniors who were their colleagues. Esther usually discusses with the respective staff and hears their version. If they choose to remain at the branch, she allows them to; otherwise she prefers taking them to new branches after promotion.

Esther also recognises the fast speed at which the business has grown as another challenge. Managing the resulting extensive branch network has not been easy. It has occasioned staff shortage and weak systems to monitor the branches. Slowly, however, monitoring systems have been established to run the organisation. The company has also increased its staff at the head office and equipped them with the necessary tools to check all the branches. For example, there is a vibrant internal audit department that ensures that the reports received at the head office are authentic.

Cash flow management is the bane of most small businesses. Most entrepreneurs do not appreciate the role of professionals or believe in acquiring the relevant tools necessary in managing cash flow. They unwittingly choose to operate in the dark as far as cash flow – the life blood of the business – is concerned. This is a recipe for disaster. As Esther observes: "If you cannot predict your cash movements, then your decisions would end up being too costly for you in the long run. I know of business people who have been compelled to borrow money from shylocks at exorbitant rates just to meet urgent business commitments. Businesses need to employ accountants who can help guide and prioritise their expenditure; otherwise they may end up paying the least important bills only to miss out on a big business opportunity."

Fortunately, Esther does not recall any major mistake that she has made in her business career.

Future of Saamchi

Esther would like to develop Saamchi into a respectable brand in the near future. She hopes that a powerful brand would allow her to diversify into other product lines under it similar to Richard Branson's Virgin business model. She also hopes to train her children to take over the running of the business.

Legacy and philanthropy

Esther advocates contributing to worthy causes and wants her legacy to be touching others' lives positively. She sees most people as having the wrong value of money. To her, money is useless if it is not used to do what it must do; for example, people should not die all around for lack of medical care, nor should friends, relatives and even staff suffer while others keep their millions.

An experience that Esther went through opened her eyes – literally. She had an eye ailment, which was diagnosed and she was subsequently advised that the best doctor to attend to her was a Dr Khan. Dr Khan worked for a mission hospital at Kikuyu in the outskirts of Nairobi. One would imagine Esther, a not so common woman, joining a long queue of the ordinary folk in a village hospital. She dreaded this experience and even ordered her secretary to arrange for a private appointment with the doctor at his wife's clinic in an up-market suburb. This was not to be. She was politely advised by his wife that the only place she could get him was at Kikuyu Mission Hospital.

Against her wish, Esther gathered enough courage to go to the hospital. What a surprise that she met! Instead of the smelly, dirty wards and compound that she had conjured up in her mind, it was impeccably clean, with organised rooms in a well-kept compound. She was treated, like all other patients, with admirable dignity and escorted from one room to the next. When she requested to pay, she was asked for a paltry KSh 750. This surprised her; indeed the facility is funded by donors. She took time to look at the list of donors. She was disappointed to find that not even a single African was on the long list yet there are well-endowed Africans in Kenya.

On women and business, Esther advocates for more entry of women in entrepreneurship as she believes that they are good business people. Says she: "Maybe due to their nurturing instincts, women are good with details. They would easily spot an unsettled or a sick child in the family as opposed to men. A mother would take just one look at her child and know that something is wrong. I believe we have brought this into business with great success. Also, and research has confirmed this, women are good at doing a number of things at once unlike men who would rather do one thing at a time. Today's business environment calls for multitasking."

As to why women are not many in big business, Esther believes it has historical and traditional reasons. There was a time when women could not get finance without their husbands' consent. This, coupled with the prejudice that their place was in the kitchen, held them back in many ways. Fortunately, this attitude is changing.

Tips for young entrepreneurs

Esther advises young people to believe that whatever they want to do is doable and that they have the capacity to make it happen. She also observes that education is good as a means to expand one's horizons. She encourages broader thinking: "I know there are those who have succeeded with little or no education. I believe that in such cases, education could have made it much easier for them to succeed. Your career in school does not necessarily determine your life career. I have met trained engineers running supermarkets and doctors heading security firms. It just goes to confirm the versatility of education. That, as they say during graduations, you have the power to do all that appertains to that degree – and much more I may add."

Young people should also cultivate an attitude that allows success. As the saying goes, 'Your attitude determines your altitude'. The young should accept that success demands hard work and sacrifice. They should know that good things come at a higher price and be willing to pay the price. The sacrifices that they may make in order to succeed are worth it in the long run.

Finally, she reminds those in the journey of success to remember that it is usually darkest towards dawn. Just when one is about to make their breakthrough, they are likely to meet even bigger obstacles. They should take heart. This just confirms that they are on the right track and success is theirs if they just keep plodding on.

Role model

Esther greatly admires Richard Branson, the founder and Chief Executive Officer of the Virgin Group of Companies. This is somebody who went into business with a human heart. He sought to provide affordable but quality solutions to people's problems in every industry that he went into. His guiding principle has been decent quality at an affordable price. He also built a brand long before branding was taught at the universities. All these for someone who dropped out of school are not only amazing but deeply inspiring. If he could do all this, do others have an excuse?

Chapter 6

Sunil Shah

Six o'clock in the morning! The congested bus park is abuzz with activity – vehicles hooting and touting for passengers, *boda boda* cyclists precariously balancing their loads, travellers, pedestrians, beggars and madmen, all jostling for the limited space, heighten the noise to a crescendo. There is brisk business for the cyclists, shoeshiners and newspaper vendors. The market traders are busy dusting up their wares ready for the day. Unmistakably, *ohangla* music, the signature tune of the town, is already blaring from every corner of the stage and the stench of raw fish permeates the dusty morning air. From the engagement, it is difficult to tell that it is Sunday morning. Welcome to Kisumu city.

This is what the writer encountered on a visit to Kisumu for an interview with Sunil Shah. A first-hand account would best describe the event: "I notice that everybody is falling for my shoes – literally. Reluctantly, I wriggle my way to an open shed and sit on this makeshift stool to get my shoes cleaned. In the meantime, I ask for the direction to United Millers Ltd. Knowing glances are thrown my way. The shoeshiner jokes, 'I thought you said you were going for a church service; is that where your church is?' he laughs. 'Just tell any *boda boda* cyclist to drop you there. Who in Kisumu does not know where United is!' he exclaims."

And thus the ride to the United Millers began, taking a steep ride downtown towards the expansive water body. In the horizon, the first rays of the morning sun were gently caressing the calm waters of Lake Victoria. Weary fishermen were dragging their boats along the shore, while others were busy repairing their fishing nets. The shoreline was dotted with half-naked but well-muscled men at different stages of the fish trade. Along the main road bordering the lake – Obote Road – stood an imposing complex belonging to United Millers Limited. As the writer further narrates, "Outside, the complex is teeming with hundreds of workers either coming for the morning shift or leaving for the day. Several branded trailers are parked outside the big iron gate. Two uniformed guards stand at the gate of the multi-storey complex. I ask for their boss. He has not arrived yet but he is expected soon. My attempt to glean some information about the company and the boss hits a brick wall. 'Why would we talk about our company to a stranger? We don't know who you are and your intentions,' the *askari* sternly puts me off. I shut up and wait."

That is the imposing 'aura' of Sunil Shah. To understand the rise and growth of United Millers, one must delve into the life and times of Sunil himself, an entrepreneur who was included in the 'Who is Who in Business' list of 1998 by the Macmillan Publishers.

Early childhood and education

Sunil Shah was born to Narshi Punja Shah and Kanchan Narshi Shah in Kibuye in the outskirts of Kisumu town in 1953, the firstborn in a family of three – two sons and a daughter. Their father, Narshi Punja Shah, was born in a village called Kajuda near Jamnagar, Gujarat, on Diwali, 8 November 1928, and was the youngest of eight children. He moved to Kenya in 1939 at the age of 11 years to join his elder brothers who had come to Kenya earlier in search of greener pastures. Comparatively, Kenya presented better opportunities to them as opposed to where they were born; Gujarat State in north-west India was a semi-desert where piped water was a far-fetched dream. The immigrants travelled by ship on the Indian Ocean, landing in Mombasa from where they moved to Maragua. They stayed there briefly before moving to Kisumu.

Narshi Shah went to the present-day Kisumu Boys' Secondary School for his primary and secondary education. When he completed high school in 1945, he joined his elder brothers in their textile business in Kisumu. Unfortunately, tragedy hit the struggling family when Narshi Shah lost, almost simultaneously, his two elder brothers, both in road accidents, leaving him to fend for the remaining members of the family.

The young Narshi Shah and his remaining brothers concentrated on their retail business, which was the lifeblood of the family. Later, they got into sugarcane farming and opened a jaggery plant in Kibos. Then they expanded into wheat, maize, sisal and dairy farming. In 1948, Narshi Shah married Kanchan Narshi, a Kenyan of Indian descent who was born and raised in Nairobi. They were blessed with three children, Sunil, Kamal and their sister Nutan. When the children got married too, Narshi ended up with an extended family that comprised his children's families: his eldest son Sunil, wife Shakuntal, their two children Sajni and Savan; his second son Kamal and son Punit; and, his daughter Nutan, her husband Arvind, their son Rohin, daughter Devina and Devina's husband Sunny.

In his days as a farmer and a Kisumu businessman, Narshi Shah would take his eldest son Sunil along with him during his farm visits. To Sunil, this was just another occasion for adventure and he barely learnt anything serious from these trips. As a youngster though, he used to look forward to these trips as a chance to escape the routine at home. He loved to experience the thrill of outdoor life.

Sunil and his younger brother Kamal spent their seven years of primary education at the Central Primary School, a public school in Kibuye in the outskirts of Kisumu Town. After primary education, his father proposed that he goes to Britain for 'O' and 'A' level education. The 15-year-old Sunil was so elated at the prospect of going abroad to study that he was not even anxious over the change in environment or even worried about the challenges that lay ahead.

Between the years 1968 and 1973, Sunil pursued his studies in a British public school. He was impressed by the standards of education in Britain, which he found quite broad and interactive. He met and made new friends during his study, some of whom were very smart in class. An average student, he enjoyed English, Mathematics, History and Geography. Although he wasn't always at the top of the class, he maintained good grades.

Sunil never gave any serious thought about his future during his school days. His focus was on enjoying every moment of his school life. Somehow, he believed that the future would be good as long as he made the best of his present occupation – schooling. His father was providing for everything that he needed and he had nothing to think of other than his studies.

Britain opened Sunil's eyes to things that were happening around him. It made him aware of his immediate environment other than class work; for example, the vibrant British media got him interested in economic issues. In effect, he started reading extensively on business and economics. His holidays were spent back in Kenya, during which he worked on the family farms.

In 1968, the year Sunil travelled to Britain for his secondary education, his family moved to Nairobi. Narshi felt that Kisumu was limiting his growth. Nairobi was the commercial hub of Kenya. Compared to Kisumu, Nairobi was vibrant. It had numerous industries that attracted the most resources and best human capital. Moreover, Narshi wanted to expand into the real estate business and the demand for housing in Kisumu was too basic to sustain this ambition. After evaluating his possibilities, he chose to wind up his Kisumu businesses and relocate to Nairobi.

After moving his family to Nairobi, Narshi teamed up with other partners and ventured into automobile and real estate business as he had planned. At the same time, he bought mining rights at the Macalda Mines in Suna-Migori. Here, with the help of an American manager, they mined copper which they took to Kasese in Uganda for smelting before exporting.

The automobile business did not do well for Narshi due to undercapitalisation. Mining was however lucrative. Unfortunately, in 1972 Idi Amin, Uganda's President then, confiscated their haul of copper en route to Kasese thereby crippling their operations. The loss was debilitating; hence, Narshi decided to sell off the mining business, opting instead to concentrate on the real estate and automobile trade.

Around the same time, there was general panic in the business scene when policies that discriminated against Asians were enacted across the East African region in a bid to effect Africanisation of the economy. While Amin ordered all Asians out of the country in 48 hours in his infamous dream speech, Kenya had passed legislation in 1967 denying trade licences to non-citizens. Cornered, the Asians started leaving the region in droves. Ironically, those who left East Africa were accorded a red-carpet welcome in England. With hindsight, Sunil believes that this was a ploy by the British Government to dupe African leaders to chase away Asian citizens, who comprised qualified artisans and skilled *dukawallas*, to go and revive their fledgling shops that were being swallowed up by fast-expanding supermarkets. To date, Asians continue to operate shops in Britain and they are very successful.

When Sunil completed his 'A' levels in 1973, he returned to Kenya to join his father in his automobile business in Nairobi's Industrial Area. Narshi and his partners had a franchise for Japanese vehicles and also did repairs at their workshop. The young Sunil opened and closed the business premises every day. Being the keyholder, he was the first to report to work and the last to leave. Sunil did not like the automobile business; he felt there was not much activity at the workshop and the showroom.

Going into business

In 1976, Narshi lost a substantial amount of money in a business deal that would change life in his family. As Sunil observed at the time: "Suddenly, there were too many creditors banging on his door for payment and being promised to come for money endlessly. This was not his habit. He was a prompt payer who hated disappointing suppliers. I also realised that he was withdrawn. Upon enquiry I found out that he had lost a lot of money to unscrupulous people. The loss totally destabilised him financially. I felt really bad. I could not fathom my father, an intelligent and relentless businessman, wearing this forlorn look of helplessness. Our family that at one time had plenty was now on the verge of bankruptcy. In my opinion, my father's mistake was veering off from the trade he had mastered, general merchant, to other areas where he had little experience. But that was not important then. Of urgency was how I could rescue our family and put them back firmly on the road to prosperity."

This challenge would herald Sunil's career. After consulting with his father about the prevailing situation, Sunil told him that he wanted to do something different. Narshi did not object and instead he threw back the gauntlet to Sunil's feet. His advice was, "I agree. If you have the courage, go to Kisumu. There, I have a derelict building on a one acre plot from where you can start." Honestly though, Sunil did not have the courage. How could he when he left

Kisumu as a schoolboy under circumstances he never understood? All the same, he packed his bags and took the historic journey back to his place of birth, Kisumu. That was in 1977.

Sunil travelled overnight and stayed with relatives in Kisumu. The next morning he drove to the premises that his father had referred to only to be met by the shock of his life: "Derelict could not begin to describe the state of the building that I found there. Overgrown weeds and bushes literally swamped the building. The rusty padlock at the gate could not open. Bats, birds and other animals screamed at my invasion of their territory. I struggled with the padlock for hours on end until I got an idea. I walked across the street to a neighbouring motor garage where I borrowed liquid oil. I poured this on the padlock and left for the day. That marked my first day at work. There was not much I could do."

The next day, the padlock easily gave in and Sunil was ushered into a desolate world of utter neglect. If this was to be his future, it was bleak indeed, so he thought.

Other than for the roof, the building was in such a state that Sunil could not make out immediately what better use he could put it into. For the moment, he felt overwhelmed. A flush of helplessness descended upon him like a dark cloud covering the sun. He sat down, took stock of what lay before him and felt blank. He did not know where to start. After gathering some courage, he went out and hired two workers to clean up the mess. As they got to work, he took a drive along the Kisumu–Kakamega road to refresh his thinking. It was a drive that would change Sunil's future forever. "The opportunity hit me like a sledgehammer between the eyes. There were farmers who were desperately selling maize and beans in the western towns. The produce, I knew, could fetch tidy sums in Nairobi. All one needed was to create a linkage between this market and Nairobi, an idea that was not far-fetched."

To actualise this idea, Sunil needed capital to set the ball rolling. Upon returning from his drive, he placed a call to his father back in Nairobi and asked him for KSh 50,000 to clean up the place and start doing something. Sunil's father somehow got this money and sent it over. According to Sunil, he could have borrowed it from his friends, as he was still in financial difficulties.

With his two workers and the balance from his father's money, Sunil went on a buying spree. They bought maize and beans, weighed and shipped them to Nairobi where Sunil used his father and brother to get him a ready market. They would put the merchandise into lorries and follow them in Sunil's car all the way to Nairobi where Sunil sold the maize to millers and the beans to traders in various market stalls. Locally, the farmers who now had a ready buyer for their produce were having a ball. They soon developed a rapport of mutual benefit and trust. Some were ready to deliver their produce at his doorstep in Kisumu as long as he promised immediate payment.

As the activities intensified, Sunil and his workers got down to work on the same procedure – weighing the produce, paying for it and packing it into lorries ready for the journey to Nairobi. The volumes soon outstripped his capacity and, unless he got some financial boost, he realised that he could not meet the demand from farmers who wanted to be paid upfront.

Pressed for more money, Sunil approached his bankers for an overdraft. His track record was good and he was pleasantly surprised when the bank handed him half a million shillings in overdraft without security. The grain business had picked up well and Sunil started thinking of other business opportunities.

Inside the premises, there lay a redundant rice mill. Sunil had this feeling that Kamal (his younger brother), although not a formally trained mechanic, was technically savvy enough to revive this mill. He immediately sent for Kamal and true to his instincts, he was not disappointed. Kamal quickly revived the derelict plant into a functional milling machine opening a new business front – rice milling. They began by milling rice for the National Irrigation Board from Ahero for a fee[23].

Sunil's reputation as a maize trader in western Kenya grew like bush fire, subsequently landing him another opportunity in the middle of 1978. Some Asian millers wanted to dispose of their milling machine. They could not think of a better buyer other than Sunil. If he could buy enough maize to sell to the millers directly, why couldn't he mill himself? In any case Nyanza was an opportunity waiting to happen as far as maize milling was concerned.

Although Sunil was interested in milling, he did not have the money to buy the machine. Luckily, the sellers understood his predicament and agreed to sell it to him on a deferred credit with not even a cent in down payment. Thus, with the sifted-maize milling machine, United Millers was born.

Now having acquired the milling machine, the long trips to Nairobi came to a halt. Sunil could now buy maize, mill, package and sell to his customers right in Kisumu and around the region. Apparently, the beckoning market was too big for his capacity. Maize milling required economies of scale to maximise returns given that prices were controlled. To seize the opportunity, he approached his bank to increase his overdraft. However, he was not lucky this time round.

Owing to the magnitude of his need, the bank, the same one that gave him unsecured facility, now insisted on security. He therefore embarked on a documentation process to provide security for the two-million overdraft that

---

23   Ahero irrigation scheme is situated in Nyando near Kisumu.

he had applied for. This experience was the beginning of an important lesson on bank security documentation. The process was long, slow and expensive.

In retrospect, Sunil believes that he got his vision to go into business during the days when he moved around with his father across his farms and businesses. This exposure planted in him the desire to start and build his own company. Although he seemed to lean towards the food industry – given that his father's background was in agriculture – he did not have milling specifically in mind. The vision of building the biggest maize-milling firm to serve the whole of Nyanza region crystallised upon moving to Kisumu and started at the onset of buying and selling of maize to millers. Once he got into the maize trade, he knew it was a matter of time before he joined the milling fray.

Production at the mill started early in 1979 and saw the birth of Jambo maize flour. The proximity to farmers was an advantage over the Nairobi competitors. Although the margins were razor-thin, efficiency and volumes kept the company afloat. In 1981, the company expanded into wheat milling and they would buy the raw material (wheat) from Kenya Farmers Association. Subsequently, they diversified in their product portfolio from milling to vegetable-oil production and have used its by-products to start new product lines.

Presently, United Millers has an assorted array of products. Among these are Jambo Maize Meal, Tropicana Wheat Flour, Unifeeds (animal feeds), Criso Vegetable Oil, Bibo Cooking Fat and Kwanga Bar Soap.

Sunil Shah is a former director of Kenya Commercial Bank. He retired in 2011 in accordance with capital market rules. He is a director of the Mall in Westlands. His father, Narshi, a real-estate developer, had commenced a project in Nairobi's Embakasi area aiming to build 1,200 housing units. Unfortunately, he did not complete the scheme. By the time of his death, he had only built 96 units. Sunil intends to complete these units.

Management strategy

The founding directors of United Millers were Sunil, his father Narshi and brother Kamal. All of them have been actively involved in its management. Unfortunately, Narshi passed on in June 2008 leaving behind Sunil and Kamal to run the show. Thus, United Millers is run by the two directors – Sunil and Kamal.

Sunil believes in hiring the best staff to run the business and pays them according to the skills and value they bring to the business. In effect, they have hired a General Manager, Finance Manager and factory managers to coordinate their operations. At the milling factory, they have packaging, sales, marketing and transport departments that ensure that their products flow from the factory to the consumers. They also have an established purchasing department that procures raw materials such as maize, wheat, other supplies and consumables.

A typical day at United Millers starts with a meeting where the directors are briefed on what happened the previous day, what is being done that day and what is planned for the next day. The directors and managers ensure that the activities are in line with the corporate vision and long term strategy. There is also periodic review of performance against budgeted targets and of the correctional measures taken.

Business challenges

A Kenyan of Asian descent, Sunil singles out the overcoming of government obstacles and prejudices as the biggest obstacle to their business progress. Particularly in the milling business, there have been too many government decrees which are counterproductive to the business. Requirements like licences for transporting and selling maize in different regions have greatly hampered business.

Raising money for expansion was also a big challenge, especially during the initial stages when they had no track record or security for bank loans. They were compelled to grow within their means by ploughing back whatever returns they got from the business. The milling industry is a high-volume business that is very competitive and favours established players. This is because the margins are thin and only big players enjoy economies of scale. Small upcoming players must be aggressive in marketing while at the same time trim costs to compete with the big players.

At the beginning of United Millers, Sunil personally went door to door marketing his new maize-flour product, Jambo. He took orders and made deliveries at the customers' premises. He also had to give huge discounts to attract new buyers and compete in the market. The 1979–1980 maize shortage, which was experienced almost immediately after they launched their milling company, was a shot in the arm to their business. Demand for maize flour was insatiable and they used to sell all that they produced at their premises. At the time, they got their supplies from the National Cereals and Produce Board (NCPB).

Family business has its challenges. According to Sunil, the ultimate commitment of all parties to the business should be to preserve the business. Disagreements are common in all enterprises, but as long as all parties act in the best interest of the business, they will overcome. Above all, partners need to have the ability and wisdom to give and take. In Sunil's family business, whenever they do not agree, they postpone the discussion to another day when matters would have cooled down or become clearer to all parties.

Future of the business within the Kisumu environment

According to Sunil, Kisumu and Nyanza region as a whole presents a great investment opportunity to serve the over 150-million market that includes Uganda, Southern Sudan, DRC, Tanzania and Rwanda. The town has a railway line, a harbour and the largest freshwater lake in Africa that connects three East African states. However, this great potential has been mired by political activism and deliberate regime neglect.

As such the hotbed of politics that is Kisumu can easily be turned into a regional business hub. Its strategic location with a proper functioning infrastructure can serve the Rift Valley, western and the greater southern Nyanza region, not to mention the neighbouring landlocked countries. Advocating positively for the people of Kisumu, Sunil observes: "These people are not lazy as envisaged; neither are they boisterous and extravagant, but certainly very hard-working. They form the majority of my staff and I would not be where I am today were it not for them. The Kisumu people are quite honest and loyal workers. I think what they need is political goodwill and a change of mindset. If that is achieved, we are going to witness an economic revolution that would rival the City of Nairobi. I personally would champion that re-awakening. Together with the leaders of Nyanza, we are already working on a master plan that should midwife the change that we want."

Presently, there are only two family members in the business, Kamal and Sunil. Their succession plan entails expanding ownership of the company to include employees and ultimately public listing at the securities market.

Marriage and family

Sunil married Shakuntalal in 1979. He was introduced to Shakuntalal, a Kenyan of Indian descent, by a common friend. She was born and bred in the coastal town of Mombasa. Together they have two children, a daughter, Sajni, and a son, Savan. Sajni went on to work in the banking industry in Britain, while Savan graduated from the university in 2008. He is now doing internship with Standard Chartered Bank.

Sunil believes that family members should only join the family business if they have an interest in it. However, he intends to train his children in the business should they show interest; after all, it is the responsibility of parents to guide their children on socio-economic, education and religious matters.

Regarding his family, Sunil acknowledges that his wife has been the pillar of the family. She has dedicated all her time in bringing up the children. In effect, he observes that women play an important role in the upbringing of children, as they influence their character especially their spirituality and education.

While observing that women in Kenya have played a tremendous role in business, a majority of them are the proprietors of small businesses. Most of their businesses never grow into big organisations because they spend most of the time taking care of family chores. They also do not have enough time and resources to do more. In the Asian communities, women are more of homemakers than breadwinners, although this is now changing. Many women now want to pursue careers of their own choice and compete equally with men.

And on family life he urges couples to exercise tolerance: "It is pointless to fight due to financial problems. These will always be there in every family at different times. What matters is how you handle them. A successful family is the one that stands together during bad and good times."

Social and charity activities

Narshibhai Punja Shah (Sunil's father) was an avid philanthropist. He played an active role in many philanthropic organisations such as Visa Oshwal Vanik Community (VOVC) of Kisumu and Nairobi and the Oshwal Education and Relief Board (OERB). He was also a founder member of the Lions Club of Kisumu. To date, he remains the highest donor to the OERB. Together with others, they renovated the Cutchi Gujarat Shiv Mandir on Race Course Road in Nairobi. In April 1998, he organised an Eye Camp in Kisumu where over 14,000 patients were treated. In December 2003, he built and provided for the Kisumu Visa Oshwal Community, a Jain Deraser (temple for followers of Jainism).

Like his father, Sunil is engaged in numerous charity support programmes. He has registered a foundation in his name which he intends to use to reach out to the less fortunate members of the society. He insists on social responsibility and socially responsible behaviour for his company.

Ultimately, Sunil would like to leave behind a legacy of philanthropy. In addition, he has on the cards a project that should turn Kisumu into the preferred business destination in the Eastern Africa region: "Kisumu is strategically located to serve the market of South Sudan, Rwanda, Uganda, Tanzania and DRC. All it takes is to improve the rail, air and water infrastructure and convince investors that the market is ready for them and they will come. That is something I have researched on and I'm committed to achieving. It will be my legacy to the people of this region." Looking back, Sunil would like to spend more time with his family and engage more in philanthropic activities: "I sacrificed my life and family time for the business. I have also not had enough time to help the less fortunate members of the society. That is the reason why I have registered a foundation to dedicate more time to this cause that I believe can and will improve humanity."

Role models

Philosophically, Sunil admires Mahatma Gandhi because he changed the world. He was a revolutionary who struggled and achieved great success for his people without using force. He gave his people what they dearly yearned for – freedom; freedom is the beginning of self discovery and one of the most prized possessions in life is the freedom to choose what to do and pursue one's dreams unhindered.

Locally, Sunil is a great fan of Hon Raila Odinga: "I admire and respect the ideals Raila stands for. I believe he has achieved a lot for the people of Kenya in terms of their freedom and for that he has paid dearly. He is a selfless man."

Tips for entrepreneurs

According to Sunil, running a business requires commitment, perseverance and dedication; success is a product of hard work. There are no short cuts. He believes that most people are wallowing in misery and helplessness due to their failure to embrace hard work as the route to take them to their desired destination. For one to be successful, they must embrace dedication, focus, honesty and above all, God first.

Sunil abhors the culture of handouts that has turned otherwise able people into beggars. He advises the youth that they should expect to work for their upkeep and they should forget altogether easy options that promise heaven at no cost. Such expectations never come to fruition. At the same time, he appeals to the government to support the youth to get into business through provision of working capital, tax incentives and lowering the cost of getting into business.

Chapter 7

Benard O Otundo and Njoroge Keige

When they were studying at the university together, Dr Benard Onkundi Otundo and Dr Njoroge Keige shared the same dream of running a business some day. They were part of an ambitious group of business-minded students in their class who had given themselves a target of becoming successful business owners within ten years of graduating. They were then studying pharmacy at the University of Nairobi. As fate would have it, Ben and Njoroge ended up as business partners in Omaera Pharmaceuticals Limited, a company they started in 1993 at a time when pharmacists would work for years in multinational companies before going into business.

Ben and Njoroge took a different path. They decided to go into business straightaway; hence, they would be starting from scratch doing all the work themselves, from making orders to delivering cartons of drugs to customers in *matatus*. This appeared strange to many of their peers considering they were graduate doctors. Some of their competitors were also sceptical about their long term prospects as they had seen many indigenous-owned wholesaling businesses fail.

Like many other start-ups they faced problems getting finance and struggled with cash flow problems. They had to plough every cent back into the business in order to grow, which meant that in the early years they had no social lives to speak of and could not afford any luxuries. But giving up was never an option.

All the hard work eventually paid off. By 2008, Ben and Njoroge were sitting at the apex of a large and respected company in the pharmaceutical industry. Omaera Pharmaceuticals enjoyed 10 percent of the total pharmaceutical business in Kenya and was the third largest distributor for GlaxoSmithKline (GSK), the market leader in the pharmaceutical industry in Kenya. In addition, it has employed a team that consists of 350 people, 10 of whom are pharmacists and 50 are graduates from leading universities worldwide. The business has also expanded into Tanzania where its presence is significant.

Ben's early childhood and education

Benard Onkundi Otundo's journey to Omaera Pharmaceuticals began in 1964 in Kisii County, Nyanza region of Kenya, where he was born into a polygamous family of Aloysius Otundo. He was the fourth born in a family of six children, five boys and one girl. Their father's first wife and her children lived in Kisii together with Ben's mother, Agnes Moraa, who was a peasant farmer.

Ben's father worked in the cooperative movement for a long time. "He was one of the people who were trained and started off the cooperative movement in post-independent Kenya. When we were growing up, my father moved around a lot and worked in major towns like Bungoma, Kisumu and Nairobi." However, the boys stayed with him. During the holidays he would sometimes send them to Kisii to help their mother work on their coffee farm.

"With all this movement, I only spent my formative years in Kisii where I also attended nursery school," remembers Ben. When he joined his father he found himself attending various primary schools starting with Commonwealth Primary in Bungoma and finally sitting for his Certificate of Primary Education (CPE) examinations at Nairobi South Primary School in 1978. He was a bright student and did well in school.

Ben's father valued education greatly, perhaps because he was forced to drop out in Form Two at St Mary's Yala to take care of the family when his own father died. He would cane his children if they performed poorly in school, especially the boys who stayed with him.

When the examination results were announced, Ben had obtained 35 points and was subsequently admitted to Lenana School in Nairobi for his 'O' level education. Here he continued to do well in his studies and also got involved in sports, particularly rugby and hockey. After the four years of 'O' level, he graduated from Lenana with a Division One of 9 points. Since he had gravitated towards the sciences, he found admission at Mang'u High School in Thika, where he was to study for his 'A' levels.

While in Mang'u, he played hockey. Ben had also come to like rugby, which he had started playing while at Lenana School, but the game was not played at Mang'u. "I even noticed that the students had never seen a rugby ball. So, I convinced the headmaster to buy one with which I trained a group of students in the game.

"Nevertheless, Mang'u students were so studious that they had little interest in sports. We lived a 'triangle' form of life where we left the dormitory, went to have meals, then went to the classroom and back to the dormitory every day. Only a small fraction played the available games – basketball, football and hockey. As rugby was not available at Mang'u, I had settled for hockey."

The school hockey team would often play against other schools and this is how he met Njoroge who was a the hockey captain at Chania High School. Ben was the hockey assistant captain of Mang'u.

Ben tried to change the sporting situation by getting a few teachers interested in these sports. These were the teachers who always had been keen on sports but had been discouraged from organising students for the various games, as they had never seen them take an interest. Perhaps this was due to pressure from their families to do well in academics. "After my initiative, a lot of students ended up taking an interest in sports and still maintained good results, proving that life was not just about books," says Ben. The problem seemed to have been transmitted to the present education system where there is too much focus on passing exams.

When it came to selection of careers to pursue at the university, Ben chose medicine out of peer pressure. "At the time I joined university, out of 150 students who were enrolled for medicine. Fifty were from Mang'u. Being renowned as a science school, little did students know that one can also do other courses like commerce. All they knew was engineering and medicine," says Ben.

"After two months, I dropped medicine because I didn't like the course. I met and consulted many people who had done these professional courses, some of whom told me that given a chance they would have chosen something else. Those who were lucky managed to dò their preferred degrees later in life but this is not what I wanted.

"Right from primary school, my mind had been business-oriented. In our neighbourhood in Nairobi I had witnessed how one Indian family was doing very well while an equally brilliant group of civil servants consisting of professionals like engineers was struggling in life within the same neighbourhood. From my observation, I thought going into business would make my life easier."

After dropping medicine Ben enrolled for a Bachelor of Pharmacy course which Njoroge was also taking. "My father was very upset, which resulted in a bitter exchange of words between us. Like many parents, my father wanted to boast that there was a doctor in the family! I actually wanted to do Bachelor of Commerce, but my father had said that the only way he was going to allow me to drop medicine was if I stayed in the Faculty of Medicine. This is how I ended up doing pharmacy," recalls Ben.

What Ben did not like about medicine then was the pressure that was put on students. "I found the pressure to do too much in a short time worse than in military discipline. It was a system where lecturers thought that we students could never be cleverer than them and communication between them and us was one way. The handling of students in a course like medicine needs to be slightly different because of all the stress under which people work. Students need to be given some level of flexibility at certain ages especially at the university level," says Ben.

Upon completion of the course, Ben knew he had to go through the mandatory internship period of three months at a government institution. He had nevertheless made up his mind to join the private sector immediately afterwards. He had no intention of staying in the civil service.

Njoroge's early childhood and education

Njoroge Keige was born in 1966 in Kandara, Murang'a County, the fourth born in a family of ten children, five boys and five girls. His father worked as an estate manager in the coffee farms while his mother took care of their seven-acre farm where they grew coffee and subsistence crops like maize, beans and potatoes. "I had a typical rural childhood where one started working on family *shambas*[24] at an early age, and herding the cows and cutting grass to feed them among other chores," says Njoroge.

When he reached school-going age, he attended Rukira Primary School which was a walking distance from his home. "In the morning I would wake up and milk the cows, feed them, go to school, come home for lunch and do a quick chore before going back to school. In the evening, I would attend to various duties before doing my homework at night," he says.

"In those days a lot of families could not afford shoes for their children, so I went to school barefoot and only wore shoes on Sundays," remembers Njoroge. He used to get into a lot of fights because he hated being ridiculed and would fight back. They also had the usual sibling rivalry but were close nonetheless. "We would have our fights but basically we would take care of each other. There was also that hierarchy in our family that we respected and a sense of responsibility always prevailed." Njoroge also recalls that the family had a bicycle which he loved to ride.

Being an estate manager, Njoroge's father worked in the coffee farm where he was employed during the week and came home on weekends. It is his mother who handled the day-to-day affairs of the home. Although she was strict, their father was the disciplinarian. "While my mum would beat us if we did something wrong, she still would defer the offence to be reported to father when he came home on Saturday. So we would be punished twice."

Njoroge's father was also very strict when it came to his children's education. They would get a beating if they got poor results in school, which must have paid off because all Njoroge's siblings made it to university. "There were no two ways about it – you either learnt or learnt. As a result, our family became the most educated in the village."

Upon completing the primary level, Njoroge went to Thika High School for

24   A *shamba* is a typical household garden usually used to provide subsistence for a family, especially food.

his secondary education, one of the best schools in Kenya at the time. It was a boarding school. "There was a good environment; discipline and education were taken very seriously, which gave me a good background." When the 'O' level examinations were announced, he came out among the top students who attained good results in the school. He had also behaved himself most of the time.

For his 'A' levels, Njoroge went to Chania High School also in Thika and near his home area. It was while at high school that Njoroge met Ben. As Njoroge recounts, "We both played hockey and we would meet as competitors. We first met in 1983 when he was the hockey assistant captain of Mang'u High School and I was the captain at Chania. In those days Thika High and Mang'u were at par and sometimes Thika would beat Mang'u in the 'A' level exams. Standards went down after we left."

The coming together of Ben and Njoroge

Upon completion of his 'A' levels in 1984, Njoroge got a clerical job at the Coffee Board of Kenya (CBK). Coincidentally, Ben also got a job at the same place. This not only cemented their friendship, but it also sealed their fate. What happened was that Njoroge got a job first at the CBK and told Ben about it. "I also got a job at CBK, but when I reported for work, I was made to carry *gunias* (sacks) half the morning yet I had been employed as a clerk. I resolved not to come back the next day but not without reporting the incident first. At around noon I was called and informed that there had been a mistake," says Ben. Therefore, he continued with the work.

That is how Ben's and Njoroge's paths converged at the Coffee Board of Kenya. They gravitated towards each other mainly due to their age; "We were the only two youngsters who had joined the CBK that year after 'A' level. The other workers were either graduates (who were very few) or clerks who had worked there for years," says Njoroge.

After almost two years at CBK, they were both admitted to the Faculty of Medicine at the University of Nairobi in 1986. As fate would have it, they both ended up studying for a Bachelor of Pharmacy degree.

By that time, the government had made it mandatory for anyone joining university to undergo basic military training at the National Youth Service (NYS). Subsequently, Ben left CBK earlier to join the training. Njoroge was exempted from the training due to a medical condition. He was to join Ben later at the university after the training.

"At the university we had a lot of fun. We were the clowns of the class; we were considered not to be serious students," says Ben. They worked together at the Nairobi University Pharmacy Students Association where Njoroge was the chairman and Ben was the editor of the student magazine. They mainly worked together soliciting advertisements from various companies.

Their studies were interrupted midstream when the university was closed for an extended period of time as a result of a riot. During this period Njoroge, Ben and another friend tried their hand at business. The plan was that Ben would bring bananas from Kisii where he was born and the trio would sell them at Wakulima Market in Nairobi.[25] They burnt their fingers in this first venture.

When Ben and his two colleagues took the bananas to Wakulima Market, the buyers knew that these new traders were young and green in the business, as they did not seem to understand the market. "The traders only bought a few of the bananas and told us that they would return the next day when the prices would have gone down. This sent me and my colleagues into a panic and we had to make a quick decision. We decided to sell the rest of the bananas at a throwaway price. What we got from this sale did not even cover our investment. It is only later that we came to learn our mistake. In the first place, we should have realised that green bananas could keep for a few days so they could not have got spoilt overnight. However, the logistics would have been tricky for us because if we left them overnight we would have had to hire a guard," says Ben.

After this fiasco they called it quits. "We were relying on our savings and a bit of 'boom'[26]; we were left broke. Thus, we did not do another trip," adds Njoroge.

Ben and Njoroge graduated from the university in June 1990 and went to do their internship in separate places. Njoroge did his internship in Nairobi while Ben went to Kakamega. The one year internship was structured such that trainees did three months each in a hospital, the industry and a retail pharmacy. Njoroge first worked at Kenyatta National Hospital then Kam Pharmacy and then SmithKline Beecham (now called GSK). After that he worked with the government and was posted to the Drug Analysis Research Unit. "Work at the unit mostly involved random inspections of drugs from companies that had tendered to supply the government. We analysed them to establish whether they met the required specifications," says Njoroge.

At his civil service posting, he was in job group K earning around KSh 7,000 a month. While working, he shared a one-bedroomed house with his, late brother Peter Keige, who was a lecturer at the University of Nairobi's Lower

---

25 Wakulima Market is the largest fresh-produce retail and wholesale outlet in Nairobi where fruits, vegetables and cereals are traded from all over the country.

26 Boom was the term used to refer to the student subsistence allowance that was paid every semester.

Kabete Campus. Life in employment was very different from the previous one of luxury at the university where students got an allowance (boom) and ate well. "At the university, we ate sausages, eggs, bread, with plenty of butter and jam, and washed our hands with hot coffee after eating chicken. Students would argue, 'Why go to the room to look for soap when the coffee is just here?' When I started working, I realised that I could not afford the kind of life I was living in college. A bit of readjustment was necessary, which was not so easy," says Njoroge.

Njoroge found the analyst's job boring and quit after a year. Fortunately, a friend who was working in a retail pharmacy situated along Jogoo Road in Nairobi got a job with a multinational company thereby creating a vacancy at the shop. He tipped Njoroge about the vacancy. Njoroge walked in one day and asked for the job and was hired at a salary of around KSh 16,000 per month. "I found this new job a little more interesting because people with many different problems would come to consult me. Then, I would dispense medicine. Basically I was in charge of operations at the pharmacy as the owner was not there most of the time," says Njoroge. This involved ordering the drugs, checking the accounts and managing the seven employees. He stayed a year and left when they started their company.

While working at the pharmacy, Njoroge was also running a small stationery shop that he had inherited from his sister who had left the country for Germany soon after Njoroge graduated from the university. She had since got married there and asked him to look after the business situated along Kirinyaga Road in Nairobi. "That shop still runs and mostly supplies Omaera and a few other related companies," says Njoroge.

Meanwhile, Ben was posted to Kakamega Provincial Hospital for six months for his internship. During this time, he also did locums on weekends. After the internship, he moved to ET Monks, a retail pharmacy in Nairobi, and then he moved to GSK. After getting registered as a pharmacist in 1991 he worked for about a year at a retail pharmacy in Nairobi on a net monthly salary of KSh 16,000. His daily duties involved dispensing medicines and giving advice to customers.

"I used to like marketing, so I left and joined Servier International, a French pharmaceutical company, as a medical representative," recalls Ben. At the time, he was living with his brother in Umoja.

Birth of Omaera Pharmaceuticals

"When I went to work for the French company, I had started actualising the idea of starting a pharmacy and was looking for money. There was a graduate loan scheme being offered by Pan African Bank followed thereafter by Kenya

Commercial Bank (KCB). One applicant would get KSh 150,000; two or more applicants would be given KSh 350,000. I applied to KCB," says Ben.

Having been with Njoroge and seeing what kind of a person and how hard-working he was, Ben approached him. "I told him that I had already registered the name and all we needed to do was to get the money. With assistance from my sister and Njoroge's brother (the university lecturer), we got the business plan done and all the paperwork prepared," remembers Ben. They also modified the earlier application that Ben had done to reflect the new 50:50 ownership.

"Preparing the business plan was tough because business or cash flow projections were not taught in pharmacy school. In fact, it is my late brother – an accounts lecturer, who helped us on those aspects," says Njoroge.

As the money was too little for them to afford the steep rents and goodwill within the city centre, they opened a pharmacy in Ngumo, a middle class residential estate near Kenyatta Market off Mbagathi Road in Nairobi in January 1993. The pharmacy was situated opposite Shadrack Kimalel Primary School. "Although it was a small room, we conformed to pharmacy rules which dictate that one must create a dispensary where prescription drugs are kept. Therefore, we had the premises renovated to create another room inside," says Njoroge.

The location of the business eventually turned out to be their biggest disadvantage. They had bought stock in 1992 on the eve of the general election, an uncertain time. However, they were determined to go ahead and start the business.

"Fortunately, this loan had no collateral involved such that if the worst came to the worst the bank could not attach anything from us," says Ben. Although this made them brave to face risks, they had no intention of defaulting in the manner some people who had taken the same loans a few months earlier had done after they misused the money. Ben and Njoroge had been warned by the bank not to do the same. "All the same, we were driven by determination to succeed even though we did not have business training.

"For the next four years, we never took a holiday. Instead, we focused all our energies on the business. As luck would have it, prices went up in the first three months of 1993 because of inflation. This really helped us because our stock almost tripled in value," says Ben.

Both partners were still employed when they started the business. Initially they hired a Form Four school leaver to stay in the shop during the day. Then they would take over in the evenings and weekends. Sometimes their siblings would help. However, this arrangement did not last. "We noticed a pattern where whenever we were not at the shop, the sales would be very low. Once in a while one of us would pass by the shop in the middle of the day only to find the assistant sitting on a stool outside the shop knitting," recalls Ben. That is when they realised that they needed to be in the business full-time.

However, the business was still so small that it could not support both of them. Njoroge was the first to resign from his job to run their business. He had been having some problems at the chemist where he was working and was ready to leave. Ben narrates, "Some drugs went missing and the boss could not find the culprit; so he decided to cut everyone's salary to cover the loss. Njoroge refused to have his salary deducted and he consequently left. He then consulted me and we discussed our business. In the end, we both agreed that the way we were running our retail chemist it was heading nowhere – notwithstanding the fact that it was starting to show signs of improvement. If we were to grow, we needed a professional who was also hard-working to run it," says Ben. Thus, Njoroge went to run the shop.

While Njoroge was running the business, Ben continued working for Servier International; as he was earning more, they agreed that he would stay in employment. "Initially the business could not even pay me what I had been earning at my previous job. It could only pay me KSh 8,000. Therefore, the initial months in the business were really about survival," says Njoroge.

During this time, the two partners worked from 8.00 am to 10.00 pm seven days a week to get the business running. Even then, the sales were pretty low. With this kind of schedule they had no social life either and in any case every spare cent went into the business. "We tried to sensitise people about our presence in the market by giving out leaflets at the nearby bus stop, but the pickup was very slow. Moreover, the location was a disadvantage because the pharmacy was actually facing the Kibera slum and was a distance from the nearest shopping centre (Kenyatta Market) where there was traffic," says Njoroge.

"Already we had started paying the principle on the loan. A point reached where we realised that these repayments, as well as the usual business expenses like rent and telephone bills, would start eating into the stock. These difficulties forced us to rethink our initial strategy of focusing purely on the retail trade. Therefore, we decided to try wholesaling after a few months. We had to think of diversifying," says Njoroge. They went into wholesaling starting on a very small scale with just three or four products which they would sell to other chemists.

"As a company, we were not known in the market, so we first targeted friends and former classmates. We had to persuade them to buy from our business since they were already established and didn't really need to buy from us," says Njoroge.

In the wholesale business, the margins were razor-thin as they had to sell at the same price as those who supplied to their clients. However, the wholesale trade had the potential of much higher volumes than retail. As he went about his employment duties, Ben used the opportunity to start approaching institutions where they could supply drugs. "We were targeting institutional clinics which stocked large amounts of medicines. Our first customers were staff clinics for Barclays Bank and Serena Hotel," says Njoroge.

When they got their first order from Barclays Bank staff clinic for KSh 80,000 they were excited. But getting credit to fulfil the order became another hurdle that they had to overcome. "While we could afford to buy a little quantity of a single item, to supply a wholesale client with the little money we had been earning from retail sales, KSh 80,000 was almost our entire cash flow. We just could not afford it. This is when we realised that friends and money do not always mix," says Njoroge.

He continues, "We started approaching friends after KCB refused to fund us insisting that we should provide security. For the earlier loan, KCB had been given a grant from the Government of Kenya to cover it; so there was no risk to them if anyone defaulted. In any case even if we had the security it could not be charged in the 3–4 days deadline that Barclays Bank clinic had given us to supply the drugs. KCB suggested that we should ask Barclays to write a letter indicating they would pay KCB directly. However, this being our first big order we did not want to start involving the customer," says Njoroge.

That's when they decided to involve friends. Many of the friends they approached turned them down despite showing them the LPO, which indicated that they would be paid in two weeks. Nevertheless, they finally got money from some friends until they had the entire amount.

After this experience, they became real wholesalers because the company that had supplied the order recognised them. "When you buy a large quantity like that the company recognises you; the next time they would be willing to give you a day or two of credit period," says Njoroge. Although they had now started proper wholesaling it was still very difficult because they had to buy most of their supplies in cash. The pharmaceutical industry is credit-based with an average period of 60 days, so buying supplies in cash and having to wait for payment created cash flow problems. "At one point, we would run out of money and had to stop buying until someone paid. This balancing was very tricky," says Njoroge.

"We started marketing ourselves aggressively to suppliers, showing them that we were worth taking a risk on and giving them our history. Fortunately, a few listened and one of the main ones was to become our biggest competitor. He was the first one to really give us a reasonable amount of credit thereby taking a big risk."

Normally, institutional orders contained a wide variety of drugs from different pharmaceutical companies and whenever they got the order they had to supply everything in the LPO. But when dealing with chemists they decided to specialise; they would only market the products of the manufacturers and suppliers who agreed to give them credit. This is how their business started growing. "One relationship would lead to another and as we approached new companies we would use our existing suppliers as references for our payment history. Slowly we started creating a name. We created trust among our suppliers and with time most companies were willing to give us credit," says Njoroge.

By then Ben had come into the business full time. What prompted his decision to join the business was that big orders had started coming in. He was now needed at the Ngumo shop where Njoroge had only one employee to assist him. "One time we got a very big consignment. When Njoroge and an employee were busy receiving the goods, the delivery person took one carton back. We only realised that a carton was missing in the evening when we were both doing the reconciliations. Thus, with the business showing signs of picking, we thought it would be more prudent if both of us were there," says Njoroge.

When a business is small everything is at one's fingertips because they are involved in everything. Prices of any product, costs of anything from the telephone to the soap used in the washroom were all in the head. Hence, doing paperwork was another big issue. "Although we compiled our cash positions and sales on a daily basis, we were not really sure if we were making a profit. We knew the basics of trying to calculate our sales every single day, but we were not accountants. We needed someone to crunch the numbers and come up with a profit and loss statement. Moreover, we were so busy with the business that we would do the paperwork from 10.00 pm after we had closed the shop. We would then try and balance invoices so that we could demand the correct payments from clients," says Njoroge.

Generally, the first two years of the business were very difficult in terms of finance and also lack of a social life. "I remember my girlfriend used to take my shirts with a torn collar to a tailor at Kenyatta Market to turn them inside out so that I could get another six months out of them. Buying new clothes then was completely out of the question," says Njoroge.

Despite being perpetually broke, giving up was never an option. "It was a struggle but we also had fun. When you get into wholesaling, even if you only stock one product, the whole shop looks full. Interestingly this attracted customers to the shop. People in Ngumo estate used to buy drugs from town, but when they started seeing delivery vans coming and delivering several cartons at the shop, they started coming in," says Njoroge.

As the business grew, Ben and Njoroge applied for a second telephone line to handle the volume of wholesale business. "Interestingly enough, retail customers who previously would be very impatient when we were doing very little business and had all the time to serve them were now willing to wait as we took wholesale orders over the phone," says Njoroge. In this way the retail side of the business also picked up.

The wholesale business was also boosted by crises in the neighbouring countries. "We found ourselves doing a lot of supplies to NGOs in Rwanda and Somalia in addition to our regular customers. This helped us to pay the KSh 350,000 loan faster. It was a five-year loan, but we repaid it in three years," says Ben.

Financing continued to be a big problem, but was especially acute at the beginning. This is when Ben and Njoroge approached many banks for possible financing arrangements with no luck. "No bank was willing to listen to us without collateral," says Njoroge. It was not until 1995, two years after they started, that they were able to get a bank loan. That is when they heard about a product from Barclays Bank run under the Overseas Development Agency (ODA) programme which had given a guarantee to the bank. In this facility, borrowers got double of what they deposited in cash, treasury bills or any other facility in the bank. Ben and Njoroge deposited a cash cover of KSh 2 million with the bank and got a KSh 4 million loan. "It was not as good as what we would have wanted, but the bank had still funded us to the tune of KSh 2 million. It was a turning point for the business because we hired more employees – accountants, delivery people and sales people," says Njoroge.

One of the conditions of the Barclays Bank loan was that they undergo training. This was a godsend opportunity because it was one of the areas where they had major challenges, especially in the area of finance. "As pharmacists we were running the business using common sense. We had no training in financial management. All we knew was that you had to balance your money somehow. Ben would carry some of the books and I would carry others; we would check all the invoice books and do manual totalling to make sure that the sales figure the accountant gave us was correct," says Njoroge. Thus, they went for the training from which they benefitted greatly; it was an eye-opener for them and it made them appreciate the value of training.

This training was being facilitated by Kenya Management Assistance Programme (K-MAP) which was established in 1986 to assist small and medium enterprises (SMEs) by tapping into the human resources of large- and medium-scale businesses based in Kenya in the form of technical and managerial training and counselling. It was the brainchild of Victor Pratt, a Kenyan-based entrepreneur, who believed that successful businesses should assist small and fledgling enterprises to develop and grow. "The training covered all the areas in a small business with emphasis on control systems because this is the main reason why many businesses collapse. Other areas that the training covered were marketing, structuring of an organisation, running a finance department by a non-financial expert, and financial reporting structures," narrates Njoroge.

The aspect on financial reporting structures was particularly important. "We used to have accountants who would still not have given us the profit and loss statement by the 20th of the month citing the fact that there was so much work. As we were also very busy, we believed them. However, during the training we were told that if an accountant was not giving reports by the 5th of the following month, then they were not doing their work," says Njoroge.

Another benefit of the training was that it made them realise that so many other businesses were facing similar challenges. "We came across people of all ages and status. Some of them were in their 60s with considerably old businesses, but had been running them wrongly for all those years. However, because they were so hands-on in their management of cash, their businesses had managed to survive," says Njoroge.

Immediately after the training, they sponsored a customer service course for their staff. They also hired a consultant to restructure their finance department. The finance staff agreed on targets with the consultant, but they could not achieve them over a three-month period. Ultimately they fired them and hired new staff.

Rapid growth of Omaera

From 1995, the business grew very fast. In 1997 the company grew fourfold as a result of accurately identifying and serving a niche that turned out to be very lucrative. "We wanted to come in and stabilise prices in a small way and help other pharmacy graduates who had difficulty accessing credit like we had experienced when we were starting. Thus, we negotiated with our suppliers to give their small businesses credit. These small businesses were the ones that helped us to achieve rapid growth," says Ben.

"Once the wholesale business took off, the growth was very rapid. We ended up occupying the entire basement in the Ngumo shop until we outgrew the premises. The location was also not convenient in terms of parking space for the delivery trucks. Thus, we moved to Tom Mboya Street in the city centre," explains Njoroge.

The location where they chose had a backstreet with a back entrance where they could receive goods. The premises had 4,000 square feet of space. They used the same concept where part of the downstairs was a retail shop and the rest were offices. Upstairs was the store. They had also computerised their systems before they moved from Ngumo. It was a first among the general wholesalers because some of our competitors were ten times bigger than us and had been in the industry longer but had not yet computerised," says Njoroge.

Computerisation would achieve two main goals: first it reduced the mountains of paperwork and, secondly, it reduced pilferage. The latter is one of the biggest problems in the industry even today. "By having inventory online you could check stock in real time. Before computerisation it would take at least a day before we knew that we had lost an item in order to start investigating. With the new system we cut this lead time. On the accounting side, immediately we invoiced a customer, our balance went up by that amount which was faster than maintaining ledgers manually," says Njoroge.

Ben and Njoroge had been trying to get the right accounting software without success. Dorcas, Njoroge's wife, who had an Information Communications Technology (ICT) background came into the business to assist them. "She had more knowledge in the field; so it was easier to choose the appropriate package," says Njoroge. Ben's wife, Lillian, also came in at the same time and took charge of their stores.

The entry of their spouses into the business was timely. Omaera Pharmaceuticals had started countrywide operations which meant that Njoroge and Ben would spend a lot of time in the field marketing. Thus, says Ben, "We needed people we could trust to take care of the back end of the business."

Before joining Omaera Pharmaceuticals as IT manager, Dorcas taught for some time in Nyeri after graduating from Kenyatta University and then joined the insurance industry. She relocated to Nairobi when she married Njoroge. Lillian was also a trained teacher and became the stores and warehousing manager at Omaera. The original plan had been to bring in the two spouses to continue running the Ngumo retail office once Ben and Njoroge shifted their base to the city centre. However, this plan changed as there were bigger challenges in the Tom Mboya office and they had to move there.

Knowing the pitfalls of family businesses, the four of them had a session before their wives formally joined the business. This session was to discuss how to separate work from personal affairs and to clearly define the role of each spouse in the company. As Njoroge explains: "We were very focused when they were coming in; the four of us sat down to agree on the basic rules about separating social life from the business, that when we meet in the office we stay focused on the work no matter what else is going on. We made them understand that Ben and I were retaining the positions of directors and they were coming in as employees. We tried to discuss in advance the dangers that we thought would come like petty jealousies because we had seen other businesses go haywire when the spouses came in."

After this first meeting they had several others to discuss the issue of staying focused on the business. The arrangement worked quite well although there were some instances where the wives would compete creating minor disagreements. Dorcas eventually left the business and went to start her own business of selling clothes. She also takes care of some other family interests like real estate. Ben's wife Lillian is still working at Omaera.

Moving into the city centre helped the business in several ways. One, they benefited from walk-in retail customers and, two, they were now taken more seriously as a business, partly as a result of achieving a long sought-after goal of getting the GSK business just before they moved to Tom Mboya Street. GSK is the biggest pharmaceutical company in Kenya and Omaera was getting their drugs through the top GSK distributor. "To improve margins and compete against others we needed to get the drugs directly from GSK. As long as we couldn't do that, we were still perceived as small players in the industry," says Njoroge.

Moreover, Omaera customers also challenged them saying if they got the GSK business then they would buy everything from them; they would not be forced to buy GSK's products from other distributors who gave them the best deal because they were direct distributors. "Although GSK had enough distributors and were not keen on getting more, we had to get that account and join the big boys' league so as to be taken seriously in the market," says Njoroge. When conventional methods of getting the business failed, such as booking appointments and meeting with finance managers, we tried the social route through a members' club. Thus, they joined the club where the Managing Director was a member.

At the Tom Mboya office, the focus of the business shifted to countrywide marketing. Eventually, Omaera was selling drugs all over Kenya. In 1995, Ben and Njoroge had opened a branch in Mombasa called Omaera Pharmaceuticals Mombasa Limited but it did not pick. "The business was not run well. We got into a lot of debts. Thus, we had to close shop," says Ben. A year later they opened another retail branch in Ukunda at the South Coast to exploit the tourism business.

"Normally business owners get a lot of pressure from family members who want to join their companies. We were no exception. We experienced such pressure at a time when we were still developing our working relationship. So we thought it better to keep the family members at arm's length but still support them," says Ben. Hence they opened individual retail pharmacies for this purpose – to help their families; Ben's was in Kisii and Njoroge's was in Juja, which he later moved to Gatundu. However, the main business would always take priority. Each of them could get a large order and use their personal pharmacies to do the business, but they were aware that if they did, ultimately the core business will fail and both of them will lose out.

To revive their business at the South Coast, which had been seriously affected by the Likoni clashes in 1997, they partnered with another pharmacist based in Mombasa called Dr Mwasi. "He grew the company progressively as a separate distribution business. However, the margins from the business were not so much and we considered the possibility of setting up branches," says Ben.

At the time, they had outgrown what their bank could give them in terms of financing. So they started shopping for another bank. The new bank still insisted on security which they were unable to provide. For them to provide security it meant removing the money from the business to go and buy a house or land in a good area in Nairobi which then the bank would discount downwards. What would be the point?

In 1998, they moved their head office from Tom Mboya Street to the third floor of Paramount Plaza near Globe Cinema roundabout. The premises had become too small and there were also security concerns. Their new office premises was 5,000 square feet of space. A year later in 2000 they expanded and took the entire first floor. By then they had 50 employees in Nairobi (with 40 at the factory) and 25 in Mombasa. Two years later saw major expansion of their retail network across the country and they both opened personal pharmacies in more towns during this period.

In the coast region Omaera has branches in Mombasa, Ukunda, Voi, Mariakani, Mtwapa, Kilifi and Malindi. The Ngumo branch in Nairobi is still in operation, which complements the head office in Nairobi. Other towns where Omaera branches are include Meru, Nyeri, Nanyuki, Gatundu, Kisii, Sotik, Bomet and Kisumu. In some of these towns there are also the pharmacies owned by the two partners as individuals. The company has a client base of over 2,500 that includes staff clinics, hospitals, chemists, government and large retail chains.

In Dar es Salaam the company has a business called Add Value African Investments which started in 1998. It deals with importation and distribution in Tanzania. After the year 2000, it diversified into surgical and medical equipment. The core business however is still pharmaceuticals distribution and retail, which brings in 85 percent of the revenue.

Diversifying into manufacturing

In 1996, Ben and Njoroge went into manufacturing. They reckoned that, although generics had acquired a bad name and were associated with poor quality and counterfeit drugs, they were a very affordable alternative for poor people in Africa who cannot afford patented drugs. As an example, many people are aware that Panadol, a popular pain killer is a paracetamol. "A tablet costs KSh 5. I can manufacture a tin of 1,000 paracetamol tablets and sell it in the market for KSh 200, which means that the cost of producing each tablet is 20 cents. This makes it far cheaper than the popular drug and I would still be making money," says Ben.

He further explains: "What the big pharmaceutical companies do is to initially claim a premium for the research they carried out to create the drug. Thereafter, however, the price never really comes down even when the patent expires. By the time the patent expires, and sometimes it can be as long as 15 years, they've not only recouped their research costs, but have also made a lot of profit." During the patent period no one else is allowed to manufacture the drug.

For the manufacturing line, Ben and Njoroge formed a new company called Sphinx Pharmaceuticals Limited. They brought in a friend called Dr Kopiyo who had experience in production and had a similar work ethic to theirs. They also brought on board another couple as investors. The bulk of the financing for putting up the manufacturing plant came from the distribution operation. "We had to sacrifice once more and didn't pay ourselves dividends in order to grow the company," says Ben. In the first year, the factory did the repackaging of products such as glycerin and surgical spirit. In the second year it started producing oral syrups. Then they started branding some of their premium products like cough syrups, nutritional supplements (nutrition is a big problem in Africa), antibiotics, anti-malarial drugs and veterinary products.

Manufacturing had its challenges, the main one being getting qualified people with the required production skills. "People will have the relevant academic papers but on the ground they can't produce the way you want. To keep costs low you have to manage the process very well, which requires people who are meticulous in their work and who can follow a precise formula every time. For example, if a product has to go through 10 processes and nine of them are done correctly but someone does one step incorrectly, either due to laziness or haste, the product is wasted and this costs the company money. Such an error could be as simple as cooling or heating ingredients at the wrong temperature or stirring the mixture for 15 minutes instead of 20," explains Ben.

Company and management structure

At the top of the company management structure are Ben and Njoroge. They are directors and are also involved in the day-to-day management of the company. They alternate in various stations. "When one partner is in head office, the other is at the factory, in the field checking operations and visiting customers, or in Tanzania," says Ben. The main role of the two directors is to focus on problems and find solutions.

Under them are five departmental heads who report to the general manager. These departments are: Warehousing and Distribution, Information Technology (IT), Accounts, Marketing, and Sales. Each department head has an assistant. The Sales Department normally handles local orders, while Marketing deals with importation of products from various companies worldwide. The role of Marketing is to create demand for these products in order to increase margins. They comprise the medical reps who visit doctors and buyers in institutions to highlight unique features of products and create awareness so that the doctors can prescribe the drugs to their patients. In total the company has 170 employees.

Ben and Njoroge share similar views when it comes to management and this is one of the main reasons their partnership has thrived. Theirs is one of the few cases where friends have managed to succeed in business and worked in a partnership while their friendship has remained intact. "We both appreciate that a business has to have control systems and that people should be hired based on competency; that is, not because you know them or they are relatives or friends," says Njoroge.

He further explains: "From the very beginning we both drew a salary which most business people do not do. This is because we knew the importance of not mixing personal and business money," says Njoroge. "We draw the line and keep social affairs out of the office. However, sometimes we would end up mixing the two because during our formative years we were always together; we used to socialise together and go to the same parties; our business and social lives were intertwined. In addition, our families are good friends, but when we are in the office business takes precedence."

Business challenges

Usually, pharmacists would be employed for years and only start their own pharmacies after they had accumulated enough money to buy a delivery van and hire people to do the manual work of delivering cartons to customers. Ben and Njoroge had no vehicle at the beginning and would deliver cartons of drugs in *matatus*. This was a main challenge especially when many of their peers expressed scepticism about their business. Nevertheless, they carried on determined to make their business work.

Some people also tried to sow seeds of suspicion between them with a view to turning the two partners against each other, especially because they were from different ethnic groups. "People would find me somewhere carrying goods and instead of finding out what I was doing, they would call Ben and ask him if he was aware of where I was. The same thing would also happen when Ben was out making deliveries," recalls Njoroge. But the partners stayed focused. With trust, which is the main thing that has held them together, they could not be separated. As Ben observes, "A partnership is like a marriage and some people will say negative things. The only way to keep it intact is to think positive about your partner."

Division of labour has also been a challenge. Both partners do not have specific roles; none of them is responsible for a specific part of the business. During the early days, if a delivery needed to be made and one person was out, the other just did it. "Even with the growth of business, we just continue to do what needs to be done on a day-to-day basis. Although Ben is good in marketing and I am better at numbers and control systems, it doesn't mean that I won't do the marketing if it's required," says Njoroge.

Managing cash flow has been a permanent problem because some clients always take advantage of the credit period. Others take advantage of disasters and political instability to delay or default on payments. An example is the post-election violence that rocked the country early in 2008 when some customers used it as a reason for not paying even when their businesses had gone back to normal. "But it is the competitiveness in the industry that fuels this indiscipline," says Ben, "if you do not give customers credit, they will go somewhere else. We tried setting up a local association, Kenya Pharmaceutical Distributors Association (KPDA), with the aim of exchanging information on who owes what and who is becoming a bad debtor. However, it did not succeed in its initial role."

The future of the business

Their vision is to make Omaera a very strong player in the region. In effect, they plan to build a retail pharmacy chain in the region. They are also exploring other areas in the health care industry which they can get into. In the long run, they plan to separate ownership from the management of the business and empower their managers. The second step is to list the company at the Nairobi Securities Exchange. Ben plans to go into semi-retirement by the age of 50 and by that time he will gradually get out of the day-to-day running of the business. "At this stage, it is critical for me to prepare a strong management team so that we just talk numbers and the expansion of the business," says Ben.

While their children can work in the company, they will not automatically manage it. "By the time the children are ready for management roles, the business will have moved to the next stage (of separating shareholding and management) and the position at the top will not necessarily be occupied by a shareholder or pharmacist," both Ben and Njoroge aver. And if any of their children does a business course, it will not be automatic that they get the top job. They would have to compete with everybody else and prove themselves. Their decision is based on the realisation that family-owned businesses have limitations; children usually have a very different approach to it.

To get more lucrative tenders from donors, government and international NGOs, which buy huge volumes of drugs and equipment, they plan to expand their manufacturing operations by putting up a state-of-the-art factory in Athi River where they own a 10-acre piece of land. A strategic partnership with an established, more experienced international firm, where they sell a stake in Sphinx Pharmaceuticals Limited, is also an option that they are exploring.

Marriage and family

Njoroge met his wife Dorcas Ndugi while in his fourth year at the university when the 1989 national census was being done. Njoroge was employed as an enumerator and Dorcas, who was then in her first year at Kenyatta University (KU) doing a degree in education, was a supervisor. The couple has three children aged 14, 10 and 6 years.

Best and worst moments

According to Ben, his highest achievement is bringing together shareholders of diverse backgrounds and different ethnic groups to work together and build a successful business. His worst failure is when he lost millions in a garment-manufacturing company in the Export Processing Zone (EPZ) Mombasa, a business he had got into with four friends including Fred Rabongo, founder of Impulse Promotions (see Chapter 10). "When we lost the money, we were trying to export textiles to the US under the African Growth and Opportunity Act (AGOA) trade agreement," says Ben.

Tips for aspiring entrepreneurs

Ben and Njoroge have braved all obstacles to establish one of the most successful business partnerships as well as pharmaceutical enterprises in Kenya. As they share the secrets of their success, they also offer a few tips to budding and aspiring entrepreneurs. One of them is developing an idea sufficiently of the kind of business one intends to venture into. Njoroge reiterates the importance of focusing on the business idea and working hard to achieve the set goals. Ben particularly recommends that entrepreneurs should do feasibility studies before starting their business because this makes it easier to plan on how to exploit the existing opportunities in the industry: "You must have a fairly good idea of the business you want to get into because it forms the basis for managing the business. If you don't understand the underlying principles in terms of what opportunities exist, you may get into a field where opportunities are exhausted and the players so big that it makes no sense to take them on. Never stop working on the research and development part of your business because what you collect in research informs every move you make."

Financial discipline, honesty and hard work are all critical ingredients for success. Training for self and staff on the various aspects of the business (products and services) is also useful.

Ben also advises parents to listen to their children and assist them to achieve what they wish to undertake in life. As he observes, "Most parents are reluctant to let their children choose their own professions. What children hear out there is that so and so is a doctor or an engineer. But the person who did Bachelor of Arts (BA), who used to be looked down upon at the university, is the MD of the company."

On financing the business, Ben regrets that, "While the bank is expected to be your number one friend when you get into business, this is never or rarely the case. Banks only identify with successful people, not those on their way to success." Thus, he advises budding entrepreneurs to look for like-minded people and other sources like savings and credit societies (Saccos) to finance them.

Social activities

"When we were starting our business, we were young and had a lot of energy. For us three hours sleep in a day was enough. Soon we were registering success and started having just a little money which we could spend as individuals," says Njoroge. Due to the need to expand their business, they bought a second-hand car – a Toyota station wagon – which they used to make deliveries for the business and in the evening would use it when socialising. "When we went out together, depending on which side of town we ended up, the one whose house was furthest would drop the other and take the car," remembers Njoroge.

Njoroge still plays hockey socially and tries to play twice a week at the Nairobi Club where he is a member of the hockey team. He also does precision shooting for sport and used to compete. Nowadays, he does it more for fun. He previously tried golf but realised that he was not patient enough to walk for three hours. Ben's favourite holiday destination is South Africa. "Every year I take the children on holiday when they are on summer vacation between July and August. I prefer to take them to a different country every year for them to understand different cultures and become aware of how the rest of the world is," says Ben. Njoroge usually takes his holidays locally, visiting different parts of Kenya.

Role models

Ben's role model is Nelson Mandela because he forgave the people who took away his youth. He also handed over power voluntarily, a very rare thing in Africa. He also admires Bill Gates for revolutionalising an entire industry and Michael Joseph who also revolutionalised the telecommunication industry through the Safaricom network and has had a big impact on the growth of the Kenyan economy.

Chapter 8

Mogambi Mogaka

Whether it is Uhuru Superstores, Ouru Discount Centre or OuruPower Limited, one cannot miss out on this brand of low-price supermarkets that are to be found all over Nyanza and western Kenya. Using an American business model, the supermarket chain has grown from a single commodity to a multimillion business that is the pioneer in the concept of store brand ownership in Kenya. This highly successful concept is the brainchild of ZN Mogaka, popularly known as Mogambi.

Mogambi Mogaka, the youthful-looking towering Kisii businessman, picked the concept of store brand ownership from the United States where he studied and worked for more than a decade. This was a common business feature. In this concept, retailers negotiate with manufacturers to provide them with unbranded products which they in turn brand with their store names and sell at lower prices without hurting the original brand. Retailers do this to avoid the cost associated with big brands. Typically, in the pharmaceutical industry the concept comes in as generic drugs.

When Mogambi introduced this idea, it was well received in this part of rural Kenya judging from the overwhelming success of the Ouru chain stores. This has seen him spread his business tentacles into real estate where he takes pride in the ownership of some of the most prestigious commercial and residential apartments in Kisii town. To appreciate this success, one has to delve deep into Mogambi's life.

Early childhood and education

A second son to Joseph Mogaka and Priska K Mogaka, the enterprising Mogambi was born in 1956 and raised in a polygamous family among, sixteen other siblings. His father, originally a rural shopkeeper and a small-scale farmer, worked hard to ensure a modest upkeep for his large family. Typical of those days, amenities were at their basic. Things like shoes were a luxury that the first time Mogambi recalls wearing shoes was when it was an entry requirement at secondary school. The school uniform at primary school level comprised a single pair of hand-stitched clothes with the usual patches that he would put on for the whole week.

For his lower primary, Mogambi was enrolled at Ibacho DEB[27] Primary School in Kisii. During this time, there were no pre-primary schools. One just walked straight to Standard One. To determine whether a child was old enough for this class, they had to be subjected to a mandatory test of reaching for their left ear with the right hand over their head. All through lower primary school, Mogambi does not recall anything out of the ordinary that shaped his life other than the hard work and stringent discipline that he had to adhere to both at home and in school.

A typical day started early in the morning: plough the fields, pick pyrethrum, support in milking the cows, get the milk and head off to school, delivering milk along the way. At school, pupils had to do manual work that included cutting grass, tending flowers and sweeping the classes before settling down for the lessons. Class work was equally thorough, but it was appropriately balanced with extra-curricular activities such as physical education, music and games.

At midday, pupils would break for lunch and run the full distance home to prepare their own lunch. Lateness was not condoned. They had to be fast. This was difficult given that they relied on firewood for cooking as the use of cooking gas was not widespread. Surprisingly, this routine was to repeat itself during Mogaka's first year in college in the United States where his lessons ended at 12.30 pm and he had to report for work at 1.00 pm. This left him with only 30 minutes to rush to the cafeteria, grab his lunch and punch in for work. It was a typical military routine, lessons that he took early in life. He was never to spend more than 30 minutes break for lunch; in most cases there would be no break at all. It was only in high school where this was an exception, and later in his semi-retirement.

After school, Mogambi was expected to collect the empty milk containers, drop them home and head to the market centre where his father had a shop. Here, he took care of the household chores that included cleaning the house, preparing meals and fetching water from the river. This demanding routine progressively took a toll on his ambitions. Gradually, he developed low self esteem whereby he started thinking that he was not cut out for big things. Moreover, he had no role models in the village to look up to. The best person one could admire was a P1 teacher. In the circumstances, he easily resigned to the fate that the best he could become was a school teacher.

This resignation had a knock-on effect on Mogambi's class work. He came to accept that he was just another average human being with no special abilities and nothing much to offer in life. In fact, his father must have had more faith in him than he had, for he proposed that, for his Standard Five, he should

---

27   DEB refers to District Education Board and is used for schools that were founded by the now defunct district education boards with no religious sponsorship. In other words, they are public schools.

join St. Mary's Mosocho, one of the leading primary schools in the country. Mogambi went ahead and did the interview. Unfortunately, he was not admitted, which confirmed his ineptitude. He felt that he was a true failure. Deflated, he continued with his education at Ibacho.

With such low self esteem, Mogambi was not surprised when he twice failed the national examinations for his end of primary school in Standard Seven. Fortunately, his father still believed in him and got him another interview, this time at a missionary school, Kamagambo Mixed Adventist Secondary School in South Nyanza District. The interview was being done in Kisii town. He arrived for the interview early in the morning and noticed that there were hundreds of other students from all over the greater South Nyanza for the same interview. This scared him stiff. Looking at the crowd, he felt that his chances, if any, were indeed slim. Surprisingly, against all odds, he got admission to Kamagambo. This school was to forever change his life. It is where he experienced a paradigm shift.

Kamagambo Secondary proved to be a great learning experience for Mogambi. It was a beautiful school to behold, with well-tended gardens and manicured lawns. It had electricity, a borehole and tapped water. For once, there was no more fetching water from the river or reading under candle-lights. And the food too was great. While at home the meals consisted mainly of cooked maize meal (*ugali*) and vegetables, Kamagambo offered variety. Besides the normal diet, students had rice with beans, tea with a buttered slice of bread and potatoes with porridge (soup). They also had the popular *magira* for power – a meal of ground peanuts. For a villager like Mogambi, this was heaven. Being an Adventist school, Mogambi found Kamagambo too sensitive on religious matters, a setback for a person who was not very religious despite his mother taking him for Sabbath occasionally along with the other children. But he had to fit in.

The student community at Kamagambo came from all over East Africa. For the first time Mogambi had a chance to meet people from different communities in Kenya as well as others from Uganda, Tanzania and Burundi. For a while, he was not sure if he would fit in this diverse community or be able to compete academically. Being just a villager amongst these sophisticated urban dwellers was overwhelming. But he had little choice. For the next four years, this was to be his community. He had to learn how to interact with them, socially and academically. They played together, argued and sometimes fought. Somehow, through experience, he came to learn and appreciate their diversity. Paradoxically, their fears and Mogambi's were similar. They all wanted to do well and excel. In church, they were taught that they were 'one in Christ'. Eventually, he learnt to fit in.

The daily routine at Kamagambo was not different from what Mogambi had been used to from way back in primary school. They woke up at 5.00 am and started classes by 6.00 am. Morning lessons ended at 7.45 am when they would break for breakfast and resume classes at 8.45 am which ended at 12.00 pm. Manual work was from 2.00 pm to 3.30 pm. This included general cleanliness and maintenance of the compound. The school had a system where part of one's tuition was paid for by working. The boss, and every student had one, decided how much one would be paid per hour. Remuneration was based on output. There are those who earned more by working fewer hours while others had to work longer hours to earn equal pay. The hard-working students added less money for their tuition. According to Mogambi, this was a great programme which in hindsight he admires. "Incidentally, it's this system that I use in my business. At OuruPower, you earn based on your output," he adds. Naturally, as a student, he hated it.

One day, Mogambi's deskmate, PK Oroko (who was to become one of the country's top ophthalmologists practising in the UK), asked him, "What would you like to be after school?" Mogambi found this question odd since they were just in Form One and had three more years to go. Mogambi told him that he had not given it much thought. What he knew, though, was that he would do his best to get a Division Three, which would guarantee him an entry into a teaching college. In other words, he wanted to train as a teacher, for that is what he felt he could achieve.

A bemused Oroko graphically took his time to explain how he would spend a little more time studying at the university. After graduating with a degree, he explained, it would only take him six months to earn the amount Mogambi would have earned since leaving school at Form Four. Mathematically, this made a lot of sense; just a few more years in college and earn more money. Seriously though, Mogambi doubted if he had the pedigree to make it to university, let alone to do a profession of his choice. All the same, Oroko got him thinking. "Could it be possible?" he wondered.

Mogambi's low self esteem melted away miraculously with the arrival of a Mathematics teacher – Elisha Luyeho – from Tanzania, when Mogambi was in Form Two. Mr Luyeho, together with his wife, had had a chance to study at Andrews University, an Adventist University in the United States. He would give his students talks on what one would call paradigm shift. Usually, he would sit the students down and tell them about their potential and how best they could realise it. He emphasised that the students had to be good in their academic work and, more importantly, they should prepare to go overseas for further studies. He shared his experiences in the US with the students and showed them his school pictures. Over a three-year period, he had taken the students through every aspect of his former school and life in the US in general.

Meanwhile Oroko, who was to be Mogambi's deskmate for all the four years of secondary school at Kamagambo as well as his best friend, had proved to be a great Mathematics student. Mogambi started to learn from him and soon he realised that he wasn't doing too badly in Mathematics after all. Oroko was to be his biggest academic competitor. However, despite the rivalry, they maintained their friendship which endured for many years. Mogambi admits that Oroko would always have a special place in his heart for he opened a new chapter in his life. He made him see the endless possibilities in life at a time when he was seriously handicapped by his own low self esteem and lack of self confidence.

Mathematics brought Mogambi closer to Mr Luyeho, the Mathematics teacher. Mr Luyeho strongly recommended that Mogambi should consider applying to Andrews University after he was done with secondary school, emphasising that it was what one learnt outside the classroom that was invaluable. At the time, going to America appeared a far-fetched pipe dream. But Mogambi kept hope alive. It may happen, he kept telling himself.

Another major transformation took place when Mogambi was in Form Three. At the start of Form Three, students were supposed to choose their subjects for the final examinations. Kamagambo School had only three streams to choose from: commerce, science or the arts. Mogambi was not good in arts; so it was not an option. He liked science, but he did not like the science teacher, a missionary who was mainly in charge of the school farm. He used to stand in whenever there was no regular science teacher. With this particular teacher, Mogambi knew that he stood little chance of making it in sciences. Left with no choice, he chose commerce.

For three weeks, Mogambi plodded through trying his best to keep pace with the demands of typing and bookkeeping. Clearly, this was not his cup of tea. He was neither apt in catching the accounting principles nor had he the desire to grasp the maze of economic theories. He enjoyed science and its practical approach as opposed to the lullabies that he was now being subjected to.

Then out of the blue, word went round, from the older students, that a former genius science teacher, Mr Tegler, was coming back to teach science at Kamagambo. Mogambi's seniors urged him to drop commerce and join the science stream. With Mr Tegler, they assured Mogambi, he could reach for the stars. With this assurance, Mogambi heeded their advice and moved to the science class. True to the advice, Mr Tegler did not disappoint. He transformed Mogambi, the lacklustre student, to a top science student in one year.

Looking back, Mogambi owes his transformation to the three people he met at Kamagambo; Mr Tegler, Mr Luyeho, and his deskmate and colleague Oroko. Mogambi was to religiously work under these two teachers and come the final EACE examinations,[28] he surprised many by setting a sterling record in Mathematics and sciences for his school. This record prevailed for a long time. Such performance coming from a self-confessed average student was a confirmation that attitude, determination and hard work are significant in everything that one does.

Experience after school

Immediately after completing Form Four, Mogambi migrated to Nairobi. At the time, Nairobi was experiencing rural–urban migration with thousands of people pouring into the capital city in search of employment. Even though Mogambi had not received his examination results, he was lucky to get a job in the Industrial Area with the Ministry of Labour and Industrial Training where he worked between January and April 1975. His job was to file the name cards of trainees in alphabetical order. He found the work less challenging as it could be done by anybody who knew the alphabet. Surprisingly, getting the job was such a big deal.

Not many people were as lucky as Mogambi was. During the period that he worked at Industrial Area, he stayed in Eastleigh with a cousin. Every morning, he would join a flood of casual workers and job seekers that thronged the streets and streamed into Industrial Area on foot. This four-month period was an eye-opener to him. He witnessed the deplorable living conditions of these people, a condition that surpassed the hard village life. Boarding a bus was out of the question, as they could not afford it. He saw people walk for miles from their dwelling places to Industrial Area, only to camp outside factories, hoping to be picked for some menial job for the day. A few lucky ones could afford *githeri*[29] for lunch. The majority, hungry and battered from head to soul, just lay sprawled on the ground outside the factories waiting for the appropriate time for their trek back home. Mogambi did not understand why they chose to sleep outside factories the whole day instead of going back home after failing to get picked for a day's job.

One of Mogambi's uncles who had just finished high school was among this group. On a good day, he would get something. More often than not, he went home empty-handed, wretched but determined to give it a try the next

---

28   East African Certificate of Education.

29   A simple meal of boiled maize and beans often in varying proportions.

day. Although Mogambi was particularly lucky not to be in such a situation, he did not like what he was seeing. By comparison, Kamagambo School seemed like heaven. He could not envisage himself living a lower standard of life.

Mogambi's work experience could have been nothing but boring were it not for his boss who apparently liked his attitude and started giving him some of his assignments. He also gave him the freedom to learn from others. One of the areas that he found fascinating was the telephone; he used to marvel at the complex telephone exchange system. One day, he watched as the operator picked the receiver, answered calls and by moving along cables, transferred the calls to different extensions. This mesmerised him. The dexterity was just amazing. He was even more dumbfounded when he later learnt that the operator, a Mr Musyoka, was visually impaired. He could not imagine a visually impaired man doing what he could not do with his total vision!

This was an experience that stuck with Mogambi for a long time. Coincidentally, he was to encounter a similar situation almost six years later in the United States when he met another visually impaired man who could disassemble and re-assemble an entire motor engine. During an interview at Texaco Oil Company in New York State towards the end of 1980, he came across the visually impaired gentleman while being taken around in their labs. He was transfixed for a good 20 minutes looking at him. Incredible! What can't a man do with determination!

When the results of the EACE examinations came out in March 1975, Mogambi did not disappoint. Following his outstanding performance, he got admission to the prestigious Njoro High School for his 'A' level studies. Nevertheless, he did not stay long; he left Njoro when he got his admission letter to Andrews University in Michigan State, USA, following a response to his earlier application. He was overjoyed and apprehensive at the same time, as the fee was quite high. Given the financial burden that his father was under, it was doubtful whether he would be able to send him to America.

Mogambi was pleasantly surprised when his father readily agreed. He knew this was a great sacrifice on his father's part and he had to reciprocate in a way. Although he did not voice it then, he vowed inwardly to do his best in his studies, come back home and make him proud. During those days, those who went to America knew what they went for and were prepared to return upon completion of their studies; they went to study with the unequivocal understanding that they would come back to the country upon graduation. In later years, the intentions changed with most of those going abroad motivated by the desire to seek out greener pastures and vowing never to return. In fact, they would swear from the onset that they would never return home. It was puzzling what they were running away from when they had enough opportunities in the country.

As soon as word spread that one of their own was on his way to America for further studies, Mogambi instantly became the pride of the village. No one in his village had ever gone to America. Unknown to Mogambi, his father had gone around the village seeing his friends, colleagues, family members, neighbours and the community at large soliciting for funds to send him to school. As Mogambi recalls, a neighbour at Ibacho village, Mr Mosota, told him, "For you, *Nyaboro* (that was Mogambi's nickname), I will sell one of my chickens if that is what it takes to send you to school." And Mosota, like many other villagers, did contribute to Mogambi's education. He was therefore a product of his community.

The fundraising effort realised seventy thousand shillings, which was enough for Mogambi's air ticket and some pocket money. By this time, Mogambi's father had relocated to Kisii town. He had partnered with one of Mogambi's uncles, George Mageto, and others to buy an Asian firm then called Ebrahim Kassim and Sons. Mageto had been an accountant who had worked for Ebrahim Kassim for many years. Being the time of Africanisation of businesses when Asians were compelled to sell their businesses to indigenous Kenyans, Ebrahim Kassim opted to sell the business to his trusted accountant. Since Mageto could not raise the purchase price, he contacted his brother-in-law, Mogambi's father, and together with others they bought the business and renamed it Masaba General Stores.

A family farewell was organised for Mogambi and the day of departure arrived. His family travelled to see him off in Nairobi. As Mogambi's father could not afford to pay travel expenses for all those who wanted to see him off, only his mother, his stepmother, his father and his elder brother left Kisii for Nairobi. In Nairobi, they were joined by two of Mogambi's uncles who were working in Nairobi, namely Sibota and Maragia. It is this modest entourage that saw Mogambi off at the Jomo Kenyatta International Airport. In a moment, the plane disappeared into the clouds leaving the family members frantically waving at the skies. That was in 1975 and Mogambi was only nineteen years old.

Life in the US and the out-of-class lessons

Upon arrival in the United States, the young Mogambi was amazed by the order of life. As he had been promised, he was picked from the airport, chauffeured to the college and dropped at the boys' hostel. All he did at the reception was to mention his name and all the details of his accommodation were rolled out. To Mogambi, this was indeed a different world.

At the time Mogambi left for the United States, there had been a bandwagon of Kenyans that had flown out in the 1970s to seek greener pastures. Contrary to popular belief, it was not easy for one to work and pay their college tuition. A majority of foreign students dropped out of college to work on menial jobs just to sustain themselves. For one who was born and bred in Ibacho, a remote village in Kisii, and whose life primarily revolved around house chores and milking cows, Mogambi would not find it that hard. He grew up in the heart of the village where his father ran a shop. Besides the house chores, he also doubled as his father's assistant at the shop. He had clearly seen it all. Maybe this was where he honed his business skills that came to handsomely reward him later in life.

At the college, Mogambi was taken upstairs and ushered into a suite. It had two rooms connected with a bathroom which had a shower and a toilet. Each room had a double-decker bed, a study area, a cabinet and a telephone. Mogambi's room had an extra bed. They were five in this suite. He was shown his bed, his work area, and his cabinet. He took time to appreciate all this luxury – hot shower, a toilet, a telephone, all for him! 'Wasn't this too good to be true?' he wondered.

That this was a new world was confirmed more vividly when he walked out of his room one day to find female and male students hugging and kissing in the lobby with an administrator watching. Mogambi could not believe what he saw. He thought this was unchristian – especially because the university was supposed to be an Adventist institution! At Kamagambo they were very strict about the social interaction between girls and boys. There were separate dining halls and dormitories. One could not sit together with, or just get suspiciously close to, a person of the opposite sex without attracting the ire of the administration. Here he was, watching 'unbridled romance' in broad daylight! It was later that he learnt and got used to the liberty of the American people. Of course, he came to accept it as part of the wonders of this new world. He also came to learn that hugging was not a romantic encounter but a way of greeting in the American society.

Mogambi got to America in September 1975 at the beginning of autumn; winter was just around the corner. The temperatures started dropping. On one chilly day, he walked from his hostel to the student centre when suddenly his ears started itching. He dashed to the nearest bathroom, looked at himself in the mirror but could not see anything wrong with his ears. The itching grew unbearable. He rushed to the university clinic for medical attention. The doctor exclaimed, saying that he had frostbite. "Boy, how dare you walk out of your room without covering your ears?" he admonished. By that time, a scald had developed – just like when one pours hot water on the skin. He was shocked. Although he had warm clothes on and the sun was shining outside, he found himself burnt. He didn't know that the cold could actually burn!

To survive the cold, Mogambi needed an entirely new winter wardrobe. Trouble was that he did not have the money. Sensing his dilemma, a friend took him to the Adventist Community Services Centre, located off campus. The centre catered for the poor. Mogambi was able to pick all the clothing that he needed absolutely free. He got shoes, boots, pairs of trousers, shirts, sweaters, jackets and inner wear, everything that he needed for all seasons, not just winter. The centre was to be Mogambi's 'shop' of choice for the next four years. It was supported by community members who donated anything that they did not need. After receiving the donations the centre then cleaned the items, arranged them and gave them to the deserving members for free. Mogambi could not just believe the selflessness of the community. Coming from a society where one had to give something to get what was rightfully theirs, let alone getting anything valuable for free, this was really amazing.

Other than the weather, Mogambi's main challenge was to adjust to the cultural shock while at the same time keeping pace with his studies. As he would realise, there was a lot of learning to do, especially out of the classroom. Lesson one would be on integrity and honouring credit. As he found out, in the US one would rather go hungry than mess up their creditworthiness because one could not do anything without credit. This he learnt the hard way. While in the US one could get credit to the equivalent of up to Ksh 10 million purely on one's creditworthiness and ability to repay, accessing credit in Kenya has remained a nightmare as most banks have insisted on property to secure their loans. Mogambi wishes that the Kenyan society would put similar value on integrity and severely punish wilful credit default, as is the case with the issuing of bouncing cheques, something that was unacceptable in the US. The Kenyan society could be paying a needlessly heavy price for this lack of integrity.

Work ethic is something else that Mogambi learnt in the US outside the classroom. He observed the Americans working diligently. Everybody, including the lowest-ranked person in the organisation, wanted to be the best. Work was quantified and timed. One had to produce a certain amount of work in a given amount of time. That was fixed. This was not comparable to what was happening in Kenya. In Kenya, it was frustrating to see workers expecting to be paid just for making appearances at their work stations without specific output to lay claim on.

As the financial burden bore down on him, Mogambi had to look for work to supplement his upkeep. He already had a part-time job at the campus, working on a production line. As a student one was allowed to work twenty hours per week on campus. But this was not enough to meet Mogambi's expenses. At this juncture, he was prepared to do anything to earn more money for his upkeep.

When he learnt that picking fruits was available to those who had the strength, he took it up. During his free time, he would walk over to the nearby farms and pick strawberries, apples and peaches. All one had to do was to look out for a sign saying 'Pick your own fruits', walk in, pick a basket, head to the farm, pick as much as one could, get it weighed and they would get cash payments on the spot. This became Mogambi's weekend job. On a good day, he could take home as much as twenty dollars – a tidy sum by any measure at the time.

Mogambi had to balance both work and academics to get the best out of each. Work experience in the US taught him that one got paid for what they produced. Picking fruits was hard work, back-breaking, but it was not any different from what he used to do as he grew up. While others complained, Mogambi continued to pick fruits and enjoyed every bit of it.

The additional menial work earned Mogambi some extra money, but it was not enough to enable him to keep enjoying the luxuries of Andrews University hostel. To keep afloat, he had to seek cheaper accommodation off campus. Small rooms were available within the surrounding community to students at subsidised rates. Therefore, Mogambi hit the road once again, this time looking for cheap accommodation off campus. Most of the facilities that he found, though subsidised, were still too expensive for him. He literally combed the surrounding homes, but he could not get a bargain. He had given up and was on his way back to campus when he met a retired old lady who was staying with her daughter probably in her mid-forties. Either they were ready to listen or he was just too desperate, but he found himself pouring out his heart to them. Perhaps out of pity or just plain generosity, Mogambi got accommodation in their basement for free. All he had to do to reciprocate this gesture was to take care of their yard, work hard in school and maintain good grades. To him, that was chicken feed. What Mogambi saw in his hostesses were people who wanted him to succeed. In fact, it became his home till he moved out of Michigan in 1977. What this experience with the hostesses taught Mogambi was a valuable lesson on generosity and giving to the disadvantaged.

Mogambi's work experience in the US also imprinted in him the value of research as a tool of managing innovation and growth. When he started running his nascent business back home in Kisii, Mogambi continued to employ research as a tool to introduce new products in his stores. They would go out and ask their clients what they would have liked to have and the product attributes that they would have preferred before commissioning manufacturers to produce the respective products for supplying.

On his own – looking for sponsors

Mogambi quickly adapted to life in the US. He kept close touch with the people at home too. During his second year at the university in 1976, he got a shock of his life in the form of a letter from his father. Ironically, he had anticipated its contents only that he didn't realise how soon it would come. In the letter, his father enumerated to him his overwhelming financial obligations with a conclusion that he was indeed unable to keep up paying his fees at the university.

This was discouraging news, but Mogambi could not give up this study opportunity and just return home. He had in his mind that his entire community had contributed generously, each from their meagre earnings, to accord him this opportunity. He could not let them down. He had to fight and protect this hard-won chance. Yet the odds were stacked against him. Working and paying his tuition was out of the question. He had seen his colleagues who tried that route flounder in their studies and finally give up to concentrate on their survival. He vowed not to join them.

The alternatives were not easy. He sought sponsors from all over the world. Eventually, luck smiled at him when Rattansi Educational Trust, based in Nairobi, heeded his request and agreed to partially support his studies on condition that he would return to Kenya upon completion of his degree course. Quickly, he confirmed to them that he would return; in any case, he had no intention whatsoever of staying in the US after his studies.

Although a godsend gesture, the Rattansi scholarship was hardly enough. Mogambi was advised by friends to relocate and transfer from the high-cost Michigan State to the lower-cost southern states. Consequently, upon completion of his pre-engineering course at Andrews University in 1977, he applied for admission in one of the colleges in the southern states. He got admission to the prestigious Tuskegee Institute in Alabama where he enrolled for a BSc degree in Mechanical Engineering. Tuskegee was founded by the great black American educationist and human rights advocate, Booker T Washington. The university is famed for the scientific exploits of George Washington Carver, a co-founder and a scientist who was able to extract hundreds of products from peanuts.

This tactical move would earn Mogambi some reprieve but not enough to let him rest on his laurels. His next option was to seek scholarships from US firms and organisations, as Mr Luyeho had advised him early at Kamagambo. Once again he got lucky. An opportunity presented itself in the form of a General Motors (GM) scholarship. This renowned motor company was coming to Tuskegee Institute to look for two top engineering students to give scholarships. The

Dean of Engineering was requested to forward names of five top students for interview. The selection was based on past academic performance. Expectedly, Mogambi was among the five. Still the battle was wide; only two would qualify for this award and he was determined to be one of them.

On the interview day, Mogambi went into the interview room excited but apprehensive. He knew this was the opportunity that he had been longing for, a chance of a lifetime that Mr Luyeho had prepared him for. Mentally, he was not alone at the interview but with his mentor, Mr Luyeho. The interviewers looked at one's academic performance, one's future career interests and how those tied up with GM's interests. Mogambi was up to the challenge and he easily landed the prestigious GM scholarship. This by extension also accorded him an opportunity to work for GM during his summer holidays, as a professional engineering intern, exposing him to the world's best engine research laboratories.

Mogambi completed his undergraduate studies in 1979 and enrolled at Auburn University graduate school for his MSc in Mechanical Engineering. He joined Cummins Engine Company, in Indiana, as a Research Engineer in January 1981. While working at Cummins, he enrolled in a business school attending evening classes. He would finally complete his MBA at Butler University in 1983 after a two-year stint.

Marriage and family

On his way back home in 1979, after graduating with his BSc degree, Mogambi passed through New Jersey to see a Kenyan friend, Joash Munda Oluoch, with whom he had studied at Andrews University and who had since relocated. Munda would mention to him that there was a Kenyan lady who was studying at Rutgers University in New Jersey whom he would have liked Mogambi to meet. Unfortunately, his flight was on the next day and he had to travel home without meeting her. However, he had a chance to talk to her over the phone.

Once back at Auburn University after this break, Mogambi kept in touch with Kemuma, this mystery girl. Those days Kenyan students were rare in the US and few were interested in forging close relationships. Mogambi's New Jersey female friend, Kemuma, had also been tipped about this Kenyan student who incidentally came from her home area. She was equally anxious to meet him. Naturally, both were apprehensive of what would become of their first meeting. After communicating for some time, they met and both were not disappointed. The slender elegant girl easily fell for the tall charming Kenyan engineer with an American accent. The rest was history.

The union between Mogambi and Kemuma blossomed soon after their graduation in 1981. They married on 20 December 1980 and a week later they moved to Indiana. This marriage would blossom into a serious business partnership that was to become the OuruPower Limited in Kisii town. Interestingly, Mogambi got employed at Cummins immediately upon graduation and Kemuma, who graduated at the same time, also got a job at the same place. While Mogambi started working at Cummins in January 1981, his wife joined the same company in the finance department two weeks later. Since they were both working with the same company and had no children yet, they found themselves with a lot of free time. Moreover, both of them did not drink. Hanging out was therefore not a priority. To fill up their free time, they weighed various business opportunities, finally settling on real estate.

Just like elsewhere in the world, in the US real estate is a big business. The interest rates are quite low, which allows investors to take mortgages and make a small margin by renting out the properties. Locally, this would not be feasible owing to the high interest rates. The Mogambis got into business by buying run-down properties, cleaning them up, renting them or selling them at a profit. Money begets money. Once in business, their instincts soon picked out another opportunity. Going to art exhibitions, which were held every weekend in different parts of the country, they observed that Americans liked soapstone carvings. Incidentally, these stones came from Kisii, their home area.

All it took was a phone call to his father giving instructions to ship a batch of the same on the next available plane and serious business began. They soon discovered that hawking was not unique to Kenya; that is, if it involved moving around with one's wares to look for customers. On Fridays after work, the Mogambis would pack their car with these carvings and hit the road on to the next art show. They would not be back until Sunday evening, normally around 9.00 pm. One thing they learnt was to enjoy this experience. Consequently, they always looked forward to it every weekend.

Two years down their marriage, the Mogambis were blessed with their first baby, a girl they named Moraa, after Mogambi's ailing grandmother. In 1979, when he had returned home, he had gone to see his ailing grandmother. She did not believe that she would live long enough for them to meet again. So she asked Mogambi to name his first girl after her – Moraa. Miraculously, she lived on (and is still alive as at the time of writing this book).

Two years later, Moraa was followed by another girl, Mogotu, also named after Mogambi's same grandmother. Lastly they got Samora. Samora was born just after President Samora Machel of Mozambique, a renowned African liberator, died in a plane crash in October 1986.[30] The Mogambis hoped

---

30   Samora Machel was the first President of Mozambique who led his country from independence in 1975 until his death in 1986, when his presidential aircraft crashed in the mountainous border region with South Africa. Machel was renowned as a military commander and revolutionary socialist leader.

that their son would also grow to be a liberator like Machel. All the children accompanied their parents when they travelled back home to Kenya in 1992 and attended the local schools. However, since they are US citizens, they flew back to their 'motherland' to pursue various courses at the graduate level and careers. At only 25 years of age, Mogotu graduated from the University of Colorado with a PhD degree in Chemical Engineering.

As a family, the Mogambis have never had difficulty with the children. Mogambi has particularly been lucky when it comes to bringing up the children as his wife was there to do most of the parenting. As he admits, he cannot profess advice to young parents about handling children. All he can remember is that before retiring to bed, they made it mandatory to read a bedtime story to the kids, regardless of their age. They also ensured that there were plenty of children's books, educational toys and games for their enjoyment. This was primarily their entertainment.

When it came to their studies, they were also somewhat blessed. The first-born daughter is a *bookworm*. She got extremely good grades in early primary. Subsequently, she was seconded to a special group of students with higher learning abilities. Maybe this rubbed off on her siblings as they tried to keep pace with her. In effect, the parents never had to force any of them to go to school or prioritise their education. Fortunately, all of them have successfully advanced in their education.

About meeting a partner, Mogambi says he is lucky that a friend recommended a good partner to him. He advises that it may be appropriate to pair up with a person with similar ambitions and stage in life. Says he, "Partners recommended by others can be good. Friends who have the interest of both parties may come in handy in marriage proposals. While chance meetings may work and are definitely common, they offer little opportunity for due diligence or a background check." He hastens to add: "You are likely to experience discordance if you are ready to settle while your partner is just beginning to experience life. One may enjoy partying the whole night while the other one may prefer spending a restful night at home. Such differences may strain the union."

Choosing entrepreneurship over career

Mogambi had a successful career as an engineer spanning over eleven years at Cummins Engineering Company in Columbus, Indiana. As a professional he worked through various departments at different levels of the company – research engineer, a senior engineer, a technical specialist, and as a technical advisor. Earlier, he had also worked as a production engineer at Detroit Diesel Allison, a division of General Motors Inc. in Detroit, Michigan, during his summer internships. Moreover, he has had a chance to publish many articles in professional journals, some of which qualified to be included in SAE transactions. These transactions are a permanent record of papers with immense future importance. Finally, he also earned two patents/innovations from the US Patent Office for his research work.[31]

When the Mogambi family packed their bags ready to return to Kenya sometime in 1986, Mogambi had a teaching job offer at the University of Nairobi and also from the University of Eastern Africa, Baraton. However, after deliberating as a family, they agreed that the time was not right for them to return. So, they unpacked and continued with their stay in the US. Six years later the family did eventually make their way back home. To Mogambi, returning home was always on the cards. It was a matter of 'when' not 'if'. This explains the reason he regularly travelled and invested in property back home. Indeed, by the mid-1980s the Mogambis had built two self-contained houses in the upmarket Milimani area of Kisii town.

Finally, the Mogambis returned home in 1992. Back home, the two professionals were not keen on salaried employment although their resumés (or CVs) would have landed them envious positions in either the public or the private sectors. They had decided that business was the way to go. Their experience in the US, both as employees and part-time business people, had taught them that financial freedom lay in business. Luckily, Mogambi had gone through business school in preparation for a management position within his company; he had realised that he stood a better chance if he topped up his technical degree with an MBA. Although he did not get the management position, the knowledge gained would come in handy in his entrepreneurship undertaking.

Mogambi set out to be financially independent by the age of 50. To achieve that, the Mogambis set up *Enterprise Uhuru*, their vehicle to financial independence. *Uhuru*, a Kiswahili word for independence, was appropriate and aptly reflected their vision. Unfortunately, *Uhuru* was a protected name in Kenya and they were denied registration. Undeterred, they corrupted the name to come up with *Ouru*, a local equivalent of *Uhuru*. This time, it got registered.

The preferred business destination then was Nairobi, the capital city. Most entrepreneurs believed that Nairobi was the business hub. The Mogambis however went against the grain. Their exposure in the US had taught them otherwise. They felt that great opportunities existed right where they were – Kisii. Defying popular opinion and advice, they went to settle in Kisii and made it their business base.

---

31   These achievements are well documented in the Internet and can be viewed by searching using the keyword 'ZN MOGAKA'.

The Mogambis had watched Wal-Mart,[32] the leading American retail chain, grow into a gigantic enterprise by focusing on offering lower prices to the rural population. They felt that they could replicate the same in Kisii. With time, they have been vindicated. Their success proves that those migrating to cities are actually running away from opportunities.

At the time the Mogambis decided to set up business in Kisii, the town was small and deprived of serious investments. They got thinking on the opportunities that they could explore. One of them was real estate, where they already had some investments. However, they felt that the demand for houses would not be significant unless there were other investments that would bring people to this town. Trading appeared more feasible given the huge rural population who were craving fair pricing. Here again there was a snag. The few manufacturers in the country had already identified and appointed distributors countrywide. Newcomers were forced to buy from the appointed distributors. Thus, they felt, there was no way their low price model could work if they were to buy from distributors.

Just as they were debating and weighing their options, Overseas Trading Company (OTC), a transport company that covered almost the whole of East Africa, suddenly went under leaving a building in the middle of the town vacant. Without a second thought, they acquired the building. Since they had decided on trading, they knew that this building would be useful. Almost simultaneously they saw an opening in selling cement which they could acquire directly from the manufacturers.

The Mogambis caused uproar in the town when they brought their first batch of 150 bags of cement and started selling at Ksh 160 per bag while the competition was selling at Ksh 168. Those were the days of price controls whereby the government set a price ceiling. As a retailer, however, one was not stopped from giving discounts to their clients. Borrowing from the Wal-Mart model, they chose to ignore the haggling that was the order and gave a straight discount. The margins were razor-thin. They announced their discounted prices through posters all over town.

After registering success with cement, they later moved to groceries. At the time groceries were synonymous with East Africa Industries, which was later renamed Unilever. The Mogambis became their agents in 1995. Unfortunately, Unilever's model did not match their vision of lower-priced products. Besides, they were just one of their many agents; hence, there was no way they could negotiate price cuts. Nevertheless, they still managed to move to number one in Unilever's national sales by 1996.

---

32   Wal-Mart is the largest international discount retail chain founded in 1962 by Sam Walton. By 2005, it had an annual turnover of USD 312.4 billion (KSh 25 trillion), with more than 6,200 facilities around the world.

The Mogambis' experience with Unilever made them see the unmet need for yellow cooking fat in the region. Every year-end, there would be a shortage of Cowboy, Unilever's yellow-fat brand. They sought to fill this gap with a different supplier. They applied to Bidco Oil Refineries, an edible oil and hygiene products manufacturer based in Thika, but they never responded. Their persistent search unearthed a manufacturer called Pwani Oil Products Ltd, then a small factory in Mombasa. Pwani was making a yellow cooking fat called Frymate, but it did not have a market for it. This was an opportunity for the Mogambis to negotiate a lower price and to take on Cowboy and Chipsy. They marketed Frymate as their brand using their resources and in a few short years, it was a household name in the region commanding over 50 percent of the market share.

With the success of Frymate, the Mogambis were ready to move on to the next product. Soap, a by-product of fat production, was the next battleground. They went back to Pwani Oil Products and implored them to get them laundry bar soap. They agreed and after a few trials they came up with the *Ndume* bar soap brand. *Ndume* is a Kiswahili word for bull. Metaphorically, the soap drew its strength from the bull. This was heralded by a pompous launch through roadshows and radio commercials. The new soap shot to the top of bar soaps in the region within no time.

As expected, this irked the competition. In a blind rush to catch up, Bidco launched a new brand – *Bull* – complete with a bull's head as the logo exactly like the Mogambis products. Now the typical rural customer could not tell the difference between the two. But the Mogambis had themselves to blame. By overlooking the registration of the brand and logo they had exposed themselves to the competition. Consequently, the opportunistic competition had it easy riding on their success. Nevertheless, they learnt their lesson. Moreover, they took personal satisfaction that the big boys were now feeling the heat. *Ndume* and *Bull* are still the dominant brands in the region.

Another opportunity emerged in 1998. The Mogambis noticed that there were only two brands in the baking flour industry – *Swan* and *Exe*. The manufacturers of these two brands could not sell to them directly. Naturally, in line with their vision of lower prices, they sought alternatives. Mr Ragu of Midland Emporium in Kisumu, one of their suppliers, advised them to talk to Pembe Flour Mills. He got wind of the fact that they were looking to expand their market; and the Mogambis were looking for an alternative brand. This proved to be a perfect match. In no time, they struck up a working relationship.

Using their tested model, the Mogambis marketed *Pembe* as one of their brands. They waged war on *Swan* and *Exe*, giving free samples of *Pembe*, conducting roadshows and live demonstrations all at their expense. Eventually,

Pembe became the preferred baking flour with more than 50 percent of the market share in the region, a position it still retains. The Mogambis were to repeat this model for various items including *Rhino* cement, sweets and drinks, among others. The model worked well for them and they created their own 'brands' and they became exclusive distributors of these brands. Consequently, they were able to offer low prices to their customers.

In 2004, they led the Mukwano Industries debut and launched a successful onslaught in the Kenyan market despite the Ugandan company's fears that Kenya had bigger boys that would frustrate their entry. Presently, Ouru Super Stores and Discount Centre are ranked seventh among Mukwano's top distributors in Kenya, Uganda, Tanzania, Rwanda, Burundi and Sudan.

All along the Mogambis had been selling the Eveready brand of dry-cell batteries as a service to their clients after they were refused distributorship. They however noted a preferential shift to cheaper Chinese batteries as the *kadogo* economy took hold. *Kadogo* economy is the euphemism for consumer preference for smaller product packages. They noted that these batteries were not approved and were substandard. In fact, they leaked during usage posing a danger to both the customers and their equipment. Their only advantage was the low price which was almost half that of Eveready products, the local competition. From this, the Mogambis saw another opportunity beckoning.

From their observation, they decided to get better alternatives to the cheap and dangerous batteries. Mogambi visited various Chinese battery-manufacturing factories, took samples and returned to test and analyse them. He gave the samples to the Kenya Bureau of Standards (KBS) for evaluation and sent others to SGS in Hong Kong, and Intertek International, a UK certification company. The results from all these laboratories were fantastic. The last stage was the customer. The Mogambis took a sample group, gave them the approved samples and sought the customers' feedback. It worked and finally they had what they wanted.

Following the satisfactory results, the Mogambis commissioned the manufacturer to make the selected batteries under their own brand. This time, the brand was duly registered with the legal protection in place. The new battery, called *OuruPower Battery*, was unveiled in July 2007. To market it, they partnered with *New Star Television*, a local TV station based in Kisii which covers the entire region. They sponsored a 13-series programme called 'Power Box' that featured the salient attributes of the battery such as zero leakage, lower cost, and local and international certification. The Mogambis have been pleasantly surprised by the results of this campaign. In *OuruPower Battery*, the Mogambis had another winner.

Besides low-priced products, the Mogambis debut in the Kisii business scene has had an impact on customer service. Previously, shop owners were complacent. They treated the customers as a bother. Since shops were few, the customers endured this ridicule. The Mogambis not only increased choices, but they also improved on customer service. For example, when they started, goods were sourced from Nakuru and Kisumu. Presently, the goods leave Kisii to go to all these towns and beyond.

The Mogambis have also revolutionised business as a profession. Initially seen as a form of retirement or the last option for school dropouts, presently the young professionals in Kisii admire business. They have inspired a lot of youth to set up shops modelled after their businesses.

Business capitalisation and strategy

The Mogambis had no problem with start-up capital. For over ten years, Mogambi and his wife worked as professionals in the US. At the same time, they ran part-time businesses. They used the derived funds to invest in real estate in Kisii. The savings gave them the initial capital while their investments in real estate in Kisii gave them the necessary security to access bank overdrafts. Supplier credit and bank facilities supported their growth. Having learnt in the US that integrity is critical in business and is a life pillar, such sources of funds were not hard to come by. In turn, they extended this credit facility to some of their valued customers, empowering them to grow without a bank facility.

As for their business strategy, the Mogambis have adopted measured growth and price leadership. They decided from the onset to grow gradually and to offer their clients competitive prices. Starting with cement, they have progressively but conservatively added other products after thorough vetting. Against all odds, they have managed to stick to the Wal-Mart model of low pricing. This has compelled them to shun the established brands that sell through distributors because they are inflexible as far as pricing is concerned.

Also, their approach has been multi-pronged. First, they identify a manufacturer of a substitute product to the major national brands. Next they evaluate the performance of the product with a select group of customers. Finally, if it is acceptable, they commission the manufacturer to produce it for them and where possible under their own brand. An example of such a brand is the *OuruPower* battery. If such an arrangement is not possible, then they negotiate for discounts and place orders for the product(s) under the manufacturer's brand. They then market the product in different media at their cost. They also engage in roadshows, freebies and door-to-door marketing. The new products are placed strategically at their front shop with personnel on standby to explain their features.

Business management and structure

The multimillion Ouru stores, though complex in operations, still retain the family business model with two directors, Mogambi and his wife Kemuma. Except for elaborate computerised sales and finance departments, the other departments are basically informal.

The Mogambis have a loose organisational structure from the two directors to the ordinary employees. They have around one hundred employees, all operating at the same location. However, they run on an open-door policy where anyone has easy access to the management.

The company has set up an effective distribution network covering all of Nyanza, Western and parts of the Rift Valley Regions. These distribution points are more like the company's branches and their job is to service them. They are to be found in every key market centre. In effect, the company has a sales team that is comprised of more than ten branded trucks that deliver products to their clientele. Most of the orders are received by telephone and are delivered immediately at no added cost.

Mogambi is a hands-on manager. This has been necessitated by lack of work ethics in the workforce. And this, according to him, has been a hindrance in furthering the company's growth. However, he feels that for the company to sustain the growth momentum, time has come to bring in professionals and re-position the company differently so as to meet future challenges.

Business challenges

Mogambi holds that business is not 'a walk in the park'. Citing the success of OuruPower, he observes that it has not been without challenges. He admits that one of the initial challenges was their inability to procure leading brands from the suppliers/manufacturers. Since they could not get products directly from the suppliers/manufacturers, it was impossible to implement their model of lower prices. They had to get alternative suppliers and products.

Another sticking challenge came from unethical business practices by competitors who resented their onslaught into the market with cheaper substitutes. Whenever they introduced a new product, their competitors went on overdrive to discredit the product using malicious propaganda about the product's integrity, approval and efficacy.

An example was in the launch of the *Rhino* cement manufactured by Athi River Mining Company, which saw the epitome of this fight. Given that the brand was unknown and the Mogambis were the only one selling it at a lower price, their competitors started a campaign of maligning the product as dust that could not build a stable house. However, they countered this propaganda by commissioning and building a nine-storey building right in the middle of the town in the full view of their clients using Rhino cement. To date, the building stands strong and the rumour dissipated. Mogambi learnt from this: that sometimes to win clients' confidence, one may have to demonstrate product efficacy. *The taste of the pudding is in the eating.* Since then their customers have come to believe in them and what they say. It is this trust that OuruPower must strive to maintain by providing genuinely good quality products at affordable prices.

Mogambi attributes dedication, commitment, vision, focus, honesty, integrity and hard work as his pillars to success. He also rates highly family support that saw them scrounge enough money to allow him to start his studies abroad. He believes that without the support from their suppliers, agents, customers and staff, they would not be where they are today. As he says, "Our partners' trust in us has fuelled our growth. Our network has grown as a result. It's a multiplier effect."

Mogambi credits the successful introduction of *OuruPower* battery brand under their own brand name as so far their biggest success story and a major leap on their journey to creating their own brands. This project involved all phases of product introduction including selecting, testing, evaluation, procurement, marketing and advertising. In less than one year, it had become the preferred brand in the region. They have been pleasantly surprised by the market response. This shows that it is possible to shatter old myths about established brands and create new and better brands.

On the flip side, however, Mogambi remembers painfully the failure of a venture that he put his heart into while in the US – running a restaurant. After living in the US for a long time, the Mogambis noticed that most people ate in the restaurants. They used this as their excuse to venture into the restaurant business back home in Kisii. In a short period, they realised what a terrible mistake they had made. They had not done proper research as due diligence would require. The surrounding community did not command enough disposable income to patronise the middle-class hotel that they had set up.

With hindsight, Mogambi realised that the failure was a major lesson. First, they resolved never to deal in short shelf-life products. Secondly, they realised that one must have control of stock to survive in business. And lastly, one must know their customers before they decide to offer them a product or a service.

The Mogambis also learnt when to quit. Although the restaurant business was their pet project, they accepted that they were unable to continue. They closed the venture soon enough to stem losses. Thus, they took this lesson to heart and moved on.

Mogambi believes that the future for OuruPower is bright; their vision is simply to be the best. They want to develop the brand more and set up various companies using the Virgin model, based on The Virgin Group of Companies where every brand develops into a distinct company. For example, the *OuruPower* batteries should evolve into a different company separate from OuruPower Limited.

Looking back, Mogambi would change nothing in his business leanings. Probably what he may consider this time round is a different approach. For example, he thinks that he would prefer the Virgin model where one builds companies under one brand as opposed to the current model, which has seen brands being built under one company. This Mogambi believes is a far better approach. If they had taken that approach, they could be having several different companies running on their own in several different industries.

Ultimately, Mogambi expects the general public, who are their customers, to get a slice of the cake when the envisaged group of companies finally lists at the securities market. This will also take care of the thorny issue of succession. By the time the company lists, it will not be a family business. However, the corporate governance structures must first be in place.

Mogambi would like to be remembered as having contributed in some little way to uplift the standard of living of the people in his locality. He wants to be remembered for having left his region better than he found it. Thus, his contribution would have inspired others to reach for the stars.

Tips for young entrepreneurs

Mogambi advises young entrepreneurs to start small. "Just do one thing. We started with only one item, cement, and did this for a whole year. This gave us time to learn and upgrade our systems as the volumes increased. It also gave us an edge since we concentrated all our resources on one thing."

He also advises upcoming entrepreneurs to go into business only if they are prepared to sacrifice: "Sacrifice and more sacrifice is the password in business. Remember everything has a price and good things inevitably are dearer. Running your own business, though good, is much more demanding. Believe in yourself. Have a plan and confidently execute it. Work hard and keep your eye on the prize. Above all maintain a high degree of integrity. Be a good learner. Learn from your successes and failures."

Mogambi does not believe that employment is the panacea to eliminating poverty and desperation in the society. What the youth – boys and girls – need is to make a decent living. Employment is just but one option. Business is the other. The country should improve credit access so that the youth have a choice other than employment. For those in employment, he advises that they should save to invest later in their businesses.

He also believes that attaining business goals is achievable. The Google founders and the Bill Gates of this world did not have property to use as collateral. Their ideas were financed by venture capitalists, people who had money and belief in the entrepreneur's ideas. But most importantly, the venture capitalists knew that their money was safe because society and government regulations tied one's future to one's credit rating. The consequences of messing up one's credit rating are too severe to contemplate. He holds that Kenya should move in that direction, where access to credit is based on one's creditworthiness.

Mogambi also wants leaders to show the youth that they can make a decent living running their own business. Says he: "Traditionally, businesses have been associated with those who couldn't make the grade in school. We must turn that around and show our youth that owning a business is a worthy pursuit. Let's make business an attractive venture. Above all, make credit available to them to pursue their passion."

Role models

Mogambi's role models betray his American leaning. Top on the list is Sam Walton of Wal-Mart Inc. Walton started with the famed small store in a rural town in the Deep South that quickly grew into a giant store. Walton's calling was in low prices. He battled major brands to give his customers the best prices. Wal-Mart became the largest employer and retailer in the world, employing more people than the top ten traditional large companies in America combined.

Mogambi also has deep respect and admiration for Bill Gates of Microsoft and Richard Branson, the maverick founder of Virgin Group. Says he: "These entrepreneurs have several things in common which I admire. They all come from humble backgrounds, are all self-made, had an idea, set up their own companies with the sole purpose of getting cheaper options for the consumer and won big."

According to Mogambi, as far as possible, young people should be accorded an opportunity first in a formal work environment to gain experience on how organisations are run before they venture out on their own. Running a company is a complex issue that involves human, technical and legal demands that a green-horn may not grapple with easily. "I'm what I am because of the opportunity I got to live and work in a unique environment."

Chapter 9

Mary Elizabeth Okelo

Her mellow voice, motherly mien and cool demeanour make Mary Elizabeth Okelo a most interesting person. She is so approachable and easy to get along with that it is difficult to associate her with the rough and tumble of the business world that she's part of. She is renowned for starting and building from scratch an institution that is the envy of the corporate world. It is not until she stands that the unmistakable towering Mary – she stands at six feet tall – commands an air of authority around her. Her height alone sets her apart from the average and has earned her jeers and accolades alike.

As a young girl growing up amidst a conservative society, she was jeered at for being tall, often being called a giraffe. She had little choice but to live up to the society's expectations. Peer bullying notwithstanding, she rose to give even more significance to her height through solid achievements in her family life, career and business.

Mary is reputed for having broken through the glass ceiling as far as women's achievements are concerned. She has in her stable an enviable list of firsts. She rose to the pinnacle of an international bank, Barclays, to clinch the coveted honour of being named the first African woman bank manager. Barclays Bank also seconded her as the first woman advisor to the President of the African Development Bank – Abidjan. Her crusade for women empowerment would later see her leave the comfort of Barclays to be the founder and first chair of Kenya Women Finance Trust. Later, she was to be named the first woman Vice-President of the Women World Banking (based in New York).

After a successful career, Mary went on to co-found the Makini Group of Schools of which she became the Executive Director. The group is a beacon of success attracting both local and international acclaim and highly rated in national examinations. The unparalleled success of Makini Group of Schools as private schools, has rung far and wide, capturing the interest of Columbia University which commissioned a study on the institution in 2002. This illustrates a success story of an African woman entrepreneur.

Early life and education

Mary Okelo was born Elizabeth Mary Awori in Busia, a town on the Kenya–Uganda border, to Canon Jeremiah Musungu Awori and Mariam Awori. She was the 14th born in a family of 17 children, sandwiched between two strong sisters, Christine and Grace. Christine, who would later become a lawyer by profession, showed her mettle in grasping legal matters from a tender age. She was the one who used to argue out her siblings' cases whenever they erred. Grace, who was equally strong, later turned out to be an administrator.

Growing up between the two left Mary in a rather weak position. Naturally, her parents, specifically her father, had to protect her in a way especially due to the fact that she was named after his mother. Although Mary enjoyed a special status with her father, she had little choice than to keep up with the pace that he had set for her other siblings, a number of whom rose to become successful public figures.

Mary's attachment to her family is evident from the many family pictures that adorn her office capped by a giant poster of the Awori family. One unique characteristic in the family was the realisation of the salient abilities exhibited by Awori's offspring as they grew up. Many of Mary's siblings were to register outstanding success in all spheres of life. This seemingly endless list of sibling success could be attributed to Mary's father who was success-driven and let the family members pursue their interests and dreams. He would support whatever one showed an interest in, whether it was music, sports or academics. He even bought a guitar for Mary's elder brother at a time when many parents had a negative view of music.

Success traits seem to have come far within the Awori heritage. Mary's grandmother, after whom she's named, was a strong and unique personality in her own way. She had defied the age-old tradition of wife inheritance way back in the 19th century; she had declined to be inherited upon the death of her husband. Such was the self-belief and determination that was to be the characteristic of the Awori lineage.

An incident that could illustrate and define the Awori family took place when Mary was young. One of their cows attempted to jump over a barbed wire fence. It tripped and the wire ripped its lower abdomen open, exposing its intestines. Mary's mother and one of her brothers held down the animal, pushed back the intestines and sewed-up the injury. The cow finally healed. This was not only unbelievable but also a show of amazing bravery. Suffice it to say that the said brother was to be the first Kenyan doctor to perform a kidney transplant – the late Professor Nelson Awori. He was not only a medical doctor but also a university lecturer. Such was the freedom in the Awori family to pursue one's dreams.

Mary was undoubtedly a child of privilege having been born into an able family. This is contrary to what would be commonly expected as conditions for building achievers; as the old adage goes, 'Necessity is the mother of invention'. The fact that the Awori children were not brought up in scarcity or in dire straits did not deter them from achieving phenomenal success. Indeed, they came to stand out uniquely as examples of those who have managed to build on a privileged platform and attain gigantic proportions of success, consequently disproving the usual spoilt-child syndrome where children raised in plenty turn into ruins. To this extent, therefore, Mary was never pampered.

Their father, Canon Awori, was a farmer, church leader and a relentless businessman who loved and cared for his family. As a farmer, he was so passionate in what he did that his farm was used for demonstration whenever new crops were being introduced in the area. On his farm, one could find trees for building poles, cotton, *wimbi* (millet) and his favourite foods – cassava and rice. He was a believer in self-sufficiency and greatly abhorred credit; were he to rise, he would be perturbed at the amount of debt that the country owes.

Canon Awori was also an astute businessman and was among the first people in the district to own a car; actually, there were only two then. An avid trader, he used the car to transport his wares to Bungoma Market from Kabula. He also engaged in sugar business after obtaining a permit from the colonial government. Initially, he used to transport sugar in hired trucks from Nambale in Uganda to his shop in the village. Later, he bought his own lorry.

Canon Awori loved music and animals. His church was a music powerhouse, a medium he successfully used to attract the largely sceptical African audience. At his home, he initiated a project in which he tried to rear various types of animals – a kind of a conservancy or sanctuary. In this sanctuary he had dik dik, tortoise, guinea fowl, cranes and monkeys, among others. From these animals, he drew values that he would pass on to his children; for example, unlike human beings, animals don't lie and this was an indictment to the extent that Canon Awori hated dishonesty. He would relentlessly instil into his children the virtues of honesty and integrity. These virtues would be useful to Mary in her life as an employee and later as an entrepreneur. In particular, her reputation would play a big role at the beginning of the school venture.

As a council representative, Canon Awori championed the principle of meritocracy in public appointments as opposed to tribal or clan considerations. Hence he advocated pay for value, which is akin to performance contracting that has come to be applied in government. He was also committed to education, especially girl-child education, at a time when schooling for girls was a rarity. He ensured that all his children had the best start in life when it came to education. Notably, all his children went to the best schools locally and abroad. At one time, four of them were at Makerere while another studied law at the University of Dar es Salaam, the best law school in the region at the time. Another went to Harvard while others attended the Ivy League universities in Europe. With such a father the Awori children had no option but to strive to be achievers. As Mary grew up, her brothers and sisters were excelling in whatever they were doing and she was compelled to follow suit.

Another significant factor that may have contributed to the success of the Awori children is the fact that their upbringing placed them at a vantage position. Their grandfather, and later their father, hosted varied guests, mostly missionaries and evangelists. Therefore they learnt to socialise with different people and to appreciate their cultures, which exposed them to various cultures at a fairly early age. This exposure would come in handy in Mary's career as well as business interactions.

Nevertheless, Mary's father did not let his status spoil the children. Although he had many workers, the children were required to do their own chores and earn their keep. He would not hesitate to remind his children that the workers, vehicles and anything in their household was his and not theirs. They had to work to get their own. Consequently, he never gave money to his children. They had to earn it. They used to work for a pay from him – for instance collecting seeds for his forestry projects, and cleaning and feeding the animals that he kept in the sanctuary.

As a Christian and church leader, Canon Awori had a lot of faith in God and strongly believed in prayers. He prayed every morning and evening and taught his children the same. Mary grew up under her father's influence, a legacy that would contribute to her success in later life. Throughout her life and in all that she undertook, she has come to draw a lot of power and inspiration from her religion. She contends that being a believer and having faith in God is a pivotal source of power for any budding entrepreneur. When all else fails, at least one gets comfort from the knowledge that there is a supreme being who cares for them and would not let harm come their way. In effect, she credits her strong faith in God and biblical principles for her achievements.

Growing up in Canon Awori's home was the best gift one could get in this highly competitive world. A very ambitious man himself, Mary's father encouraged his children to compete with the best. He would not tolerate failures, and personally charted out the career path of his children. Anybody who dared come second in their class had better present a convincing reason and be ready to make it up in the next exam or squarely face his wrath. When it came to success, the Aworis really had no choice.

In later years the Awori name came to ring all over the East African economic and political scene, featuring in the who's who list – from WWW Awori to Willis Awori. The late Wycliffe Wasya Work Awori (WWW Awori) was a freedom fighter in Kenya and an aggressive businessman who made his first million in his early twenties. He is remembered as the man who went to Britain in 1946 to convince Kenyatta to return to Kenya. He would later provide his car to ferry the English lawyer Noel Pritt and others to and from Kapenguria during the infamous Kapenguria trials. Wycliffe is also remembered as the last Secretary-General of the Kenya African Union (KAU) before it was proscribed in 1953 and the founding editor of one of the earliest newspapers in Kenya, *Radio Posta*.

Moody Awori, another of Awori's sons, also got into politics and business. Not only would he leave behind an impeccable development record in his Funyula Constituency (which he represented for a record 25 years in Parliament), but he also had a successful national political life, as he rose to become Kenya's ninth Vice-President.[33] During the political transition in 2002, he chaired the NARC Summit, a top party organ that brought together the heads of the affiliate parties. He is also an extremely successful businessman with interests in insurance, banking and real estate.

Another member of the Awori family who has made a contribution in the corporate world is Joshua Ayienga Awori. Joshua is credited with the exemplary management of the international conglomerate, Caltex Oil Company. A similar striking performance from the Awori scion was that of the late Hannington Awori who by design chaired boards of several blue-chip companies such as East Africa Industries (later Unilever Group), Standard Chartered Bank, Nation Media Group and Mabati Rolling Mills. Another Awori, Ernest Awori, a civil engineer, had a distinguished career with outstanding success and is remembered for the work he did in Uganda and at the Kenyatta National Hospital, the largest referral hospital in the East and Central Africa region. The accomplishment of the late Prof Nelson Wanyama Awori is another success story in the Aworis stable. He is credited as the first African in the East Africa region to perform a kidney transplant.

Mary's other siblings have also done well in their fields. Henry Awori, played a pivotal role as the Commissioner of Insurance, while retired sister Winfred Odera Awori ran a catering college in Nairobi. Grace Wakhungu Awori became a senior civil servant. Christine Awori, who married a prominent High Court Judge, Justice Andrew Hayanga, is a celebrated lawyer and a human rights activist. The outspoken Aggrey Awori rose to become a senior politician in Uganda. He is a Member of Parliament and at one time aspired for the presidency. Willis Awori, another brother to Mary, is a human resource practitioner.

For Mary, growing up in a rural village and being the daughter of a church

---

33   Others before Moody's Vice-Presidency were: 1. Jaramogi Oginga Odinga (1964–66); 2. Joseph Murumbi (1966–67); 3. Daniel arap Moi (1967–78); 4. Mwai Kibaki (1978–88); 5. Josephat Karanja (1988–89); 6. George Saitoti (1989–2002); 7. Musalia Mudavadi (2002–3); 8. Michael Wamalwa Kijana (2003–04).

leader had its ups and downs. To begin with, the moral standards were very high. As children of a pastor, people expected them to be morally perfect, almost like angels. This was a big challenge. However, it also made them aspire for higher ideals in life.

In school, Mary grew to be a celebrated sportsperson. Both her parents loved and promoted sports in the family. Canon Awori believed in sports; his philosophy was "A healthy mind in a healthy body". Thus, his emphasis on sports was more than casual. He was a soccer enthusiast and had music as his hobby. He would insist that his children pursue all their sporting events and would support such undertakings both morally and financially. Mary's mother was an athlete. It is therefore not surprising that Aggrey participated and won a medal in the Olympics in Rome and Tokyo. Hannington also participated in the Commonwealth Games. At Butere Girls, Mary was in the first netball team.

That Mary went to the best schools at the time was not accidental, but it was through merit. She deserved every opportunity she got. She was chosen to be among the first thirteen girls to start the Alliance Girls' 'A' level class. The chances were few and the administration was quite strict on the qualification criteria. At the time, everything was done above board; corruption was minimal. One had to merit the opportunity. Mary would not be admitted to such a competitive school simply for being a Canon's daughter. She had the credentials and got the chance which she also utilised well enough to gain admission at Makerere University. Among her peers at Alliance Girls' High School was the first lady judge, Justice Effie Owuor, the first woman Deputy Vice Chancellor, Prof Farida Karani and the first woman Chief Inspector of Schools and also Permanent Secretary in the Ministry of Education, the late Elizabeth Masiga.

Career in banking

Like most youngsters graduating from college with a deluge of opportunities beckoning, Mary was confused as to what career to pursue when she finally graduated from Makerere University with an honours degree in history. At first, she toyed with the idea of becoming a diplomat. Being the go-getter, she went ahead to join the public service in the Ministry of Foreign Affairs, only to discover soon enough that diplomacy was not her cup of tea; she was too direct and perhaps undiplomatic, according to her self assessment.

Bored with the diplomatic etiquette, Mary sought out a greater challenge in the then prestigious but exclusive male domain, the banking world. Despite the competition, her outstanding credentials won her a coveted position in Barclays Bank in Nairobi. Indeed Barclays was a welcome home for the ambitious young girl who subsequently became the first African female bank management trainee.

This was a tough call by any chance but she was determined to make it a success. It was her upbringing that gave Mary the confidence to survive, and actually flourish, in the banking career that at the time was totally unfriendly to women. Soon, she proved her mettle and was recommended for work/study scholarship in the Barclays London office.

London, the new terrain, came with its challenges. To start with, Mary encountered a radical shift in weather – very cold compared to the tropical African weather. Luckily, she did not have to contend with a cultural shock having lived and interacted with the Europeans back home. She however had to struggle to keep pace with the fast life. A lot of things were different, from the weather to food and culture. There were also issues of attitude. Race bias was also a shocker given that the Europeans she had lived with back home did not exhibit this bias. She had to pull up her socks literally.

Fortunately, her upbringing and schooling had prepared her for these challenges and she easily adjusted. She also got assistance from her elder sister who was also studying in London, although she opted to stay on her own. She chose from the onset to ignore any negative forces, rise above pettiness and focus on her goal. Over time, she came to win her colleagues' respect.

Mary returned from London not only with a diploma in banking and the prized offshore experience, but also with a husband and a child. She had charmed her way into the heart of an electrical engineering student named Pius Okelo who was pursuing his PhD at Imperial College. The two wedded in London in 1968, an occasion that was attended by several of her siblings and Kenyans from all walks of life including the High Commissioner. When she met Pius, she knew right away that she had found her mate. They fell in love in London, married right there in London and lived happily for 36 years until Pius' demise in November 2006.

Typical of the time, Mary's employer was not amused when she got her first baby, perhaps fearing that she might become a homemaker and not the career woman that they had invested in. In spite of the misgivings and the lovely blues enveloping the newly wedded, the two lovebirds did not lose their focus on what took them to London: academics. Both Mary and Pius bagged their Diploma and Doctorate respectively before jetting back to their motherland in 1970. Specifically, Mary, now a mother, was determined to make a success of her career as she came to take leadership in the male-dominated banking world.

Mary worked so hard for Barclays that she used to be referred to as Mrs

Barclays. As the first woman bank manager, she had to succeed if not for herself then for the womenfolk! During this transient time immediately after independence, the attitude and atmosphere at Barclays was different. The majority of those who could afford banking services were the settlers and most Africans were bankless. The general feeling was that Africans were inferior. It was at this time that Mary encountered one ugly incident. She had no choice but to confront her European boss for the way he treated staff. He exhibited an arrogance that belittled staff and made them feel useless. She did not like it and she felt that this arrogance was just a cover for his own inadequacies which he was projecting on innocent staff.

Fed up with the nagging boss, she one day summoned her courage, walked into the office and told him to his face what she felt about his management style and racist attitude. The boss was shocked that an African woman could take him to account. He was dumbfounded, as he didn't expect it. Unfortunately, he reported her to his seniors for insubordination but Mary stood her ground. Naturally, they could not work together thereafter and she was transferred to another branch, but the message hit home.

Mary was not going to be a pushover in this game. She knew henceforth that she was going to face a lot of resistance in her career. Sometimes she would have to deal with a conservative lot – the relic of colonial mentality. She had failed as a diplomat due to her forthright approach and she wasn't ready to compromise her ideals to keep the job, neither was she prepared to lose it – not before she had made a statement for the women whom she clearly represented. She therefore devised a strategy to survive in the organisation. She had to be tough but tactical.

Slowly but systematically, Mary began to stamp her mark at Barclays. The reality that a woman was in charge dawned on her employer when she declined to take her staff loan – which was extended to her on account of her seniority – until the same facility was extended to fellow women in the bank. She felt that the decision to avail to her a loan was biased and discriminative against the other women. This was duly honoured.

Progressively, Mary's consistent challenge on the establishment's thinking was admired by friends and loathed by foes. Her enlightened seniors quickly noticed her noble crusade and promoted her to the position of branch manager in Nakuru. Unfortunately, Mary had to decline this promotional transfer citing her family responsibilities. She had learnt the importance of family responsibilities from her father who always gave priority to his family. He would not hesitate to sacrifice his career ambitions at the altar of his family; for instance, he did forgo an opportunity for a scholarship in Australia due to his family obligations.

According to Mary, this particular sacrifice and the many more they made for the family came to pay dividends through their children. They are better people due to these sacrifices that they made as a family in their upbringing. She is saddened by those sacrificing their families in blind financial pursuits and she opines, "Remember, at the end of the day, everything you do is for them, so why not take care of their interests first?"

Despite the small hiccup, Mary finally became the first woman bank manager in 1977. Another rude shock awaited her. When she took over as the branch manager, some clients – mainly white – would walk into the office, find her seated, and still ask for the manager. They simply could not believe that this black woman sitting in the manager's office could, in the remotest possibility, be the manager. A bemused Mary would politely inform them that she was the one in charge. With time, they came to accept her and later appreciated and respected her work. She admits that converting the sceptical clients and winning their respect was quite a challenge.

One of the lessons that Mary learnt at Barclays was that one has to stand his or her ground and fight for whatever they believe in, but they have to be strategic about it. "You don't have to be confrontational all the time. Some situations demand that you fight back while others may not. You should learn to evaluate situations and respond appropriately so that you achieve what you want at the end of the day."

At Barclays, she was able to encourage women to work hard and become managers. Consequently, she started Barclays Bank Women Association through which she was able to mentor other women so that they could become managers. Her effort bore fruits as now there are many women bank managers.

Mary finally left employment in 1992 to join her pet project – Makini Group of Schools started in 1978 – as the Executive Director. At the time, she was Vice-President of Women World Banking in New York and a senior advisor to the President of African Development Bank in Abidjan, and was now going to head a primary school. This was a paradox that many a friend and foe found hard to believe. Despite their misgivings, she was undeterred as she followed her passion for children.

By moving from Barclays, she was not leaving her comfort zone, neither had she been frustrated. Although while at Barclays she bought a car, a house and could afford to live well, this was a comfort zone and was far from being a luxury to her as she was brought up with all these items. Work pressures were always there, but these were nothing that she could not handle. According to her, she felt that she had made her mark as an employee and it was time for a change and possibly to go for bigger challenges. She is happy with her track record at Barclays because she stayed long enough to challenge the policies and practices that were discriminative to women.

Makini Group of Schools

Mary's grandfather, Awori Khatamoga, was a man only four feet tall. However, he had a gift of running. He was such a fast runner that he created an occupation as an elephant hunter from it. Although she was born long after he had passed on, Mary greatly admired him from the stories that she heard about him. She found his exploits as an elephant hunter and an ivory trader way back in the 19th century quite inspirational given his small body size compared with the huge animals that he hunted down. From his story she learnt something about vision: irrespective of one's physical size, one can kill 'elephants'. Success demands vision, big dreams and the courage to realise them. Out of this she derived the belief that she is both visionary and courageous enough to live big dreams.

According to an interview she gave to researchers from Columbia University, Mary grew more interested in education as a respite from the pressures of the financial world. In the late 1970s, she had a friend named Mrs Motion who had recently opened one of Kenya's first private schools. Mary used to visit her a lot at the school as a break from banking. Struck by Mary's interest and passion in education she advised her to start a school. She hinted to her that it was good business and besides it would go a long way in fulfilling her passion. Needless to say, Mrs Motion became Mary's mentor in her fledgling school venture.

Apart from schools, Mary had always been passionate about children and education. She felt then and still does that the Kenyan society has little room for talented children; that it is a society that is more comfortable with average people than super-achievers. Unwittingly, people judge others by the average standards; for example, why would the system insist on eight years of primary education while there are children who can cover the course in less time? Through this standardised thinking, the society pulls down those who excel and are above average.

Through Makini, a Kiswahili word for diligence and hard work, Mary thought she would settle some of the discomfort that was nagging her with regard to children's education. Thus, to a great extent, Makini School is a model learning institution. It has a unique blend of staff and incorporates sports and other extra-curricular activities intricately into the daily programme. The curriculum is broad enough to capture most spheres of learning and is not confined to academics.

In the late 1970s, private schools, if any, were very few. Public schools were still the rave, as the public still had a lot of faith in the public institutions. Mary however had noticed a nascent deterioration in education standards in public schools. A few discerning parents too were slowly awakening to this decline coupled with pressure on public schools. In particular, Mary observed a growing middle class and the parents seeking better schools for their children. Although this opportunity was not glaringly apparent at the time, she suspected that it was just a matter of time before an explosion in the demand for private schools was experienced. Her premonition was vindicated.

The school started with only eight nursery-school children from the Okelos' old family house off Ngong Road in 1978. It grew steadily as satisfied parents refused to withdraw their children to other schools upon completion of one class, demanding instead that they add a new class. From this experience Mary learnt the importance of uncompromised quality of service to one's clients. Parents were unwilling to transfer their children to new schools because they felt that they were getting good value at the school.

At the beginning, the school business borrowed heavily from Mary and her husband's reputation. She was a respected and successful banker while Okelo – an engineer and a university lecturer – had his clout too. From this experience, Mary believes that start-ups with no visible track records can survive on the good reputation of the owners. While it is possible that one may not have experience in a certain field, at least every adult has a history and a track record whether from school, college or former workplaces. The goodwill one carries from their previous stations will be a boost to one's new undertaking. When clients believe that one is capable, they will trust them even at the initial stages.

The school grew very fast in all facets. Teething problems quickly sprouted; the increasing demand for classrooms took its toll on the Okelos finances. Their savings, which formed the seed capital, were quickly running out as they acquired surrounding plots to put up buildings that could accommodate the growing number of students. Relying on Mary's banking experience, they drafted a proposal for a bank loan to supplement their savings. This was granted after providing the requisite security and signing multiple personal guarantees.

Nevertheless, they had to be more careful with their resources. Thrift would become even more useful at the height of the crisis experienced in 2000 when the Kenyan economy was severely depressed. To steer from the storm, Mary had to change tack. As the Chief Financial Officer and in lieu of the construction cost overruns at their Lang'ata complex project, lower than expected revenues across the board and realities of a depressed economy, Mary fell back on her father's lesson one – thrift. All but the necessary expenditure was cut. Further expansion was curtailed. The only department that survived the cut was the core resources – teachers and school supplies. No matter the circumstances, she was not ready to compromise on the quality of education.

From experience, Mary concurs that it may be quite difficult but not impossible for new businesses to access financing from banks. For example, although the Okelos had a bankable proposal, they were not spared the stringent requirements for collateral security.

Growth and management strategy

From the beginning, the growth of Makini School was fuelled mainly by word of mouth and referrals by parents. This was later reinforced by their rising standing in the KCPE rankings. Mary did little advertising. Parental referrals and impressive performance at the national level were the school's strongest ambassadors, which proved the commitment to high standards.

For ease in administration, Mary categorised the schools into Makini Lower Primary School, Makini Middle Primary School and Makini Upper Primary School, each with its headteacher, which translated into Makini Group of Schools. By 2008, the school had 300 teaching and non-teaching staff, five campuses and a college. There are also over 50 buses that ferry students to and from school.

Mary brought to Makini a management experience that had been nurtured at home, honed in school and matured at Barclays Bank. She is passionate in whatever she does, emphatic and approachable. A great communicator with the nurturing instincts of a mother, Mary inspires her staff to excel.

As the team leader, she believes that every human being is unique and talented. She therefore lets her staff explore their potential and even make mistakes. She is not the know-it-all type of manager, but one who only shows the way and lets people do it their way. According to her colleagues, Mary is a team player, assertive and unassuming but can be aggressive when there is need to achieve her goals.

Mary, a humble mother of three, credits the success of the school to hard work, focus, determination and divine intervention. The management encourages and rewards success besides involving all stakeholders in determining the quality of the processes and products; for example, recruitment is on merit, there is training and development of staff and particularly involvement of parents through the Parents Teachers Association (PTA) in overseeing operations. Makini also pays well to attract the right staff and to motivate them.

Makini has been a beneficiary of a high-calibre management team consisting of Mary, Okelo (her late husband), an excellent and highly qualified board, and direct involvement of parents. This is supported by a team of competent and motivated staff. In addition, Makini had the first mover advantage. Started at a time when there was little interest in private schools, it had several years to build core staff and their brand before there was much competition.

Another strength that Makini has is a clear market niche. The first private schools in Kenya focused on serving the elite, mostly foreigners, embassies and UN staff. Makini strategically focused on the middle-class Kenyans who, as the Okelos have been vindicated, form the majority in the market. Their pricing is reasonable to attract their target group. This niche has proved big, loyal and elastic enough to sustain the business even in times of crisis.

The Makini success can also be traced to a unique learning environment and unrestrained investment on facilities. The school has excellent multimedia libraries and high-class laboratories. The classrooms are similarly well maintained and supplied. The schools have attractive buildings decorated with murals on well-manicured grounds. Additional facilities include swimming pools and gyms, which present a recipe for exciting and cheerful surroundings, something that is seriously lacking among the space-starved competitors.

In the longer term, Mary and her board have not settled on any one strategy for the progress of the school. The Columbia University research suggested that the school could borrow from among the following options to drive the school forward. These include but are not limited to consolidation, incremental expansion, aggressive expansion or Makini franchises.

The consolidation strategy is where future expansion of the schools would be stopped and all resources concentrated on improving the existing amenities and rounding out their management team. Incremental expansion may entail opening satellite locations in various points around the city to reduce on transport costs and maximise on accessibility and customer convenience. Aggressive expansion is where the board has the option to leverage the strong Makini brand name throughout East Africa and seek out new investors to inject capital and expertise to realise such a growth. Finally, Makini franchises is where the family can maintain ownership of the existing schools but give out licences at a fee to those entrepreneurs who would like to run schools under the Makini brand. This would be a possibility due to the strong brand name.

Mary would like to maintain the Makini Group of Schools as a family business. Already she is grooming her three children to take over the reins of the business. They are members of the board of directors. However, the future is open and they can take any appropriate route. As she says, "Business is dynamic and we cannot afford to be rigid."

Management structure

Makini School is run by a competent board of directors comprising the owners – Mary, her three children and their spouses, all of whom are professionals in their own fields – and other co-opted board members. The co-opted members are called to the board in light of their strengths in their respective fields. The board works closely with the PTA.

Then there is the administration, a distinct unit completely separate from the academic side of the business and tasked with implementing the board's policies. Within the administration there are various departments – Finance, Operations, Procurement and Supplies, and Human Resources. The latter department is tasked with ensuring that the school's human resource demands are matched with the relevant personnel. Hiring is professional and takes care of the need of the particular field. Mary is a believer in being slow to hire so that one gets the right staff than hurry and get the wrong staff which one is forced to fire almost immediately.

Mary admits that firing can be difficult. It can be messy unless one follows the rules and tries to be strict but fair; that is, being professional. However, employees have to know the rules of the game, which should strictly be enforced. A strict administrator will not hesitate to fire an errant employee. At Makini, staff turnover, especially on disciplinary grounds, is common due to strict enforcement.

Through professionalism, Mary has built a distinct Makini School that stands as its own brand and is not dependent on individuals. Makini should always remain Makini with its distinct values irrespective of who is the leader.

Challenges

No worthy dream is without hiccups. Makini has had and continues to have enough of them. To begin with, the school operates in an unstable society where political risks are inherent. One cannot simply predict policy changes where overnight declarations can easily derail a venture of this magnitude; for example, the government declared a policy that not more than 15 percent of students from private primary schools would be admitted to the elite national secondary schools. Such a policy would cripple private schools.

Growth in itself had its share of teething problems. At the school level, the deteriorating economic status of the Kenyan middle class in the late 1990s had significant impact on the growth projections of the school. Although a conservative five percent annual growth in students had been predicted, the actual growth was way below, while the number of parents defaulting on fees dramatically increased from two percent to over 15 percent during the same period.

At the macroeconomic level, sourcing for funds for expansion remains a challenge. Despite Mary's financial background, the strict security requirements and the cost of credit can be unpredictable and prohibitive; for instance, the IFC dollar-denominated loan that the school took to expand into secondary education by putting up the Lang'ata complex.

The Kenyan economy took a plunge in the second half of the 1990s seriously eroding the exchanges rates. This was exacerbated by the unexpectedly slow construction progress (due to the type of soil in Lang'ata). Consequently, the anticipated international baccalaureate programme that had been planned to cushion the school from the foreign exchange exposure on the loan did not take off in good time. Out of the blue, Mary was facing a crisis of gigantic proportions in repaying the loan with the weakened shilling and no dollar inflows. Luckily, once again Mary tapped into her long banking experience to re-negotiate a principal repayment moratorium.[34]

Mary has a seemingly inexhaustible list of challenges – the HIV/Aids prevalence, power rationing, government bureaucracy and corruption, land acquisition, and poor roads that occasion periodic vehicle breakdowns. Prevalence of HIV/Aids has taken away many parents, leaving promising children destitute. As a school, Makini tries to step in and ensure that the children do not drop out of school. The financial implication is however prohibitive given the numbers involved.

A major challenge has been in making tough decisions. Business is about making choices and tough decisions almost on a daily basis. Makini has been no exception to this rule. Fortunately, the enterprising Mary is no stranger to making hard choices. She had to make a choice to marry in London and have a family, something that was frowned upon by her employer. Later, she took Barclays head-on in women financing and employment, confronted her egoistic boss and declined a loan until and unless fellow women enjoyed the same facility. Even the choice to leave the comfort of employment to run a primary school was by any means bold. These and many more tough decisions prepared Mary well enough to face the business world.

As Mary points out, deciding whether to expand into a secondary school was one of the toughest choices they had to make as a board. On the face of it, the return on investment did not justify the move. Investing in a secondary school would not only require a bigger resource outlay due to such requirements as science laboratories, advanced libraries and sporting facilities, but it would

---

34   This is an arrangement that allows non-payment of the principal loan amount for a period of time. During the moratorium only interest due is payable by the borrower. This scenario can also be attributed to the underdeveloped financial market that lacks such facilities like foreign exchange hedging mechanism.

also call for upgraded teaching resources with a direct cost implication. But there was dire need for more secondary schools in the country.

Initially, Mary was wary of expanding into a secondary school as she thought it would jeopardise the existing business; from her experience, the returns were potentially lower compared to continued expansion of the primary schools. Her husband however insisted on this expansion. It was later that she came to see the expansion as a worthy contribution to national education.

Mary had to make another landmark tough decision in the year 2000. The school was facing a financial crunch due to the cost overruns in the Lang'ata project and the falling revenues across the board. Logically, the management moved to restructure the financial facilities in view of the slow collections. However, the longstanding banking partner could not heed their request. Difficult as it was, Mary had to move to another bank.

Around the same time, the business had to trim its operations. The technical college near the city centre, though successful in terms of enrolment, was not generating enough cash due to expensive teachers' salaries and the inherent costs of running a technical college. It was subsequently converted into a commercial marketing college and a primary school, the proven moneymakers.

Family and marriage

In a family of 17, sibling rivalry and competition could easily rear its ugly head, but not in Canon Awori's household. He applied one principle that did not allow this rivalry to fester – fairness. He treated all his children equally. Mary took up this legacy.

Mary and Pius were blessed with two sons and a daughter all of whom have a great relationship with one another. Besides attending reputable colleges in Europe and obtaining second degrees, they are married and have settled in their families.

The firstborn is Joseph Okelo, an economist. He worked for an American company, Cargill, in the human resources department before joining the school full-time. The second born, Lawrence, rose to head the auditing team at British American Tobacco (BAT) but is an engineer by profession. The one and only daughter, Claire Niala, studied Osteopathic Medicine and Naturopathy. Mary fondly remembers her exploits during her young age. They travelled a lot together. According to Mary, the little girl had an amazing grasp of issues. At one point, she recalls an incident when they went to Tokyo, Japan, a complex city with road signs written in Japanese. They had to rely on her vivid memory to guide them through. She was only nine years then. She also remembers a time when Claire's sharp wit got her elevated from economy to first-class after she impressed the flight attendant.

All the children have taken an active role in the running of the school both as directors and in various management roles. Joseph heads the Makini Marketing College. He is married to Patricia, a computer graphics designer who runs her own company, Willart. Lawrence is married to Christine whom he met at Manchester University. Christine has a degree in catering. Dr Claire is married to Alistar Beurnette, an engineer and technical director of the school. He took up what the late Dr Okelo was doing for the school.

Mary admits that her children are her greatest inspiration and joy. Parenting was not easy, especially bringing up the children into becoming responsible adults. But through prayer and leading by example she succeeded. When it comes to marriage, Mary is confident that their moral barometer will guide them; she believes that they will follow their moral instinct when meeting and maintaining friendships. If, for example, one believes that stealing is wrong, one cannot marry somebody who is a thief.

On marriage and family, Mary thinks that couples who fight over money are missing the point. Family is a partnership where people must share responsibilities as well as finances. In her household, they rarely disagreed over family finances. They approached finances with the understanding that they are supposed to be common resources.

Evidently, Mary's family has broken the tribal and racial barriers when it comes to their marriages. This could be traced to the multicultural upbringing that was pioneered by her grandfather. He not only traded with the Arabs, but he also housed the early missionaries on their way to and from Uganda. Mary's children, having had the unique opportunity of being brought up in Nairobi and later going to school in Europe, easily broke the cultural barriers in their search for partners.

Tips for entrepreneurs

From her endless list of challenges, one wonders how Mary came to stay on top and ride the crest of success Apart from watching the business grow, she is also watching over the growth of another generation in the Okelo scion, a clear indication of success. She has a handful of tips for budding as well as aspiring entrepreneurs.

First is focus and getting priorities right: "When you know where you are going, you will get there no matter the obstacles. Just don't compromise the things you believe in for an easy way out. To succeed, one has also to prioritise."

Secondly is abiding by the rules: "Follow the rules of the profession that you are in. Business, just like games, has rules. Those who break the rules cannot be judged winners. One of the rules to success is commitment to good quality." Mary's commitment to quality right from the beginning, including designing processes that would guarantee the best in quality, ensured the success of Makini School.

Third is time management. From the onset, Mary attached a lot of value to her time. In her view, one has a choice either to spend the time they have in this world or invest it. She chose the latter and the outcome is evident.

Leading by example is another trait that contributes to success both at the family level and in business. "Children can read the actions of adults more than their empty rhetoric. It serves absolutely no purpose to reprimand your children against drug abuse, for instance, while you puff away in the house in their full view." Parents should teach their children through actions and not just words.

Other important pillars of success are honesty and integrity. She notes: "Our family did not condone dishonesty in any form. We were schooled in the narrow path that success follows hard work. Young people should concentrate on building a respectable reputation. It is a strong selling point for any budding entrepreneur."

For the successful people, she urges them to mentor others. It is the mentor spirit that will eventually change society: "Be a mentor to those around you. As already mentioned, our school venture was strongly recommended to us by a family friend – Mrs Motion – who was also running her own school. It's hardly expected that a business person would prop up a competitor, but that's what happened. At Makini, we try to mentor others. For example, we have supported some of our teachers who leave to go and start their own schools."

Patience, teamwork, tolerance and competitiveness are values that would comfortably see one through life. Mary learned these values while in school at Alliance and in Makerere. In sports, she learnt teamwork, competitiveness and the essence of preparation; they had to work as a team to achieve the goal of winning; they had to be competitive at the same time to beat the opponents, and they had to prepare adequately to succeed whereby the team had to train many times over just to be ready for a match that would take less than an hour. Mary's advice, particularly to the young, is that they should accept the fact that success takes time and demands preparation. "Those who join business for a quick return are setting themselves up for failure. They should have patience to wait for the fruits of their effort to ripen."

A believer in transformational leadership, Mary recommends continuous change for even established businesses. She advises people to be ready to learn and change with the times. "Business growth is a process that continuously evolves. Keep changing to be relevant. Update your products and systems regularly to keep up with the times."

Another piece of valuable advice for entrepreneurs is passion in whatever business one chooses to engage in and to give one's best: "Follow your heart. Work with all your heart as if it is your own business. I'm a believer in honesty and therefore do not support acts in employment that defraud your employer. Give your employer what they are paying you for and much more."

For those in employment, Mary believes that one can only transfer the work ethic they have acquired to their business. It would be impossible for one to all of a sudden become a stickler for punctuality and time having spent ten or more years in employment carelessly throwing away time in the guise of fooling the employer.

Most importantly, an aspiring entrepreneur must always be vigilant to spot an opportunity at the right time. Although pioneering has its challenges, it is a better bet compared to late entry.

On financing business, Mary advises that entrepreneurs must look first into their own resources to set up and maybe get funding along the way. Personal savings and family support are just but among the few options available at this stage. "We had these clay piggy banks given to us at the first christening where we were supposed to keep all our savings. From this, we learnt from a tender age to always keep something for a rainy day, a habit that will come in handy both at the start and in the running of Makini Schools," counsels Mary.

Women and business

If there is one thing Mary holds dear it is the welfare of fellow women. Being a woman, Mary has first-hand experience in the unbalanced treatment that they go through. From her experience at her previous workplace, she found herself a champion of women affairs. Ever since, she has built on this platform to lead and to advise on gender improvement initiatives.

Mary believes that women are equal to any task. She attributes their poor showing in business to family pressure, skewed allocation of resources and lack of opportunities. She also believes that the security requirements do not favour women since in most African cultures, properties such as land are only inherited by men. As she observes: "It's instructive to note that women are the proprietors of most small enterprises which they rely on to feed their families. However, these enterprises never grow beyond certain limits due to overdependence on them for family needs and lack of financing. Remember, until recently, financial institutions were insisting on approval from husbands for women to be given loans."

The trappings

Success comes with its rewards otherwise it would not be worth the hassle. This starts with financial independence and the freedom to buy, hire and live the way one wants. One can take their children to the best schools, their family on holidays and above all give back to the society. Like many successful people, Mary is not averse to a little luxury. She drives a state-of-the-art Mercedes Benz, the ultimate status symbol. To her, the Benz accords her class, comfort, prestige, reliability and safety. On the standby, she has a four wheel Range Rover for the rough terrain and upcountry travels; she is a village girl who loves travelling upcountry for holidays.

Her Nairobi home is in the leafy suburbs of Karen. The upmarket Karen residential area has magnificent houses with large compounds and beautiful landscaping. Residents here keep horses and other expensive pets. It is the confirmed address for Kenya's who's who. The aura reminds Mary of her village upbringing: "You know I was born and bred in the village. Back then, I enjoyed taking a leisurely walk in the forest while listening to the chirping birds. The Karen environment closely resembles where I grew up."

Mary has been airborne for the better part of her adult life. She kicked off with the Barclays airlift in her mid-twenties and has literally traversed the world both in business and leisure travel. She always travels first class, not just because she can afford it but also to get the best of her travelling hours. As she spends quite some time in the air, she needs to work, relax and enjoy every bit of it.

Her credentials are such that many private and public institutions including UN agencies want to have her on their board of directors. She has had to turn down some invitations to boards and invitations to other numerous occasions in order to focus on her school business. Nevertheless, she sits on the boards of about 10 companies some of which are public, charitable and private. Wherever she serves, she believes she makes a positive contribution in their activities. She also consults for a number of organisations on women, finance and education as well as gender issues, errands that are handsomely rewarding in finance, status and privileges.

Mary considers one of her greatest achievements as her family – with her only regret in life being that she was not able to get many children. Nevertheless, the three children allowed her space to pursue other goals, something that may have been difficult if she had more considering the reaction from her employer – Barclays Bank – when she became pregnant and eventually got her first baby.

Mary's life is a testimony of sacrifice, perseverance and determination. "I challenged a lot of fundamental beliefs and archaic ways of doing things. This taught me one thing – to always push your limits and expand your boundaries."

One thing that Mary abhors is pretenders or double-faced characters. She believes in originality and has no respect for those who wear masks. She holds that people should not pretend to be what they are not.

Mary has had many firsts, which has won her many awards and honours. She has previously won the Africa Enterprise Award and has been bestowed the Moran of the Burning Spear (MBS) by the President.

Best and worst moments

Mary's best moments have been the times spent with her family and they have been many. Her worst moment was when she lost her husband: "Together we were working on great plans for the school, one of which was expanding it into a university. It was devastating to lose him at that time. Sadly, it happened and we had to slow down some plans. We therefore decided to strengthen the school as it is first before considering further expansion."

Chapter 10

Fred Rabongo

When the Minister of Labour appointed Fred Rabongo as the acting Managing Trustee of the National Social Security Fund (NSSF) in August 2008, the decision may have generated some controversy. However, many people who know Fred Rabongo were amused by media reports referring to him as a public relations consultant. The reality was that at just 40 years of age this founder of Impulse Promotions Limited had carved for himself an enviable niche in the marketing industry and had also won the respect of his peers. In September 2008 Fred was nominated for the coveted annual Warrior Award of the Marketing Society of Kenya (MSK). This award recognises individuals who have made outstanding contributions to the field of marketing in Kenya.

Fred Rabongo founded his flagship business in 1995. The company grew to become top in its field, handling below the line (BTL) marketing projects for a range of blue-chip clients in Kenya. Such clients included Safaricom, East African Breweries Limited (EABL), Delmonte Kenya, Ketepa Limited, Coca-Cola Company and Unilever. It has over 100 employees and offers a wide range of services such as product launches, sales and merchandising, consumer competitions/promotions, event management, and roadshows/street parades. Its operations are nationwide covering six key regions – Nairobi, Mount Kenya, South Rift, Western, Nyanza and Coast.

Perhaps the reason Fred is not known outside marketing circles is because he prefers to stay out of the limelight and instead in the foreground of his company. Outside the marketing field, he has diversified into real estate, digital advertising and commercial cleaning services.

Early life and childhood

Fred Rabongo was born in 1968 in Nakuru into a polygamous family. He was the firstborn of his mother's ten children comprising eight boys and two girls. His stepmother also had ten children, seven girls and three boys. Fred's mother, Margaret Awino (or simply Peggy) was a primary school teacher in Nakuru, while the stepmother lived with her children at their rural home. His father, Eliud Rabongo, worked with the police force. With this physical separation, Fred never really experienced the whole family living together, neither was he exposed to the tension that often characterises polygamous families. "Nevertheless, the two families came together during such occasions as Christmas when we would also visit our grandparents," says Fred.

"Another factor that acted as a family barrier was that we were considerably spaced out such that we hardly grew up together. When one was in primary school another would be in secondary school. Although we were close as a family, the age difference between us was wide; for instance, the gap between my last born sister and I meant that we would have a father-daughter kind of relationship – when I was 40, she was still a teenager," says Fred. It was not surprising therefore that, during school holidays, some of the children would go to visit other relatives.

In his childhood, Fred moved around a lot owing to the nature of his father's occupation as a court prosecutor. In total he attended six different primary schools in Migori, Kendu Bay, Nairobi, Homa Bay, Rongo and Kisii. While one would expect that all this relocating would have an adverse effect on his studies, this was not the case. On the contrary, he maintained good performances and scored high academic grades. As he observed: "When you learn in the same school and you're always number one, you think you're the brightest. When I was in the Nyanza schools I was always among the top three in my class. Then I went to Kisii and for the first time I was not in the top 10. So either I had been affected by all the moving or the standards there were higher. But it prepared me to know that I was probably not as good as I had previously thought."

Fred and four of his siblings grew up in urban areas as they moved with their father on his transfers. The last five siblings grew up in their rural home in Mbita, Suba District in Homa Bay County, where their father settled after retirement. "During this time when my father was moving from one place to another, court prosecutors were perceived to be people who would influence cases in court and, together with CID officers, they were subjected to frequent transfers," says Fred. "Whenever he was transferred, I would move with him. At some point, this became too much and I opted to stay with my mother in the schools where she taught."

Early exposure to different cultures as well as learning environments was most important to Fred. The experience taught him the value of humility and learning from others because in a world full of competition he would not always be the best. This is a lesson that he has carried with him. Even today, he always seeks to learn from people who are older, more experienced and more successful than he is. Such interactions have not only resulted in solid friendships but they have helped to propel him to the success that he was to achieve.

The constant changes of environment in his childhood also became visible in Fred's working life. He is not afraid to try new things. Largely driven by the need to pull his large family out of poverty, he has over the years tried different jobs including teaching, selling clothes, dealing in dress fabrics and office equipment on commission, and marketing. All this was before starting his company.

Fred's father did not earn much in the police force (court prosecutors were drawn from police officers). Therefore, the family was not well off. "It is still puzzling how our parents managed to bring up all of us considering the size of the family," comments Fred, "perhaps one of the factors that helped was that primary education at the time, especially the early 1970s and part of the 1980s, was free. It was only when I was in Form Four that I experienced a school fees problem. Before that, I had not noticed any difficulties."

When he was admitted for 'A' level studies at Baringo High School, lady luck smiled on him in Form Six when former President Daniel arap Moi paid school fees for all the students for the whole year. "I was also bought school uniform. Both gestures reduced the burden on my parents significantly," Fred remembers with nostalgia. Moi also did the same for two other schools in his home area – Sacho and Kabarnet. Ultimately, Fred was to shoulder the responsibility of educating some of his siblings when he started working.

Before joining Baringo High School, Fred had attended Maranda High School in Bondo District of Siaya County for his 'O' levels. After sitting the Kenya Certificate of Education (KCE) examinations, he obtained Division One. "I was number two amongst the one hundred and twenty candidates. My score was also among the highest in the whole province for that year. I followed up this sterling performance at Baringo High School where I was one of the two leading candidates in the Kenya Advanced Certificate of Education (KACE) examinations. Nevertheless, the school did not do well that year," says Fred.

Fred's mother was a disciplinarian. Consequently, all through primary and secondary school, Fred was under strict discipline. While other boys generally picked up all sorts of mischief such as smoking, drinking and sneaking out of school, he steered clear of such activities. Generally, he was a model student and was made a prefect in Form One, Form Four and later in Forms Five and Six. However, he was suspended once while in secondary school because of fighting. Fred recalls: "What happened was that a bigger boy had whacked my head against a wall. I took a stone and hit him in retaliation, something that earned me a two-week suspension. After the suspension, I was given the worst punishment at the school – to uproot a tree trunk. Although I was unable to do it, the teachers forgave me anyway."

Despite the fact that Fred's father was a serious footballer who even played in his adult years, Fred was not into sports. His brothers were also good football players and were members of their respective school teams. This however changed at the university where his roommate Fred Ouko introduced him to rugby. The roommate had played the game at Nairobi School. Fred loved it instantly and ended up playing for Black Blad, the Kenyatta University team, as a scrum. Later, he played for Nakuru RFC while at Afraha High School where he was posted for teaching practice. "Indeed, I am the one who started rugby at Afraha School and later at Kajiado where I was later posted as a teacher," says Fred.

Before joining Kenyatta University (popularly referred to as KU), Fred had always dreamed of doing a Bachelor of Commerce degree. However, he was admitted for a Bachelor of Education (BEd) degree course in which he was to take linguistics, literature and economics. As he progressed in his course, he later changed to business education and economics. On completing the course he learned that he had been posted to teach at Ol Kejuado High School in Kajiado County. He was inclined to refuse the posting, especially because it was classified as a hardship area. "When you finish campus you want to be posted to Nairobi or Mombasa and not a rural school," he says. However, his resolve changed when he met a friend who had graduated from KU a year earlier and was teaching at the school. She encouraged him to visit and see the school for himself before turning down the posting.

"When I visited the school, I could not believe what I saw. The school had first class facilities and was not as bad as I had thought. Perhaps they had such facilities because they wanted to encourage teachers to go to such places. I was allocated a three-bedroom house fully furnished with a fridge, bed, cooker and sofa set," he recollects. This was a dream house for a fresh university graduate and proved to be the decisive factor for him. He took up the offer and taught economics, accounts and business education. As one of the only two business teachers in the school, he was utilised to the hilt and ended up teaching students from Form One to Form Four.

The downside of the teaching job was the meagre salary (KSh 4,040 per month) and the delays in payment of the same that the teachers and civil servants were experiencing at that time. For the first three months, he did not receive a cent. "Every weekend I would travel to Nairobi and get KSh 1,000 from my cousin, Otieno Kajwang, a young lawyer then. With this money, I would purchase food for the week and pay for my transport back to Kajiado.[35] It was really a difficult time for me," says Fred.

By this time his father had left the police force and was carrying out some business. Having worked in the courts and with the police for a long time, he had initially started a business that was related to court cases such as process

---

35   Otieno Kajwang, a lawyer, was to later become the Member of Parliament for Mbita Constituency. Following the disputed 2007 elections, he was appointed cabinet minister in the resulting coalition government in 2008. He served as Minister of State for Immigration and Registration of Persons.

serving. "The biggest problem my father faced was chasing payments from clients. After some time he found himself being owed a lot of money. Thus, the business did not do well and he really struggled to make ends meet," says Fred.

Thereafter, his father gave up, went to his rural home in Mbita and started a *matatu* business. Fred's mother had sought a transfer from Nakuru and was teaching in a school in Mbita as well. The business however lasted only a year due to the terrible roads. "My father then bought a fishing boat and went into business. It also did not do well as he was ripped off by the people he hired to do the actual fishing and remit the proceeds to him," Fred remembers. It was while in this business that his father died in 1990. He had opted for early retirement to start a business. Subsequently, the responsibility of taking care of the family fell squarely on young Fred's shoulders who was then 22 years old.

Getting into business amid career demands

While Fred's father was struggling with his businesses, the family had real problems coming up with school fees for the children. "Although I had started working, my KSh 4,040 monthly salary was hardly enough to take care of my needs, let alone help my parents. My siblings were constantly being sent home for lack of school fees; some even spent a whole term away from school. When I saw that my mother could not manage with her even smaller salary, I was naturally distressed. This is what drove me into business," says Fred.

After three months of teaching without a salary, Fred decided to get an acquaintance at TSC to chase the payment for him. Eventually, he was successful and received a total of KSh 11,000 when the money was released. At the time, this amount seemed like a lot of money. "Thus, I decided to start a business with that money to supplement my salary and help my family with school fees. Immediately, I started going to Namanga, one of Kenya's border towns with Tanzania, to buy dress materials which I would sell to tailors in Nairobi," says Fred.

Such trade was not allowed; it was *magendo* (illegal). To effectively operate, Fred explains: "*Matatu* drivers would sneak them into the country for me because if the police found them they would be confiscated." Fred's market for the fabrics consisted of tailors in Kenyatta, Uhuru, Jericho and Umoja markets. Chiffon was the in-thing at the time. On the first trip, he made a really good profit. "I was buying a three-metre length of fabric for KSh 150 and selling it for KSh 300. Business thrived so much that some customers would tell me to leave the materials with them and collect payment on my next trip."

With the money that he made from the sale of contraband fabrics, Fred decided to expand his sources. He sent friends who worked with Kenya Airways to buy suits for women from India and the UK. "At that time there were very good suits for women called Zeki. I would buy each for KSh 2,000 and sell for KSh 3,000."

Due to the demands of his business, Fred was in Nairobi most weekends. "I would leave Kajiado before 6.00 am on Saturday, arrive at Namanga by 7.00 am, shop for fabrics and be in Nairobi by midday. Then I would go round to my clients selling the fabrics and collecting payments for materials left the previous week. This way I was able to discover what my clients liked. One such discovery was that other than chiffon fabrics, the most popular items were the Zeki suits." Fred was also selling men's trousers and leather jackets from India. Each week he would take the remaining fabrics back to the school and sell them to fellow teachers who could afford to buy. He would also sell them to the nearby *Kwa DC* area where people had money. This was the District headquarters for all government ministries. There were many potential customers with money like district heads, among others. Within a short time his business was bringing in more money than his salary, enabling him to pay school fees for his siblings. This really helped the family after the death of their father.

Despite the thriving of the business, it was not all rosy. There were numerous problems with logistics. "Some people disappeared or refused to pay altogether, which interfered with my stock levels. Also, some of my 'business friends' who procured stocks for me could only go to London or Mumbai when they had flights scheduled to go there; thus, I could not get stocks as regularly as I would have wished."

With the proceeds from his business, he bought a new sofa set and gave the one that he had been provided with the house to another teacher. It cost KSh 30,000 and was the most expensive item he had ever bought. He also bought a carpet.

Soon after that, while visiting his girlfriend, a fellow student from his university days who had been posted to Mombasa, Fred found out that there was a private school looking for a teacher in economics and accounts. The Deputy Headmaster in the school turned out to be a friend he knew also from his university days in KU. At the time economics teachers were quite difficult to get. He was offered a monthly salary of KSh 13,000, triple what he was earning with TSC. He resigned immediately and reported to Memon Villa Secondary School in Mombasa ready to begin teaching the following school term. The year was 1991.

The distance factor (from the border town and Nairobi) now made it very difficult for Fred to continue with his fabrics business, so he decided to do something else to supplement his income. He got a part-time gig selling office equipment such as fax machines and telephones on commission. "My new employer had no problem with me having another job as long as I hit my targets," says Fred. In most days, teaching ended at 3.00 pm. He would leave the school and do the rounds seeing clients until 5.00 pm. He would also utilise free time during the day when he didn't have classes to push sales. This way, he juggled the two jobs for some time.

However, the additional income was not sufficient to cater for his siblings' school fees. The family still had many money problems. "Therefore, I opted to take on a third job that involved doing private tuition on weekends. My days were now packed from morning till night and even the weekends. As a result, I had no social life. In any case, I could not afford it because I had a lot of family responsibilities," says Fred.

To save on living expenses, Fred was sharing a four-bedroom house in Ganjoni with two other bachelors, Bob Opee and Moses Omolo, with whom they split the KSh 8,000 rent. Moses was also a trained teacher but had left teaching and was doing shipping, while Bob had a sales job at Eveready East Africa Limited. "I was determined to get a serious sales job and had gone for several interviews. However, I always got regrets after the prospective employers found out that I was a teacher with little experience in sales," says Fred.

When Eveready advertised for sales jobs, Fred decided to apply. Bob offered to introduce him to his boss, the Sales and Marketing Manager known as Odhiambo (he has since died), in Nairobi. They met in Odhiambo's house on a Sunday and he proceeded to interview him. "Why do you want to do sales?" he asked Fred. "I have always wanted to be a salesman and I love marketing," Fred replied. Odhiambo retorted, "If I were you, I'd start by selling books." And when he learned that Fred had gone for other interviews on the sales job he said, "If they didn't take you we won't. Eveready does not take rejects." The blunt comment was all the more depressing for Fred because he and Bob had spent the whole of the previous day looking for Odhiambo and had only managed to get him on Sunday. To make matters worse, Fred had to take the 9.00 pm bus back to Mombasa in order to make it to class the next morning, but because the session with Odhiambo lasted so long, he missed the bus.

Sometime later, Fred applied for a job as administration manager at McCann Erickson. By then he was desperate to move to Nairobi as both his friends (and housemates) had found jobs with multinationals in the capital city. Moses was first when he joined Maersk, a global shipping company. Then Bob left

Eveready and joined Gillette. "We all really wanted to move to Nairobi and had this practice where whenever any of us returned from an interview in Nairobi, usually around 4.00 am in the morning, he would wake the others up and they would discuss how the interview went until daybreak."

At McCann, Fred was interviewed by two people. The first was the General Manager, Rose Kimotho, who was later to found Regional Reach, the flagship behind Kameme FM and later K24.[36] The other interviewer was Ndirangu wa Maina, the General Manager of McCann Response, a firm that carried out marketing research. Ndirangu later bought this division and renamed it Consumer Insight. "I did not get the job," he says.

At that time McCann Erickson had another division called McCann Epic (events, promotions, in-stores and competitions) which was headed by Philip Gachago as General Manager. Gachago was the first to move with a McCann department. Someone referred Fred to him when he was just about to do so. Before moving, the agreement was that McCann would continue to support the new company in the initial stages. Therefore, struggling to get the business started would not be an issue.

After interviewing Fred, Gachago hired him. "During the interview, which was held at McCann, Gachago made it clear to me that he was leaving with the department. They would nevertheless continue staying in the McCann premises for some time, about a week or two, making preparations for the move as they registered Gap Promotions," says Fred. Patrick Mutuma soon joined them and the trio got the new company started in 1993. Fred was put in charge of merchandising at a monthly salary of KSh 25,000, while Mutuma handled promotions.

The pioneer in the industry was a company called Marketing Support Services and it was the largest player in the market. Another company was Enza which later changed its name to Azen. But as Gap grew it overshadowed these companies and became synonymous with below the line (BTL) marketing services in Kenya. Impulse Promotions, which Fred started later, became the leading agency.

"On leaving with the department, the arrangement was that McCann would give all below the line marketing jobs to Gap in exchange for the usual 18–20 percent agency fees. We even moved with some of the furniture we had been using at McCann. Bulk photocopying was also still done at McCann. For a while we ran it like it was part of McCann," says Fred.

Gap Promotions' first base was in Hurlingham. With rapid growth, it later moved to Upper Hill after a few months. To get started it had inherited McCann clients such as Eveready, Unilever and the Coca-Cola companies. As

---

36 Kameme FM was the first vernacular FM radio station in Kenya while K24 was the first 24-hour local news television channel.

the company found its feet it completely detached itself from McCann and was not relying on referrals from the latter to survive.

Although Fred was mainly responsible for marketing, he also got involved in promotions. "I had certain dedicated accounts like Coca-Cola and Eveready for whom I would handle not only merchandising but also any competitions and promotions that they had." The most challenging aspect of the job was that his teaching background had not prepared him for a management position in marketing where he had many people in various towns reporting to him. "This management aspect turned out to be like baptism by fire. I was put at the helm and needed to travel all over the country. Nevertheless, I learnt quickly on-the-job and within a short time, I was the next in line after Gachago; even Patrick was now reporting to me," he says.

The best part of the job was that he got to interact with the 'who is who' in marketing because Gap was handling some of the biggest companies in the market. From such meetings, Fred observed that, "Dealing with such senior managers makes you grow because you start behaving like them; but it also humbles you."

After two years at Gap Promotions, Fred joined Esso, an oil company, to do merchandising. At Esso, he was offered double remuneration which amounted to a monthly salary of KSh 50,000. The job offer came together with another one from Rose Kimotho who had by then left McCann to start her own company, Regional Reach. "While on leave from Gap, I helped her do one promotion at Regional Reach for Blue Band. After the promotion, I was not sure whether I wanted to join the company full time. Rose wanted me to help her set up the new company. Ironically the person at Esso with whom I was negotiating the move was Rose's sister, Mary Kimotho. I believe they must have talked because the next thing Mary was asking me to decide which of the two jobs I really wanted. It was not easy for me to choose given my youthful age. While Rose was offering me a car, Mary at Esso was offering to double my salary," says Fred.

Finally he chose Esso and put in his resignation at Gap. The main reason he chose Esso was because he had always wanted to work for an oil company. He felt that his career prospects would be better in that industry.

At Esso, Fred's first position was a marketing assistant and he later became the marketing analyst. At that time fuel stations did not have convenience stores, which were to become a common feature. Fred's main task at Esso was to roll these out in the company's retail outlets. "Total was actually the first company to implement the concept, but they had small shops. These shops were not really convenience stores of the scale that came later. At Esso I was able to raise the income of the first real convenience store – the Chequered Flag – by 60 percent. I did this by involving the input of the other employees and rewarding them with vouchers. They would go to the station and fill in score cards. Chequered Flag was not an Esso concept. It had already been introduced by others. But the Chequered Flag was mainly known as a garage rather than a convenience store. But the C-store concept was Esso's," says Fred.

While he was working at Esso, Fred's mother passed away in 1991. By this time he was financially stable, able to educate his siblings without difficulty and to support his stepmother financially aided by his brothers.

Throughout Fred's career, two years seemed to be the amount of time that he would spend in one job before getting restless and seeking new challenges. After two years at Esso he was sending out job applications. He was offered two jobs as Marketing Manager with Ryce Motors (which is part of the Sameer Group) and Synresins Limited. He chose to join Ryce Motors. "However, I did not stay at Ryce for long. I felt uncomfortable with the working environment. Meetings would often be transacted in the Hindi language which I did not understand. Within a month, I called Synresins and they gave me the job." However, the same thing happened there. "Imagine going all the way to Nakuru with your boss to see a client and they switch to Hindi. This is a serious meeting and you're not supposed to say anything!" exclaims Fred.

Fed up with this state of affairs and wishing he had stayed at Esso, Fred resigned after three months and decided to start his own business with a little money that he had saved while working at Esso. Around the same time he was offered a job at SmithKline Beecham (now GlaxoSmithKline). However, he turned down the job offer as he had already made up his mind not to go back to employment.

Birth of Impulse Promotions

Fred first started toying with the idea of starting his own BTL marketing company when he was working at Gap Promotions. "Gap had so many clients that the company was in almost every product range. There were also a lot of promotions that it was not able to do because of conflict of interest." Often a potential client would approach the company but they could not take the job because they were already working with the competition. "I could see that there was a large market for these services," he says.

Fred had a friend called Maxwell Owuor, an interior designer, who was operating from his house in Westlands, a Nairobi suburb. By day he would convert the house into an office. He agreed to let Fred use the same premises for Impulse Promotions. "During the day we would put our files in the cabinet in the living room and at night we would transfer them to the bedroom and put the plates and other crockery back in the cabinet," says Fred. Although he had his own home where he used to spend the nights, because he was using Maxwell's house as an office during the day, he split the rent with him. In addition, he got his own telephone lines but they shared a secretary, Julia Waikwa. With the two telephone lines, he started the business which cost him KSh 5,000.

At the time he started Impulse Promotions, Fred had accumulated savings of KSh 150,000. "Knowing well that it would be some time before any business came along, I kept the money aside to pay rent, my upkeep and the salary of the secretary," he says. The initial period of getting the business on its feet involved working 12-hour days. He would be in the office by 6.15 am daily, something he commemorates by having all his vehicles bearing 615 on the number plate. He would spend the day handwriting proposals (because they did not have a computer) and attending meetings with potential clients. He would then leave the office at around 6.00–7.00 pm and go to the computer room at Kenyatta University to type proposals until 10.00 pm assisted by his wife Edna Wangui who was then a lecturer at the university. They also did not have a printer, so Fred would save his work on diskettes and go to a bureau to print and bind the proposals. Eventually they decided to buy a computer and printer in anticipation of some jobs coming in. After this, they were now doing all the proposals in the office. They still had no clients three months after Fred got into the business.

"I was prepared to stay only six months without an income. Meanwhile, I was extremely frugal keeping expenses to a minimum," he narrates. He approached Ndirangu wa Maina who was still at McCann and asked for referrals after explaining that he had gone into business. Fred naturally expected a favourable reaction from someone he had worked with before and who knew his capability. However, Ndirangu's reaction surprised him. "He told me that I could not be helped." Retrieving a McCann company profile, he asked Fred: "Show me what work Impulse Promotions has done before I can help you." "I asked him, 'Where do I get a company profile when I have just started the business?'" says Fred. He only had to rely on the experience he had acquired at Gap. Despite pointing out the fact that in the past they had done work similar to what he was now asking for, Ndirangu was not swayed. Fred left his office a very dejected man.

"But I think the experience with Ndirangu made me stronger. I realised that I could not rely on the people I had worked with in the past to give me business and that it was not going to be as easy as I had previously thought." Most of the clients that he had worked with before would say, "We know you've done this, but as Fred Rabongo; what have you done as Impulse Promotions?" Everyone wanted him to produce a company profile before they could give him work. "This proved to be my biggest challenge during these initial stages."

Fred's breakthrough came when Gavin Bell, then the General Manager at Holiday Inn and later the proprietor of Kengeles chain of restaurants, asked him to organise the hotel's New Year promotion. "Bell wanted an event that would help sell all available seats on New Year's Eve. I worked with Daewoo Motors, which offered to give branded material as prizes in the raffle. Two weeks before, Impulse Promotions displayed a Daewoo Cielo and this helped sell tickets as people must have thought it was to be won. Jerry Okungu, who was in Nation Media Group, and Ali Mohammed, an advertising manager at the *Standard,* offered free advertisements. The client was happy. I had also identified a children's home where part of the proceeds from the event would go, which they put in the adverts as well. Coca-Cola had given the banners. Therefore, the client only paid for the radio advertisements. Seats were sold out within the first few days. This was my first project and it was very successful," says Fred. The job earned him KSh 360,000.

With that money, Fred was able to rent his own offices on Wood Avenue in Kilimani. Although they were sublet, the premises were bigger as they provided the use of two rooms. In addition to the secretary, Fred also hired another employee, Richard Owade, and put him in charge of promotions while he focused on marketing and business development. Now that he could say he had done one project successfully, he approached Unilever whom he had worked with at Gap Promotions and asked for a job. "I was still at the stage where someone had to have a lot of trust in the service provider. Potential clients still felt like they were taking a risk hiring me. The representative from Unilever visited our offices and he was not impressed. All the same, he decided to give me a small job to brand their offices, which earned us KSh 200,000," says Fred.

Their next job was a distribution drive for House of Manji biscuits and Kokozi (lozenges) which involved selling bicycles. They bought bicycles specifically for this project and hired people to do the promotion mainly targeting kiosks. "This was very challenging because some people disappeared with both the bicycles and the stock. Accounting for the money was also another major problem because some went and sold goods on credit after we had told them not to. I ended up in court with one of the hired hands after I caught up with him in Kiambu." This was a headache and proved to be one of the most difficult jobs that he had ever done. Subsequently, he swore off selling bicycles for good. Although convinced that selling bicycles is a viable business, Fred quips: "I would not advise anyone to adopt it unless they're able to put controls into it."

From there Impulse Promotions grew rapidly. It grew to such levels that the average single job handled by the company is KSh 3 million, although it handles all jobs irrespective of size, some for as little as KSh 50,000. This growth has been fuelled by three main strategies: keeping costs to a minimum, aggressive marketing to get new business, and striving to satisfy existing clients.

Diversifying into other businesses

Around the year 2004/5 Fred partnered with four friends including Ben Otundo, who co-owns Omaera Pharmaceuticals Limited, Yesse Achoki, and Mohammed Nyaoga to form an apparel company at EPZ Mombasa called Chandu EPZ. "At that time EPZs were being cushioned by the government in terms of expenses. We realised that these industries were only being run by Indians; so why not get into the business? We also found that the volumes were usually quite high; for instance, a customer could order one million trousers. Although the industry suffered frequent employee strikes, we felt that as long as we treated our employees well we would manage."

Starting off required a lot of money, but they found an EPZ company being sold by Barclays Bank in Mombasa and got a good deal on the price. The company had around 400 machine operators and another 50 supervisors, accounts, human resources and management staff. Ben Otundo and Fred were the largest shareholders with 60 percent between them.

None of the partners had experience in the industry, but they were determined to run it professionally. "We hired consultants and professional staff. We brought in an overall supervisor from Sri Lanka who had years of experience in this business. The supervisor took me to Sri Lanka to interview other supervisors and I ended up selecting eight people in different lines like cutting and packaging. We rented for them a furnished house with a cook in Nyali, Mombasa, where they lived relatively well," says Fred.

Although the deliveries were being made direct to the US, Chandu EPZ was still getting most of the orders from China. What the Chinese would do was to get orders beyond their quota and send part of them to Kenya and other countries. This meant that the profit margins for those subcontracted were reduced. Also, being under contract to a Chinese firm, all accessories, including buttons that could be obtained locally, would be sourced from China.

Even the labels 'Made in Kenya' and the price tags came from China. As Fred explained: "This is what happens with a lot of these Kenyan EPZ firms. Very few get direct orders from the US market. The main reason for this is that if you went to compete directly with Chinese firms in the US market, they'll beat you in pricing every time. So they get the jobs but because they are not allowed to exceed their quota, they go to other countries where they do the actual manufacturing. This is why Chinese firms are everywhere."

Based on the above *modus operandi*, the Chinese firm that contracted Chandu EPZ would dictate the styles and provide the fabric and accessories which Chandu would pay for. Chandu staff would do the stitching and ironing of finished garments and a representative of the Chinese firm, who was permanently stationed in the factory as a supervisor, would inspect them. The finished garments would then be packed and shipped to supermarket chains like Wal-Mart in the US. "The Chinese would also be accompanied by buyers to do spot checks in our factory. At some point they would even get jobs using Chandu's name, but we did not mind because we wanted jobs with huge volumes." Much as they wanted to grow the company, they lost many jobs because they could not do certain styles, as they lacked the relevant machinery. Fred had to travel with one of the partners to Dubai to buy more machines and a generator to combat the frequent power blackouts.

Among the five partners, they would alternate with one of them going to Mombasa for one week to oversee the business. "At one point one of the partners, who had a clearing and forwarding firm in Mombasa, offered to stay there longer. As the rest of us were all so busy with other things we thought it was a blessing," says Fred. The most crucial aspect of the business was ensuring there were sufficient funds available to pay staff; usually, the staff were paid weekly to avert strikes that would be detrimental to a business with characteristic tight delivery deadlines.

By this time Fred and the Mombasa-based partner were travelling to Dubai to purchase machinery. The partners had pumped in excess of KSh 50 million into the business. The salary bill per week was KSh 2 million. Whenever the cash flow was poor, usually as a result of delays in payments for orders, one of the five shareholders would volunteer to meet salary expenses out of his pocket and have the amount converted into shares. The Mombasa based partner seems to have taken advantage of this arrangement. "Staff had not been paid for one week and had threatened to go on strike the following week. Unknown to us he convinced the Chinese supervisor to give us KSh 4 million to cover salaries for two weeks. Meanwhile the rest of us had also sent what we could and managed to raise the same amount. Later we discovered that he had used the extra KSh 4 million for his own purposes. He promised to pay but didn't.

Mistrust set in and when there was another salary crisis no one wanted to send money. In the process of investigating and checking the books we discovered that he had written cheques to himself and withdrawn money amounting to another KSh 2 million. We had made this partner the chairman because he was older than all of us and we trusted him."

By then the company was in serious debt and employees went on strike over unpaid salaries. Fred cut his losses and got out of the business. As Fred bitterly put it: "We had big plans and so we had ploughed back into the business all our earnings to buy machines and do more styles. I had personally invested millions of shillings but I felt so betrayed especially since the business had picked up but I just walked away. I didn't want anything to do with the business after that."

Fred felt the loss of his investment in Chandu EPZ deeply. They had been in business for only one year by the time they called it a day. While the idea was sound, and indeed everything was sound except the management, they seemed to have trusted too much to a point of not checking the business records. Fred learnt some important lessons from the saga: "Running an EPZ company is very difficult and the tight deadlines make it worse; so you must be present on a daily basis. Before you get into business with someone it's important to know them well. It put me off getting into business with friends. The funny thing is that I've started several businesses with friends and none has picked up."

Where he cannot run a business alone, Fred has resorted to getting people who are professionals in a certain area as business partners. This is what he did with Forbes Media, a firm in the digital advertising business which he set up in 2005. "In this case, George Wasike had the original idea into which I bought. Then I brought in Jonah Mutuku to run it on a day-to-day basis." They also incorporated a fourth partner to come and run the business as the managing director as they wanted someone who was more aggressive. Fred owns a 40 percent stake in the company. "As indoor digital advertising has not really picked up in Kenya because it has not been well understood, we decided to diversify into outdoor advertising," says Fred.

Fred's decision to get into outdoor advertising is ironical because when Stanley Kinyanjui, founder of Magnate Ventures, a leading outdoor advertising firm, approached him a few years back to join him in the business, he had refused because he thought the market for outdoor advertising was saturated. "Kinyanjui had proposed that Impulse Promotions and Magnate Ventures merge in order to build synergies but I was not keen. At that time Kinyanjui was not yet doing billboards; he was doing posters and similar things. Around the same time, a lot of people also approached me wanting to join forces in outdoor advertising. I turned down the offers, something that I would later regret. I thought that the market was saturated. However, what happened was that when the big players came in, they quickly muzzled the smaller companies which fell by the wayside," says Fred. When all is said and done, Fred's vision for Forbes Media is to continue diversifying into all aspects of media.

Fred later ventured into real estate, a business which his wife Patricia Mwihaki Rabongo[37] came to be also actively involved in. He would buy land, build and sell residential properties. In one of the projects, he put up nine houses which he sold for KSh 16 million each, raking in 80 percent profit. His aspiration is to make the real estate business a fully fledged company also dealing with commercial properties: "I want to import a concept from Dubai where I put up a high-rise office complex then offer offices for sale because in Kenya people mostly lease offices in such high-rise buildings."

Fred also has a cleaning company called Impulse Holdings which he started in 2003. Most of its employees are based at client's offices, but there are two employees based at the same location in Kilimani where Impulse Promotions has its headquarters. The cleaning company shares accounting staff with Impulse Promotions.

Other than businesses, Fred has also invested in the securities market and has shares in a number of listed companies. He also has minority shareholding in a few companies in the hotel, promotional materials production and advertising industries in which he is not involved in their day-to-day management.

Strategies for growth and management style

As a business, Impulse Promotions has generally grown fast attaining up to 30 percent in 2007. Fred financed growth in the business by ploughing back the profits. One of the strategies that he applied in achieving growth is keeping costs to the minimum. When it comes to costs, Fred runs a tight ship. "I realised that in most businesses the problem is cash flow. Therefore, I believe that if you were to cut your costs, you would be able to make more profits and ease cash flow problems," says Fred.

One of Fred's key cost-cutting strategies is to never ask for a deposit from a client before doing a job. "To us, this is a minimal risk because most of our clients are blue-chip firms; hence, we are confident that we will be paid after doing a job. We cost projects from the beginning and know how much we will make. Then we try to do the work at a lower cost than that in a bid to increase our profits from each job," says Fred.

To do this successfully, Fred uses cost cutting as a tool to reward employees

---

37   Before he married Patricia, Fred was married to Edna Wangui. The couple later split up in 2000. They had no children. Edna left for the United States to study and later settled there.

who save the company money. "Every project manager comes to me with his costing of each project and I often cut it down. We then work with it and succeed. If we have agreed on the costs of each project and we save money then I give the project manager part of what we have saved. The employees like the strategy and this is another reason why we are able to make more profits on projects," says Fred.

Another strategy to realise this kind of growth is where project managers who each handle specific accounts are given annual targets defining how much they must grow their business. Those who meet targets are rewarded with commissions. "We have a commission based on whether or not you have performed and another based on whether or not you have brought in new business. If you bring in business you get 10 percent of the gross proceeds," says Fred.

Fred's single-minded focus on cost cutting has influenced his management style and he is a hands-on manager. "There is no expenditure that passes without my approval. I sign all cheques and even vet the monthly shopping, something that prompts complaints from staff because they say I should leave some things to Geoffrey Pesa (the General Manager). I strongly believe that it helps to keep costs under control." However, to ensure that the business runs smoothly, Fred devised a system with his bank where money can be released for urgent obligations when he is absent or travelling.

Employing qualified personnel has also been a key factor in helping to grow the business. "All my senior-level employees are graduates, some with second degrees. This helps because they are people who understand things faster. All that counts in attracting and retaining such calibre of employees is how I treat them." Fred had to study for an executive MBA degree with a bias in marketing, which he obtained from Moi University. "I felt intimidated because all my senior staff had MBAs making me the least schooled. In the MBA course, I found the marketing units familiar, but was challenged by the human resources bits."

The office culture at Impulse Promotions is quite informal. Employees do not address him as 'sir' or 'Mr Rabongo'. "Despite the free atmosphere, the employees know that I am a no-nonsense person when it comes to work and I push them hard. I do not compromise when it comes to work. Each project is assigned to a project manager who is responsible for its success or failure. If one's project does well they get a commission which is calculated on the gross estimate (the figure billed to the client) which makes it a lot of money. Thus, how the project managers marshal and motivate the people below them to get the project done is up to them because they are the ones who take on the entire responsibility for the project."

The management structure of the company is relatively flat with few layers of authority. Fred and his wife Patricia are shareholders and directors in the business. Patricia is a television engineer with the national broadcaster KBC and does not play an active role in the day-to-day operations of the company. In his role as chief executive, Fred has two officers reporting directly to him, namely the General Manager and Client Service Director. The General Manager basically runs the office and handles the day-to-day administrative aspects of the business as well as the human resources issues. The GM also takes on projects during extremely busy periods.

At the next level are four project managers who report to the Client Service Director and in his absence to the General Manager. There are also regional supervisors who oversee the five regions that the company covers – Nairobi, Mt Kenya, Coast, Western/Nyanza and South Rift. Mt Kenya region is run from the Nyeri office, Coast from an office in Mombasa, Western/Nyanza from the Kisumu office, and the South Rift from the Eldoret office. Nairobi, the headquarters of the company, has two regional supervisors. There is also a regional supervisor based in Nakuru although without an office. At the lowest tier are over 350 merchandisers who are on one-year contracts. The bulk of them are stationed in Nairobi. The company also hires promoters on a project-by-project basis. Even with the flat structure, Fred believes in observing protocol and in dealing with lower-level employees through the managers he has appointed to oversee them so as not to undermine the respective managers. "Despite his hands-on management style, Fred is open and has time for any employee who needs to see him. Even when he's not involved in interviewing potential promoters, he makes time to have a talk with them about the project and his expectations from the employees," says Geoffrey.

The company has an office in the UK which Fred started with his brother, Collins Rabongo, who resides there. However, the office has not quite picked up. "We started the office to carry out a specific job for East African Breweries Limited (EABL) which we came close to clinching but missed it. As it is registered, I hope to use it someday."

Impulse had also opened an office in Tanzania, but it had to be closed after two years. Thus, the company does not have any offices in the region which, according to Fred, is a major disadvantage. "Although I have tried going out to get some work in the region, it has not been a success. But I think this could perhaps be attributed to use of the wrong approach. We must stop being myopic and open business all over the region," he says.

At the beginning of every year, the senior managers hold a brainstorming session outside the office for three days, which also serves as a retreat. The meeting is usually attended by the CEO, General Manager, Client Service Director and the project managers. "During these sessions, we do a projection for the year, arrive at the growth percentage to push for, discuss the projects we did the previous year, deal with areas of failure, and explore new areas into which the company could get into." The retreat also serves as a forum to reward exceptional performance. Merchandisers in each project who performed well the previous year are also invited and enjoy the games and other festivities after the formal part of the retreat is over. "Most significantly, the retreat is about team-building where we interact amongst ourselves. Everyone, from the senior to the junior, looks forward to it because it is fun," says Julie Njeri, a secretary at the firm.

Maintaining a good relationship with clients has also been a key factor in the company's success. As Fred observes, "If you have good clients and things are going wrong they will tell you instead of waiting to criticise you. Then, you have a chance to correct mistakes and strengthen the team. We build strong relationships with clients by being their friends beyond the business dealings. Sometimes we have social outings like a drink or lunch, or watch a rugby game together."

Prayer has also played a key role in the success of the company. "Above all else my wife and I pray daily before going to work that we run the business well so that it grows. This is probably one of the main reasons why we are able to do things the correct way because God will lead you to do things the right way."

When it comes to networking, Fred does not network in a formal structured way such as membership in a group or clubs. But he holds frequent consultations with friends and other marketers. "I do not believe in members' clubs. Networking is based on those you know who know those you do not know. So if I need to speak to someone I do not know, I just look for any of my friends who knows that person."

Business challenges

Growing the business has not been smooth sailing all the way. Fred has faced a number of challenges, the main one being competition from small mushrooming agencies. As he has observed, "People see the success you have made and they want to get into the industry but many want to use short cuts. They don't offer the same exemplary service. This makes people think promotions don't work, not realising they were dealing with quacks. These agencies are also able to charge much lower because their overheads are low. We have offices all over and have to pay rent and so we charge more."

Cash flow is another major challenge as many of the big clients they take jobs from are poor payers. However, he has tried to overcome this challenge by applying cost cutting measures.

Getting and keeping qualified staff is another major challenge. "Our biggest strength is having good diligent workers. But good people will always be poached by other companies and are expensive to keep. Sometimes it boils down to the relationship that I have with them. They approach me and tell me that someone tried to poach them, and that they refused to leave the company. Once an employee mentions this to me, then I know how to improve their terms though not immediately because then it becomes a blackmailing tool. Over time, I have discovered that commissions help to keep the staff. While many entrepreneurs want to keep everything for themselves, if you help people to make money as they are making money for you, then you will keep them," says Fred.

Fred has observed that the industry has changed tremendously since those heady days when clients would give him a free hand to conceptualise and create promotions. Creativity is no longer the driving force. The best part of the job was writing proposals for new promotions. Now the clients have pre-determined ideas and only want a company that will execute them. "Clients just tell you 'Go and do this and give us a quote'. They come with a set mind having already decided which prizes are to be won. They think they know what is best or want to cut costs and are looking for the cheapest company. This has changed the industry negatively and there is less creativity with the same campaigns being copied by different companies like the Win-a-double-cabin-pickup promotion."

Best and worst business moments

Fred's worst business promotion was a Population Services International (PSI) Trust Condom promotion in 2003. The project manager who handled the promotion was inexperienced and ended up mismanaging the project. "Being his first major project, I felt that we gave him too much leeway without close supervision. So we also failed. He ended up making mistakes that were really unforgivable, such as agreeing with the client to do promotions in particular outlets then changing the outlets without communicating to the client. In the end, it looked like we were cheating and were not doing the promotion. I sacked the project manager immediately, but of course we also lost the client. Unfortunately, it was also our first job with PSI and they were extremely disappointed because I had been highly recommended from all quarters."

Another big mistake that Fred made was getting involved in a promotion for a fight between Congestina Achieng and an American opponent. He was approached by the late Tom Nyamunde and another promoter to run a joint promotion. "They lured me into doing the promotion together only to realise later that they had conned me. The promotion entailed doing the tickets and looking for endorsement from various media houses. Kenya Broadcasting Corporation (KBC) agreed to pay KSh 500,000 to get exclusive rights to broadcast the fight. We also did SMS promotion in which people were to win prizes." However, the American fighter turned out to be a hoax and they found someone else whom Congestina defeated in their bout. As Fred recalled: "The promoters got the money from the sale of tickets, the sponsorship money and the SMS promotion and then took off after the fight. They did not pay Congestina and left me to handle the mess. It was chaotic. The media was on my neck and wanted to do bad reports on me. I ended up paying all the expenses together with the company which was doing the SMS promotion. The Betting Control and Licensing Board weren't going to license any more promotions for us until we paid the prizes which were worth KSh 1.5 million. The owner of the company which did the SMS promotion paid KSh 900,000 from his pocket and I paid KSh 600,000. I also paid tickets for the judges and the plane ticket for the boxer who fought Congestina. In the end I lost over one million shillings."

What Fred learned from this experience is that no matter how good a business proposal sounds to him, he can only deal with established companies.

Marriage and family

The Rabongos have two daughters, Kyle Hawi Rabongo and Courtney Wendo Rabongo. The couple got married in 2006. Due to the demands of his work, balancing work and family life has constantly posed a major challenge for him. His workday usually ends at 7.00 pm but often he has another meeting scheduled after that or needs to meet clients socially. When they are working on a major proposal, he works late sometimes till 9.00 or 10.00 pm. "By this time, my children have slept; so sometimes I have to go home during the day to see them. Sunday is the family day. I normally switch off my phone and spend the whole day with my wife and children."

Surprisingly, as much as he has helped his siblings, especially in paying their way through school, Fred feels he has failed in a major way when it comes to his family. What drove him to business in the first place was an effort to lift the family out of poverty. "However, I have not been able to make my younger siblings rise to where I am. I believe that that's what brothers are there for." Citing the example of Indian communities, he observes, "They bring up their brothers and ensure they reach the same economic level of success." Rather than bring his siblings into his businesses, Fred prefers to help them set up their own outfits. However, he brought one of his stepbrothers to work with him at Impulse Promotions for a short period as the family prepared to send him to India for an undergraduate course. Another of his stepbrothers took up work in Nairobi as a marketer. Most of his stepsisters got married and settled near their rural home.

Due to Fred's success as a marketer his siblings wanted to emulate him and three ended up in marketing. The brother who immediately follows him lives in Switzerland where his wife works but his business is in the United Kingdom (UK) so he shuttles his time between the two countries. Fred has another brother whom he's tried to help by starting a business for him. He invested KSh 300,000 to set up a bureau with a cybercafé, typing, photocopy, binding and telephone services but he opted to sublet the business to someone else and earn rent on the premises.

Another brother opted to stay and work in the UK after finishing his degree course. Yet another settled in the United States although Fred hoped he would return to Kenya some day. As he put it: "All you can do is go there and get a car and live comfortably but you can only succeed up to a certain level. Even my brother in the UK has some businesses here because people here are more receptive to you unlike abroad where people always look at you as an outsider. You can't do serious business out there and not find resistance."

One of Fred's sisters is married and lives as a housewife. "She didn't pass Form Four. I tried to persuade her to repeat the class so that I could take her to university. I told her in the Kenya we live in currently you need to be a graduate to be competitive. She was living with my aunt but she took off from there and got married. She's not working and I want her to be independent. When my father died my stepmother would have been able to help out if she was working just like my mother, a fact I came to realise later."

Two more of his brothers are doing university degree courses in Malaysia. "They both wanted to study marketing but I said no. They see you've made a success of something and they think that's the only thing they can do. Now I understand why parents impose courses on their children. There's an age where you're given the freedom to choose but you must also be guided. I told my stepbrother he couldn't study marketing because three of my brothers had already done this course and I felt he should do something else. I gave him time to choose another course but he couldn't come up with an alternative so I encouraged him to study law because a lawyer in the family would be good."

The future of Impulse Promotions

"Over the years, Fred has managed the company in a hands-on style, often getting involved in all aspects of the business. He would be found in the bars where promotions are being carried out or he would be on the roads in the morning when fliers are being distributed," says Geoffrey. Eventually, this changed and he started delegating a lot more, especially owing to the fact that the business was expanding and that the company is now staffed with reliable and competent people who could handle things well. This left Fred to run other businesses.

"I would not wish for a relative to take over the running of Impulse Promotions. I would prefer if the business could be run professionally." He sees himself eventually employing a managing director to run the business on a day-to-day basis while he retains the position of a director. In effect, he set out to groom Geoffrey Pesa, the General Manager, to take over as MD. Geoffrey first worked at Impulse Promotions in 1997 while still in college; he was the team leader in a promotion for a newly imported juice brand. By the time he left to do an MBA in Australia, he had risen to a project manager position. He returned to the company in the same position and was eventually promoted to General Manager.

"My perception of the person to succeed me is one who is a good administrator, good at decision making, hardworking and creative in the sense of coming up with concepts." Ultimately, his dream is to float the company at the Nairobi Securities Exchange. Regional expansion is another big priority for him: "My vision for Impulse is to be a Pan-African marketing firm."

The trappings

The family lives in one of the town houses that Fred built in Lavington having moved from Runda because Patricia felt that Runda was too cold for their newborn daughter, Courtney. When Fred bought his first car, a Nissan B14, he was working at Esso. As he grew his business, he came to own a number of cars including a Range Rover Vogue and a Mercedes Benz.

As far as holidaying is concerned, Fred finds his work demands limiting. Although he can certainly afford it, he rarely makes time to go on holiday. If he goes, he does not take more than two weeks. He usually goes to South Africa or the UK; he has two brothers in the latter. However, it is not strange for him to take even three years before he goes on holiday.

Tips for aspiring entrepreneurs

Having been involved in numerous business ventures that spanned many parts of the country, Fred has some tips for aspiring and newly established entrepreneurs. One of the most important is having clear goals and a vision.

"You can only succeed in business or in life if you have a vision and a goal about where you want to be in life. You must have long term goals broken into short term goals that are then broken down into strategies. Goals go beyond dreams and visions. Even when I was employed, I've never worked for two years in the same job. This is because I had set goals for myself – going into each job with what I want to achieve in five years in mind. Whenever I saw I was not getting there after two years, I shifted gears."

For employees who aspire to management positions in a company, Fred advises them to learn the business much more deeply than a person who is just working to earn a salary: "You need to start thinking: What are the managers doing? How do they behave and handle issues? This helps you to practise similar traits and move to the next level." Similarly, people in business should look at more successful business people to understand how they do things.

Another important thing is planning. As Fred puts it: "Above all else you must plan if you want to succeed and believe in yourself. If I am employed, do I believe that one day I can be the managing director? Most people who don't believe in themselves never get there. If I believe I can be a multi-millionaire, I will be. If you don't believe in yourself other people will not believe in you. But when you believe in yourself you're able to convince others that you can do something even when you can't and they help you to achieve your goals like when a bank gives you money."

"Diversification is also important because millionaires do not stick to doing just one thing," says Fred. "However, it is important for one to build the first business that they start and entrench themselves in the industry. Build your cash cow to the core so that even when you leave the business, it is still strong. As you diversify, don't keep jumping from one thing to another trying to do everything because you'll achieve nothing. Try and diversify within the same industry."

Employees are also important. They are the lifeblood of any business and it is important to pay them well and motivate them. "These are the people who bring in the money."

Social and charity activities

Fred believes that corporate social responsibility (CSR) is important and Impulse Promotions sponsors two students to study in India every year, contributes to children's homes, and assists HIV/Aids orphans mainly in the slums. The company also supports Rhino Charge, the annual motor race where four-wheel-drive vehicles navigate Kenya's roughest terrain to raise money for Rhino Ark, a charity working to construct a perimeter fence around the Aberdare National Park. The Park is a sanctuary for the endangered Black Rhino and an important water catchment area providing water to the Tana and Athi Rivers.

Role models

Fred's mentor is Evans Kidero, the former Chief Executive of Mumias Sugar Company. "I discuss most of my businesses or what I want to do with him sometimes even without knowing since we are good friends. Our families know each other and we visit each other often. Evans is also into real estate like me and before I start something I consult him."

Entrepreneurs that Fred admires include Ben Otundo of Omaera Pharmaceuticals. "Like me, Ben started from scratch and he's been able to move his business to another level." He also admires Equity Bank founder Peter Munga and James Mwangi, the CEO. "They were able to take risks in an industry that until then had been choked by mistrust and the inability of banks to listen to entrepreneurs and grow with them. Even though they are aggressive, their approach to business is very down to earth. I believe that if all banks in Kenya were like Equity, the country would go very far." One of the reasons that Fred cites is the cash flow problem in businesses. "The main reason why businesses flop is cash flow. You may grow, but what happens when you have local purchase orders (LPOs) that you cannot service because banks cannot lend you the money in good time on account of the LPOs? Equity Bank has been able to assist SMEs get loans with LPOs," concludes Fred.

Awards and achievements

The highest achievement that Fred earned in recognition was the International Business Management Award won by Impulse Promotions in 2005. The award was given by the Foundation for Excellence in Business Practice based in Geneva. The best campaign he has ever done is Mavuno Kenya Mzima for EABL. "It was the biggest promotion of its time with KSh 60 million worth of prizes. We ran it very well and it was very successful. We were doing in-bar activations covering 4,000 bars using 500 people at the same time countrywide."

As mentioned in the opening paragraph, Fred was appointed acting Managing Trustee of NSSF. Although he had no experience in public service, the purpose was to bring the change that NSSF so badly needed. He was to help clean up the rot in the place since it was riddled with corruption, to instil the private sector culture into the fund and to inject fresh young blood. The Minister was categorical that he wanted someone from outside the system to perform this role.

Chapter 11

Evelyn Mungai

Catherine Munkumba, a Zambian, was doing a six-month flower arrangement course in London when she read about Evelyn College of Design in a magazine. After the course, she travelled to Kenya and went to find out where this school was. Upon finding the school, she did an interview and a tour of the school. She was so impressed with what she saw that she went ahead and enrolled. She didn't even bother looking at other schools. On completion of her design course at Evelyn's, she decided to open up her own business in Kenya called Mihatchi Designers specialising in African wear.

Munkumba is just one of hundreds of students from Kenya and other African countries who have had their training at the Evelyn College of Design and have gone on to become successful designers and businesswomen. The college, founded in 1976, is synonymous with fashion and interior design in the region. Among its alumni are top designers who have made names for themselves both locally and internationally, for instance at the Smirnoff Fashion Awards and the M-Net Face of Africa contest. They include Sally Karago of Macensal and Susan Omino of House of Brides. The name behind this design institution is Evelyn Mungai Eldon.

Nevertheless, starting the first design college in East Africa is far from Evelyn Mungai's only accomplishment. Her first business, a recruitment and secretarial agency which she started in 1970 while still in her early twenties, was the first such business owned by an African. She has also dabbled in publishing and microfinance, and has been involved in property development. She holds various board memberships and engages in charity activities as a Rotary Club member. Most remarkably, a modest lifestyle that is devoid of flamboyancy belies her enormous achievement as an accomplished entrepreneur.

Tracing the roots

Evelyn Mungai comes from a long line of achievers, so her boundless energy is not surprising. Her great-grandmother, Medrin Wanjiru wa Rara, who is her role model, was a landowner and successful businesswoman in the 1900s at a time when few women owned land. A pioneer settler, she owned large tracts of land in the modern-day Nairobi City around the Globe Cinema area. However, the scramble for land by white settlers in the 1900s saw her lose most of it and was forced to settle for a twelve-acre plot in Karai, Ndeiya Location in Kiambu County, which is still the subject of a land dispute more than 100 years later.

Medrin's troubles began with the arrival of John Ainsworth, one of the first field administrators of the East African Protectorate (later renamed Kenya) in Nairobi. His career in East Africa had began as an agent of the Imperial British East Africa Company (IBEACo) in 1889 and ended 31 years later when he retired as the Protectorate's first Chief Commissioner. Despite his relatively junior position, his decisions and opinions had a major effect on the most important issues in the region at that time – labour, land and development.[38] 1901 found Ainsworth encouraging white settlers to take over land around Nairobi. Historical records show that Sandbach Baker fenced off 5,000 acres of land which now includes Muthaiga and parts of Parklands.

Colonel Ewart Grogan, a renegade soldier who had arrived from a hunting mission in Mozambique in 1904, also pitched tent. His arrival and subsequent actions were a turning point in Nairobi's history. Grogan fenced off all the land that comprises Kirinyaga Road and Kijabe Street, extending all the way to the modern-day Chiromo Campus of the University of Nairobi. He dished out part of Wanjiru's land to Major CGR Ringer and his business partner R Aylmer Winearls who built the Norfolk Hotel which opened its doors on 25 December 1904. A century later, Wanjiru's name hardly rings a bell having been eclipsed by the eventual rise of Nairobi to its present-day urban status. Perhaps the only reminder that Wanjiru owned part of the city is the Globe Cinema Bridge which some old-timers still refer to as *Ndaraca ya Wanjiru*, meaning Wanjiru's bridge.[39] This is the bridge over Nairobi River.

After losing the Nairobi land, Wanjiru wa Rara was resettled by IBEACo on a twelve-acre plot in Karai, Ndeiya. By the 1920s she had established herself back in Nairobi and constructed houses for rent in Pumwani which today still benefit her descendants. While still in Nairobi, Wanjiru wa Rara accommodated the young Jomo Kenyatta and other veteran freedom fighters. Kenyatta had just arrived in Nairobi as a water-metre reader.

After independence, Wanjiru continued to pay the annual land rent of KSh 60 as required by law on the Ndeiya plot for a long time until the plot was formally handed to her on condition that she purchased the same. Subsequently, she paid KSh 2,400 with the understanding that a title deed would be issued. But in a classic illustration of post-independence land-grabbing and bureaucracy, the title deed to the Karai plot was issued to the wrong person and her third

---

38   Maxon, RM (1980) *John Ainsworth and the Making of Kenya*, University Press of America (Lanham MD).

39   *The People*, April 19–25, 1996

-generation descendants are still engaged in a tedious legal battle to correct this mistake.

Wanjiru wa Rara was widowed while still very young. The same misfortune was to later befall both her granddaughter Marjorie and great-granddaughter Evelyn. Rather than break them, losing their loved ones just seemed to fuel their determination to succeed and take care of their families as single mothers. By the time Wanjiru wa Rara died in 1971 she was a wealthy landowner. Evelyn recalls going to see her in Pumwani.

Evelyn also recalls that her great-grandmother was a generous woman. She would always give her grandmother money. Contrary to traditional practice where fathers helped their sons when they got married, it was Wanjiru wa Rara who helped settle her son-in-law – Ishmael Ithong'o – when he married her only daughter Gladys Wambui (Evelyn's grandmother). When they married, they were living in Pumwani. Wanjiru bought land for them in Kanyariri, near Kikuyu, where they settled. She also built for them a fantastic house. She's the one who gave them a foundation. She would help everybody using her income from rental houses in Pumwani. Evelyn's mother continues to collect rent from the same houses.

Wanjiru was very strong. Having been widowed early in her marriage, she had to do everything by herself. Indeed, she accomplished everything by her own effort. Due to Evelyn's industrious nature, many people in her family drew a resemblance between her and her great-grandmother. They often alluded that she reminded them of her, and that she had taken after her. Evelyn herself was also widowed at a very early age.

Ishmael Ithong'o was one of the very first Christians to be converted and subsequently educated by Canon Harry Leakey in Lower Kabete. He was also one of the first Kenyans to go to London for further education. Upon his return, he worked as an interpreter at the Kenya Law Courts. This exposure made him value education and he was determined to give the only child he had with Gladys – Marjorie Gachigi, Evelyn's mother – the best education he could give. He sent her to Gayanza High School in Uganda, then one of the best schools in East Africa. Upon her return she married Evelyn's father, Noah Kimenyi, who had just graduated from King's College Budo (KCB) also in Uganda.

King's College Budo was then a school for the elite in Uganda; it was the Eaton of Africa. In fact the Kabaka of Buganda was Kimenyi's schoolmate. After completing his education Kimenyi was employed at the law courts like his father before him. Evelyn's mother was a housewife for many years but later worked at Kenyatta National Hospital as a housekeeper in charge of the medical students. Both parents had no other siblings although Ishmael (Evelyn's maternal grandfather) later married a second wife with whom they had other children. Ishmael wanted more children but his wife kept miscarrying. In such circumstances, it was understandable for a man to take another wife; and in those days, it was traditional for the first wife to help choose the second wife. Gladys dutifully helped her husband bring in her co-wife. Little did she know that her husband would change after this marriage for the worse.

Although the estrangement was not always apparent to Evelyn when she was growing up, she noticed friction between the two families. She and her siblings were not close to her grandfather's second family even though they lived on the same piece of land as her grandmother Gladys. Nevertheless, Evelyn remembers her grandmother as a lovely woman and very hardworking, and forgiving. Unfortunately, she must have died of a lonely heart. Evelyn is cynical about a polygamous family; there will always be tension. Despite his relationship with her grandmother, Evelyn still adored her grandfather.

Moreover, Evelyn was very close to her grandparents and formed a bond with them such that they often consulted her when making decisions even though she had an older brother who would naturally be expected to take on the leadership role. But this was not without arousing complains from her siblings who thought that she was regarded as the favourite one. This inclination was perhaps because she was of upright character as she did not join them in tree-climbing and stealing their grandmother's fruits. She may have acquired a sense of responsibility from an early age which sometimes makes one quite proper. In any case, both her parents were very strict and didn't spare the rod if their children misbehaved.

Early childhood and education

Evelyn Karungari was born in Cura Village, Kiambu, in Central Kenya, where she was also raised. She was the second-born child and first daughter of Noah Kimenyi and Marjorie Gachigi in a family of nine children, seven boys and two girls. Her childhood was ordinary and she grew up herding goats with her brothers and taking care of her grandfather's cattle. Generally, she was regarded as a tomboy because of spending so much time with her brothers and cousins.

Evelyn's grandparents on both sides valued education, a progressive attitude particularly for those days. Having had the benefit of education themselves, they wanted the same for their children, a benefit which was passed on to their grandchildren, so Evelyn had no difficulty getting an education.

She had her early education at Cura Primary School where she attended

Standards One to Eight. However, this was a difficult period as it was during the *Mau Mau* war. People were herded into fortified communal villages, but her family escaped that. Evelyn was too young to understand what the unrest was all about. She did not know that the *Mau Mau* insurgents were fighting for independence. She recalls chilling encounters of the *Mau Mau* fighters following people into the school. Due to insecurity, they all went to live with Evelyn's grandfather where they stayed in the same compound within Cura village. Shooting would be heard every night. Evelyn's grandfather would shoot in the air every time they heard shots.

The first time Evelyn was away from home was when she joined Mary Leakey Girls' School in Kabete which was a boarding school. She probably would have been sent to Uganda following in the footsteps of her grandparent, but during this time, people felt that there were equally good schools in Kenya.

After completing secondary school, she joined Kianda Finishing School for Girls. At that time, *finishing school* was a colonial relic where white settlers took their daughters to learn deportment, how to dress and conduct genteel conversation, foreign languages, dance and other social graces. One would wonder why an African girl needed to go to *finishing school*. Evelyn wanted to do something with her life and her parents told her that before she even thought of what she wanted to do, she should just go and get finished off, learn languages and music appreciation. Later, the school became a college offering secretarial and business courses.

Kianda students came from extremely wealthy families, examples of which were the Block family and the Manji family; the former owned the Block Hotels and the latter owned the House of Manji, the largest biscuit manufacturer in the country. The students would be picked and dropped from school by drivers, while Evelyn would be taken to school by her grandfather and then find her own way home at the end of the day. Although her grandparents were wealthy, her own parents were not equally rich. Despite this, and being the first and only African student at the school, she did not feel disadvantaged or inferior. Strangely enough she never heard any racial slur directed at her and neither did she regard the other students as white or see them as being different.

Evelyn was at the school for three years. By the time she was leaving, other African girls had begun to join the institution including the daughters of James Gichuru and Eliud Mathu, both renowned nationalists.[40] Both young women had just come from abroad – the United States and England respectively – where they were schooling. They represented the new African elite.

It was while at Kianda that Evelyn met her future husband, Arthur

---

40   James Gichuru had founded the Kenya African Union (KAU) in 1944 and later stepped down as chairman in June 1947 in favour of Jomo Kenyatta. Eliud Mathu was the first black Kenyan to be appointed to the colonial legislature in 1944.

Wagithuka Mungai, in 1962. This was just a year before Kenya was granted full independence from Britain. Arthur had just come back from studying in the United States where he had obtained a Masters degree in economics. She met him through a cousin, Edmund Njonjo, and they clicked straightaway. In any case, they were both starting out – Edmund with the Kenya Government and Evelyn with East African Common Services Organisation (EACSO). They grew together from that point onwards.

A career stint and entry into business

While searching for a job, Evelyn was accompanied during her interviews by her school tutor, an Irish woman named Miss Curran. This was the only way that European employers would believe that an African could speak their mother tongue effectively and do shorthand with speed and the required accuracy. At that time there were no African secretaries and wherever Evelyn would go people would say, "You mean an African can do shorthand?" Subsequently, she became a promotional tool for Kianda. And she did not disappoint. Following her success, the school started to source for people to sponsor African girls for the courses in readiness to take over jobs from expatriate secretaries.

Evelyn got her first job at EACSO as a secretary. After a while, she was promoted to the post of Assistant Recruitment Manager for the three countries of Kenya, Uganda and Tanzania. With the promotion came a good salary and greater responsibility. She worked at EACSO for eight years and later served shortly in the private sector, in personnel training.

She was by then married to Arthur Mungai and was expecting their first child, Eric. While on maternity leave, Evelyn decided that she wanted more time with her baby and thought of trying temporary jobs. She registered with some of the personnel services companies in Nairobi which sent her to work in various places on temporary basis. This experience opened a new opportunity for her. She decided not to go back to employment but to do what she had come to know best, dealing with personnel recruitment. She set up her own personnel selection agency. That is how Speedway Bureau came to be in 1970.

With Speedway Bureau, Evelyn had founded what was to be the first African-owned personnel selection agency. At the time she was still in her twenties. It was very challenging because she did not have any capital and could not afford to rent an office. Fortunately, some Asian friends offered her the use of their small office, she was allocated a corner with a desk. The office was on Duke Street (later renamed Luthuli Avenue) in downtown Nairobi. As she did not have any money to buy a filing cabinet, she used to lock all her files at night in a suitcase at the corner. "It's amazing really when I look back, I can't believe that I had such confidence," says Evelyn. The office had only one telephone line, but the Asian friends allowed her to use it free of charge.

"It was constantly engaged however, so I started putting two adverts in the *East African Standard* newspaper. One advert asked employers to come to me and I would put a second advert saying I had the staff. I started getting companies calling me and also started registering personnel. Then I would put the two together," she says. To popularise her business, she visited various companies to sell her services to them. From the very beginning she knew that quality is what would differentiate her business. Other personnel selection companies relied on references, but Evelyn went a step further and thoroughly tested and vetted potential employees. She was very confident that anyone she sent out was qualified for the job. She knew that her reputation was very important if the companies were to come back to her.

Arthur supported her significantly during this initial stage of the business. His support proved to be crucial because without it she may have been tempted to give up when the going got tough. She was juggling a demanding business and a young child while she was still so young herself. "You've got your own doubts at some stage and all it takes is the person closest to you to say you must be mad to start a business in your twenties. But he never said that and I'll forever be grateful because from an early age I had someone at home believing in me which helped to give me confidence that I could do it and I was able to transfer that confidence to the business," she says.

Evelyn's husband not only supported her fully when she started the business, but very often she leaned on him for advice. He played a key role in terms of advising her, supporting her and listening to her crazy ideas. Never did he tell her that it cannot be done. Many a time she felt like giving up because business could be very difficult, but he would always tell her, "You can do it". Whatever challenges she faced they discussed them together. Evelyn realised that he had a very good business brain and was good with figures which she was not. They made a tremendous team because they pooled whatever they earned and did things together. Together they bought their first house and together they got him started and running his own businesses even though he was a civil servant.[41]

After a year into the business, she was doing fairly well. She was now able to move into her own offices. At the time, Electricity House on Harambee Avenue was being built and vacant offices in the building were being advertised in the newspapers for renting. She applied and surprisingly found out that Speedway Bureau had been allocated space by the property managers. When she read from the newspaper advert on the allocation, she was very excited. It was quite a big space and she partitioned it to create spacious offices that

---

41   Among other businesses, Arthur was in the hotel business and he was a part owner of the then Grosvenor Hotel and Grosvenor Properties.

could accommodate the company adequately. For the very first time she had an office to herself, which had a boardroom, a testing /interviewing centre, a proper reception and a place to make tea. She would now be able to hire a personal assistant and a messenger.

From this time on, there was no looking back for Evelyn. The companies she had contacted now started to seek her services and word spread among the business community that Speedway was the place to go. The success at this time could be attributed to her emphasis on recruiting only high quality staff for her clients. Her personal assistant was also very efficient. They made a good team and placed hundreds of people in various jobs. Speedway also offered additional services like getting work permits for expatriates to come from abroad on short contracts to train Africans. This helped her to get clients, among them top law firms, blue-chip companies and embassies.

The media also started writing about Speedway as people's imagination got caught by this young woman and what she was doing. On Speedway's second anniversary, Evelyn hosted a party for major clients and the event caught media attention which boosted the business. This was a very exciting time for Evelyn as an idea that she had started slowly became very big. She still meets people who tell her that she placed them in a certain job and helped them make something of themselves.

On the home front, things were also going very well for the couple. They had moved from the government house in Upper Hill where they had been living from the time they got married to their own home in Kitisuru which they bought in 1973. At the time they didn't have enough money and they spent time trying to figure out how they would buy it. Fortunately, Arthur had a good relationship with his bank manager, so they decided to go and ask for a loan. However, they needed to make a deposit on the property. Evelyn had been saving a little money for some time and had something like KSh 50,000, a large sum of money in those days. This was the money they used for the deposit.

Evelyn's first experience with the banks was when she faced challenges in the business, the main one being cash flow. As the company grew, she had more and more employees placed in various companies who needed to be paid weekly, yet she invoiced the companies they worked for on a monthly basis. Every Friday, the employees would submit their worksheet for the week and she had to pay them. The challenge was where to get the money to pay them because she had to pay the bills like everybody else in the business and wait for thirty days for the clients to pay. Since she could not ask her clients to treat her differently, as she had her credibility to think of, she decided to go to her bank and ask for money to pay the staff. This proved to be the biggest challenge, especially when she was starting out.

Her first encounter with the bank was memorable. The bank manager told her to put down her requirements and to present a proposal. At that time she required KSh 16,000, which was a lot of money then. Nevertheless, the bank manager gave her the overdraft facility despite having no security. This was surprising given the prejudices that were prevalent at the time – she had no collateral, she was a woman, she was very young and she was an African. Basically, she had everything going against her. Later, she came to learn that the manager was able to give her the overdraft without security because of the confidence that she displayed; he decided to bank on her. Consequently, she stayed with that bank for a long time.

Evelyn grew the business slowly by ploughing back her earnings into it. Initially her typical working day was 8.00 am to 6.00 pm, but as the business grew bigger, she had to work longer hours. She ran Speedway Bureau exclusively for six years and it became very successful, attracting many other people who started similar businesses, eventually saturating the market. With all the media attention and people saying that she was successful, others started getting the idea that this was the business to be in, a typical Kenyan phenomenon. As more people started similar bureaus, profit margins got eroded. That is when she decided to do something else.

The birth of Evelyn College of Design

The business into which Evelyn got after Speedway Bureau was in fashion design although, interesting enough, she's not and never was a designer. Nevertheless, she loves design and she is very artistic.

While interviewing people for Speedway Bureau, she often met people who were not good in office work and would ask them why they got into this line of work. Many told her that they wanted to be dress or interior designers but there were no colleges offering design courses in Kenya. Therefore, when the time came to move away from Speedway, she realised that this was a totally unexploited field; hence, she decided to start a school of fashion design. This, as she called it, was her unique feasibility study.

At the time, she knew nothing about design. Nevertheless, in a classic example of 'flying by the seat of your pants', Evelyn went ahead and advertised for students. Miraculously she got people responding to the adverts. She recruited two expatriate teachers who came in at the same time as the students. She had decided to run the school out of the premises of the soon to-be-closed Speedway Bureau. She started with just one class. Initially all the teachers were expatriates because there were no Kenyan designers at that time. But these expatriates were the ones responsible for the initial success of Evelyn

College of Design because the work ethic that they adopted was brilliant. It was wonderful to see their commitment.

Within six months, the demand for the course had increased and Evelyn started shopping for bigger premises outside the city centre. She saw a property at Riara Road off Ngong Road and informed Arthur that she wanted to purchase it for the school. He didn't tell her that she was crazy, but instead asked her how she was going to do it. She suggested they borrow money from the bank and that's what they did. This is where Evelyn College of Design stayed for the next twenty-five years.

The property on which the college stood was a one-acre piece of land, spacious with landscaped gardens and was very suitable for both learning and the fashion shows. In addition, Evelyn could add extra buildings because it was their property and the environment was wonderful – it was out of town and the students and teachers were very happy there.

The early years of the college coincided with the reign of Idi Amin in Uganda when many people were fleeing the country or looking for opportunities elsewhere. This meant that half of the students were from Uganda and so they were housed by the college. Today, the majority of the alumni are from Uganda. The college also attracted many students from other African countries, mostly through word of mouth, because as the only player in the market then, it hardly used to advertise.

Evelyn also started an interior design course but had to discontinue it because the intake was very slow. People were not familiar with what interior design was and for her it was sad, as this was during the coffee boom in the late 1970s when people had lots of money. She would go to people's houses and see the inappropriate colour schemes that had been applied. If only they could employ the services of an interior designer! However, the course was reintroduced in the 1990s and became very popular, ranking at par with fashion design. People are now more conscious of how their homes look and architects know that to be successful in whatever they do, they need interior designers. Today, Evelyn College has about twenty teachers in addition to other administrative staff. It has an average annual intake of 150 students. The fashion design course takes a total of eight terms or two and a half years.

Diversifying the businesses

By the early 1980s the Evelyn College of Design was established and chugging along smoothly. True to her nature, Evelyn became restless and was looking for a new challenge. She now wanted to reach out to women and thought the way to do that was to have a voice through a publication. One who loved reading and writing, she launched *Presence* magazine through which she started reaching out to people. She describes the magazine as one of the best times of her life.

However, although she was in publishing for ten years, she concedes that there was no money in it. They were permanently hustling for advertising. If anything, the magazine took away a lot of her money. When she sees people going into publishing thinking there is money, she shudders. From her experience, there is no money in it, at least not in Kenya. One may have the best content and everybody buying a copy but it's nearly impossible to generate enough advertising to keep afloat, which explains why a lot of publications go under.

Nevertheless, her greatest achievement with the magazine was informing women about their rights. Targeting middle-class women, it became a platform during the women's decade conference (in 1985) to talk about the issues they were dealing with and the Beijing conference for women which came soon after that.[42] It was not a feminist magazine but a forum for women to feel good about themselves with even serious issues like abortion or reproductive health written in a way that women could relate to. Evelyn even had a column in it, 'My Presence World', which was very inspirational to women.

Through the magazine, Evelyn got to travel all over the world attending international forums as Publisher of *Presence*, interacting with other publishers, politicians and people in the media, and sharing what she learnt with her readers. As it were, it became a good entry point into other things for which she has no regrets.

At around the time when she was Vice-Person of Africa Business Round-table (ABR), the private sector arm of African Development Bank (ADB), Evelyn started a company for the import and export of handicrafts called Evikar International, but it never got off the ground. Subsequently, she got into property development and microfinance around 2003. Her interest in the latter began when she was the Vice-Chair of Kenya Women Finance Trust (KWFT) in its formative stages. KWFT's idea was borne out of the fact that women had no access to credit. She felt that although she had been lucky to be able to access credit from banks, a majority of women had always had a problem particularly when it came to collateral. They were certainly disadvantaged. She felt that it would be useful to have a body that would help them, so she sat

---

42 The United Nations Decade for Women (1976–1985) was as a result of a recommendation by the first World Conference on Women, held in Mexico City in 1975. The decade sought to address the needs of women in the world with a tripartite theme of equality, peace and development. This culminated in a world conference held in Nairobi in 1985 to review the achievements of the Decade for Women and to create a ten-year action plan for the advancement of women. The resulting document was *Forward-Looking Strategies*.

down with a group of women and decided to form KWFT. These included Mary Okelo, currently the proprietor of Makini Group of Schools and the late Veronica Nyamodi, a lawyer.

KWFT worked out very well and Evelyn is very proud to have been part of it. The institution grew to be the largest in the country in microfinance. By December 2006, it had a network of 121 offices and an annual disbursement in excess of KSh 3 billion. Evelyn later became a director of Pride Africa, another microfinance organisation, which eventually morphed into a company called Microfinance Partners Limited. She became the chairperson of the latter, which exposed her to the actual operations of a microfinance company. This company had branches in Kenya, Uganda and Tanzania. Now she came to learn how microfinance was helping people irrespective of gender. This is how she got the idea for Faida Biashara.

Evelyn started by first doing a feasibility study to determine an appropriate place to locate Faida Biashara, which would be based on the need for micro-finance services. She settled on Ongata Rongai in Kajiado County followed by two satellite branches at Southlands in Lang'ata and Kasarani both in Nairobi. Starting with seed money of KSh 3 million, the company grew tremendously and they started another branch at Wangige in Kiambu County, another busy commercial centre. By then the company had been operating and growing for a year. The clientele's needs were overwhelming. The growth was faster than anticipated and the source of money for on-lending became a challenge.

Consequently, Evelyn talked to the Minister for Finance at the time and he was ready to provide them with money. However, she was not ready for a large business. Thus, she decided to give it a break and focus on the property development company. Although a rapidly growing company is the dream of many entrepreneurs, in microfinance the main challenge is to keep up with clients' demands. If one is not ready to serve their needs, then they are being unfair to them. Even if one decides not to engage any more clients, the ones they have qualify for bigger loans as they grow and one has to grow with them in terms of being able to pump in more money. When she decided to pull out she passed on the company's clients to other microfinance institutions.

However, Evelyn has not given up on this idea. She feels that she will go back to it at some point. Right now she is comfortable in property development to which she wants to give all her attention as it is a steadily growing industry. She decided to get into property development and focused on the upmarket, high quality finished homes. She had spent some time looking for a suitable property before realising that she was sitting on an acre of prime land where Evelyn College of Design was located along Riara Road. She then decided to relocate the school to Lavington and put up her first project on the land. The result was 32 apartments with amenities like a swimming pool and a gymnasium.

While embarking on property development, she wanted to create a country-feel through landscaped gardens. The emphasis was on quality – spacious rooms and high quality finishes. The complex was named Cedar Springs. In a classic illustration of the growth of the real estate industry, the same apartments were going for KSh 10 to 12 million each double their original price three years later. She was to follow this up with a second project located directly opposite the first. Both were developed under Speedway Investments, a company she set up with her son Eric as the CEO. Their strategy was to build and sell as opposed to renting out. Interestingly, this was Eric's idea. Evelyn was for putting up apartments to generate rental income for her retirement. Eric predicted that there would be a glut in the market and they would be stuck with the apartments. This happens in the market often. They however carved a niche for their market by developing properties that have landscaping with their signature waterfall in the garden, play areas for children and high-quality interior finishes. Many developers do not care about quality. As a result, they created such a demand that they had a waiting list for the next project, also comprising 32 apartments.

For the second project, Evelyn signed a contract with the contractor stipulating that he was responsible for dealing with plumbers, electricians and other workers to complete the project on time and within the budget. This meant that Eric did not have the headache of monitoring workers to keep pilferage to a minimum, a big problem in the construction industry which can really escalate the costs of building.

Family and business

Three years after Eric was born, Evelyn gave birth to their second child, a girl called Wacuka. Unfortunately, in 1978 tragedy struck when Arthur died, leaving Evelyn a widow at a young age. Wacuka was just 10 years old and Eric was 13. By the time he died Arthur had gone up the ranks in the civil service to the position of Commissioner of Customs and Excise. Thus, the family lived a comfortable life. Many women left in such a situation with a young family to take care of single-handedly have seen their quality of life deteriorate, but Evelyn was determined to maintain her children in the manner they had been accustomed to. When her husband died, she went out of her way to ensure that nothing else changed about the way they lived; for example, the children continued to attend the same schools. In fact, the family drew closer together because they only had each other.

Like her great-grandmother, Wanjiru wa Rara, losing her husband made her stronger in a way. Those who know her attest to the fact that Evelyn really came into her own after this period. It is when she showed her true leadership abilities and her capacity for hard work. She later met and married Mike Eldon in 1995 after being widowed for eighteen years.

Evelyn started *Presence* when Wacuka was in Sarah Lawrence College in New York (one of the top schools in the US). After graduation, Wacuka took over the daily running of the magazine as Managing Editor. Working with her daughter was very refreshing as she brought youthful dimension into the magazine. She was not only able to interact very well with the young workforce, but she also knew about generating advertising revenue and also brought a fresh perspective in terms of content. Wacuka later returned to New York where she studied for her Master's degree at the New York University. She later worked in the New York Committee for Protection of Journalists (NYCPJ) for a few years, returned to Kenya in 2006, and briefly worked for the Kenya Government. She then went to work as a media consultant with part-time engagements at the Evelyn College of Design as a Business Development Manager.

Eric took up the position of Chief Executive Officer of the property development company. He deals with the technical side and day-to-day operations that involve architects, quantity surveyors, contractors and other professionals who are hired for each project. Evelyn plays a key role of getting the initial financing for the projects. "If you had told me I would become a developer, I would have said you must be kidding but I've discovered that it's a very exciting field. My love of interiors and the artistic part of me is now coming out," she says. Speedway Investments has a project manager, accountants and support staff.

Eric is married and the couple has three children: Karungari, Githuku and Muthoni. His wife trained at Evelyn College of Design and briefly worked there as a teacher before she left to start her own fashion design business under the label African Inspirations.

Management style and strategy

Evelyn's management style is hands-on with regard to the administrative and financial matters. The technical side is handled by the college principal, a qualified designer and administrator. She gives her staff, particularly the head of the school, a free hand to deal with the students and parents. However, she is available when it comes to critical issues. She also holds quarterly management meetings.

Evelyn is the chairperson of the company which has a board of directors made up of family members. Other than the principal there is a general manager who reports directly to her. Under him are an administrator and a director of admissions who also manages the hostel for the students.

Members of Evelyn's family have worked in the business, although she admits that working with relatives is not necessarily the best thing. However, whenever she has worked with them she has made it clear that they are employees. When they are in the office, they are not related and she ensures that she does not deal with them directly. With regard to Eric and Wacuka, each of them has their own role and they must make their operations profitable. For example, Wacuka managed *Presence* (the women's lifestyle magazine that Evelyn published in the 1980s) and Eric dealt with the property company, Speedway Investments. She likes them getting involved in business because eventually she'd like to feel she can ease herself out and let them carry on.

Evelyn feels that it has been a pleasure working with Eric because he's managed to do some of the things that she would otherwise not have done. He knows it's a family business and brings a lot of enthusiasm into it. He knows that if he falls, the family falls. Everybody understands why they are where they are. The family has regular meetings to be able to understand each other.

During the early years when Wacuka started working in the family business, Evelyn was tempted to discuss office matters at home. She told her mother, "Mum, as soon as we get home that's the end of office stuff; we don't talk about it here." Thereafter, they trained themselves not to discuss office matters until it became the norm. No matter how crucial the situation becomes, they do not discuss business issues as a family at home. Even on weekends they do not talk business. That waits until office hours, otherwise they are likely to be consumed by business matters and forget how to be a family. They all respect that and it has worked very well for them. It has strengthened their bond as a family.

To ensure that her children are independent, each person gets a salary when they work with her. "I always tell them this is your salary and allowances; sink or swim. And this avoids a situation where they come begging for money for petrol, to pay an electricity bill or other expenses which can create room for conflict and dependency. Of course if the company turns out dividends they get a share of that as well," she says.

Evelyn is not flamboyant and nothing about her even hints at the wealth she has accumulated over the years or her success in business. She drives a simple Nissan Saloon car, which surprises those who expect to see her in a big flashy vehicle. Catherine Munkumba, a past student of Evelyn College of Design and one who has known Evelyn for some time, describes her personality as one on the quieter side, but one who is very assertive and hardworking.

Best and worst moment in business

Evelyn says the best times of her life in business were when she was publishing *Presence* magazine. She loved reading, writing and reaching out to people through the magazine.

Incidentally, it was while publishing *Presence* that Evelyn made the biggest mistake of her working life. She used to give the publication to the printers and then realised that the bill was too high. She decided to set up a fully fledged printing press. This was a nightmare and the worst mistake she ever made. She borrowed money to buy it but knew nothing about printing presses. Before long, her workforce took her to the cleaners and she just ended up pouring more money into it. Says she: "It was costly to buy and maintain printing presses, which did not bring a return. The whole investment was a total loss." Little did she know that the best thing would have been to outsource. She lost millions of shillings.

This costly mistake taught her an important lesson: that one does not have to do everything themselves and sometimes it is best to outsource. This is a lesson that will come in handy when Evelyn College of Design gets its own clothing line. It will not need to start a manufacturing company; Evelyn knows nothing about manufacturing. She will give it to the experts and put her mark-up. She will then demand quality from people who are conversant with manufacturing. This is what a lot of people do; for example, Marks and Spencer, a leading UK clothing retailer, which is in the business of selling clothes and outsources manufacturing in India and elsewhere. They simply give their requirements.

Future of the business

Unlike many African entrepreneurs whose businesses die with them, Evelyn has designed a well thought-out succession plan which involves working side by side with her children to teach them the ropes while she is still active in the business and ensure that they can comfortably take over once she retires. Involving them from an early stage means they understand the whole concept and dynamics of the business, and the challenges. When she will make an exit, she knows that the business will be in good hands. Even if the children let it go down, she will be confident that she had done her best to prepare them well aware that nothing is guaranteed in life.

Eric got involved in the college as soon as he came back from the United States where he studied for a Bachelor's degree in Business Management. He is very entrepreneurial. He started out at the college working as operations director and dabbled in the entertainment industry when he and two colleagues opened the Jazz Bar at Yaya Centre which they later closed. He later became the Chief Executive of Speedway Investments – the family's property company. He is a natural when it comes to real estate; he took to the business instantly like a duck to water. He seems to have inherited this trait from his late father, Arthur, who was also very keen on building.

Speedway Investments will continue to focus on the high end of the property market, but Evelyn does not rule out getting into other areas like low-income housing or commercial property. Her vision is to become the best property developer in the country offering quality that stands out. She believes in building houses that she can be comfortable living in and not a house that is built very quickly and after a few years starts falling to pieces.

Other than starting a clothing line under Evelyn College of Design, Evelyn's dream is to turn the college into a university offering degrees in design. Currently, her students have to go abroad to obtain a degree. She also feels very strongly about promoting the ethnic line and taking the best local arts and crafts, and blending them to create a uniquely Kenyan clothing line internationally as a way of maximising the Evelyn brand.

Evelyn has often expressed the desire to slow down, retire and let her children take over. However, she is still taking on more and more projects. As Eric observes, "I think her idea of retirement is to just come into the office a few times a week!" Evelyn herself cannot explain what drives her endless quest for new projects: "Entrepreneurs are restless souls. I like a lot of pressure, things happening at the same time; I operate better that way. If one thing is doing well then I find it's too quiet. I start asking: Where can I direct my energy? Seeking for opportunities all the time is how I end up doing other things."

Challenges as entrepreneur

Evelyn is one person who's never intimidated by anything. Some people give up even before they start when they see the obstacles before them. According to her son, Eric, her confidence is infectious because it helps one to see that this mountain is climbable.

At the beginning when she founded Speedway Bureau in the early 1970s, Evelyn faced the challenge of racism and her youth which she had to overcome. "I was in my twenties and very young and most of the personnel managers were white and very senior people. I would make an appointment and sometimes have to wait for a while before they could see me. But I would tell them to try me and not come back if they didn't like my services," she says.

Another major challenge is finance. When putting up the Cedar Springs complex, Evelyn had problems getting financing for the project. Being their first project and given that at the time there was no explosion in real estate developments, there was bound to be a problem. Evelyn packaged the whole deal and started going round to banks starting with her bank. But she would get answers like "we're not ready yet" or "the figures don't read right", probably as a way of turning her down.

One bank was very receptive but it had never financed property and needed to first create a mortgage division to handle such a request. The process proved to be long and bureaucratic and by the time the financing came through two years later, Speedway Investments had already completed its first project with financing from Shelter Afrique. The loan from this bank ended up being used for the second project. Shelter Afrique looked at the project proposal and funded 50 percent. They raised the balance by doing pre-sales – asking prospective buyers of the apartments to commit a 10 percent deposit on the sale price. Shelter Afrique also gave a wonderful project officer who worked with Evelyn's professionals.

The project took eighteen months to complete. Evelyn was also fortunate to have good architects who believed in the dream and did not ask for money upfront before doing the architectural bit of it. Thus, she got a good professional team. And for banking on them the architects were used for the second project. In addition, they referred them to many other potential clients as their work is also of high calibre.

After completing the first project Evelyn invited the first bank, which had declined to finance it, for the official opening. They were very impressed by the project but wondered why she had not approached them. They were shocked to hear that she had actually approached them, but they had declined to finance the project. "They later came to see me to find out how they had failed and I told them it was because they weren't willing to take a risk. It was the most amazing thing having these bank people sitting in my office taking notes on how they had failed to finance us," she says.

Another challenge is pursuing one's dream blindly. Despite the fact that Evelyn enjoyed publishing *Presence*, it was an overall loss. In every business one has to be practical, realistic and weigh the direction the business is going. If it is not bringing in profits and all one is getting are deficits, they should just walk away and do something else. The entrepreneurial spirit is fundamental. Even if doing something is fun, how long can one lose money in the process? She admits that shutting down the magazine was a hard decision to make, especially letting go of loyal staff although some were absorbed into the college.

A perennial challenge for Evelyn is staff. She is ever seeking to get good, honest staff that is able to keep up with her energy. She is perceived as a workaholic, but she doesn't see herself that way. She sees herself as a perfectionist and someone who works very hard. She demands the same of the people she works with. Whenever she finds shortcomings in the respective staff, they part company.

Charity and social work

A major part of Evelyn's life is her charity work especially the socio-economic project she started in her native Cura village when she was Chairperson of the Rotary Club of Nairobi (another first as she was the first woman to ever hold this post). She engaged an NGO to promote tissue-culture bananas in the village as a way of boosting incomes. Later they started a bee-keeping project with 200 hives for 40 farmers. She also got water into the village through her Rotary friends, and started a home for HIV/Aids orphans sponsored by international benefactors.

Partly because of the success of the Cura project, Evelyn briefly tried her hands in politics in 2007 when she sought election as the Member of Parliament for Kikuyu Constituency. However, Eric and her husband Mike prefer that she stayed out of politics altogether. Eric particularly thinks that it is a thankless effort. With the murk of politics, he does not want anyone he loves involved in it. Although she has not decided whether to try politics again in future, either way she will continue with her charity work which is a large part of what she wants her legacy to be: "To me it's not about personal success but whose life you've touched along the way."

Evelyn usually takes a break from her hectic schedule to relax and rejuvenate by reading, swimming, watching movies and travelling. Her home in Runda, one of Nairobi's leafy suburbs, is her haven. It has a swimming pool and pool house used for entertaining guests. She has turned it into a celebration of African art, design and fabric. Its walls are adorned with artefacts collected on her travels all over the continent. Her favourite holiday destination is Mombasa, which she likes for its climate, the atmosphere and the fact that she does not have to hassle through several airports to get there.

Tips for aspiring entrepreneurs

Evelyn advises young entrepreneurs to believe in what they are doing because business is never easy. She attributes the reputation of the school of design to her staying put in the business. Says she: "In business you can give up at times but the fact that I've been able to hang on even when things are really bad is why students keep on coming. People we've trained or who have been teachers here see the kind of money coming in and start their own institutions and take away our students by charging lower fees. But I keep on saying I'll not let go because there'll be better times tomorrow."

She continues: "Never hesitate to realise your dreams and put your ideas into practice. I've met a lot of people with fantastic ideas but they keep talking and don't do anything about them. There are many opportunities in Kenya; you just need to tap into them and don't be discouraged by challenges. When you fall pick yourself up and go for it knowing the next time around you'll become a better business person learning through your mistakes. Falling is not a failure, it's just a process."

Regarding financing of business through bank loans, she says: "Even if one bank does not believe in you go to another one but you must believe in your dream." Especially for women entrepreneurs, she urges them to have confidence, as she thinks that if there is something that women lack, it is confidence and a belief in themselves as business people. "Women should not think about themselves as women when venturing into business, but as people and to remove the feeling that because I'm a woman the doors will forever be shut. If you are turned away with your business idea, know that it's simply because it's not a good business proposal. Go refine it and go to the next person and remove the feeling that I'll never be listened to because I'm a woman. People pick up on this. Have the confidence to defend your business ideas."

Role models

Evelyn's role model is her great-grandmother, Wanjiru wa Rara, because of what she was able to do more than a century ago when it was unheard of for women to even think about business. There are three entrepreneurs she respects. First is Richard Branson because of his very unorthodox ways of doing business; challenges he has had in his business life, and making a success of himself. "I've read his book and he's tremendously inspirational because he's not confined himself to one business; he's a restless soul and he's not afraid of failure."

She also admired the late Anita Roddick, founder of the vast Body Shop network of cosmetics stores because she started her business very small and when she had a young family. However, she believed in what she was doing and became a huge success internationally. More than anything else, she went for quality and this is why she became such a great success.

Another person whom Evelyn admires is Bill Gates because he's using his millions to help others through his Bill and Melinda Gates Foundation.

Annex

Evelyn's leadership roles
- Project Director, Cura Rotary Community Corps: an integrated rural development initiative aimed at village empowerment
- Advisory Board member, US-Africa Small Business Network: US-based initiative promoting African business in the US
- Trustee, President's Award Scheme: Kenya Chapter of Duke of Edinburgh's Award Scheme
- Board of Advisors, Whale Hunters Foundation
- African Leadership Foundation

Past responsibilities
- Chairperson, Transparency International, Kenya Chapter: The global anti-corruption watchdog
- Chairperson, Rotary Club of Nairobi
- Assistant Governor, Rotary District 9200
- President, All Africa Businesswomen Association (AABA): Promotes development of African businesswomen in the formal sector
- Vice-chairperson, Africa Business Roundtable: Private sector arm of African Development Bank (ADB)
- Board member, African Project Development Facility: Part of IFC, the private sector development arm of the World Bank
- Board member, Kenya Film Corporation
- Board member, Voluntary Agency Development Assistance (VADA)

Chapter 12

Myke Rabar

Not long ago a career as a disk jockey (DJ or deejay) was not one that many parents would have been enthusiastic about. Deejays were often associated with flashy lifestyles, wasteful spending and indulgence. One man has however shown that spinning the disks as a deejay can be a serious career and a stepping stone to big things. Myke Rabar, founder of *HomeBoyz* Entertainment Limited has demonstrated that there is serious money to be made in the entertainment industry. His example so inspired his two younger brothers Alph Rabar and John Rabar that they decided to join him in the business. Ultimately, the last three sons in the Rabar family were to sit at the apex of an enviable entertainment business that was to encompass a DJ Academy and a radio station that in just six months from inception, became the most popular in the youth market.

HomeBoyz were also to make their mark on the international entertainment scene with their enormous project that involved the production of a 52-episode animated series for children. This project was undertaken in partnership with Tiger Aspect, one of the UK's most successful independent television production houses. The series, called Tinga Tinga Tales, was launched on the BBC's pre-school channel CBeebies in February 2010 and was also sold to Playhouse Disney. This project was groundbreaking for Kenya as it involved building the first fully equipped animation studios in the country employing local designers, writers, musicians and animators.

While these achievements are noteworthy, perhaps the most inspiring aspect of Myke Rabar's story is the way he and his brothers have maintained a serious profile in an industry known for destroying its best talent through flashy lifestyles, free booze and other trappings that have ended the career of many a promising deejay. *HomeBoyz* has gone on to build a reputation for innovation which keeps them ahead of competitors eager to copy what they've done. *HomeBoyz* DJs are the pioneers in Radio Mix in Kenya; they introduced Kenya's first video mixing TV show (H_2O) and are the first and only DJ outfit to start their own radio station. They have organised events for some of East Africa's biggest companies including East African Breweries Limited (EABL), Zain (later renamed Airtel), Coca-Cola, Unilever, MTV Base Africa and Nation Media Group. They also organised concerts for international stars like The Lost Boyz, Coolio, Shaggy, Sean Paul and Akon (in Tanzania). All this adds up to a business that has been dubbed 'the most influential entertainment powerhouse in East Africa'. To understand *HomeBoyz*, it is essential that one delves into the background of its founder – Myke Rabar.

Early childhood and education

Myke Rabar's journey began in Nairobi in 1970 when he was born into a polygamous family. Born as the sixth of the eight children of Wilson Rabar and Janet Auma comprising four boys and four girls, and two stepsisters, Myke spent part of his childhood in Parklands area where the family initially lived. It was an average family in terms of income; hence they generally did not lack in basic necessities. As his father worked for Kenya Railways while his mother was in publishing, they lived in the staff houses in Parklands. Later, the family moved to South B, another middle-class suburb in Nairobi.

During his early childhood Myke found himself mostly hanging out with his friends and age mates in the estate because his elder brother was six years older and his brothers Alph and John were far younger. With more than forty families living in the staff quarters in Parklands, there was no shortage of playmates. Most of Myke's playmates were in the same primary school with him, so they pretty knew much of everyone else in the 'hood'. After school, he would always be in someone else's house. Nevertheless, his parents were strict and the children avoided getting into trouble as much as possible.

When he reached school-going age, Myke went to Parklands Primary School and completed the primary phase in 1980. Thereafter, he went to Highway Secondary School in South B, Nairobi, for his 'O' level education and later in Nairobi School for his 'A' levels where he graduated in 1989. He did well academically and was usually in the top three all through primary and high school. At the primary school examinations, he obtained 36 points while at 'O' level he graduated with a Division One.

Myke was naturally curious and was always trying to discover new things. This is the trait that he attributes to having enabled him to achieve all he has. "As a child, I would dismantle the radio to see what was inside and find out where the noise was coming from. Whenever our TV got a problem, I was the one who would sit with the technician as he fixed it or with the mechanic who used to fix my uncle's car. I asked a lot of questions all the time," says Myke.

All through high school, Myke nurtured a dream of doing electrical engineering at the university. "I really wanted to become an engineer. While other people dream of flying an aeroplane, I wanted to build the engine. Understanding how things worked was what would make my day. However, the first time I sat the 'A' level exams I did not get the required grades and opted to repeat the class. On repeating, I still didn't make it and was instead admitted for a meteorology degree at the University of Nairobi (UoN) in 1991," says Myke. "I chose meteorology as a second fiddle because it had elements of Mathematics and Physics." As he was studying for his meteorology degree at the university, he took some electronics courses on the side at a commercial college in Nairobi.

Growing up Myke was surrounded by music and developed an interest from an early age. His father loved music and had a gramophone and a lot of records. His favourite music was Lingala and Dholuo music. "He knew all the songs and would play music every weekend. He'd call me to play the music for him when he had guests because it was very manual and you needed to turn each record to play the other side. I remember my mum used to get so upset because I was sitting there playing music instead of reading or playing, but I really enjoyed it," says Myke. He also had an uncle living in Mombasa who had lots of records that he would often leave at their house and Myke would spend hours listening to them. His uncle's taste in music was more modern like Boney M and Donna Summer.

There was a tradition at Parklands Primary School that after completing Standard Seven, the pupils would hold a leavers' party. It was during such an occasion that Myke played music outside their home for the first time. "One of my friends had a brother who had disco equipment, which we used. Again I found myself experimenting with deejaying for the first time," says Myke. In that era, there were no CDs (compact discs); music was recorded on long-playing phonograph records (LPs).

It was while he was in Form One in 1981 that Myke bought his first record at Assanands Music Store for KSh 17. At the time, a song by 'D' Train called 'You're the One for Me' was a big hit. And while in high school he and his friends in South B would collect music cassettes and compete to see who had the latest music. They would get relatives living in the US to record the latest music playing on radio stations there and send the cassettes to Kenya. "We spent our entire holiday just exchanging music. All we had was KBC radio so when you had a tape from London you were the man. My mum knew if she wanted to find me I'd be in someone's servant quarter dubbing music," says Myke.

It was from this adventurous undertaking in music that Myke discovered that he could make money by selling the cassettes to the *matatu* crew in South B Estate at KSh 100 each.

Highway Secondary School had an impact on Myke. It introduced him to a wide range of people and exposed him to diverse cultures. "With the multiracial environment at the school coupled with my outgoing character, I found myself making friends with Asians. This experience provided a strong basis of how

I would relate with people later in life. It also helped me to understand how to deal with people from other communities, which was significant especially when I went to the United Kingdom for further education after my undergraduate studies. When you find yourself in a foreign country and you are the only Kenyan, you feel cut off and unable to relate, always conscious about being black. My experience at Highway made my cultural transition while in Europe easy."

The start of deejaying – studies and career

During his days at the University of Nairobi, Myke frequented disco clubs such as Visions and Carnivore which were popular with campus students. Most of his friends who accompanied him would busy themselves partying, having fun and chasing girls. But he would be at the club for an entirely different reason – to observe the resident deejays do their thing and he would try to pick up a few tips. For hours all night, Myke remembers: "I would just sit and observe the deejays' hands working on the turntables, wondering how they blended one song into another. When it was time to go home my friends knew they would find me at the deejays' table."

Before joining the university, Myke had hooked up with a group called Bad Boys that played music at weddings and other social functions. It was based in Nairobi West, the neighbouring estate. "My parents had a major issue with me staying out all night when I was just sixteen. But due to my passion and determination, I kept following the group; after all, my grades did not suffer and I was still an A-student.

"I started by helping to carry and set up the equipment. Eventually, the group started letting me play for a short time just before the main DJ came in. This way I picked up some experience. However, clubs like Visions still wouldn't let me play despite my experience."

After observing the deejays in the big clubs for a while, Myke became a little proactive and would always request for a chance to spin. Despite frequent rejections, he never gave up. He was so keen to play that money wasn't an issue; he was ready to play for free which was often the case once clubs started giving him the chance. At Visions, he proposed that the club holds a campus night on a day that it never used to open. If they allowed him to play, he promised to pack the club with students. At that time only Bubbles had a campus night. Visions did not have time for students and it is Myke and his friends who kicked off campus nights. These campus nights became increasingly popular and the concept was later picked up by other clubs.

Visions Club agreed to Myke's proposal. "I started by deejaying and promoting the club at the same time. Part of the agreement was that I would not be paid for the first month, an arrangement that I did not mind; in any case, I was ready to pay the club just to tell people that I worked at Visions. I rallied all my friends with whom I did a small campaign in campus for the special days. On the first Thursday, they had about 500 people paying to get into the club. It registered great success." He was to later start Karaoke Night at Green Corner Restaurant which was held on Saturdays.

Soon Myke was earning good money. In his second year at the university, he bought a second-hand car with the earnings. He also had a TV which he kept in his room, a rare thing for students at the time. Most of the students only aspired to own a boom box (music system) which had to be the biggest and the best.[43] "It was primarily an ego thing."

In those days, being a deejay was really 'cool'. All the girls wanted to date them. The deejays were paid well, had many perks and were celebrities in their own right. A well-known deejay was DJ Babs of the Carnivore, a real celeb! Nevertheless, the environment exposed one to temptation of negative lifestyle – drugs, alcohol (which would be free-flowing) and womanising. Such a lifestyle has ruined many a DJ's promising career. Being financially independent early can ruin someone because they can buy all the alcohol, drugs and have as many girls as they want. Although he has built his career within the party scene, unlike many deejays Myke does not take alcohol. Like many teenagers, he had experimented with it but did not pick the habit. Thus, he ended up not drinking. His brothers John and Alph do not drink either.

"When my earnings from deejaying improved, I started buying my own equipment, especially turntables and speakers, which I used to perform during the weekends in private parties and weddings. I became so busy that I never had time for anything else, which was probably a good thing because it kept my mind off negative influences. Even when I went to a club I was either working or watching the DJ, leaving me with no time for drinking or womanising." In fact, he would drive his friends home as they would all be high. "For me, sitting in a bar drinking was a complete waste of time. I would rather be somewhere dubbing a cassette," says Mike.

Like many people at the time, Myke's parents were also not supportive of this lifestyle. It wasn't until his final year at the university that they made their peace with his chosen career because this is what it had clearly become. What helped was that they could see the financial rewards that came with it. In fact, Myke had become independent early. It was while he was in high school that his parents gave him pocket money for the last time.

---

43   The music system was referred to as a 'boom box' because it was purchased with the student's subsistence allowance called 'boom'. Usually it was the first item that one bought with the first boom.

With his parents now condoning his 'career', Myke bought equipment gradually and took over the servant's quarters in their South B home. It became his storage area and studio. He would spend hours inside the small room practising or in the backyard building his own speakers. He would collect old components (drivers, hoofers and tweeters) and get a carpenter to cut the wood for him to build the cabinets. It was a way of getting speakers cheaply, which enabled him to create his own designs for the boxes housing the drivers. "The activity would take a whole day and when my parents saw this level of dedication, they realised I was not doing it out of mischief. It was serious business for me."

The *Bad Boys* group would often call him to play at gigs. He would collect the equipment, take a driver who would help him set it up and return the equipment late at night. It had started out with Myke playing for a short time before the *Bad Boys* deejays took over. But sometimes they would not show up at all and he would be happy to play for the entire function. He was still doing it for free; for him, this was part of gaining experience and learning the craft. "It even got to the point where I could arrange transport, go for a meeting with a client, and do the entire setting up and gig by myself."

He was also doing some gigs under a group called *The Crew* which he had set up with friends in Lang'ata. Previously he had been doing everything solo – from transporting his equipment to the venue, setting up and playing. After some time, he asked four friends to assist him. Initially they only helped with setting up the equipment, but after a while he started training them to deejay. At the time, his younger brothers Alph and John, had not yet taken an interest in the business. "They had no interest in what I was doing and thought I was nuts. Later, they were to suddenly get sucked in," observes Myke.

However, Alph and John do not agree with Myke's observation. Both trace their interest in what Myke was doing during their time in high school. "I thought I was too young to get involved in the business. So I just observed. It was not until I got into the university that I involved myself fully in the business. Having tried my hand in deejaying, I found that I could not only just do it, but it was also fun and could help me earn extra pocket money. I was well received in the industry and after my undergraduate studies, I decided to do it full time," counters John. On his part, Alph would sneak into the servant's quarter where Myke kept his equipment and try his hand at deejaying. For months he carried out his clandestine activities using a master key that he had made. "On one occasion, Myke caught me and gave me a good tongue-lashing. Turntables were expensive and Myke was worried that I would mishandle the equipment," says Alph. It was not until just before he left for the UK that Myke gave Alph a bigger role in deejaying. This is how Alph cut his teeth in the business.

Myke continued juggling his own fledgling DJ business and playing for the *Bad Boys* until the latter started having disagreements amongst themselves. Subsequently, they decided to wind up the business. Myke bought some of their equipment to augment his business. "Also, when I realised that the *Bad Boys* had a huge following, I decided to use part of the name. I changed my group's name from *The Crew* to *HomeBoyz*. The name 'boyz' would be fundamental to the survival of my business." By this time Alph and John were getting more involved in the business. John was studying at Egerton University for a Bachelor of Science (BSc) degree in Horticulture and would come to Nairobi every weekend to join them.

It was during his final year at the university that Myke made up his mind not to be employed but instead to pursue a career in music. With knowledge that his current degree was not going to be very useful, he focused on his deejaying work. "While I was not going to fail my exams, I was not going to spend too much time trying to get a first-class either," says Myke

Three months after graduating from the university in 1994, he moved out of home to a servant's quarter in South B. "I was probably earning as much as my mother if not more. I earned money by playing at weddings on Saturdays and in clubs on weekends. I also played at karaoke, and earned considerable money by mixing and selling tapes to *matatus* and individuals." He would record many of the tapes while playing in clubs. He was often approached by revellers with some offering as much as KSh 1,000 for a well-mixed cassette. Thereafter, he became a resident DJ at Visions and would play throughout the week. Thus, he was extremely busy and had no social life basically; however, he did not mind because music was his passion. He played every chance he got.

Having made up his mind to concentrate on music, Myke was resolved that he would not be using this meteorological degree and would instead pursue Sound Engineering. Understanding how things worked had fascinated Myke since his childhood. It was this curiosity that made him dismantle items such as radios and iron boxes. This trait having manifested itself so early, it had spilled over into music. At the time he was leaving university, the CD technology was getting into the market and he now wondered how CDs were made and the process of recording music. He figured out that a degree course in sound engineering would help him to learn this stuff. Unfortunately, there was no institution that offered a degree in deejaying at the time and this influenced his choice of further studies.

Less than a year after graduating from the University of Nairobi, Myke was off to the UK to start the three-year degree course in Sound Engineering at the SAE Institute. He sold his car and some sound equipment to finance the trip. While in the UK, he took up some jobs to earn money for tuition and upkeep. Lady luck had smiled on him and he got a job on the second day after landing in the UK playing at an African club. His schedule was gruelling but he was happy to be earning money doing what he enjoyed. He would work from Friday to Sunday at the club and attend classes during the week. To add to an already full plate he started consulting for some clubs.

Getting into music full-time

While Myke was in the UK from 1995 to 1998, John and Alph managed *HomeBoyz*. John was still at Egerton University, Njoro. Alph was doing a computer engineering course at a college in Nairobi. Capital FM had just been launched. John and Alph asked for and got a slot to play their music on the radio station. "Although we were not being paid for it, we did not mind as we really wanted the exposure. The station had a lot of roadshows and other events to which they would invite the *HomeBoyz* to play. With time, they became like their official deejays. This is what kept the band alive for the three years that I was away. The partnership was also instrumental in growing the *HomeBoyz* brand."

After three years the *HomeBoyz* deejays were poached by Kiss 100. For some time after that there was a game of musical chairs when *HomeBoyz* had shows on Nation FM (later Easy FM), Capital FM and back to Kiss 100 where they were to perform for a long time. They got a five-hour Saturday night show on Kiss 100 in addition to playing on *HomeBoyz* Radio which was launched in 2008.

Meanwhile, assured that the deejay outfit was in good hands, Myke could focus on his work and studies in the UK. A large part of his training was practical and involved attending and working in huge concerts. Students would get free concert tickets because they would provide cheap labour. While many students stayed in front enjoying the main act, Myke would always be found backstage with the engineers. "For me, the excitement was derived from finding out what type of equipment the mixer would be using; hence, my hero would be the sound engineer and not the artiste." He would spend two days with the engineers and ask all sorts of technical questions, eager to learn as much as he could. Initially he volunteered, but later he started getting paid when he enrolled with an agency that supplied labour to such concerts. As he observed: "In the UK, people were specialised. You could get people who only cleaned male toilets. In the music industry there were sound engineers who specialised by genre such that a guy mixed rock music only or jazz only. You could get a designer who only designed sets using satin fabric and he would get a lot of work even though he did nothing else. By contrast, event organisers in Kenya do everything from designing sets, lighting, decorations, and often double up as masters of ceremony."

After three years in the UK, Myke returned to find that his brothers had done a sterling job sustaining the *HomeBoyz* brand while he was away. He decided that his first priority would be to build on the strong brand and take the DJ outfit to the next level. However, implementing the ideas he had picked up while in the UK proved to be an uphill task. "I was so exposed that there were things I wanted us to do as a deejay outfit but the radio stations could not understand where we were coming from. I wanted to do more events (especially in clubs) and concerts, and launch a DJ academy. However, I could not do such things on my own. Getting people to resonate with this thinking became difficult and it got to the point where radio stations got scared of the *HomeBoyz* because we were growing so fast. As the stations still needed us, they decided to curtail our growth by reducing our exposure."

In Myke's absence Alph had taken charge of the administrative work while John headlined their events and did the actual deejaying. Upon return, Myke decided to take up the role of marketing and finding new gigs for the group. He handled the overall strategy which involved looking for new areas that the business could venture into and people they could partner with. He also focused on building capacity in terms of getting new equipment, some of which he had bought while he was abroad; he had discovered where to get good but affordable equipment in the UK (sometimes people paid to have the equipment taken off their hands because it was obsolete in the market but still relevant in Kenya). Myke was quick to take advantage of such opportunities.

Myke had also gained some valuable experience on how to set up a radio station during a job he had taken up for a couple of months as he waited for some equipment he had shipped from the UK to arrive. The job involved sound engineering for Epsilon Broadcasting which was building radio stations in Uganda, Tanzania, Rwanda and Burundi. But as it turned out, they would have to wait for another ten years before getting a licence to broadcast.

Diversifying the business

While he was in the UK, Myke would hire a stall on some market days and sell CDs. This made him keen to open a music shop when he returned to Kenya. That dream came true when *HomeBoyz* opened a shop at Nakumatt Prestige on Ngong Road called The Boxx in 2005. However, after a year in operation, the outlet had to close down. "It was too expensive to maintain. Between paying rent for the premises and pilferage (which was very common), we hardly made any profits." Another factor had to do with culture. "The culture of buying music in the country was virtually non-existent. The customers complained that our prices were very high. While the wholesale price of a CD was KSh 700, we sold the same at KSh 1,200. At this price there were few takers. Pirated copies were cheaper by far. Moreover, the FM stations played music around the clock, making people feel it was unnecessary to buy music," says Myke.

When opening The Boxx, *HomeBoyz* expected that contemporary music like R&B and hip hop would sell more. However, gospel music was the fastest, moving. They were however not a mainstream gospel music store. Although they stocked a few gospel titles, they were not ready to invest in this type of music. The stock was not moving fast enough and yet they had to keep on buying new titles because the shop also had to cater for people who wanted the latest music. Because of this, they ended up with a lot of money tied up in dead stock which led to cash flow problems. "Some customers would come and request for the latest album by an artist, but when we eventually brought it, they would say they didn't want it anymore, probably because they had got it free from the Internet or dubbed it from a friend."

The hardest bit was knowing when to stop and accept that things were not working. This was because Myke was so passionate about the business. They were bleeding cash and only a trickle was coming back in form of sales. "Already we owed too much, but we had fought so hard to get into Nakumatt that we just kept pushing and hoping things would change," says Myke. They had negotiated for six months before they got a breakthrough into the supermarket; which had a model stipulating that all its branches must be similar, and meant that a supplier had to supply to all branches. In their case, they were expected to roll out The Boxx across all Nakumatt branches, an investment that was beyond their means. But the chain's management was understanding and gave them six months to do it. Nakumatt did not own any of the stock and only charged rent for the space and took a commission on sales.

For quality and uniformity purposes they had to use the chain's contractors when building their shop which was expensive. Setting up the shop alone cost KSh 4 million (which didn't include the cost of buying stock). In the end, they had no choice but to shut down. As Myke reflected, "We had a good idea but we were not ready for it. It made sense to partner with such a large retail outlet because one of my long term plans was to set up a record label and I knew the one thing that kills music sales in this market is poor distribution. We competed with a foreign-owned music store to get into Nakumatt and they decided to give it to a local business. I was worried that if we pulled out, we'd never get another chance. They could see the numbers and knew what we were going through because all our sales went through their tills. They were very understanding when we decided to pull out."

After shutting down the shop they were given shelf space. However, without an attendant in place the problem of pilferage persisted. With nowhere to sample the music before buying, people would return the CDs after a few days saying they were not playing. "The supermarket had a no-questions-asked return policy and would take the CDs back and put them into the inventory. Needless to say, the CDs would not be saleable afterwards, thereby increasing the losses. Apparently, some people were being dishonest by dubbing CDs then returning them," says Myke.

The business made such huge losses that the venture almost shut down *HomeBoyz* altogether including their flagship deejaying outfit. What Myke learnt from this experience is that, while thinking far ahead is good, it can kill a business in the short term due to the logistics of implementation. The devil is always in the details and implementation has to be given a lot of thought before diving into a new venture.

Another venture that did not really take off was the all-girl crew called HomeGalz which they launched in 2000. "The concept was easy to sell and the girls became popular. However, the girls had personal issues because of parents and boyfriends who could not accept a job that involved staying out all night in clubs. Most lived at home because they were all young (aged between 18 and 25 years) which translates to too much pressure from the families. In Kenya the perception is that such a job is about being wayward and is for losers." Seeing girls deejaying was such a novel concept that the crew had travelled to as far as Dubai for gigs. They had to abandon it after a year and a half.

HomeBoyz later opened a deejay academy to train people in the craft. The shift in focus to training was a natural progression because they were in an industry where, as market leaders, people would copy what they were doing and undercut them on price. Moreover, Myke wanted to help others especially in view of the hassle that he went through trying to learn the craft of deejaying. While critics have argued that they were creating competition for themselves, Myke did not worry about that: "If we don't train them, someone else will. So we might as well reap from them when we can. We also realised that our strong brand would make it easier to draw in students than the next guy who opens a college across the road."

Other successful ventures included SoundTraxx Touring, studios and Aktivate. SoundTraxx is a company that was formed to hire out sound equipment, including the huge trucks on which the equipment is mounted. They had accumulated so much equipment that they wanted to utilise it fully. They were also getting queries from people who just wanted to hire the equipment without the deejays. *HomeBoyz* also started producing video mixing TV music shows (such as H_2O) and started building studios eventually putting up seven studios in its Baricho Road base in Nairobi. This enabled them to start producing radio commercials in-house. Aktivate is the outfit that handles roadshows, experiential marketing, and product launches.

A less successful venture is their record label *HomeBoyz* Records (Producshizzle). "From interacting with audiences for so long, we had good knowledge of how crowds react to songs. There's a certain style, tempo and groove that a crowd relates to. We could tell when a new song had too much bass, the vocals were too high or it was mixed badly. In the same way we could tell which song would become an instant hit." But the way to make money off a record label is by publishing and distributing music. CDs of contemporary hip hop and R&B music, which *HomeBoyz* specialises in, are very slow compared to the River Road market which specialises in audio cassettes.

While gospel singers and artists who sing vernacular can sell albums in the hundreds of thousands, only a few contemporary artists are able to sell 10,000 CDs. Since *HomeBoyz* have opted to specialise in contemporary music, they got stuck in a low-volume market. Currently their focus is recording albums for artists and not owning artists as a record label. Among the artists that they have recorded are Nameless and Jua Kali.

An exception was the signing of the pop group SEMA, a result of Kenya's first-ever reality TV music talent search, the Coca-Cola Pop Stars. *HomeBoyz* were involved in writing the lyrics, recording, production, mastering, CD printing, marketing and distribution. When the group broke up *HomeBoyz* lost a lot of money. They thought that if the group was well packaged, they could command a premium on album sales. This was supposed to be a long term investment but the group didn't last and *HomeBoyz* were left with stacks of SEMA albums in their stores. As Myke explained: "Once you sign on an artiste you invest everything right from where he lives to what he eats, how he looks, how he's seen, in short, you control the image of that artist. After we signed on SEMA we used to pay their salaries and pay for their upkeep, do all the PR work like photo ops and album signings, get for them gigs, organise trips and so on."

Myke believes that the group broke up because they were just too young and could not handle the fame and pressure of being suddenly thrust into the media spotlight. They were complete strangers who were put together and expected to perform without knowing each other's background or whether they had chemistry as a group, a recipe for disaster. "First there were personality issues. Secondly, they could sing but had never struggled to build a career in music, get someone to record their music, or hustled to get gigs. They did not know the value of getting that signing, took a lot for granted, had very high expectations and expected an instant life of luxury. When you're 18 years old and a nobody one day and the next in front of 50,000 people screaming for you, it goes to your head immediately."

If *HomeBoyz* were to sign a group or an artiste again, they would work with existing mature artistes who have struggled and who know what it takes to be an artiste. It is only when they have had this experience that they can appreciate the help given to them.

In August 2008 *HomeBoyz* Entertainment landed its biggest commercial project to date which entailed producing a 52-episode animated series for children in partnership with Tiger Aspect, one of the UK's most successful independent television production houses. The project was commissioned by CBeebies in the UK and Disney's Playhouse channel in the US. The series, called Tinga Tinga Tales, marked the debut of *HomeBoyz* into the global entertainment scene. The project was also groundbreaking for the country as it involved building and equipping the first fully equipped animation studios in Kenya employing local designers, writers, musicians and animators.

Based on African folk stories and illustrating a growing appetite for African animation in the international entertainment scene, Tinga Tinga Tales was designed to entertain children all over the world retelling how their favourite animals came to be – why the lion roars, why the crocodile has a bumpy back, and why the hippo has no hair. These are examples of the themes of the stories in the series.

Recognising that the sound for the show was going to play a vital role, Claudia Lloyd, Tiger Aspect Head of Animation and Children's programming, went looking for appropriate sounds. "Just as with the visual style and the stories, we wanted the sound to come from Africa, but we couldn't find a sound house capable of producing all aspects of animation sound. *HomeBoyz* is a fantastic outfit specialising in live music and radio production and Myke Rabar was very keen to expand their expertise and knowledge," she said in a press statement announcing the project. Says Myke, "They came to Kenya scouting for a studio to handle the project. I think they chose us because we had the space, a musical background and, we were already doing both TV and audio production. Naturally, we were the most strategic partner."

In the subsequent arrangement, Eric Wainaina (a prominent contemporary Kenyan musician) was to produce the music for the soundtrack. Key *HomeBoyz* personnel were trained in the UK and in Kenya prior to commencing the project which took a year to finalise.

In July 2008 *HomeBoyz* also partnered with Warner Bros in the US to produce a video game.

The birth of *HomeBoyz* Radio

After twelve years of hosting shows on other FM stations, Myke actualised the dream of launching a radio station, which he had harboured since 1998 when he came back from the UK. The station, known as *HomeBoyz* Radio, was started in 2008 and became a tool for promoting all the *HomeBoyz* brands. "In its unique form, radio provides the ears and eyes and makes you sell yourselves to the public. I was especially of the view that if people believed we could do so well in radio, then we could sell the academy and other services." For years, only the likes of Patrick Quarcoo, Chris Kirubi and SK Macharia were ever heard launching a radio station. Now came a couple of unknown entities competing with the big boys.

Another factor that motivated Myke to launch a radio station was that when he returned, he found that radio stations in Kenya were not ready for the things he wanted to do like starting a deejay academy. There was considerable delay in rolling it out due to bureaucracy in getting the frequency, a common problem in the country. "We have always wanted to launch a radio and TV unit because we know what we want to achieve, but we could not do it on someone else's terms or turf. Within six months of its launch, *HomeBoyz* Radio became the number one station in the youth segment. This was probably the best moment of my career."

The station's core market is with the 18–25-year olds, urban, middle-class, predominantly male listeners. They have plans to start a second radio station catering for older people aged over thirty. The proposed station's edge would be music of the yesteryears that they have kept from their deejaying days and is never played on other stations, either because they do not have it or presenters are too young to remember good music from the old day. "There is an audience that is not being catered for. I did weddings for people ten years ago and still have those CDs. These people are not listening to us because currently we don't have a product for them."

Organisational and management structure

The *HomeBoyz* Entertainment group has four shareholders – Myke, Alph, John and Rose (Myke's wife). It has 90 employees and is organised into five divisions, namely the DJ Agency, DJ Academy, Radio, TV and the record label. Radio generates the most revenue. SoundTraxx and Events are under the DJ Agency. The three brothers sit in management teams of the group's divisions.

The company was restructured so that Aktivate, which was previously under Events, stood on its own, SoundTraxx was also made independent, and TV now included the audio studios. "The whole idea is to ensure that these divisions were completely separate and independent. With each of the divisions becoming a strong brand on its own, it would grow the business. Previously, the profit centres were all merged which made it difficult for us to see what the best areas were. When each division is separate as a profit-making unit it will be easier to manage and analyse to see the divisions that are our best areas in terms of making money." They are currently hunting for investors to partner with and start a TV station. The three directors-cum-brothers pay themselves modest salaries and no dividends as every spare cent is ploughed back into the business.

A business with such volatility as in the entertainment field requires stringent management of cash flow to ensure there is enough money to keep it running on a day-to-day basis. Rose has been pivotal to the success of the business in this respect. The decision that she joins the business happened almost by accident. She was an auditor working for PricewaterhouseCoopers (PwC) and one day while on leave in 2005 she decided to help out in the office. She realised they were struggling with one main problem – cash flow. "The company was making money and they were able to invoice, but they were not very efficient when it came to collecting such that a lot of cash was held up by debtors," says Rose.

Streamlining expenditure was another problem. "This business is cash intensive with a lot of money being spent on a daily basis by casuals in the field. Myke was very busy on the technical side and would sometimes just sign vouchers without scrutinising each expense to verify that it was in fact necessary," she says. As a result, despite the business making money, expenses were too high. In other words, the business was draining cash which was affecting their ability to reinvest profits.

When Rose interrogated the accountant, he became edgy. Eventually, he left without giving any notice and she had no choice but to step in and take control of the company's finances. The first thing she did was to cut the lead time in collecting payments owed to them and getting clients to stick to the agreed credit period of 30–45 days. "As I needed to build rapport with clients, I called them up and introduced myself telling them that I was the one now doing the accounts. I just kept reminding them to pay their outstanding amounts and agreed on a payment schedule with those who had problems paying. Once clients were up to date it was a matter of staying on top of what we had invoiced and ensuring we stuck to the credit terms," she says.

This arrangement worked really well. Although Rose started out by volunteering her services, the company started paying her a salary after a few months. Surprisingly, she had studied for a BSc degree in horticulture at

Egerton University, the same course that John Rabar was to do later. Nothing in her early years suggested that she would end up in the accounting profession. "When I was just about to finish my degree course, the big accounting firms came recruiting and I did the aptitude test. I had no accounting background and I had to do Certified Public Accountant (CPA) courses from scratch while working. With the subsequent examinations, I found it really hard. I worked as an auditor with PwC for nine years before ending up at *HomeBoyz*. With hindsight, it was as if I was being directed into accounting because I would need to use these skills to help my husband," Rose reminisces. "My experience at PwC helped a lot at *HomeBoyz*, in the grand scheme of things perhaps this was meant to be."

In addition to using her skills to make a direct contribution to her family's business, Rose was also happy to work in an environment where she could dictate her working hours which gave her more time with her family especially her daughters Tracie and Hawi. At the time of writing this book, she was still nursing Hawi who was six months old. Rose often left the office by 3.00 pm, something she would not have been able to do in her previous job.

For Myke, having his wife in the business was a relief as he could now concentrate on the other aspects of the business without worrying about the finances. The fact that he finds himself working and living together with his spouse does not pose any difficulties. As he put it: "One of our biggest strengths as *HomeBoyz* has been to have on board people who have the interests of the business as their main priority all the time. I know Rose will take care of the finances so I don't have to worry about missing shillings or cents which affects a lot of businesses. When we're in the office we stick to business. If anything, working together has probably made our relationship stronger because given the type of work I do, frequent travel and the hours I put into it, if she didn't understand what I did she probably would not cope. By being in the business she fully understands, which has helped to manage the relationship at home."

Myke is in the field most of the time and this gives Rose a free hand to run the office without too much interference. Moreover, he knows that she does a good job. Whenever there is a disagreement, which is rare, it has to do with spending money to reinvest in the business. Rose is an accountant, very conservative, and usually wants to play it safe while Myke is a risk-taker always wanting to spend more and expand the business in a different direction. In such instances, the couple usually strikes a deal to invest in phases rather than all at once. This is a win-win for both of them because Myke knows he will get the money he needs to invest and Rose can manage their cash flow to avoid a negative impact on the business.

Rose says that Myke is a hands-on person in the business, and is understanding and supportive of his employees. He makes time for everybody, which creates problems because he has so many meetings on some days that it prevents him from getting his own work done. In such instances, he is forced to work late to catch up. He is also very forward looking and everything he is doing today stems from ideas he has had for years. "We moved house recently and I was going through old documents from 10 years ago. I came across brochures with the logo for the radio station which he created and the experiential company *HomeBoyz* Aktivate which does roadshows. When I look back, I remember that he used to talk about all these things while in campus and when he was in the UK. He has a grand plan which he's actualising step-by-step; it's always been a question of timing and getting things like financing in place. Even now he's always thinking about new ideas," she says.

When it comes to John and Alph, they play more or less the same roles in the business that each played in 1998 when Myke came back from the UK. John is in charge of radio, Alph is in charge of the studios (which involve production of radio commercials and the animation project) while Myke handles long term strategy and marketing. He looks for new opportunities and partnerships to grow the business. "John is the creative; Alph is the doer. If you want anything sorted out Alph would be the person to do it. While John and I are the creative ones, Rose and Alph are the ones good at executing or seeing that the ideas come to life," says Myke. John concurs: "I particularly get excited when it comes to formulating concepts, proposals and ideas. Once we have landed the job I will tend to get bored with the finer details like getting a licence for an event and so on."

Many entrepreneurs find it difficult to work with relatives especially after suffering unpleasant experiences. With cases of such experiences, some have even sworn never to assign relatives any positions in their businesses. Maintaining discipline is a challenge in an environment where it is hard to fire a relative who proves to be incompetent or a slacker. However, the *HomeBoyz* have managed to stay focused and build a thriving business. "Although we have disagreements, we respect each other's point of view in the manner in which we were brought up. At the end of the day I respect Myke, Rose and Alph because they are all older than me. In addition, we have created an environment where everyone gets to have their say and it works," says John.

Business challenges

Over the years, the *HomeBoyz* business has faced a number of challenges. One of these challenges has been competition. Previously, they used to be a household name in weddings. In addition to cheaper deejays, the craze for African music that is performed live by groups like Kayamba Africa has affected their market. Kayamba Africa used to partner with *HomeBoyz* to do wedding gigs where Kayamba would hire equipment from *HomeBoyz* and the latter would provide the deejays for the evening party. Later, Kayamba bought their own equipment and started their own deejay outfit called Kayamba Deejays, which allowed them to offer clients an all-inclusive package. "We found it difficult to compete with something like that. The whole business of live performance was obviously more attractive than a deejay at a reception."

For them, like any other business faced with increased competition, the challenge is to keep reinventing itself in order to stay relevant in the market. "We were using younger persons to provide the element of freshness, using computers to deejay, and video mixing using screens so that people can see what you are doing. This becomes a different experience for the consumer."

Another key challenge, especially which most entrepreneurs face, has to do with staff. There is frequent poaching of radio presenters in the industry and Myke knows he cannot compete with such stations as Capital FM, Kiss 100 or Easy FM in terms of salaries. It has reached the point where some radio presenters command higher salaries than many CEOs of medium-sized companies (earning over KSh 700,000 per month). In the event that being passionate about the station is not enough to keep presenters from leaving, *HomeBoyz* Radio has structured the station around the music. "People listen to us because of the music and not the personalities."

Getting the right people to manage the business the way an entrepreneur wants is one of the biggest challenges. And so is being able to pay for such talent. Of the *HomeBoyz*, Myke observed: "Convincing qualified personnel to come and work for us is a challenge because the perception of the entertainment sector is that it's very informal. Even your own bank doubts you and they can see the millions in your account. For us the challenge has been to project the image of a serious company which is now happening because of the kind of alliances we've formed."

Financing has also been a major challenge. The only financing that *HomeBoyz* got from banks was KSh 2.5 million to buy two generators. "Despite applying for loans several times to purchase equipment, we have not been successful because banks do not take our business seriously. They consider entertainment as a hobby and not a business. If we had procured bank financing, perhaps we would have been bigger. The Boxx could still be running, Radio would have come earlier, and the TV station would have been set up."

Another financial challenge in the entertainment industry is that it is risky, which makes it difficult to plan for revenues. Things change overnight for good or for bad leading to sudden windfalls or terrible losses. With regard to a windfall, says Myke: "Someone with a Hollywood budget could walk in and say they want to produce a film for six months for which they would hire our studios." An example of a windfall was Tusker Project Fame where *HomeBoyz* managed all the parties for the project including the eviction parties for 10 weeks. They also did a lot of work for the mobile phone companies such as roadshows when Celtel rebranded to Zain. However, events are generally difficult to plan around as they get cancelled often. The only divisions with predictable revenues are the DJ Academy where they have a regular intake of 32 students for an eight-week course and advertising revenues for radio because most advertisers buy space in blocks for six months.

Working together as a couple could have been less of a challenge to Myke, but how to avoid discussing office matters at home is a bigger one. Usually, the earliest time Myke comes home is 8.00 pm and he focuses all his attention on the children. After they have gone to sleep, he starts discussing business; he is very passionate about the business. If it were not for Rose, they would never switch off and spend some quality time together in the evenings. "Sometimes I have to make a deliberate effort and stop discussion of work otherwise we would discuss work for 24 hours. That is the kind of a person Myke is," says Rose.

Another significant challenge is the constantly changing technology. "The entertainment industry is the kind that is technologically dependent. You have to keep investing in new things to stay on top of the game. Partnership with people like Tiger Aspect was very helpful to our business. They chose the company because it had the right equipment such that they did not have to bring in a lot more."

The future of the *HomeBoyz* business

With all the other areas that *HomeBoyz* has diversified into, Myke has no time to deejay as he is busy with the financial, strategic and administrative aspects of their growing entertainment business. Considering that playing music was his life for years, this may have taken away a piece of him though he believes he is still a techie: "I totally miss it but someone has to run the business. Just like with any business you have to go through the processes and eventually I'll be able to employ people who can do this and go back to playing music. I love recording and mixing live bands and I'm still very hands-on in terms of handling the technical aspects of big shows like the Akon one we did in Tanzania. [44] This involves set-up, wiring the studios, recording, mixing, enhancing the quality of the sound and pictures, and picking the right hardware and software."

Myke's vision is to sell a stake in the business to a strategic investor and make the company public. He already had offers from people who wanted to buy

---

[44] Akon is a hip hop musician from USA. He disappointed his Kenyan fans in 2008 when he cancelled shows in the country three times and eventually performed in Tanzania.

into the business. As he put it: "The whole essence of business is to grow and make it attractive to investors as long as you don't lose control over it. With an injection of capital I can get the TV station up and running, have more radio stations, build more studios, and create an equivalent of MIT (Massachusetts Institute of Technology) in Africa."

Myke's dream is to leave the day-to-day running of the business to professionals and focus on strategic expansion of the business as a director. He aspires to get into media in a big way – print (magazines and online content), radio and television. "I want to have the capacity to positively influence lives through entertainment. I should be able to take two weeks away for a strategy meeting which I can't do right now. I want to be able to just sit down and plan where to take the company, like opening a branch in Uganda, Tanzania, UK, US, plan how to take programming from Kenya to those markets and how to get strategic alliances to help me achieve all this. I want to steer the vision of the company and let other people run it."

The brothers say that *HomeBoyz*'s legacy is to show people that they can build a future in any sector no matter how informal, as long as they take it seriously. "When we were getting into the industry, the DJ role models were reputed to live flashy lifestyles. We changed all this and showed people that deejaying was a serious business. Our parents were not enthusiastic and would often wonder why we did not get into more serious careers. However, they later changed to be our biggest supporters," says Alph. Their mother watches every episode of H_2O and listens to John's radio shows every day.

Many deejays do deejaying not as a career but for fame. "But for us, this is something we love to do. I'm not interested to be in the spotlight, I prefer staying in the background. My satisfaction comes from knowing I have done an event that was successful," says Alph. He says that the change in perception of deejaying as a career is visible in their DJ Academy. "Because we've shown that deejaying is a serious career and you can make money in it, 70 percent of our students are actually brought here by their parents, showing that they support their children's choice of career."

HomeBoyz are also trendsetters in the industry. "We were the first people to offer more than one service (deejaying) when it came to music. We provided a template that came to be copied by a lot of other entertainment companies in the country," says John. Now that they made it to the top, staying on top is another challenge. "While it is hard to get to the top, staying there is the hardest bit because there will always be other people wanting to copy what you are doing. The challenge is to keep coming up with new ideas and to be innovative all the time. The support that we give each other as directors and the bond that we have as brothers really helps us to overcome setbacks," he adds.

Tips for aspiring entrepreneurs

With his years of experience in business, Myke has a number of tips for upcoming and aspiring entrepreneurs: "It's always good to live your dream but there are some things the Kenyan market is not ready for and instead of pounding your head against the wall, look for something else to do and when the time is right go back to your idea. In my case I knew deejaying would not pay the bills and if I stayed as a deejay the rest of my life I would not get to do the things I wanted. But if I could use deejaying to do other things like road-shows I could get there. People thought I was mad to start doing roadshows but this is what the industry understands and I was using my equipment and deejay skills in the process."

Myke also advises that it is good to know when to change something that's not working and do it differently. "Something may not be working because it's in the wrong location or the product is not suited to the market; find out what's preventing it from not working and fine tune it."

An example was when they set up The Boxx to sell music. Myke observed that the future of selling music lies on the Internet. Selling from a physical location was slowly dying off. However, the problem in Kenya was how to get people to pay for the music sold through the Internet because most people do not have credit cards. Whereas low Internet usage was a hindrance, once the challenge is overcome, the business would be profitable.

Myke also advises against having a rigid business plan. An entrepreneur should always be open to new ideas. "I've tried many things; some have worked and some are still under way. A business plan should only give you a direction but you don't have to live by it. Have an open approach to business and take calculated risks. Take the Tiger Aspect project; we poured so much money into the pilot but I knew that if it didn't kick off I would put the equipment back into the studios for the other stuff we were doing."

Myke believes if you have a gift, use it and you will be rewarded. His whole life has revolved around music. In an interview with the now defunct *Adams* magazine he said: "I have been lucky that through music, I have rubbed shoulders with people I never dreamt I would be able to meet. I have toured the whole world with my turntables. Recently, Richard Branson had a party here and I spent an evening with a man who has made history. So I feel humbled to have this gift."

Equally, he advises people to pursue their aspirations out of passion. When they decided to dwell on the high-end contemporary other than the popular gospel music, it was passion that was the driving force. If Myke is not passionate about something, he doesn't do it no matter how much money there is. As he reflected: "I know if I went to River Road I'd make a lot of money but my heart is not in it. I always do things first and foremost because I'm passionate about them and I'm driven by the music, not the money."

Even if something fails the first time, Myke believes he can do it in the future just differently. Giving up and saying something cannot be done is not in his vocabulary. Things fail because the market is not ready or the person doing it didn't understand the market, which does not mean that an idea is not viable in the future.

Another important aspect of business is building confidence, even with forward planning, such that others can join in taking a risk, as happened with the Tinga Tinga project. "For Tiger Aspect, deciding to come to Africa to produce this series was already a big risk and the post-election violence had resulted in cancellation of the entire project. It took a lot of wooing including doing all sorts of risk assessment before they came on board again because these companies plan five years in advance. When you work with them you realise what planning is all about. They know in 2020 which production they'll be doing and who they'll be working with. They've got a very systematic way of doing things."

Another important tip is to focus on one's strengths rather than weaknesses. As John, Myke's brother, observed: "For a company to succeed you have to understand the strengths and weaknesses of the people you work with and exploit the strengths and don't focus on the weaknesses. For instance, my strength is not in animation or video production, that's Alph's thing. And we let him fly with that and give him the tools to enable him to flourish and expand it. I'm in charge of radio and do 15-hour shifts every day of the week but I don't even notice because that's my thing and I'm passionate about it."

Delegating is also important both on a managerial and departmental level. "You would break your back trying to do everything. Therefore, it is important to build a good team and make sure everyone understands their job description," he adds.

Last but not least there is cash flow, a fundamental part of a business, and a financial challenge to an entrepreneur. According to Myke, business owners should live within their means and should not overstretch themselves. "Risks are important but calculate them. You can't be too careful."

Likes and dislikes

Myke has a collection of over 2,000 CDs, all of them original. He would never buy a pirated copy because he takes pride in having original CDs in his collection. While in the UK, he observed that people took pride in their music collections and would show them off to friends unlike in Kenya where most people have no problem buying pirated music, putting a cheap price above all else. "And this extends to all manner of things including movies, clothes and accessories. You find people proudly showing off their fake Gucci shoes." He believes this trait is what differentiates Kenyans from their neighbours in Uganda and Tanzania to the detriment of the music market. Myke explains thus: "Ugandans will proudly buy an original Chameleon CD because they believe in supporting him. They also have pride. A guy would rather spend KSh 5,000 buying an original watch than spend KSh 200 buying a fake one. But Kenyans don't care. And yet they are generally richer than their neighbours. The people there are conscious about quality and value and they are willing to pay for it. Here, people buy a movie from the street which has bad sound and you can barely see the picture. Because it costs KSh 50 they are happy to take it. We accept very low standards."

Their flagship deejaying business has faced similar challenges where consumers care more about the price than getting a good-quality deejay. "Corporate clients care and are willing to pay for quality but they only form 20 percent of our market. We also lack an entertainment culture in this country. When people go to a bar the first question they ask is how much is the beer, not who is playing, so the clubs don't think the deejay is important. To the club owners' music is music; it can come off a computer. They say that hiring a professional deejay eats into their profits. Consumers in countries like the UK are very different and go to clubs because of who is playing, leading to competition amongst clubs to hire these deejays. You'll find a deejay who does two hours in one club then moves to another and he moves with 500 people. It's not just deejays but even people like chefs. Some chefs are held in such high standing that they can change the status of a business overnight just by being hired. So people there appreciate such skills but here it's always about who is the cheapest. Consumers are driven by price."

Social activities

Music has kept Myke grounded to an extent that it drives everything he does. However, he travels a lot, at least once a month. Before getting their second baby, Rose and Tracie would accompany him sometimes and they would combine work with a holiday. His definition of a holiday is anywhere with lots of sun and a swimming pool where he can relax.

Role models

One of Myke's role models is Richard Branson because he went on a non-traditional tangent with his magazine and music distribution business. He also admires Sean 'Puffy' Combs because he has taken something intangible, created a strong brand around it and built an empire. According to his observation: "Other artistes make money from endorsements but they are using their profiles, not their brains, and once they stop being hot the endorsements dry up. He's gone beyond that and has his own clothing line, has created his own TV shows; he's all over the place."

Locally, Myke admires Patrick Quarcoo for his open approach to business. He believes that entrepreneurs can learn a lot from him. "He's got the balls to try things that no one else attempts."

Chapter 13

Jonathan Somen

The day 4 June 2007 was special for two brothers, David and Jonathan Somen. Picture this: The bell goes and the brothers pop champagne to usher in a new dawn in the Kenyan stock market and to start a new chapter at the Nairobi Securities Exchange (NSE). The mood at the bourse is electric, although the anxiety amongst the majority traditional investors is discernible. Enter the technology kid into a rather conservative market of predominantly 'brick and mortar' companies. A new company in Information and Communication Technology (ICT) and computers was joining the club.

During this occasion, the air was clouded with a mix of apprehension and excitement reminiscent of an intimate family affair. David and Jonathan's baby – AccessKenya – was taking a giant step into adulthood and the 'loving parents' could not help but look back with appreciation at the pains and joys of nurturing it. From a family outfit that started in a single room in 1994, it was now a corporate entity that was taking the bold step of being listed at the NSE. And given the stringent requirements before a company is listed (key among them profitability, specific performance benchmarks and a satisfactory due diligence), this was indeed a seal of approval for the young entrepreneurs. What began as an idea between two brothers metamorphosed into a communication company, an Internet Service Provider (ISP) in 2001 and finally into a fully integrated ICT company with a public stature in 2006.

In a way, AccessKenya Group, the brainchild of the Somen brothers, is a first on many fronts. While most Kenyan enterprises fizzle out in the first five years, AccessKenya not only grew but also leapt from a family outfit into a public company within six years. Its listing at the NSE through an IPO generated a remarkable response from the public as evidenced by an oversubscription of shares (363 percent). This was a great success.

After this, it acquired Open View Business Systems to complete the technology service chain from Internet connectivity and networking to provision/maintenance of software and hardware. The Group continues to grow steadily both on the ground and at the securities market where it debuted at KSh 10 per share and by 2008 it was trading at an average of KSh 28 per share, a confirmation of the confidence that the public has in the visionary brothers. Jonathan, the younger Somen, doubles as co-founder and as the Managing Director of the Group.

Early childhood and education

Jonathan Somen is an alumnus of the prestigious high-cost Banda School in Nairobi. Born in Kenya on 27 June 1969 to Michael and Vera Somen, he is a second-generation Kenyan by birth whose great-grandparents settled in Kenya in 1925. Michael Somen is a lawyer of repute who rose through the ranks at the prominent law firm of Hamilton Harrison and Mathews to retire as a senior partner. Dr Vera Somen is a medical doctor.

The Somen brothers were lucky to have a father who gave them the best education money could buy. After their primary education, both David and Jonathan went to Europe for their college education. While Banda School was great and had a fantastic learning environment, schools and colleges abroad provided even better learning. In the United Kingdom (UK), Jonathan enrolled at Epsom College where he spent five years under the British system of education, arguably one of the best in the world.

While studying in the UK, Jonathan never missed an opportunity to return to Kenya during his school holidays; he would travel back home all his holidays and over time came to believe that there was no better place to spend a holiday or to live than in Kenya. Unlike the ordinary schoolboys who while their holidays away, the restless Jonathan sought ways to engage himself in constructive activities and earn some money too. Often he would find an occupation in the hospitality industry or embark on marketing his motherland as a tourist hot spot. As someone who enjoys travelling and working with people, tourism fitted his bill naturally. He also took flying lessons during the holidays and ended up satisfying his quest to soar in the sky.

As the country of his childhood, Jonathan appreciates the beauty of Kenya and has expressed no regrets in having the country as his place of growing up. As he has observed: "I had a wonderful childhood. Unlike the developed countries where space and freedom to play for children is limited, Kenya affords maximum opportunity for the young to play and just be kids. Children learn so much by playing. As a matter of fact, this is where our journey of self discovery begins. Added to this is the friendly tropical weather with abundant sunshine that makes living and working in Kenya an endless pleasure."

Jonathan would take one year off from college in 1990 to work full-time as a tour guide before returning to Bristol University (in the UK) in 1991 to pursue a degree course in economics and accounting. Three years later, he graduated and returned to Kenya where he officially took his first job in tourism, the same industry he had worked in during his summer holidays. This time he would work as a safari guide for Rhino Safaris, KLR (a tour company in the US) and finally Abercrombie & Kent.

Although working in the tourism industry is associated with adventure, the eager Jonathan found it less stimulating as time went by. It soon degenerated into a routine for him. His search for greater challenges would be rewarded when he got a new job at Kilimanjaro Water Company Limited where he joined as the Chief Operations Officer, effectively becoming the number two in the organisation. At the time, the company was the leading mineral water company in Kenya.

Going into business

The seemingly plum appointment at Kilimanjaro Water Company Limited would do little to appease the raving desire of the enterprising youth. Jonathan would confound friends and foes when he jumped ship to start a business with his elder brother, David Somen. Together, they founded Communication Solutions Limited (Commsol) in his apartment in Nairobi's Westlands. That was in 1994 and Jonathan was only 25 years old.

By starting the company, Jonathan wanted to be his own boss. As a teenager, he always insisted on being the one to drive the car. In all, one can say he always wanted to be the Chief rather than the Indian. Jonathan is fiercely competitive in his pursuits and hates losing, though he tries not to show it. This spirit is equally evident in sports. He is an accomplished squash player having played for the Kenya junior squash team at one time and ranking the 15th best player in the country.

Apparently the entrepreneurship bug bit the family a long time ago. The trailblazer was Jonathan's great-uncle, who was also the mayor of Nairobi in the 1950s. He started what came to be the beacon of modern classic furniture, the prestigious Hutchings Biemer (the business was partly named after his wife Sophie Biemer). He also served on numerous boards of both local and multinational companies. Jonathan's mother, Vera, who is a trained doctor, joined her father at his private clinic in Nairobi where she retired in 2004. Her father was called Dr Alexander Gellert. In a way, therefore, Jonathan's parents were also entrepreneurs. As Jonathan says, "The thirst for success runs through our family. I can assure you, our parents didn't push us to succeed either in school or in our careers. In school, for instance, it was my brother David who set the pace for me. He did very well, a standard I always tried to match. Other than giving us a great education, my father has been content to let us pursue our dreams. For instance, we had to dig into our own savings to start this company instead of running to him for handouts," says Jonathan.

David and Jonathan Somen were armed only with a fax machine and a telephone when they started Commsol. The company was offering callback, email and IT consultancy services. Through brainstorming, they worked on the product and when they felt that it was ready, they launched it into the market. Jonathan quips, "For every business, the defining moment comes when you hit the tarmac and meet your potential customers. This is something I do insist on even for my staff. All the planning in your office will take you nowhere if you do not get out and test the product in the market."

They started out by gradually building on the services that they were offering (emailing and consultancy) before consolidating to start what is now known as AccessKenya, a Corporate Internet Services Provider (CISP) in 2001. Internet service is a communication hub aptly named the information superhighway. At the top is the World Wide Web (www) which is the international pool of information. All other users are connected to this pool through satellite. The licensed Internet service providers (ISPs) tap into the Internet connectivity by buying bandwidth from authorised distributors before distributing it to their subscribers. The quality of Internet connectivity (mainly speeds and capacity of data transmission) is largely determined by the bandwidth, the connecting infrastructure, and the satellite capacity.

At the time, Telkom Kenya had the monopoly of providing both the backbone and the internal distribution infrastructure through Jambonet and Kenstream respectively. Following the liberalisation of the service by the Communications Commission of Kenya (CCK), individual companies could now lay their own infrastructure for Internet, data and voice connectivity. AccessKenya Group took advantage of this opening to commission a new infrastructure company, Broadband Access Limited, also known as Blue, to lay a fibre optic network that was to link its clients, an extension to its existing wireless network infrastructure that was originally launched in 2003. This would give them more control over the quality of their connectivity and service to clients. In other words, they saw this as an opportunity to control the quality of their network.

The two brothers' experience while offering email and callback services had pointed them to a gap in Internet services. There was the gaping void involving the CISPs whereby the existing players were not addressing the specific needs of corporate clients, and which they decided to fill. Thus, they recognised and took up the opportunity. Theirs was the typical 'fly by the seat of your pants' growth; one day it was a concept, within months it had grown to become a full-fledged business.

After listing on the securities market, AccessKenya Group's performance did not disappoint. It continued to grow steadily both on the ground and at the stock; whereas it debuted at KSh 10 per share, by 2008 it was trading at an average of KSh 28 per unit, a confirmation as to the confidence the public has in the visionary brothers. At the beginning, investors were justifiably apprehensive as AccessKenya had come hot on the heels after the unceremonious exit of African Lakes Technologies (ALTECH) from the securities market, coupled with the much-hyped Internet bubble in the United States. In addition, African Online, the pioneer Internet service provider with an imposing public presence, had somehow lost its market aggression slowly receding to the background. It was against this uncertainty that AccessKenya entered the Internet fray.

Since the floating of AccessKenya Group's shares on the NSE in 2007, within one year the company was worth over KSh 6 billion, with the Somens controlling 33.7 percent of the shareholding. Jonathan, the Managing Director, was barely 40 years old at the time. The company he had co-founded a short while earlier had not only crossed the divide from a family business to a public company, but it had also been firmly placed on the driving seat of technological innovation in Kenya and beyond.

Management style and growth strategy

That AccessKenya is the corporate communication hub is evident at their Museum Hill offices, which also serve as the headquarters. A bevy of technosavvy youth, their tables dotted with the latest gadgets in communication, skilfully glide through the office at a frenetic pace. Their dressing too reflects the changing times. One would be forgiven for mistaking the office for a catwalk parade. Situated strategically at the far end is Jonathan's office. Unlike the no go zone traditional manager's office, the staff often pop into his office to casually discuss delicate issues while standing. Speed and innovation is the password here and that could as well be their distinctive advantage.

At the time of listing, AccessKenya Group's Board of Directors comprised people who were highly competent and were leading professionals in their various fields. They were led by Michael Somen. Others in the Board were Mungai Ngaruiya, Ngugi Kiuna, Eddy Njoroge (Managing Director of KenGen) and Michael Turner. Both David and Jonathan were executive directors with Jonathan being in charge of local operations while David was the director specifically in charge of Mergers and Acquisitions, Investor Relations as well as being the primary driver for many strategic initiatives. David also ran their UK business, a managed IT services company.

In 2010, there were some changes among the members of the Board, which saw the replacement of Michael Somen as Chairman by Daniel Ndonye, a widely experienced person in corporate affairs who had held a number of senior positions in financial institutions inside and outside Kenya. The replacement of Michael came after the company adopted a Charter that covers all governance matters, roles and responsibilities, as well as definitions and qualifications related to the running of the Board; the Charter disqualified Michael from holding the chairman's seat. At the time he stepped down, Michael had been at the helm for over 10 years. He remained as a director in the company. Other board members were: Jonathan Somen (Managing Director), Titus Naikuni (Kenya Airways Chief Executive), Paras Shah, David Somen and Michael Turner. This board was reconstituted at the right time when the Group was continuing with rapid expansion. According to Jonathan, the board added diversity and leadership insight into the organisation.

AccessKenya has a system in place that is responsive to the needs of its customers. They listen carefully to their clients and design products that meet their needs. Listening and responding to customer needs constitutes their strengths in the market. They also make sure that the speed of response to customer complaints is systematic and fast. That is why they created distinctive departments to cater for specific demands. The company is an organised system grouped into departments, which include the following: Finance, Administration, Corporate Sales, Residential Sales, Marketing, Network Operations, Engineering, Help Desk, Field Services, Corporate Communications, Installations, Telemarketing and Yello (the company's voice service).

With headquarters in Nairobi, AccessKenya has established offices in Mombasa and representatives in Nakuru, Kisumu and Eldoret to effectively service upcountry clients. According to Jonathan, it is more effective to organise a team into groups with specific leaders to optimise on resources and improve task-specific focus.

From inception, the company has stayed on the cutting edge of technology. As Jonathan says, "We vowed from the onset to invest in the best equipment that can give unmatched quality of service to our clients. We also do not spare investment on bandwidth. We buy what can service our customers without compromising quality. In 2003 we started Blue to provide infrastructure for the local loop or last mile to the client. This has taken us a step further in controlling the quality of our local connectivity and ultimately more of the end-to-end solution for clients. This allows us to respond appropriately and quickly to client needs without having to rely on third parties."

Service quality is enhanced by the calibre of staff that the company hires. It gets the best in the market and tries as much as possible to give them an environment and tools that can make them deliver the best quality of service. The company has also invested heavily in training to ensure that not only does the team get a good working environment with good packages, but also it is updated with skills.

As part of their strategy, AccessKenya is open to outsourcing and acquisitions, what Jonathan calls lateral growth. According to him, while every organisation needs organic growth since it's the natural way to grow, time may not be limited with regard to the technology business, hence the necessity to consider the adoption or acquisition of established companies offering related services as part of the growth strategy. In effect, the company continually evaluates the needs of its clients and looks at competitors or industry peers offering similar products. Those that they can grow in-house they do, but others they outsource or acquire. As Jonathan explains: "For example, we felt that some of our clients did not have up-to-date machines that could afford them maximum Internet benefit in their premises. This limitation was compromising on our quality as well as a business opportunity. To meet this need, we acquired Open View Business Systems of Henry and Lucy Njoroge. This single acquisition enabled us to offer Internet network solutions for clients on their Local Area Network which was an excellent value addition over and above our traditional business of Internet connectivity."

Open View Business Systems would become a subsidiary of the Access Group with its own structure and an independent Managing Director, a sales team and technical staff. The Managing Director was the previous proprietor, Henry Njoroge. He would now report to Jonathan, the Group Managing Director.

Another strategy that AccessKenya adopted is niche marketing with corporate focus; that is, its ISP product is focused on corporate clientele. This is where the company works with corporate organisations to understand their needs and design their products to meet that need. For example, organisations want high speeds, quick response to problems, reliability and consistency. They also want assurance that the service provider will be there to address their need any time it arises. They don't want to be kept waiting and want to keep pace with the technological developments and its compatibility with their systems. Consequently, the company positioned itself in such a way that it could address these needs adequately.

It was while dealing with corporate clients that the company identified the need to serve individual customers. Through research, they realised that more and more people were either working from home or wanted to work from home. That is how they came up with the home product into which they diversified.

This area involving home products has registered tremendous growth, having achieved over 4,500 residential customers by the end of 2010.

Business challenges

AccessKenya Group's biggest headache has been managing growth. As Jonathan observed in 2008, "We have been growing by over 75 percent every year for the past five years. With such a growth rate, your resources, both human and financial, are strained. You need to upgrade your human resources, buy more bandwidth and basically review and upgrade your systems and equipment to keep up with the growth otherwise you will disappoint your customers."

Like all organisations, AccessKenya has not been spared the challenge of managing cash flow, the bane of most start-ups. The management realised early enough that they needed robust accounting software that would give them an accurate and up-to-date performance of their debt portfolio. They knew that cash flow problem is the Achilles heel of young organisations and decided to tighten their credit control. Their core services were prepaid, which helped them with their credit focus. Nevertheless, at times they had to be sensitive to the needs of their clients and extended credit.

According to Jonathan, running a family business with his elder brother was not a challenge, even during the formative stages. As he says, "We have been fortunate that the family members involved in the business are professionals who not only merit their positions but also deliver value to the shareholders. I have a great professional relationship with my brother David. We grew up together and understand each other well. My wife, who is also the marketing manager, is a professional who understands that I'm the boss around here but she is definitely the boss at home."

When AccessKenya ceased to be a family business, they expanded their board and brought in competent members to professionalise its running. Prior to going public, they had appointed additional board members who represented the group of investors who not only injected capital into the business but also brought in invaluable managerial experience. Later, they brought in a non-family member as the Managing Director of the Internet business who also deputised Jonathan whenever he was away.

At the initial stages, the enterprising brothers faced the daunting task of raising the licence fee of KSh 1.2 million, which was a lot of money back then. As they believed strongly in the future of the business, they sacrificed and raised it through their savings. This amount was lowered in subsequent years, something that would encourage more investors into the ICT sector.

Another hiccup that AccessKenya experienced was at Telkom Kenya, the bureaucratic monopoly with the exclusive rights of selling the bandwidth. According to Jonathan, their service was very poor. The attitude of the staff was so negative that they thought they were doing their customer a favour and their response to complaints was painfully sluggish. To beat the red tape, Jonathan and David organised a number of *nyama choma* get-together parties with the staff at Telkom. Through these, they built a rapport with them, dramatically improving the kind of service that they got from the organisation. From this experience, Jonathan observed: "It is important to know and personally understand 'who is who' in an organisation whose services are critical to your success. At least, you get to direct your problems to the right people rather than to the whole impervious organisation."

Staffing also posed a challenge. With the increase in the number of mobile telephone companies and ISPs, there was an impact on the availability of qualified personnel in the ICT sector. The new players that were coming into the market preferred to poach staff from the competition rather than training their own. AccessKenya managed to maintain their good staff through competitive remuneration and an attractive working environment.

Certainly, going public had its challenges. The red tape, the paperwork and the demands on time were overwhelming. The brothers agreed that David would follow up the process of taking the company through the IPO while Jonathan concentrated on running the company. This worked very well for them and ensured that they did not allow services to suffer while they were undergoing the process.

Like other nascent businesses, financing posed a major challenge. When they were starting the first company, Jonathan had moved out of the family house and was staying in a rented apartment such that he had to balance resources for his upkeep and for business. David was a management consultant at McKinsey and Company in the UK and Jonathan had just left employment. At the beginning, the business was financed by the savings from both brothers and angel funds from a relative. Therefore, they had savings to start them off. However, when growth demands outstripped their capital, they went to the securities market.

Jonathan considers that they were lucky to have worked and saved for their business venture aware that there are many potential entrepreneurs who face the challenge of start-up capital. Nevertheless, he believes that there are organisations in Kenya that are ready to support start-ups. If one believed in their idea and was armed with a good business plan, they could raise funds from local financial institutions. Entrepreneurs can also explore options of selling shareholding in the start-ups to raise funds and opting for the securities market.

But turning to the stock market is not that simple. Getting listed on the securities market requires a proven track record. In developed economies, there are securities markets for new companies and venture capitalists that support start-ups. Kenya could be headed in that direction. Before getting there, however, entrepreneurs have to do with what is available; hence, the banks should be more responsive to the needs of entrepreneurs with business plans and collateral.

Pillars of success

AccessKenya's rapid growth and success may have caused consternation among the competition. Jonathan attributes this success to their open-view approach; that is, having their ear on the customer. "We listen to the market, know what the market wants and then design products that meet the particular needs of the market. We also ask our staff what they think we are not doing right and what we can improve on. Through regular meetings that I or my assistant attends, the staff have a chance to voice their complaints as well as those from their clients."

AccessKenya also operates a consultative culture. There is a company improvement programme where the management consults the staff on how they can deliver more value to the customers as well as improve the working environment. These forums also allow the staff to air their feelings about the organisation. The resolutions from the meetings are taken up by the management for implementation.

Another pillar of success was their timing. AccessKenya's foray into the ISP industry was well timed. The market was ready for the product and as already mentioned, the biggest challenge was managing growth. According to Jonathan, "We were at the right place at the right time. We therefore had to maximise on the opportunity. That's why we decided to raise more funds to meet our growth needs, expanding our infrastructure and developing our human resource. After evaluation, we opted for the securities market as we felt that it was the best way to raise funds. Other than raising the funds, it was also a way of sharing out the success of the company with our clients as well as other Kenyans. Through the IPO, we now have over 30,000 shareholders, some of whom are our best clients. This has in a way improved their loyalty to the organisations. Also, the aggressive marketing glitz that preceded the listing propelled the company into the public rostrum, making the yellow and blue colours that characterise our company a household feature. In a way, the onus of running a public company has made us more transparent and diligent in our operations."

Vision and future of AccessKenya

Unlike most entrepreneurs, Jonathan does not remember anything specific that drove him into starting a business. He just wanted to be his own boss. However, he credits his parents and elder brothers, David and Mark, for moulding him to be responsible and take on challenges. "Even while we were working, we found time to share business ideas with David. We would draw different business scenarios and try to find out which one would fit with our long term strategy. This scenario casting is how we settled for IT as the industry to be in. From our evaluation, we noticed that IT was going to be the next growth front, both locally and internationally. Although we had no formal IT training, we hired the best people and learnt on the job."

Their vision at AccessKenya Group is to be the undisputed data leader in Kenya and integrate into a full ICT company providing data, voice, TV and related services.

Marriage and family

Jonathan met his wife, Petra, who is also the Marketing Manager at AccessKenya Group, sometime in 1986, during one of his breaks from college. Petra, a German, was born in Nigeria where her parents worked before they relocated to Ethiopia and finally to Kenya in 1985. Jonathan came to know her through her sister who used to hang out with his friends. However, nothing much developed between the two as their life took different paths, he going back to England for his studies and she going to Germany for five years.

The historic encounter that would change the course of their lives was at the New Year's Eve party of 1997/98 at the Diani Beach. The two acquaintances rekindled their friendship and wedding bells quickly followed. Jonathan wishes he would have met her earlier, an indication of the fondness that has developed between them. They have three children: Talia, Jaden and Noah. Jonathan says that they are typical Kenyans, who make him happy. He always looks forward to going back home to be with them.

On parenting, Jonathan believes that parents should be there for their children and mould them into what they would like them to be. For example, one cannot maintain a stern face in the house if they expect their children to be joyful and humorous. The parents should be playful with them too. He also believes that married partners can work together in business as long as both respect their boundaries. However, not everybody in the family is fit to work in the family business.

"We work well with my wife here. She is a real professional. The challenge to every family business is to bring on board the right family members to the business." With regard to the company, Petra views it as their first baby. As a family, they saw it grow.

Tips for entrepreneurs

Jonathan has a number of tips for existing and aspiring entrepreneurs, including those running family businesses. One of the key factors in the success of a business is that one should not go into it as a last resort for those who have failed elsewhere. Entrepreneurship should be among the first options for those seeking a better life: "Take for instance our case. It wasn't out of necessity. We had good jobs. We just wanted to be our own bosses and probably experience the thrill of it. Indeed, the best entrepreneurs are the ones not in it for survival. While we have successful entrepreneurs who took the plunge to survive, this should not be the case. However, this survival mentality may well limit your vision and your ability to take risks. You know, if you cannot afford to lose, you cannot take chances, which is the backbone of entrepreneurship."

Another important factor is self belief, which is critical in the success of entrepreneurs. Business is for those who have a blinding faith in themselves and their products. If one does not believe in themselves and their idea, then they should forget having their own business. Some of those who have been pushed to go into business would confess that their greatest undoing has been lack of self belief. One should particularly have belief with regard to the product or service that the entrepreneur is offering to the market: "It is upon the entrepreneur to demonstrate to the customer that their product or service best fits their needs and then be patient with them. There are those who may embrace the product immediately while others may be slow to adopt it. It is important at this stage for the entrepreneur to exhibit self belief which differentiates success and failure in entrepreneurship. Nobody can buy into your product if you don't believe and show confidence in it."

It is also important for one to enjoy what they do, as it is the only way of giving it maximum attention and staying updated with the new developments. Therefore, it becomes easy to succeed in business if one enjoys what they are doing, not just doing it for the money.

Having the right business idea is also very important. According to Jonathan, there could be thousands of unknown entrepreneurs out there who are struggling because they have not hit on the right idea. "If you hit on the right idea at the right time, the breakthrough may be sooner as opposed to plodding through with a dead idea. We were lucky to hit on an IT idea at the right time. Entrepreneurs should continually review their business ideas and try to match those ideas with the times if they are to remain relevant."

Focus is also very important. Aspiring entrepreneurs should not get sidetracked by potential opportunities. They should be single-minded as opposed to being a jack of all trades. How can one do many things if they cannot do one thing right? As Jonathan observes, "At AccessKenya, we have chosen ICT and even though we believe there are other great opportunities in Kenya, we remain in ICT. That's the only way we can give it our best shot and stay ahead in the industry."

When it comes to staffing, Jonathan advises entrepreneurs to bring on board good talent. "Success in business is driven by good employees and an able board that provides relevant leadership. Entrepreneurs should not compromise on hiring good staff. At AccessKenya, we hire the best talent, train them and try as a much as possible to give the best working environment to realise their potential."

For those running family businesses, Jonathan's advice is that they should ensure those family members that are brought into the organisation merit their positions. For example, Jonathan and David are professionals, while their father Michael, who was at the helm for ten years, is a widely respected lawyer whose experience has been invaluable to the organisation. Nevertheless, other than good fatherly advice whenever sought, he has not played a direct role in the operations of the company and served as a non-executive chairman.

On financing, Jonathan advises those running family businesses to consider going to the stock market to raise funds, as this has many economic advantages including increased visibility and public awareness. When a company lists, it not only gets tax reduction from 30 percent to 20 percent for the next 5 years (which is a government incentive to increase listing in the stock market), but it also improves on its systems for public probity.

Jonathan also has a word on cooperation in business. He believes that it is much easier to be an entrepreneur if one has someone with whom to share their ideas like he did with his brother. Entrepreneurship can be quite a lonely undertaking; hence, there are organisations whose origins are to cater for the needs of lonely entrepreneurs. "Usually, starting a business drops one from the rank of your peers in employment. Remember, in my case, I was the number two at my workplace and all of a sudden, I was my own boss, the messenger, the tea boy and everything. I was used to having a horde of staff surrounding me as opposed to being the lone ranger. This is where self belief comes in. From my experience I would recommend that you start a business with somebody to keep you company – it helps to ensure you have someone to discuss ideas with and helps to give input when needed."

Finally with regard to developing talent, Jonathan believes that while entrepreneurs may be born, one's upbringing has got to do with developing self confidence, a critical requirement for entrepreneurs. If one's parents let them pursue their desires unhindered, they can be more daring and confident as opposed to when they were over-patronised. Over-parenting, where parents want to do everything for their children, can erode their self esteem. In effect, he advises parents to let the children explore their abilities, fail and learn.

Role models

Jonathan is inspired by his father and his brothers. He also has great respect for Dr James Mwangi, the Chief Executive of Equity Bank, on whom he remarks: "He went out there, took on established players, challenged them and rewrote the book about banking in Kenya when he took banking to people in rural areas. He is a real visionary and strategic thinker."

Jonathan also admires Titus Naikuni, the Chief Executive of Kenya Airways. He views him as a clever man who has excelled everywhere he has been – at Magadi Soda and at Kenya Airways. "Like all visionaries, he sees ahead and strives to take the business there."

Social activities

Jonathan and David are in love with hair-raising speed sports. Both are sworn fans of formula-one motor sports, an indicator of their thirst for life in the fast lane. Pointedly, the two risk-takers defied tradition to plunge into full-time business at tender ages, an occupation in Kenya that has only been recommended to retirees or those unable to secure gainful employment.

Legacy

Both Jonathan and David would like to be remembered for having created a company that made a positive contribution in the country through quality service to its clients and giving its employees a great place to work and earn a living. By 2008, AccessKenya Group was employing more than 250 staff. As Jonathan remarks, "I would like to be remembered for giving employees a great place to work, an opportunity to grow and learn, and a secure and enjoyable working environment. Our legacy should be that we built a sustainable business that created thousands of jobs for Kenyans," says Jonathan.